Mexico's Search for a
New Development Strategy

Mexico's Search for a New Development Strategy

Proceedings of a Conference
Sponsored by The Ford Foundation and
The Economic Growth Center of Yale University

organized by Dwight S. Brothers and Leopoldo Solis M.

edited by Dwight S. Brothers
and Adele E. Wick

Westview Press
Boulder • San Francisco • London

This Westview softcover edition is printed on acid-free paper and bound in library-quality, coated covers that carry the highest rating of the National Association of State Textbook Administrators, in consultation with the Association of American Publishers and the Book Manufacturers' Institute.

Published in 1990 in the United States of America by Westview Press, Inc., 5500 Central Avenue, Boulder, Colorado 80301, and in the United Kingdom by Westview Press, Inc., 13 Brunswick Centre, London WC1N 1AF, England

Library of Congress Cataloging-in-Publication Data
Mexico's search for a new development strategy / edited by Dwight S.
  Brothers and Adele E. Wick.
    p. cm.
  ISBN 0-8133-7880-X
  1. Mexico—Economic policy—1970- .   I. Brothers, Dwight
S., 1929- .
II. Wick, Adele E.
HC135.M574 1990
338.972—dc20   89-27600
                                                                CIP

Printed and bound in the United States of America

The paper used in this publication meets the requirements of the American National Standard for Permanence of Paper for Printed Library Materials Z39.48-1984.

10   9   8   7   6   5   4   3   2   1

Contents

Dwight Brothers, Preface and Acknowledgments   ix

Adele Wick, Editors' Note   xv

PART I: PERSPECTIVES AND GUIDELINES

Enrique Cardenas, Contemporary Economic Problems
in Historical Perspective   1

Angus Maddison, Comparative View of Mexico's
Adjustment and Growth Problems   27

     Gustav Ranis, Comments   38

Leopoldo Solis, Social Impact of the Economic
Crisis   43

     Robert Pastor, Comments   53

Raymond Vernon, Mexico's External Environment:
Prospects for the 1990s   59

     Jesus Reyes Heroles, Comments   75

Pedro Noyola and Jaime Serra, Rebalancing
Government Direction and Market Guidance   79

     T. N. Srinivasan, Comments   89

Victor Urquidi, Broader Perspectives on
Development Problems   93

PART II: MEXICAN—U.S. RELATIONS

Hugo Margain, Mexico, the United States and the
World Economy   103

Anthony Solomon, Suggestions for Establishing a
Special Bilateral Relationship   111

Cathryn Thorup, In the Eye of the Storm: The
State of U.S.-Mexican Relations   115

PART III: DEBT, TRADE AND GROWTH

Pedro Aspe, Mexico: Foreign Debt and Economic
Growth   123

    S. T. Beza, Comments   135

Rudiger Dornbusch, Mexican Debt   141

    Angel Gurria, Comments   170

Jaime Zabludovsky, Trade Liberalization and
Macroeconomic Adjustment   173

    Koichi Hamada, Comments   198
    Juan Enriquez, Comments   202

Sweder van Wijnbergen, Growth, External Debt
and the Real Exchange Rate   207

    Willem Buiter, Comments   244
    Anne Krueger, General Comments   251

Everardo Elizondo, Private Sector Net Exports
and the Real Exchange Rate   255

    Enrique Espinoza, Comments   263

PART IV: FINANCIAL SECTOR REFORM

Dwight Brothers, Financial Sector Planning and
Mexico's New Development Strategy   271

    Jesus Marcos, Comments   302

Aristobulo de Juan, Prudential Regulation and
Financial Stabilization   307

    Francisco Suarez, Comments   325

Sergio Ghigliazza, Role of the Central Bank in
Financial Modernization   333

    William White, Comments   350

Adalberto Garcia Rocha, Distributive Effects of
Financial Policies in Mexico   359

    Sylvia Maxfield, General Comments   372

Appendix: Yale/Mexico Conference Program Plan   377

Preface and Acknowledgments

After a prolonged period of developmental retrogression Mexico appears to be poised for what will inevitably be a difficult struggle to recover lost ground. Clearly the most fundamental challenge confronting the Salinas administration is that of correctly formulating and effectively implementing a coherent strategy for guiding the country toward the objectives of financial stability, economic growth and socio-political development which have been largely subordinated to the imperatives of crisis management throughout much of the past decade.

There is under way in Mexico a determined search for the most promising strategy for achieving the country's interrelated economic policy objectives in the immediate future and throughout the 1990s. During the first several months following installation of the new administration in December of 1988 the shape of the strategy to be adopted began to emerge in the form of a series of policy pronouncements rather than as a comprehensive strategic conception. It was evident that a unique opportunity existed during this formative period for bringing together under intellectually respectable and politically neutral auspices a representative selection of Mexican and non-Mexican academicians, statesmen and other knowledgeable and involved individuals whose breadth of wisdom and variety of viewpoints could be utilized to facilitate in a timely manner the Mexican process of development strategy formulation. This was the fundamental rationale underlying the Yale/Mexico Conference.

The Conference was convened in New Haven on April 4-6, 1989. The program was organized around four themes: (1) the economic and socio-political context; (2) contemporary macroeconomic problems and policy issues; (3) alternative development strategies and policy instruments; and (4) financial sector reform agenda. Additional observations regarding U.S.-Mexico relations and the Yale-Mexico connection were made by speakers at the keynote banquet, and historical perspective was provided by a presentation made during a midpoint luncheon. The program plan, including identification of the principal contributors, is contained in the Appendix to this volume.

As indicated, the program plan provided for outstanding authorities to present commissioned papers in regular, banquet and luncheon sessions. A commentator was designated in advance for each commissioned paper, and other participants were invited to make contributions during the discussion periods. Each of the four plenary sessions was directed by distinguished chairpersons (namely Victor Urquidi, Anne Krueger, Rodney Wagner and James Tobin) who managed to fit the ambitious agenda into the allotted times while also making their own observations and providing opportunities for questions and statements from the audience.

The program was conducted according to plan in most respects, although some modifications were required to accommodate scheduling conflicts and time constraints. Another divergence from the original concept was that during the period immediately preceding the Conference a substantial number of requests were received for permission to attend. Most of these were undeniable coming as they did from interested university, governmental and international agency sources. Altogether approximately 100 people attended some or all of the Conference sessions, of whom upwards of 40 had preassigned roles and an additional 30 or so participants spoke extemporaneously. While the last-minute scheduling adjustments and the enlarged participation detracted from the orderliness of the program, for the most part these developments served to illustrate the contemporary relevance of the proceedings and to contribute to the sense of spontaneity and goodwill that permeated the entire affair.

The contributing authors were, of course, free to choose the orientations and emphases of their respective papers within the limits of the main themes. Although a few actual titles and topics diverged somewhat from anticipations, the original conception was not greatly altered. There were, however, some surprises in the ways the authors carried out their assignments and -- even more so -- in the responses to their presentations by the designated commentators and discussants who came forward from the audience.

In addition to assisting Mexico's search for a new, more viable development strategy the Conference had the following subsidiary objectives:

1.   Contributing to a wider understanding of contemporary economic and related socio-political issues and constraints;

2.   Appraising the findings and recommendations of the Bilateral Commission on future United States-Mexico relations; and,

3.   Identifying priorities for public policy research both in Mexico and elsewhere.

It was recognized, of course, that the published proceedings would be the principal means for pursuing these objectives.

The Economic Growth Center (EGC), an affiliate of the Economics Department at Yale University, was an especially appropriate sponsoring agency for the Conference because of its reputation as an outstanding research and training institution concerned with developing countries. Furthermore, an impressive number of leading Mexican economists and government officials have had prior associations with the EGC faculty while pursuing their professional degrees at Yale. The Conference provided a timely opportunity for reaffirmation of this long-standing Yale-Mexico relationship. We are grateful in this regard to The Honorable Gustavo Petricioli, Ambassador of Mexico to the United States and one of the first Mexican economists to do his professional preparation at Yale, for his thoughtful and witty remarks during the keynote banquet.

Funding for the Conference was mobilized from several sources. The Ford Foundation provided the major share of financing and the EGC contributed significant support from its own budget. These amounts were supplemented by financing made available from the participants' own institutions for travel and accommodation expenses. And numerous individuals made "in kind" contributions by foregoing honoraria.

Responsibility for organizing and administering the Conference (from enlistment of participants to program arrangements through publication of the proceedings) was assumed jointly by Leopoldo Solis and myself. Solis worked to assure support within the relevant Mexican academic, governmental and private sector circles -- including enlistment of an appropriate range of Mexican participants. My primary responsibilities were for recruitment of the desired range of non-Mexican participants and, together with Sue Brothers and Tito Vidaurri, for supervision of arrangements for hosting of the Conference. I have also assumed responsibility for publication of the proceedings volume -- with the very substantial assistance of others as indicated below.

Those invited to make the principal presentations were selected with the intention of facilitating expression of diverse viewpoints within a framework that would bring into focus convergences as well as differences in theoretical orientations, empirical analyses and policy judgments. The Conference organizers were well aware, of course, that not all pertinent topics could be covered and also that the individual authors might pursue their respective assignments in unpredictable directions. We were particularly cognizant of the fact that the program design emphasized macroeconomic and financial policy issues at the expense of proper attention to some other problem areas -- particularly agriculture, public education and various social welfare issues. Fortunately, however, this calculated deficiency in the program design was remedied to some degree by individual presentors and commentators who broadened the frame of reference and offered remarkably frank appraisals of pertinent political considerations.

Each of the Conference sessions was highly stimulating, provocative and constructive. Given the outstanding qualifications of the participants, and also the substantial efforts evidently devoted by the key people in preparing their presentations, it is not surprising that this was so. But the results nevertheless were beyond expectations not only because of the fortuitous timing of the event but also because the various contributions were remarkably complementary without being overly structured or repetitious. On the other hand, many of the points touched on by the contributors were not fully developed and the papers lack the coherence that might have been achieved had the Conference program been more narrowly focused.

In preparing their contributions for publication the authors and commentators were requested to make whatever post-Conference revisions of their papers they deemed to be necessary or appropriate. While there have been relatively few substantive changes in the original versions as presented at the Conference, the reader is assured that the revised papers represent the authors' considered judgments on the respective topics.

It is important to emphasize in this connection that the papers contained in this volume were initially drafted prior to April of 1989 during the period in which policy formulation processes with respect to Mexico's economic problems, both in domestic and external contexts, were in a state of flux. The post-Conference revisions of the papers and commentaries were, with few exceptions, completed during the May-July period, prior to completion of the negotiations between Mexican officials and the committee of bank creditors that were concluded (if somewhat ambiguously) in late July. Discussion of the governing parameters and likely prospects for these negotiations figured importantly in many of the Conference papers -- but given the somewhat disappointing outcome (at least from Mexico's point of view) the environment within which Mexico must continue to search for a viable development strategy has not been greatly altered from that which prevailed at the time the Conference participants were preparing and revising their papers.

Some of the papers as finally submitted have been edited more heavily than others to accord with the publisher's guidelines and the overall space constraint. However, care has been exercised to avoid unwarranted intrusions of either a substantive or stylistic nature. Further explanation of the editorial procedures employed is contained in a separate "Editors' Note" prepared by my colleague in this endeavor, Adele Wick.

There is one aspect of the editorial process that warrants explanation in this context, however, since I am solely responsible for the arbitrary decisions involved. In compiling this volume the papers have in some instances been reordered, reclassified or retitled in accordance with what in retrospect has seemed to be the most logical and useful organization of the materials from the readers' point of view. Consequently, this volume is not structured in strict accordance with the Conference program format. Furthermore, it has been necessary to omit from the published proceedings the work of some contributors to the Conference program because of their inability to provide suitably revised manuscripts in accordance with the governing criteria and deadlines. On the other hand, two of the principal papers in this volume were not originally presented as such at the Conference but rather in the form of commentaries which were subsequently expanded into more substantive contributions. I hope that those who may feel imposed upon by these decisions will be understanding.

It remains to acknowledge the efforts of the many people who contributed to the success of the Yale/Mexico Conference and to the relatively rapid publication of this proceedings volume. We are grateful to Steve Cox and Tom Trebat for their efforts in arranging the generous financial support from the Ford Foundation. And we wish to express our appreciation to the Economic Growth Center at Yale University for serving as host institution for the Conference, and particularly to its director, T. Paul Schultz, and business manager, Dorothy Nitschke. Special thanks are likewise due

to the many Yale faculty members (mostly affiliated with the
EGC) who served as chairpersons or commentators during the
Conference -- especially Professors Gustav Ranis, T. N.
Srinivasan, James Tobin, Willem Buiter, Koichi Hamada and
Sylvia Maxfield.

Those mainly responsible for the success of the Conference, and also for the quality and timeliness of this proceedings volume, are, of course, the authors of the various
papers and commentaries. It was indeed gratifying to have
our invitations to prospective participants so readily
accepted by such an outstanding array of highly qualified
and very busy people. Their evident efforts to deliver
excellent products and to comply with the scheduling requirements are greatly appreciated. We are indebted as well to
those who chaired the respective Conference sessions so
effectively.

All who contributed to the program, as well as the
other participants, appeared to have found the Conference
useful as well as enjoyable. It is hoped that those who
made the additional efforts in performing their post-
Conference paper revision assignments will feel adequately
rewarded by the quality and circulation of the published proceedings.

Finally, I wish to express personally my appreciation
to the individuals who have labored so diligently in facilitating the publication process. The Westview Press staff
involved in the project (namely, Spencer Carr, Lynn Arts and
Marykay Scott) have been most helpful at every juncture.
But the basic task has been performed by Colin Trass (who
provided technical assistance in re-formatting word processing diskettes), Rosalie Crosby (who single-handedly performed the arduous task of converting the edited documents
into camera-ready form) and Adele Wick (without whom the
monumental editorial task could not have been done nearly so
quickly nor with such care and cheerfulness). Indeed, it is
these latter two individuals who have done virtually all of
the really hard work involved in moving the revised manuscripts through the successive stages to publication -- and
I am extremely grateful to them.

Dwight Brothers

Editors' Note

With my less than admirable A.B.D. professional status standing more and more for "All But Daughters," I was especially delighted to shift this past summer from raising three sons to raising the style of authors in turn raising the prospects for Mexico's economic growth and development. I date my entry into home economics at the precise moment when Gary Becker asked me to draw the supply curve of women to the marriage market: I surprised both of us by answering correctly, promptly demonstrating the "as if" verities of economics by appearing to locate myself on the lower left-hand section of the curve and making a match. Because I have persistently failed, however, to meet another Chicago challenge -- the repeated admonition, "Dare to split an infinitive!" urged by a fellow graduate student -- this editing project seemed a particularly apt pursuit.

The Yale/Mexico Conference was extremely topical. Indeed, while the Brothers-Wick team was working feverishly to solve stylistical problems obstructing publication of the Conference proceedings, through debt negotiations many of the authors of the proceedings were working with fervor to solve substantive problems obstructing Mexico's economic well being. Speed was clearly a key desideratum for both sides, and although the revised papers and comments were all technically due on June 15, authors are no more malleable than bankers and two papers actually refer to the outcome of the debt negotiations at the end of July.

Nor can (or should?) authors be constrained to adhere strictly to their pre-announced topics. Commentators, for example, were quite free to stick closely to their assigned author(s) or to essay forth into essentially independent inquiries -- indeed, so fully and successfully in two instances that their comments became independent papers (see Preface and Acknowledgments for more on this point). Those contributions that maintained their standing as commentaries can be equally provocative and therefore warrant the reader's keen attention as well. I am honored and delighted to be associated with a project of such high overall merit and to have received so thorough an economics education about my neighbor to the south.

The Wick-Brothers editing principles were rather simple, with The Chicago Manual of Style and common sense in equal measure our guides. Most of the editing was done on a sentence-by-sentence and paragraph-by-paragraph basis with an ear to cadence and an eye to grammar and meaning. Our aim was to keep each author's voice distinctive, but to free meaning from tangled or cumbersome syntax. In practice we therefore became quite sensitive to such issues as "which (versus that) hunting," making certain "first" things were indeed first and trading "thus"'s and "therefore"'s just for the rhythm thus gained. The Yale/Mexico Conference was so timely that we faced the challenge of how to deal with phrases like "at the present time" (well, "now") and "during the last six years" when events were changing so fast, and decided to emphasize the "conference" nature of the book, with its convening in April the reference point for all dates. Most of the fun came from dealing with the confused metaphors. We ignored Rupert Hart-Davis' advice -- "If you're going to mix metaphors, mix them thoroughly, like a salad!" Instead, we eliminated most of them along with the occasional malaprop, with relish in some cases and reluctance in others: the book would certainly have been more colorful with its full complement of elephants, camels, angels, tents and dice.

The only consistency we imposed on the papers involved suggestions by Westview Press concerning section headings, dates (issues of style like "1970s" versus "'70's"), footnotes and references (see infra); and then such punctilios of grammar as whether or not to place a comma before the last element of a series (generally not, unless clarity dictated otherwise) and how to treat foreign phrases (like domestic ones -- no italics, no quotation marks, no underlining except in footnotes and references). Our treatment of footnotes, references, graphs, tables and data as a whole also emphasize the conference nature of the volume. Constraints as well as principles propelled our decisions. Westview Press was very flexible about all matters but footnotes, which it insisted be placed at the end of chapters. Because of spacing problems aggravated by a 10 percent reduction from the 8-1/2" x 11" standard page size, we also elected to move all tables and graphs to the rear, and apologize for any inconvenience thus occasioned the reader. Some of the graphics had to be omitted because particularly after the 10 percent reduction their quality was insufficient for the publishing technology, which required camera-ready copy. As length became a problem, we also eliminated tables and graphs that were either so amply discussed in the text that they were a tad redundant or so loosely referenced that their elimination did not jeopardize the discussion. Because many of his text and appendix tables contain data not previously available in so complete and systematic a form, we most regret the cuts in the case of Jaime Zabludovsky's contribution and encourage the interested reader to contact him for more information. Finally, not only are many of the perspectives and positions of the Conference participants at odds; so are their data. These discrepancies often reflect statistical revisions, but Mexican data can be maddening with or without revisions. Our only solution to this problem is to alert the reader to its existence.

I have certainly enjoyed converting "Mexican/Spanish English" and "Economic/Academic English" into good "American" -- like Harry Johnson, "I'd say 'good English' but that's a higher aspiration." And I am deeply impressed by the quality of these papers and the Conference as it lives here and on the tapes that were my substitute for actual attendance. The greatest summer return, however, has been the nonpecuniary reward of making some new friends, Dwight and Sue Brothers and Rosalie Crosby, with whom I have already shared much laughter and shall presently share much tequila. After listening to the tapes, I only wish I'd convinced Dwight to add to his preface Mr. Dornbusch's jokes about the good tree and the bad mother-in-law and Mr. White's anecdote about advising a ditched stranger how to find Dublin -- "If I were you, I wouldn't start from here." But, then, how would I end my own piece?

Adele Wick

PART I
PERSPECTIVES AND GUIDELINES

Contemporary Economic Problems in Historical Perspective

Enrique Cardenas
President and Professor of Economics,
Universidad de las Americas

INTRODUCTION

Mexican economic development has been closely connected to the foreign sector through most of its history. From colonial times to the present, the export sector has been instrumental in either promoting economic growth or creating recessions and crises in the balance of payments. The Mexican economy, like most other developing economies, is highly vulnerable to foreign fluctuations and to the specific behavior and composition of the export sector. This sector is fundamental essentially because of the vital necessity for a small and developing economy to generate foreign exchange revenues in order to import technologically advanced goods, especially for investment.

This paper puts into historical perspective the problems that the Mexican economy faces today, with special emphasis on the relevance of the foreign sector. It shows that in different forms and at different times, the foreign sector has strongly influenced both domestic business cycles and the model of industrial development that has been followed. Although other sectors like agriculture and finance undoubtedly help explain overall economic growth, the emphasis has been placed on the foreign sector because it somehow affects all the others and to some extent determines their behavior.

The word "hypothesis" is mentioned several times in this paper. Many assertions remain strictly hypothetical: although there are good reasons to believe that they are correct, to the best of my knowledge they have not been proved yet and consequently should be evaluated with caution. Perhaps they will inspire further research.

In addition to the usual introduction and conclusions, this paper has been divided into three sections to reflect the three main epochs of Mexico's economic and especially industrial development. The first comprises the period from colonial times to the Great Depression, when the economy clearly followed an export-led growth model. The second period starts in the 1930s and ends with the 1982 crisis when the model of development was one of import substitution. Third is the current transitional period, after which the economy must grow at a high rate sustained by both the internal and the external sectors.

THE ORIGINS

Throughout the colonial period, the economy of New Spain, especially that which involved the market, was closely related to the exploitation of the silver mines. International and domestic trade, as well as monetary circulation, were determined by the productivity of the mines. The market economy and mining activity were intertwined. Whole areas were devoted to supplying the various articles needed to work the mines, such as foodstuffs, cattle, leather and tools. The money wages paid the laborers implied the existence of a money market far before the appearance of a monetary economy in the rest of the country. Consequently, when the mining activity decreased in the first third of the seventeenth century because of the depletion of rich deposits and a shortage of mercury, a basic raw material in the productive process, a large part of the market economy turned inward simply to survive through the bad years.(1) Rather than causing a drastic decline in the standards of living of most people, the ensuing depression affected economic activities selectively so that part of the labor force had to shift to other fields, especially agriculture and crafts.

In the middle of the eighteenth century many new and rich silver deposits were discovered. Together with the supportive Bourbon Reforms, the introduction of explosives and other technological advances, this discovery created a boom in silver production, which surpassed any previous output level. In the twenty years between 1741 and 1760 silver output reached over 6 tons.(2) The linkages of mining production with other sectors were enormous. Not only did economic activity in those fields related to the mining sector surge, but the economy as a whole was stimulated because silver was not only the raw material for jewelry and other such commodities but also foreign exchange and money. The production of silver therefore implied more foreign trade and a greater circulation of money which, in the absence of other important means of payment, increased aggregate demand and had a corresponding impact on domestic output. The level of consumption and standards of living for people in mining-related sectors and the cities increased, and most of the business cycles were determined by the cycles of mining activity.

Because of its special characteristic of actually producing foreign exchange, the mining sector had linkages not only to the domestic market, but especially to foreign trade. The latter, in turn, made imported raw materials available and, more importantly, equipment for the new industries developed as a consequence of the industrial revolution. Textiles were surely the most important, but not the only, industry benefited in this fashion.

The War of Independence that broke out in 1810 abruptly interrupted the course of a rapidly growing economy. Output of silver diminished from 27 million pesos in 1812 to only 4.4 million in 1822,(3) when the war ended. Even worse, the mining productive capacity was severely damaged by the destruction of the war and by the flooding of mines that occurred as a consequence of their having been abandoned for so many years. By 1821, enormous amounts of resources were needed to bring the mines back into operation.(4)

Conventional wisdom considers the following forty years of Mexican history to have been characterized, and determined, by the continuous struggle between the conservative and liberal factions searching for a national identity and a coherent form of government. The argument follows that the economic depression in the first sixty years of the nineteenth century was to a large extent the result of this political struggle.

However, some economic historians have recently contended that such developments also had an economic cause. John Coatsworth(5) has forcefully argued that backward forms of economic organization and the lack of a cheap means of transportation hindered economic growth. A complementary explanation highlights the importance of the depression of the mining sector and the lack of financial capital. Indeed, in addition to the ordinary contraction of the mining sector and all its linked activities, the drastic drop in the production of silver implied both a reduction in the volume of international trade, at a time when it was imperative to import newly developed equipment and raw material for the growing industries, and a decrease in the means of payment available in the domestic economy, with the concomitant contractionary effect on aggregate demand.(6)

One way to gauge the real macroeconomic effects of the decrease in the production of silver is by looking at the opportunity cost of the lost revenues. If at least a quarter of the approximately 25 million pesos of annual silver production, most of which was exported, went instead to the growing industrial sector, these enterprises would have increased by 152 a year. This assertion is an extrapolation from the projects financed with only approximately 1 million pesos by the first development bank of the country, Banco de Avio, from 1830 to 1843,(7) and gives an idea of the tremendous loss caused by the fall of the mining sector in spite of the foreign investment in that activity since 1824.(8)

During the last third of the nineteenth century both Mexico's domestic market and its export sector grew. The former was stimulated by the appearance of the railroad, which enhanced internal trade and enlarged the domestic market, thus making it possible to take advantage of economies of scale and positive externalities. The mining sector also contributed by reaching its pre-independence level of production in the 1860s and continuing its growth thereafter. On the supply side, the discovery of new deposits and some technological advances in the production process like the use of electricity and a new method to refine silver ore increased production. On the demand side, the "second industrial revolution" created a market for minerals that were extracted with precious metals, so that the whole process became more productive. From 1873 to 1910 the export of mineral goods in dollars increased at a yearly rate of 3.9 percent. The linkages of mining with various other sectors of the economy, as well as its special role as producer of foreign exchange, have already been mentioned. The exportation of minerals, especially silver and gold, represented over 66 percent of all exports in the last quarter of the century. Coffee and sisal also became important export products from the 1890s on.(9)

On the other hand, the first commercial banks, founded in the 1860s, reduced the monetary dependence of the economy on mining activity, although bank notes and checking accounts were of no great significance in the money supply as a whole. Nevertheless, the foreign sector continued to exert an enormous impact on the market economy through its demand for domestically produced goods and the foreign exchange this made available. Once again, international business cycles were transmitted to the internal economy through the foreign market, as in the case of the international recession of 1884. In addition, the adoption of the gold standard by many of the most powerful countries and the increase in world silver production reduced the relative price of silver to gold in international markets, and a nominal depreciation of the Mexican peso vis-a-vis the dollar and other currencies followed. Over time, because the domestic price level increased the real depreciation of the peso was fairly small, but it still affected the economy because some prices, like wages, were sticky so that relative prices changed, especially among factors of production.(10)

The growth of the international economy at the time was probably an important factor in determining the corresponding growth of the Mexican economy. Technological advances that took place elsewhere throughout the nineteenth century were incorporated relatively quickly. For example, electric power was used in the mines as well as in lighting Mexico City before the end of the century. The refining process in the production of silver was also improved with the new technologies developed in Europe, and the "second industrial revolution" demanded new products such as lead, zinc and copper which were also produced in Mexican mines.

The development of the railroads, both a cause and an effect of growth in the mining sector, provided the necessary basis for the development of other sectors like manufacturing and trade. John Coatsworth argues that freight and passenger services explain about one-third of the productivity growth during the Porfiriato.(11)

Recent studies of the manufacturing sector have shown that the railroads were indeed instrumental in stimulating various industrial activities. Stephen Haber argues that the manufacturing sector grew rapidly during the last twenty years of the Porfiriato due to the beginnings of a process of import substitution in some basic industries such as textiles, beer, paper making, cement and steel.(12) This was made possible by the inflow of foreign capital since the middle of the century, especially from England and France, and by the availability of sufficient foreign exchange. Domestic production could be increased significantly without additional demand if domestically produced commodities replaced imports. Indeed, the domestic market was beginning to affect the overall level of economic activity, albeit on a very small scale. Still, the engine of growth continued to be the export sector constituted by mining, agriculture and, since the first years of this century, oil.

In spite of the foreign ownership of most export enterprises, the return value of their output was relatively

large. In addition to the usual forward and backward linkages, a large fiscal linkage provided the government with
resources that were returned to the domestic economy in one
way or another. The fiscal linkage became more important
when the post-revolutionary governments had the political
will and the actual power to impose higher taxes on the
foreign companies for the exploitation of the country's
natural resources. A fairly sophisticated procedure was
installed to increase taxes in mining as the international
price of the minerals rose, thus capturing a large percentage of the rents for the benefit of the nation, and to
decrease them when it fell, thus avoiding the possibility of
a heavy tax burden.(13)

The Mexican Revolution brought years of civil war,
political turmoil and economic distress. The conventional
wisdom states that the ten years of the "violent phase" of
the revolution brought a drastic decline of economic activity in basically all sectors. However, new research has
shown that this was true only in specific areas like agriculture, cattle, domestic trade and to some extent manufacturing. Important sectors like mining and oil not only did not
diminish their activity, but actually augmented their volume
of production. Moreover, instead of lasting ten years, the
reduction in output occurred over only a four year period.

On the one hand, the revolutionary factions were reluctant to attack or confiscate the production of the largely
foreign-owned export enterprises, for fear of offending the
United States, which supplied most of their weapons. Other
domestic enterprises were not destroyed by the revolutionaries because their profits could be confiscated and contribute to the revolution. Occasionally the revolutionaries
actually protected the factories to maintain this source of
income.(14)

On the other hand, World War I created a large demand
for mineral raw materials as well as oil, so that the export
sector boomed during various years of the revolution. The
value of exports increased 191 percent between 1910 and
1920.

GDP did fall between 1913 and 1916 basically because
the transportation network, and therefore commercial operations, were interrupted by the fighting. In addition, the
financial sector collapsed in these same years as a consequence of the over-issue of money by both the federal government and the revolutionary factions. The monetary system
was replaced by one in which the various means of payment
were almost worthless paper money, and the exchange rate of
these monies against the dollar abruptly depreciated.

Although the most violent years coincide with the fall in production for the above reasons, these years also coincide with the collapse of the financial system. At the end of 1916 a stabilization process put the monetary system back into place in a matter of days with fairly limited contractionary effects,(15) and perhaps the financial system collapse and this eventual recovery, not the political and social turmoil, were instrumental in determining the economy's performance. In fact, the railroad network was not restored until the 1920s, so that the transportation factor was rather stable between 1916 and the following years. It should be noted, however, that the destruction of capital was not widespread, at least in the secondary sector.

The post-revolutionary years were characterized by a slow recovery of production, institutional development and the establishment of basic economic infrastructure. It is clear, however, that the export sector was at its peak, with the production of oil, for example, at 193.4 million barrels a year in 1921, a figure that was not regained until the mid-1970s.(16) Other exports were also sizable, providing foreign exchange and fiscal revenues badly needed for the economy's recovery. Indeed, during the 1920s, the engine of growth was once again the export sector while manufacturing was regaining prewar levels of production.

The monetary and banking systems were slow to recover, thus curbing the availability of credit and means of payment. The Bank of Mexico was established in 1925 but it did not function as a central bank until 1932 as a consequence of the Great Depression.(17) New credit and financial laws were issued to modernize the banking system, and a development bank for agriculture was created in the late 1920s. The two basic economic infrastructure projects were construction of a road network and a series of dams to increase agricultural productivity. Several authors have argued that these projects, as well as the new laws and financial institutions, were the basis for the future development of the country.(18) Perhaps this is an overstatement, but roads and other infrastructure that complemented the railroad network must have improved overall productivity. A rough estimate states that productivity increases contributed 25 percent of industrial growth, partly as a result of the road network during the 1930s.(19) Indeed, the launching of these programs constituted a conscious effort on the part of the government to promote economic development and enlarge the domestic market. However, a new model of development was soon shaped by the major economic event of the Great Depression.

A DRAMATIC SHIFT IN THE PROCESS OF DEVELOPMENT

The Great Depression that hit the western world in October of 1929 had long lasting effects on the economies of many countries, as well as on the role of government in economic policy. Mexico was no exception to this phenomenon.

The foreign depression affected the Mexican economy through three different channels. First, a reduction in the demand for exports and a decline in the terms of trade diminished the capacity to import by 50.3 percent between 1929 and 1932. Second, the trade imbalance abruptly reduced central bank reserves and with them the money supply. Between 1929 and 1931 the level of reserves was almost depleted, the gold standard, which had been adopted in 1905, had to be abandoned, and the money supply diminished 60.2 percent.(20) Finally, the decrease in exports implied a corresponding reduction in fiscal revenues. In those years, about half of the domestic revenues were related to the production and exportation of minerals and oil. Consequently, given the impossibility of financing a fiscal deficit because the public was still unwilling to accept Banco de Mexico's paper money and the foreign debt had been in default since 1913, the reduction in fiscal revenues implied a decrease in government expenditure so severe that even some public employees were fired.

These three factors had the common consequence of reducing aggregate demand. The only countervailing effect was exchange rate depreciation, which tended to increase foreign demand for Mexican exports and make its imports more expensive. Nevertheless, the overall impact on production was fairly strong and real gross domestic product fell 17.6 percent between 1929 and 1932.(21)

The Great Depression was significant not only for its impact on production, employment and overall welfare, but especially for its long-lasting effects in two other areas. First, the 21.9 percent real depreciation of the exchange rate changed the terms of trade and especially the relative price of exportables and domestically produced commodities, thereby shifting domestic demand from the foreign to the internal sector and promoting through the market a process of import substitution in the modern sector.(22) During the 1930s import substitution alone contributed 36.9 percent of the increase in demand in the industrial sector. This magnitude compares quite favorably to the experience of many other Latin American countries, including Brazil, where import substitution was particularly strong in this period.(23) Second, the government acquired the basic

instruments to conduct economic policy in general and monetary policy in particular. Perhaps even more important, the
State became aware, and convinced, of its need to have a
more active role in the economy through monetary, fiscal and
exchange rate policy. Until then, commercial policy was
really the only area in which the government felt comfortable to intervene. During the 1930s, the State became more
prone to act in promoting economic growth and social welfare. Public investment in economic infrastructure and
social welfare increased respectively 140.4 percent and
161.7 percent in real terms between 1925 and 1949.(24)

This phenomenon was fairly widespread in different
forms in different societies. In many other Latin American
countries, a similar situation brought radical changes in
the process of development. The domestic sector became the
engine of growth because import substitution was both stimulated by the Depression and promoted by the State. It was
hoped that foreign-sector dependence, which had determined
domestic business cycles for so long, would be drastically
reduced by import substitution in the modern sector and
related industrial development. However, time would prove
differently.

The changes in the process of development that were originally catalyzed by the impact of the Great Depression continued during the following forty years as a result of a conscious economic policy. While the market had prompted the
changes in demand and indeed the whole shift in the process
of development from being export oriented to looking inward
in the early 1930s, it was the government that actually pursued the goal of industrializing the economy through a policy of import substitution and widespread protection of the
domestic market. This was not a real possibility until the
late 1930s, when the government actually acquired the instruments to conduct economic policy in an effective manner.
Indeed, the 1938 recession, which by some measures was as
strong as the Great Depression, was the first instance in
which the government succeeded in counteracting the foreign
shock by an expansionary monetary policy which sustained the
level of the money supply and kept production almost constant.(25)

In the decades that followed, economic policy was used
not only to minimize the impact of adverse business cycles,
but actually to create a positive economic environment that
stimulated private investment and economic growth. More specifically, the following policies were pursued.

On the supply side, quota barriers to trade were
installed to assure a high level of effective protection

both to the domestic production of consumer and to those intermediate goods that were the easiest to manufacture and consequently to substitute for imports.(26) The goal of public investment was to supply at low prices basic infrastructure like roads, dams and irrigation facilities, electricity, gas, oil, urbanization, bridges and land clearing; and this policy was very effective in providing positive externalities and creating a much larger market for the private sector. Affordable financial credit and cheap foreign exchange were provided, especially after the second half of the 1950s, as were fiscal incentives to industry and subsidies to agriculture aimed to ensure sufficient and cheap foodstuffs to the working class in order to maintain low real wages in the modern sector. Social spending, particularly on education and health, was also important in making qualified labor available.

On the demand side, the government followed a policy of financing the fiscal deficit with relatively small amounts of foreign debt and especially by printing money, thus providing a high spending environment. Protecting the domestic market forced Mexican demand to remain within the economy, at the expense of consumer welfare, and reinforced the concept of having internal demand as the major engine of growth.

As mentioned above, the policy of import substitution came partly from the will to reduce the dependence on the availability of foreign exchange as well as from the perception that external shocks and adverse business cycles were to be avoided. However, the results were not really satisfactory since the process of import substitution in Mexico, and in most other countries that followed a similar policy, happened to be <u>intensive</u> in imports. By the 1970s it was widely acknowledged that the policy of substituting imports by producing those commodities domestically required large amounts of foreign exchange, because raw materials and equipment and parts necessary for the production of those goods had to be imported. Consequently, instead of escaping from its dependence on foreign exchange, the economy became even more dependent in certain ways. However, the goal of industrializing the country and having the domestic economy at the center of the development strategy was achieved with enormous success. Real GDP increased at an average annual rate of 5.7 percent between 1931 and 1970, which in per capita income terms meant an annual increase of 2.8 percent. At the beginning of the 1970s economic growth continued, but at a slower pace, and then the oil boom overwhelmed the economy and made it grow 8.4 percent a year during the 1977-1981 period.(27)

One hypothesis is that this performance was possible essentially because large unused amounts of natural resources like land, water, minerals and oil allowed productivity increases in spite of the rapid population growth. The economies of scale realized by enlarging the cities and expanding the markets with good communications and the positive externalities created by public investment and internalized by the private sector also increased productivity.

However, this growth path was repeatedly interrupted by a series of external crises. Indeed, the behavior of the Mexican economy since the 1930s can also be studied by looking at the series of devaluations that occurred from 1931 to 1982 and formulating the hypothesis that these six devaluations have common elements so that an explanatory and predictive pattern of behavior can be drawn. At the same time, examining the causes of devaluations can uncover some structural conditions that determine and constrain the overall behavior of the economy.

With the exception of the 1954 devaluation, every external crisis was accompanied by an overexpansion of the money supply to finance the budgetary deficit, a recession in Mexico's major partner countries, a fall in the terms of trade, and an overvaluation of the currency. During the devaluation of 1982, large capital flight and heavy servicing of the foreign debt were also present. All of these factors are interrelated and all cause problems in the balance of payments.

When the government incurs budgetary deficits and overexpands the money supply, the level of demand is high and prices tend to rise. With a fixed exchange rate, the currency tends to become overvalued, there are incentives to buy abroad rather than at home, and exporters prefer to sell their products domestically. A high level of domestic income generated by large government expenditure also increases the level of import demand. Consequently, a trade deficit tends to develop. If this situation is accompanied by a reduction in prices and foreign demand for Mexican exports, foreign exchange revenues fall, precipitating a collapse in the foreign accounts and an unavoidable depreciation of the exchange rate. In other words, if the government tries to keep aggregate demand high by expanding public spending, the economy will eventually face the "external constraint," the continuous need for foreign exchange to buy the necessary raw materials, equipment and parts to keep the factories going.

When these crises occurred, unless an extraordinary source of foreign exchange could counteract the imbalance between the supply of and demand for foreign exchange, the economy had to undergo a contractionary process to diminish the level of imports. External shocks were consequently still transmitted to the internal economy even when the economic authorities showed financial discipline in not allowing budgetary deficits to get too large.

Leopoldo Solis divided the macroeconomic performance of the economy between 1935 and 1970 into two phases.(28) The first period, from 1935 to 1955, was one of growth with inflation, while the second period was characterized by growth with stable prices. The usual explanation of this change in price performance is that during the first phase the government relied heavily on deficit spending thus putting pressure on prices, while during the second period the government was more reluctant to use the money printing machine to finance public expenditure.

However, another hypothesis is that from the late 1930s to the mid-1950s, the international economy in general and Mexico's major commercial partner, the American economy, in particular experienced substantial instability due to the 1938 recession, World War II and the Korean War. The changing international situation, sometimes favorable and sometimes adverse, had drastic implications for the foreign demand for Mexican exports of goods and services, while the Mexican demand for imports was dependent on its own growth rate. The demand for Mexican exports grew rapidly because of foreign factors like wars, thereby raising Mexico's income and import demand. But when this foreign factor ceased to exist, always after a very short period of time, the availability of foreign exchange was reduced and caused a crisis in the balance of payments. This process was exacerbated when the government's policy involved budgetary deficits. While exports were increasing there was no concern for the external constraint since the supply of foreign exchange was sufficient to meet the demand; but if growth was maintained and exports collapsed, a crisis would certainly follow.

This process is very clear during the early 1940s, when as a consequence of World War II exports increased rapidly to the point where the Central Bank had to take measures to sterilize reserves and resist pressures to revalue the currency. However, when the War was over and the demand for exports drastically diminished, at first the large war-time accumulation of reserves financed the excess of imports; but eventually the reduced amount of exports caused a trade deficit and devaluation of the exchange rate in 1948-1949.

During the second phase mentioned by Solis, the international economy was fairly stable and prosperous. The volume of international trade increased considerably,(29) and
with it the demand for Mexican exports. Tourism also became
an important generator of foreign exchange. Moreover, there
was no sudden decrease in export demand or in the terms of
trade, and the government did not follow a policy of large
deficits. The relatively small current account deficit was
financed by foreign investment and both public and private
external debt. Consequently, it was possible to sustain a
fixed exchange rate and avoid overvaluation, in spite of the
fact that the agricultural sector, which had traditionally
been a net exporter, began facing in the mid 1960s a profound crisis from which it has yet to recover. Indeed, it
is possible to hypothesize that the "desarrollo estabiliza-
dor" period (1956-1970) was more the result of the absence
of external fluctuations, than of the Mexican government's
budgetary discipline. This hypothesis does not mean that
the fiscal discipline was not important; indeed, I believe
that it was a necessary, but certainly not sufficient, condition to obtain price and exchange rate stability.(30)

The decade of the 1970s was a period of substantial
financial instability in the international economy. The
financing of the Vietnam War, the collapse of the Bretton
Woods system and the oil embargo all played their role in a
financial crisis that lasted for several years. The Echeverria administration decided to insulate the economy from the
adverse foreign fluctuations, and generated large expenditure programs that pushed up prices but made the economy
grow at a rate of 6.2 percent a year between 1970 and 1976.
However, the balance of payments was bound to collapse when
the excess of public spending was not matched by additional
revenues because the proposed fiscal reform was never carried out.(31)

In the early 1970s it began to be realized both that
the export sector would soon be unable to provide sufficient
foreign exchange to keep the economy growing and that the
import substitution model of development, while effective in
terms of output growth, had not been able to reduce unemployment and improve the distribution of income.(32)

The short-run causes of the 1976 devaluation were essentially the external imbalance of the economy and neglect of
the external constraint. A high level of aggregate demand
generated basically by the internal sector and a currency
overvalued due to a domestic rate of inflation higher than
that of the United States stimulated an excess demand of
imports and prompted a devaluation of the peso. Exports

were not able to grow as rapidly as required by the economy
to provide the necessary volume of foreign exchange, so that
foreign borrowing had to finance the growing current account
deficit.

Once again, the engine of growth was the domestic sector, sustained by a high level of aggregate demand and public investment, which in those years was allocated not only
to building economic and social infrastructure, but also to
establishing public enterprises of all sorts, some in basic
areas and others in activities completely unrelated to the
government's usual sphere of action. A regression in the
process of import substitution arguably also occurred in
spite of the quantitative import restrictions, because of
the enormous economic incentives to spend abroad rather than
at home.

By this time, however, it was increasingly apparent
that some structural constraints were preventing the economy
from growing at a steady and rapid pace. The public sector
faced chronic fiscal deficits partly because of excess spending and partly because of a low fiscal burden. The availability of capital goods and parts depended heavily on foreign suppliers, population growth was depleting the natural
endowment of resources so that the ratios of land to labor
and capital to labor had reached critical levels, and the
productive plant had become chronically inefficient during
the overextended period of widespread protection. The external constraint clearly had to be eliminated for the economy
to regain steady and rapid growth.

With the rising prices of oil since the OPEC embargo,
the exploitation of Mexican deposits increased to the point
that the country stopped importing crude oil in 1973 and
instead started exporting on a modest level. Since the
beginning of the Lopez Portillo administration at the end of
1976, it was realized that the exportation of oil could eliminate the external constraint that had hindered development.

After a year of planning and the exploration and discovery of vast new oil deposits, the government adopted a strategy of very rapid growth. The private sector joined the government in this endeavor and the excess capacity available
after a year of recession was reduced. Oil exports increased
foreign exchange revenues dramatically, in effect eliminating the external constraint. Fueled by domestic demand and
the linkages created by the oil boom, the economy recom-
menced rapid growth substantially above historical levels.
Building the infrastructure to exploit the oil wealth was
one of the first large government projects, and the state
soon expanded to other areas of production as well. The

private sector, in turn, invested large amounts to increase
the productive capacity for the domestic market which was
growing along with the oil sector. Imports, especially of
capital goods and raw materials, were increasing along with
oil exports. Clearly, just as in colonial times with silver, the export of essentially one commodity was permitting
the economy grow and develop. Between 1978 and 1982 oil
exports increased from 30.7 percent to 77.6 percent of total
merchandise exports. This time, however, the oil wealth was
in the hands of Mexicans and specifically the government, so
that in principle it could basically benefit the Mexican
people.

Suddenly, as if by magic, the structural problems that
had become evident just a few years back disappeared from
the scene. Because about 30 percent of all public revenues
came from the oil sector, the oil boom provided additional
fiscal revenues that first eased the deficit situation and
then allowed an unprecedented expansion of expenditures to
over 40 percent of GDP in the early 1980s. It also supplied
large amounts of foreign exchange that permitted the importation of any kind of equipment and parts needed, so that the
capital/labor ratio and productivity increased in the second
half of the 1970s. The structural problem of international
lack of competitiveness was, however, reinforced. Although
import quotas were increased to allow the entrance of most
goods in order to raise the volume of aggregate supply and
control inflationary pressures somewhat, aggregate demand
was so large that domestic producers continued to be able to
sell whatever quantities they could produce at high prices.
In other words, the domestic market continued to be widely
protected from foreign competition.

The oil boom of 1978–1981 generated an annual growth
rate of 8.5 percent, thereby bringing about the highest
level of employment in contemporary Mexican history. Standards of living increased considerably, especially real
wages measured in terms of dollars. The much higher demand
for both domestic and foreign goods and services was instrumental in developing specific areas. The average yearly
rate of inflation over the same period was 22.4 percent,
much higher than in the United States, but relatively low
considering the overheating of the economy.

The country's rapid rate of economic growth, the temporary elimination of the external constraint, and the apparent disappearance of the above-mentioned structural problems
permitted the economy and society as a whole to behave as if
the country was very rich and developed. Of course, some
aberrations occurred, related to consumer habits as well as

to production systems. In general, an increasingly overvalued exchange rate and the availability of huge amounts of
foreign exchange stimulated the consumption of goods and services intensive in dollars, distorting the patterns of consumption and production and causing imports to grow very
rapidly. The volume of Mexico's international trade more
than quadrupled between 1976 and 1981, and the economy had
to rely increasingly on foreign investment and public and
private borrowing to finance the excess of imports over
exports.

The public foreign debt increased from $22.9 billion in
1977 to $53 billion in 1981.(33)   Banks were eager to lend
because the international financial system was fairly liquid
due to the large petrodollar deposits that flooded the financial markets as a consequence of increases in oil prices,
and Mexico had become a solvent and attractive client to the
banks due to its vast oil reserves. The private sector also
increased its borrowing from about $2 to $18 billion in the
same period.

Since 1979 the balance of payments had shown a dangerous current account deficit which threatened to become even
more serious if radical measures to diminish the demand for
imports were not taken. However, at least the president and
some of his closer advisors were not willing to accept a concomitant reduction in the economy's rate of growth. Therefore, in spite of clear signs that the international oil market was about to collapse, the government refused to devalue
the exchange rate, which by then was highly overvalued, and
a huge capital flight took place. Unofficially, it is estimated that about $14 billion left Mexico in the summer of
1981.(34)

The imbalance in the current account was unsustainable
and in February of 1982 the exchange rate was devalued almost 50 percent. However, once again the government refused
to acknowledge the situation and both capital flight and
imports of goods and services continued to grow. By the
middle of that year the exchange rate had been devalued once
more and the Central Bank's reserves were practically depleted. Consequently, an exchange control had to be established and the government had to convert the "mexdollars" or
dollar-denominated deposits into peso-denominated deposits.

Economic activity responded to this unstable situation
by showing signs of recession in the second quarter of 1982.
The government continued its expenditure policy, in spite of
the decrease in fiscal revenues and the refusal of the international banks to continue lending fresh money. Consequently, the public deficit reached a record level of almost 17

percent of GDP by the end of that year. It was financed essentially by printing money, and the money supply increased 71 percent in 1982.(35)

The change of finance ministers in the second quarter of 1982 as well as the cash flow crisis prompted a drastic, but belated shift in policy. On the one hand, the government reduced subsidies by increasing the price of controlled public goods and services. On the other hand, it declared a moratorium on the servicing of the foreign debt and reached a "stand by" agreement with IMF just before the change of administrations at the end of 1982. The main macroeconomic indicators were discouraging. Inflation was about 100 percent and rising, output growth was disappearing, the service of the foreign debt was absorbing 77 percent of merchandise exports, the exchange rate had devalued almost 80 percent during a single year, the money supply was growing at around 100 percent, and the public deficit was 17 percent of GDP.

The new government essentially faced a double challenge: it had to reduce inflation and also provide the economic conditions for sustained economic growth. In other words, the government had to control the budgetary deficit, reduce its financing through inflationary means, stabilize the exchange rate, prevent as many bankruptcies as possible, and minimize the external constraint to ensure long-term growth consistent with increases in the population and labor force. It was imperative for the government to solve the recession and at the same time make the structural changes needed for sustained economic growth.

ECONOMIC CRISIS AND STRUCTURAL CHANGE

In retrospect, the economic policy pursued during the first four years of the de la Madrid administration in an effort to solve the first challenge was orthodox and "gradualist" because the fear of social and political unrest was always present. The government tried to control inflation by decreasing both the budgetary deficit and the money supply and to reduce imports by a strong devaluation and slower economic growth. Negotiations to reduce the service of the foreign debt never became confrontational and, through several rounds of negotiations, the cash flow crisis was replaced by a longer-term commitment to pay the debt, in hopes that eventual growth in the economy would increase the capacity to pay.

Needless to say, the economic and social costs of the policies were substantial. They included acute reduction in

real wages, deterioration in basic social indicators such as
nutrition and health,(36) loss of human capital, deterioration in income distribution and the consequent impoverishment of the middle classes.(37) From 1981 to 1983, the public and private investment necessary not only for growth but
even for maintenance of the productive capacity, declined by
9 percentage points of GDP.

Although the macroeconomic policy was consistent, it
faced two basic problems. First, the depth of the crisis
was underestimated so that many of the policies, though correct in direction, were insufficient in magnitude to yield
the expected results in the appropriate time. This problem
in turn created a vicious cycle of built-in inflationary
pressure that threatened continuously to become hyperinfla-
tionary. Indeed, right at the beginning of the de la Madrid
administration, the exchange rate was devalued almost 100
percent in the hope that the peso would be sufficiently
undervalued to absorb the rise in domestic prices until
inflation could be brought completely under control.

However, the inflationary inertia inherited from the
previous year, plus the policy of increasing the prices of
controlled and public goods and services to reduce subsidies, proved to be too strong and consumed the undervaluation margin before it was possible to control the inflationary process. The government then decided to allow the
exchange rate to slide downward in order to avoid sudden
devaluations. This policy, however, implied steady import
price increases that became more and more important, especially in terms of inflationary expectations. This factor,
plus the usual price-wage mechanism and the need to maintain
positive real interest rates in order to avoid capital
flight, constituted the basis of the built-in inflationary
process.

The second macroeconomic policy problem was a series of
foreign shocks, most notably the collapse of the oil market
in 1986. The loss in foreign exchange revenues in that year
reached $8.5 billion, 39 percent of total merchandise
exports of 1985. This decline adversely affected public
finances, and the government was unable or unwilling to
reduce its spending enough to counteract the adverse impact.
Consequently, the public deficit reached 16 percent of GDP,
placing the economy back in a situation similar to that of
1982 and eliminating gains made by the the austerity efforts
during the previous three years. By then, the burden of the
foreign debt had become too heavy to bear in such adverse
external circumstances.

The government's response was to search for an unorthodox way to reduce the burden of the debt and to fight inflation. The Central Bank had to accumulate massive reserves,
and through strict monetary policies and increases in real
interest rates, it stimulated the repatriation of portfolio
capital to be invested in the stock market and treasury
bills. By September of 1987, international reserves had
reached over $15 billion, or about 60 percent of 1987's
total current account expenditures. When the stock market
collapsed in October of 1987 and uncertainty increased,
Banco de Mexico refused to use those reserves to finance
capital flight, closed the exchange market, and devalued the
exchange rate 25 percent.

After acquiring sufficient international reserves but
failing to achieve a reduction of the debt through an innovative process with zero coupon bonds, the government decided
to fight inflation through a shock program. Although similar in some respects to the ones used in Brazil and Argentina, it differed in obtaining prior agreement among the
various social groups to necessary relative price adjustments to be followed by a period of frozen prices.

The first results of Pacto de Solidaridad Economica,
the program launched in December of 1987, were quite positive: inflation decreased from 159 percent at the end of
1987 to 52 percent one year later, and unemployment and
plant closings were substantially less than anticipated.
The new administration has successfully continued the program with only slight changes so far, but concerns are rising over the problems of ending the price freeze and restor-
ing a completely flexible price system. This problem is
complicated by failure to replace the depreciated capital
stock created during the oil boom and by the uncertainty of
the debt situation. The new administration has made it
clear that the debt burden must be reduced since economic
growth with price stability is the national priority.

The de la Madrid administration also faced the challenge of solving one of the structural problems at the heart
of most economic crises: the economy's lack of international
competitiveness. The first and perhaps most important step
in that direction was the change in 1984 from import quotas
to tariffs for most commodities. Adherence to the GATT then
required the liberalization of trade in 1986.(38) Labor
unions and some businessmen opposed the policy, fearing a
disruption of the domestic market by the flood of foreign
merchandise. Other entrepreneurs, as well as segments of
the general public, reacted positively in growing recognition of the importance of a diversified export sector and

sufficient foreign exchange to pay for needed imports. Consumers were, of course, happy with the news.

The trade liberalization policy was accompanied by a realistic, if not undervalued exchange rate in order to stimulate a rapid change in demand and in patterns of production. Moreover, the reduced level of domestic demand caused by the economy's low rate of growth also provided the incentive for producers to sell abroad.

The dollar value of non-oil exports increased 74 percent between 1985 and 1987 as a result of both a prosperous American economy and the above-mentioned conditions. The expansion of non-oil exports, and particularly those of the manufacturing sector, was ample enough to counteract to a large extent the decreased oil exports. Non-oil exports accounted for over 58 percent of total exports in 1987, and the private sector exported as much as the public sector.

This successful performance has been considered a sign that the structural change needed to strengthened the Mexican economy has indeed occurred. This is without a doubt the first time in Mexican economic history that the majority of merchandise exports is composed of non-traditional exports. However, it is not yet clear to what extent the increase in exports is due essentially to the contraction of the domestic market and to what extent it is a response to the favorable exchange rate and trade liberalization. Sectors that are good exporters like the automotive industry are not highly vulnerable to fluctuations in domestic demand. Mexico's exports, like those in other countries, depend instead mostly on the income levels of its major commercial partners.

The institutional changes towards trade liberalization and the positive performance of the export sector make it clear that the Mexican economy is in a transitional period leading to a substantial structural transformation that is changing Mexico's long-term model of economic development. Indeed, the domestic economy, which suffered a drastic shift in the 1930s when the foreign sector ceased to be the engine of growth and gave way to the domestic sector as the major and most dynamic component of aggregate demand, now faces a similar change that will yield a new model of development which could last for a long time. This seems to be the beginning of the new era in which a diverse export sector expands along with a competitive internal economy, providing sufficient foreign exchange to sustain such growth and perhaps minimizing, if not eliminating, the external constraint that has provoked economic recessions, recurrent crises in the balance of payments, and corresponding devaluations of the exchange rate.

However, the modernization of industry should also be accompanied by a similar restructuring in other traditional sectors, especially agriculture. Indeed, the success of the new scheme of development depends upon a new policy that will substantially increase agricultural productivity and reconsider property rights with respect to land tenure. It is increasingly acknowledged that small plots of land, either in private holding or in a cooperative system of land tenure, yield much less than larger plots, given the state of technology and actual availability of other inputs such as water and fertilizers. The ejido system is doomed to fail as population increases, since average plot sizes in ejidos will continue to shrink, in spite of rural migration to the cities. Moreover, many characteristics of land tenure discourage investment and efforts to increase productivity, and must therefore be changed.

It is difficult to conceive of how Mexico can be successfully integrated into the world economy with such a backward agricultural sector. If a structural change equivalent to that now occurring in industry is not carried out in the more traditional sectors, the difference in levels of development and productivity between agriculture and industry will inevitably exacerbate Mexico's already acute problems of income distribution, rural migration, excessive urbanization, increasing poverty and related social distress. Continued migration will make unbearable the economic, social and political consequences of the acute problems of Mexico City and many other urban areas in the country -- problems which already absorb large amounts of resources and generate poverty and social unrest.

Other activities that will require a new and more liberal approach and could be invaluable as foreign exchange producers are tourism and fishing, which may also become important generators of employment. Mexico's natural resources for those industries are unmatched in most countries of the world, and clearly it is necessary to look at such endowments to identify opportunities for investment and growth.

The international economy is increasingly open to foreign trade in spite of some cyclical protectionist winds.(39) It may be the right time for the Mexican economy to prepare for integration into the world economy. Indeed, there is no alternative if the country is to resume high rates of economic growth in an increasingly interdependent world economy. Moreover, since the world economy appears to be undergoing reorganization into multi-country blocs, it is highly probable that eventually Mexico will have to join a

North American bloc in order to compete with Europe, Japan, China, the USSR and other such regional trading blocs that may arise. In the long run, a different option that is viable for both the United States and Mexico may not exist. Consequently, the structural change that will eventually increase productivity and competitiveness in both the industrial sector and the economy as a whole may have arrived at just the right time.

CONCLUDING REMARKS

Mexico's economic development has been characterized since colonial times by a heavy dependence on the foreign sector. For more than 400 years, the export sector was the most dynamic and important sector of the economy. Its importance derived from the country's dependence to a large extent on imported equipment, parts, raw materials and other products vital to the economy's development.

Mining was at the center of economic activity, both during the colonial period, and with some slight changes, through most of the nineteenth century. Railroads and banking also became important during the last quarter of the century, as did the growing but still small industrial sector. The Great Depression forced the first dramatic change in this model of development by stimulating a process of import substitution and, more importantly, by placing the center of economic activity in the internal sector of the economy. Economic policy consolidated this situation since the early 1940s and the economy's industrialization was quite successful. However, the technological dependence on foreign sources for capital goods and raw materials, plus external economic fluctuations, generated recurrent recessions and balance of payments crises which disrupted economic growth.

As a consequence of the 1982 crisis, the weak economic structures permitted a rapid and profound structural change now in its consolidating stage. The liberalization of trade must be accompanied by a similar policy change in traditional sectors, such as agriculture, in order to increase their productivity and take full advantage of Mexico's natural resources. The objective is to make the Mexican economy highly competitive. It is worrisome, however, that the modernization efforts of the Salinas administration apparently do not include structural changes and property rights adjustments in traditional sectors that are badly needed if the new development strategy is to succeed.

23

The preliminary results of the economy's structural changes undertaken so far are outstanding, since the export sector has become diversified and dynamic, provided the level of foreign demand is appropriate. This change is so important that it assures a new model of development that will minimize, if not eliminate, the external constraint. Indeed, the Mexican economy is undergoing a process of transition that will eventually lead to a new model of development, one characterized by a more competitive internal economy with a strong export sector and by greater involvement in world markets.

NOTES

1. David Brading, Miners and Merchants in Bourbon Mexico 1763-1810 (Cambridge: Cambridge University Press, 1971).
2. Instituto Nacional de Estadistica, Geografia e Informatica (I.N.E.G.I.), Estadisticas historicas de Mexico, Secretaria de Programacion y Presupuesto (Mexico, 1985), p. 437.
3. Urrutia de Stebelski Ma. Cristina and Guadalupe Nava Otero, "La Mineria," Mexico en el Siglo XIX (1821-1910), ed. by Ciro Cardoso, Editorial Nueva Imagen (Mexico, 1983).
4. Robert W. Randall, Real del Monte: a British Mining Venture in Mexico (Texas University Press, 1972).
5. John H. Coatsworth, "Obstacles to Economic Growth in Nineteenth Century Mexico," The American Historical Review 83:1, pp. 80-100.
6. Enrique Cardenas, "Algunas cuestiones sobre la Depresion Mexicana del XIX," Revista Lationamericana de Historia Economica y Social III (1984), pp. 3-22.
7. Robert A. Potash, El Banco de Avio de Mexico: El Fomento de la lindustria 1821-1846 (Mexico: Fondo de Cultura Economica, 1959).
8. Robert W. Randall, op. cit., Chapter IV.
9. I.N.E.G.I., op. cit., pp. 661, 663 and 686.
10. Jaime E. Zabludovsky, Money, Foreign Indebtedness and Export Performance in Porfirist Mexico (Ph.D. dissertation, Yale University, December, 1984), Chapter II.
11. J. H. Coatsworth, "Indispensable Railroads in a Backward Economy: The Case of Mexico," Journal of Economic History 39:4 (December 1979), pp. 939-960.
12. Stephen H. Haber, Industry and Underdevelopment: The Industrialization of Mexico, 1890-1940 (Stanford University Press, 1989).

24

13. Enrique Cardenas, La industrializacion mexicana durante la gran depresion (El Colegio de Mexico, 1987), p. 27.

14. Stephen H. Haber, op. cit.

15. Enrique Cardenas and Carlos Manns, "Inflation and Monetary Stabilization in Mexico During the Revolution," Journal of Development Economics 27 (1987), pp. 375-394.

16. I.N.E.G.I., op. cit., p. 455.

17. Enrique Cardenas, La industrializacion..., op. cit., Chapter 3.

18. See for example E. Krauze, et al., "La reconstruccion economica," Historia de la Revolucion Mexicana, Vol. 10 (El Colegio de Mexico, 1977), pp. 7-30, and Leopoldo Solis, La realidad economica mexicana. Retrovision y perspectivas, Siglo XXI (Mexico, 1981), pp. 76-86.

19. Enrique Cardenas, La industrializacion..., op. cit., pp. 176-183.

20. Enrique Cardenas, "The Great Depression and Industrialization: The Case of Mexico" in Rosemary Thorp, Latin America in the 1930s: The Role of the Periphery in World Crisis (MacMillan Press, 1984), p. 227.

21. Ibid., p. 227.

22. Ibid.

23. Enrique Cardenas, La industrializacion..., op. cit., pp. 112-117.

24. Ibid., pp. 99-100.

25. Enrique Cardenas, "The Great Depression and Industrialization...", op. cit., pp. 235-237.

26. Rafael Izquierdo, "El proteccionismo en Mexico," in L. Solis, La economia mexicana I analisis por sectores y distribucion, Serie de lecturas No. 4 (Mexico: F.C.E.), pp. 228-269.

27. I.N.E.G.I., Estadisticas Historicas..., op. cit., p. 311.

28. Leopoldo Solis, La realidad economica mexicana: retrovision y perspectivas, 1st ed. (Mexico, 1970), Chapter III.

29. Richard N. Cooper, The Economics of Interdependence (New York: Columbia University Press, 1968), Chapter III.

30. A preliminary report that points to this conclusion was formulated in my Economic History course in 1983 by two students, Alejandro Reynoso and Alejandro Olascoaga.

31. Leopoldo Solis, Economic Policy Reform in Mexico: A Case Study for Development Countries (New York: Pergamon Press, 1981).

32. See for example Gustav Ranis, "Se esta turnando amargo el milagro mexicano?" Demografia y Economia, Vol. VIII, No. 1, (1974), pp. 29-33, and Clark Reynolds, various works.

33. I.N.E.G.I., op. cit., p. 645.

34. Presidencia de la Republica, Unidad de la Cronica Presidencial, "Las raxones y las obras: Gobierno de Miguel de la Madrid," Cronica del sexenio 1982-1988 Primer Ano. (Mexico, 1984), p. 17. For a more detailed description of the events that led to the 1982 crisis, see the introductory chapter "La Transicion" of the first volume.

35. Banco de Mexico, Indicadorers Economicos, various issues. M2 was the money supply figure considered.

36. Nora Lusting, "Crisis economica y niveles de vida en Mexico: 1982-1985," Estudios Economicos, Vol. 2 (El Colegio de Mexico, 1987), pp. 227-249.

37. See the contributions of Leopoldo Solis and Adalberto Garcia-Rocha in this volume.

38. See Jaime Zabludovsky's paper in this volume.

39. See Raymond Vernon's paper in this volume.

Comparative View of Mexico's Adjustment and Growth Problems

Angus Maddison
Professor of Economics, University of Groningen

For the past seven years Mexico has been trying to solve five interrelated and persistent problems. This paper briefly discusses each of these concerns before turning to an analysis of concurrent external circumstances. With this framework in place, it returns to a more extensive look at Mexico's problems and prospects followed by a brief conclusion.

MEXICO'S FIVE PROBLEMS

First, after four decades (1940-1982) of sustained and very substantial growth averaging 3.1 percent a year in per capita terms, Mexico has experienced seven years of fluctuating GDP during which per capita product <u>declined</u> an average of 1.5 percent a year. Because the terms of trade worsened and a significant fraction of GDP was required to service the debt, the actual decline in income was even more severe.

Second, inflation has averaged 70 percent a year in the 1980s. This compares with an average of 10 percent in the period 1940-1980, and rates much lower in the years when Ortiz Mena was Minister of Finance.

Third, during the Lopez Portillo presidency the external debt increased to massive proportions. Since then the annual burden of foreign debt service has averaged about 6 percent of GDP because of both the debt's size and historically unprecedented real rates of interest. To meet this rising cost, Mexico has had to run a very large trade surplus and borrow even more.

Fourth, the public sector deficit reached exotic proportions during the presidency of Lopez Portillo. Eliminating the deficit has proved difficult because of the burden of foreign debt service and the adverse impact of inflation on tax collection and on the conditions for domestic borrowing.

Fifth, resource allocation is inefficient, initially due to excessive dirigisme, protection and subsidies, and more recently due to inflation and reorientation of the productive structure. Factor productivity growth has been substantially negative.

Right from the beginning of the de la Madrid administration it was clear that the problems were daunting and that the policy tasks were extremely unpleasant. However, the persistence of the problems was not foreseen, and bad luck in the seesaw of oil prices and the 1985 earthquake exacerbated the situation. The policy record has been patchy, with the biggest effort being made, courageously enough, in the election year of 1988.

The Pacto of 1988 succeeded in cutting inflation and mitigating the budget problem, and the government did quite a lot to improve long-run resource allocation by rationalizing tariffs, abolishing most import licensing and more than half of the 1,200 state enterprises. However, fixity of the exchange rate very heavily eroded the trade surplus, exchange reserves are quite low, and lags still exist in the price adjustment process. Government policy has mitigated some problems, but accentuated those of debt service. These loom larger than ever, now that the trade surplus is so slight.

The public finance position, though improved, is rather ambiguous. The government keeps three sets of books to measure the fiscal deficit. The "primary" fiscal balance is in substantial surplus, but the "financial" balance is in substantial deficit. If inflation has indeed been whipped, it is difficult to comprehend why the difference between these two fiscal concepts is equal to 13 percent of GDP. In fact, domestic expectations about the future exchange rate and future inflation are such that the government has to pay very high real interest rates to domestic lenders, who are free to move their capital over the border.

Experience suggests that even a major policy effort with high domestic political costs could not solve all the five major policy problems simultaneously. And external forces further complicate the situation.

THE EXTERNAL CIRCUMSTANCES(1)

An examination of external forces is useful in assessing the degree to which they are likely to constrain

Mexico's policy options, offer hope for change, or provide policy lessons. We may divide the external world into five parts, each of which is examined below.

The United States

Mexico has a much closer economic relationship to the United States than to other Latin American countries. The U.S. is dominant in trade, in tourism, and in movements of capital and labor.

The United States has followed an idiosyncratic policy mix since 1979, combining fiscal laxity with tight money. The consequences for other countries are themselves mixed. On the one hand, this combination has pushed up interest rates throughout the world economy, making the burden of floating-rate debt higher than it would be if the U.S. followed the fiscal norms of the other leading capitalist countries. On the other hand, the United States has had a very long expansion and runs a very large trade deficit, helping create a buoyant export market for developing countries.

One could imagine better or worse scenarios in the United States. But there are no reasonable grounds for thinking that the overall balance of U.S. policies will change for the better as far as Mexico is concerned.

Other OECD Countries

Most OECD countries have been hypercautious about the risk of inflation, keeping their economies on a slow growth track in the 1980s and running a trade surplus as a group. There is no likelihood that they will return to inflation at the 1970s' pace that made foreign borrowing look so attractive to Latin America; and there is little hope that they will accelerate their growth to a rate that would create a commodity boom.

Three elements were important in the OECD slowdown. First were the inevitable costs of adjustment to two system shocks: the collapse of the Bretton Woods agreement in 1971 with the related resumption of free mobility of private capital and the twelvefold increase in oil prices at the end of 1973. These shocks were large enough to require changes in the discretionary weapons of macroeconomic policy and in the rules of the game by which central bank and finance ministries had operated. They were large enough as well to change expectations in the private sector. By any reasonable accounting, even countries with the most sophisticated governments cannot be expected to lose output in dealing

with these shocks because they involved new risks for policy
and transitional problems in devising and learning to use
new policy weapons such as floating exchange rates. The same
adjustment problems were faced by the entrepreneurial and
trade union decision-makers whose reactions significantly
affect macroeconomic outcomes.

The second reason for slower growth was the new consensus in economic policy. It emerged as a response to events,
but it also helped mold them. Thus, when oil prices collapsed and the momentum of world inflation was broken in the
early 1980s, the new orthodoxy still continued both to
stress the dangers of expansionary policy in spite of widespread unemployment and strong payments positions and to
wait for a self-starting recovery rather than stimulating
one through policy. The proposition that OECD policymakers
have a new and distinct policy line from that in the 1950s
and 1960s is, of course, a stylized representation of reality. The "establishment view" changes over time, and is not
the same in all countries. But the ideological change in
the OECD countries has been widespread and far-ranging, and
has made output stagnation and increases in unemployment
intended outcomes of policy. This approach has been successful in stopping inflation, and the Latin American experience
of the 1980s provides confirmation that the costs of inflationary explosions are very real. The very success of the
new approach may lead to excessive caution and underexploita-
tion of the potential for growth for some years.

The third element in the OECD slowdown after 1973 was
the longer-run erosion of growth potential. Golden Age productivity performance had been very high by historical standards, more than double that of the first half of the twentieth century, that is, an annual average of 4.5 percent compared to 1.8 percent from 1900 to 1950. But this was due in
part to a series of once-and-for-all factors, like recovery
from the war in Europe and Japan, the reopening of economies
to international trade and the sizable movement of labor out
of agriculture or other less productive sectors of the economy. Moreover, as Europe and Japan modernized their capital
stock and came closer to the technological frontier, they
could no longer benefit to the same degree from the advantages of catch-up; and the pay-off on very high levels of
investment was smaller than in the past.

International Agencies

The IMF and the World Bank did not exist in pre-war
years. They play an historically unprecedented role that

has added to the buoyancy and stability of the post-war world economy.

After the 1982 debt crisis, these agencies stepped in to prevent a messy collapse in international capital markets, which had grown dramatically in the 1960s and 1970s. They preserved the legal integrity of most international debtor-creditor relationships, negotiated an involuntary flow from the banks to Latin America that would not have occurred without their intervention, and gave the creditor banks time to move to a more prudent reserve position.

An examination of the costs and benefits to both parties from this official "management" of international capital markets supports the conclusion that the creditors have fared better than the debtors. Without the IMF and World Bank, Latin American countries would almost certainly have behaved in the 1980s as they did in the 1930s, when all but Argentina and Cuba imposed moratoria on debt service, thereby forcing their creditors to write down the debt. In the 1942, 1943 and 1946 agreements, Mexico settled its debts at 10 cents on the dollar.(2)

Some palliatives may now be in the works. Unlike the earlier Baker initiative, the Brady plan from the U.S. Treasury recognizes the principle of writing down the debt burden. However, the degree of write-down envisioned seems modest in relationship to the size of the problem, and its mode of financing is not clear.

Asian Countries

The experience of the faster-growing Asian countries is pertinent if not immediately helpful for Mexico. Most conducted their economic policy more prudently in the 1970s. They were more cautious about inflation and foreign borrowing, and have smaller budget deficits, more realistic exchange rates and more export-oriented economies. Accordingly, they did not end up in the same situation as Latin America, in spite of facing similar challenges from the world economy.

Although they do not have much policy instruction to offer on how to emerge from the sort of problems Mexico now faces, for the longer term the Asian experience does carry some lessons. First, a successful policy for economic growth also requires prudent handling of conjunctural problems. Second, a greater degree of social equality makes their growth path more attractive, and would make income policies easier to mount when stabilization problems arise. Third, associated with more equality and with positive

effects on long-term productivity growth is a bigger commitment to raise the educational levels of their populations as
a whole and to offer more complete coverage at the primary
level in particular. Fourth, Asian birth control policies
have been more successful, and the effect has been to raise
savings rates and reduce poverty.

Other Latin American Experience

The collapse of the Bretton Woods agreements and the
acceleration of inflation in the early 1970s did not have
the same effect on the policymaking establishment in Latin
America as it did in the OECD countries. Many had never
seriously tried to observe the fixed rate discipline of Bretton Woods, and their exchange rates were only a fraction of
their 1950 level. National currencies had been repeatedly
devalued and high rates of inflation had become endemic.
The new disturbance was simply a variation on a familiar
theme, and was not regarded as a razor's edge situation,
calling for drastic policy change.
The direct non-price effects of the OPEC shock itself
were unfavorable for a large importer like Brazil, but they
brought windfall profits to Colombia and were fairly neutral
for self-sufficient oil producers like Argentina, Chile and
Peru. There was little effort to economize on the domestic
use of energy, and the general policy posture was one of
accommodating inflation rather than trying to break its
momentum, though there were temporary and unsuccessful monetarist experiments in Argentina and Chile. Growth continued
to be strong up to 1980 and the only recessions (in Chile
and Argentina) were due to internal causes -- the shift to
neo-conservatism from neo-Marxism and Peronism, respectively. Imports quickly expanded, and the payments problems were
met by large-scale foreign borrowing, mostly by government
from foreign banks at floating rates of interest and denominated in dollars. As interest rates remained lower than the
rate of world inflation in the 1970s, this strategy for continued growth did not seem too risky.
However, the basic parameters changed in the early
1980s. By then, the OECD countries were vigorously pushing
anti-inflationary policies. The restrictive monetary policy
initiated by the Federal Reserve pushed up interest rates
suddenly and sharply. The dollar appreciated and world
export prices began to fall. The average real interest cost
of floating-rate debt rose to nearly 16 percent from minus
8.7 percent in 1977-1980. Real interest rates remained high
thereafter, mainly because of the unusual fiscal-monetary

policy mix in the United States, where large fiscal deficits made Federal Reserve policy seem even more stringent.

Per capita foreign debt is three times as high in Latin America as in Asia and per capita exports are lower. The debt service problem is serious for all of the countries but Colombia. None has repudiated foreign debt and all have negotiated rollovers of principal payments, but they have generally paid interest in full. Given the high level of real interest rates, meeting this obligation has involved transfers that are a substantial fraction of GDP and have been financed only with the help of involuntary lending by commercial banks under pressure from the IMF. Thus creditor banks have not been forced into bankruptcy and developing countries as a whole have been able to continue to draw on the market. However, Latin America has been faced with a debt service burden without historical precedent.(3)

The domestic cost of adjustment for Latin American countries has been very heavy. Their real GDP in per capita terms has fallen since 1980 and worsened terms of trade further squeezed income. Their investment and imports have been drastically diminished. The fall in living standards and the acceleration of inflation have weakened the credibility of government to a degree that precludes most of the feasible policy options for a return to sustained growth. Productivity fell in all Latin American countries. In prolonged periods of stagnation capitalist economies generally do not experience significant declines in productivity like this, as redundant workers are laid off or plants shut down completely. But Latin America has large numbers of self-employed or family workers(4) who do not become overtly unemployed, and a good deal of labor hoarding has therefore occurred. The collapse of investment also helps explain the setbacks in productivity.

In sum, the economic problems of Latin America as a whole are quite similar to those identified at the beginning of this paper for Mexico in particular. Most countries accepted the risks of inflation and balance-of-payments difficulties with insouciance in the 1970s because they could borrow so cheaply. Like Mexico, most had inefficient resource allocation due to dirigisme and inward-looking policies. And the debt crisis of 1982, the end of voluntary capital inflows and the deceleration of inflationary momentum in OECD countries affected all of Latin America in much the same way.

Policy responses to these problems, however, have differed substantially. Three such approaches are discussed below.(5)

The Peruvian Option. This assumed that debt was the only problem. Debt service was capped at 10 percent of export earnings and other elements of policy were expansionist. The cost of a brief boom was heightened inflation, public sector deficits and resource misallocation. The result was hyperinflation, zero reserves, zero foreign credit and a very deep recession. This is a disastrous path which has legitimacy only if the country is willing to risk wrecking political institutions and believes it is the only way to induce creditors to make the massive write-down of debt that has occurred in Bolivia.(6)

The Heterodox Options of Argentina and Brazil. These assumed that inertial inflation was the key problem. In 1985 and 1986 Argentina and Brazil respectively attempted a freeze on prices, wages and the exchange rate, abolished price indexation, adopted new currency units and established debt tablitas (that is, formulae for settling private debts contracted before the controls). They neither cut demand significantly nor solved the budget problem. After a brief boom, reserves fell, the trade surplus disappeared, the currencies had to be substantially devalued and the inflationary process was rekindled. Both countries have dabbled with debt moratoria and Argentina has recently been too insolvent to meet interest payments, but neither adopted the Peruvian approach to debt. The situation in both countries is worse than it would have been in the absence of these heterodox experiments, which have eroded the scope for incomes policy, deepened domestic skepticism about the possibility of cutting inflation and exacerbated resource misallocation. Although some elements of this approach, like the fixed exchange rate and the idea of an incomes policy, were incorporated in the Mexican Pacto, it was a much more serious proposition than the Argentine-Brazilian experiments.

The Orthodox Path Pursued by Chile. The Chilean path has been more rigorous than the policies pursued by Mexico. Both budgetary expenditure cuts and tax increases were larger and the degree of privatization and trade liberalization was greater. Social and monetary policies were much tougher and substantial unemployment and two very deep recessions (15 percent declines in GDP in 1974 and 1982) were accepted as part of the cost of breaking inflationary expectations. Real devaluation has encouraged export growth, and along with extensive debt-equity swaps this has eased the debt service problem. Economic growth has been respectable in the past few years and inflation is moderate by Latin American standards. Living standards, however, are about what they were 20 years ago.

Significant mistakes compounded Chile's problems and prompted policy reversals. These errors include keeping the exchange rate fixed for too long, giving the banking sector too much freedom, and temporarily abandoning all exchange controls. But even successful pursuit of Chilean options would probably be beyond the capacity of the Mexican political system; it is clear that their harshness depended on the country's military dictatorship.

CONCLUSIONS

In the 1950s and 1960s Mexico did not share in the post-war policy orthodoxy of much of Latin America, which gave top priority to economic growth with only small attention to issues of microeconomic efficiency and little of the concern for conjunctural equilibrium or social welfare always characteristic of policy in the OECD countries. However, during the populist presidency of Echeverria in 1970-1976, Mexican policy changed; and in the subsequent administration of Lopez Portillo the government engaged in a spending spree that pushed the budget into a deficit equal to 17 percent of GDP by 1982. This led to suspension of debt service, massive capital flight and inflation. The legacy of four decades of growth with virtually no interruption was then a huge build-up of inflation, payments difficulties, social tension, fiscal-monetary disequilibria and the macroeconomic inefficiency underlying the chaos of the 1980s.

The subsequent administration of de la Madrid (1982-1988) successfully renegotiated the foreign debt and cut public investment, subsidies and real salaries in the public sector. Combined with slackened domestic demand, a sharp effective devaluation converted the trade deficit into a surplus, but it also made continued high inflation unavoidable.

Policy problems were further compounded by the massive earthquake in 1985 and the drastic fall in oil prices from $25.33 per barrel in 1985 to $11.85 in 1986. Since oil represented two-thirds of exports, the payments situation suddenly collapsed and government revenue from this source fell by 4 percent of GDP. Allowing the real exchange rate to appreciate further weakened the external balance.

In response to the new crisis, government adjustment efforts strengthened along orthodox lines -- renegotiation of the debt and fiscal austerity. It also became clear that the government was serious in its efforts to open up the economy by joining the GATT and removing import licensing. It pushed ahead with privatization of some of the sellable state enterprises, reduced government subsidies and made the remaining public enterprises pursue more realistic pricing policies.

The authorities studied the Argentine and Brazilian stabilization experiments closely, but chose not to emulate them, trying instead to break inflationary expectations by the moderately heterodox technique of an income and prices policy during the last year of the de la Madrid administration. This involved a concerted effort among the government (Ministries of Labor, Commerce and Public Finance), trade unions, business groups and peasant organizations to freeze prices voluntarily and maintain wage stability. To provide an anchor for expectations, the exchange rate was also frozen, as it had been in both the 1985-1986 experiments in Argentina and Brazil and the monetarist operations in Argentina and Chile in the 1970s. At the same time fiscal policy aimed at a primary surplus (disregarding the inflation-compensation component in government interest payments). Monetary policy remained tight and real interest rates high, and the economy was kept open with 90 percent of imports free from quantitative restrictions and subject to a maximum tariff of 20 percent.

The commitment to a fixed exchange rate was feasible due to some recovery of oil prices, an improvement in the trade surplus and accumulation of impressive exchange reserves as a result of earlier austerity. However, this new approach has yet to cut back inflation to acceptable levels and, like the exchange rate freeze, was a temporary suppressant whose after-effects will be unpleasant.

Mexico may be able to mount a milder version of Chile's orthodoxy for the first half of the present sexennio and a more viable social pact than Argentina and Brazil, but it probably needs massive debt relief in order to come up with a policy package that can restore economic growth.(7)

NOTES

1.   For a fuller analysis of background developments in the world economy, see A. Maddison, The World Economy in the Twentieth Century (Paris, OECD Development Centre, 1989).

2.   See A. Maddison, Two Crises: Latin America and Asia in 1929-38 and 1973-83, (Paris, OECD Development Centre, 1985).

3.   For historical precedents of previous transfers see H. Reisen, "The Latin American Transfer Problem in Historical Perspective", in <u>Latin America, the Caribbean and the OECD</u>, ed. by A. Maddison (Paris, OECD Development Centre, 1986).   In the 1930s, when Latin America faced a similar problem, there was widespread delinquency in payments, with eventual write-off of most debt (see Maddison, <u>Two Crises</u>).

4.   The proportion of self-employed and family workers is about 37 percent in Latin America and 13 percent in the OECD countries (see ECLAC, <u>Statistical Yearbook for Latin America, 1987</u>, p. 655.   At 50 percent, this proportion is highest in Peru, where H. de Soto, <u>El Otro Sendero</u>, has stressed the importance of the informal economy.

5.   See A. Maddison, <u>The World Economy in the Twentieth Century</u>.

6.   See J. D. Sachs, "Comprehensive Debt Retirement: The Bolivian Example," <u>Brookings Papers on Economic Activity</u>, No. 2 (1988).

7.   Editors' Note: For more references to Maddison, please see the "General Comments" by Anne Krueger, pp. 251-253.

Comments

Gustav Ranis
Professor of Economics, Yale University

This paper is a tour d'horizon, but as we have come to expect from Angus Maddison, full of nuggets of wisdom and refreshing both in content and in presentation. In a world where Northerners usually emphasize domestic adjustments in the South, and Southerners emphasize the deterioration of the international environment, this paper presents a disarmingly symmetrical treatment of the world economy in all its component parts. With respect to the "big players" it includes an interesting discussion of how the breakdown of Bretton Woods and OPEC price increases made the leaders of developed countries more cautious as their inflationary fears mounted -- with the important exception, of course, of Reagan, the "accidental Keynesian". It also emphasizes that this problem of caution was compounded by a global slowdown which would have come in any case due to the exhaustion of the post-war catch-up effect in Europe and Japan as everyone eventually had "grown back into their skins," as Raymond Goldsmith liked to put it.

Turning to the Southern countries, Maddison emphasizes that after the first oil shock really only the developed countries had to do most of the adjusting, while the developing countries, buffered by commercial bank lending in the 1970s, didn't have to adjust until after the second oil shock. Yet they clearly paid for this delay, as the paper points out, through the resulting micro-misallocations of the 1970s.

Maddison comments that LDC's never observed the fixed-rate discipline of Bretton Woods -- as if "they should have" -- even during the 1950s, when what I would consider legitimate import substitution policies were in vogue. Even the East Asians experienced such sub-phases and adopted movable peg policies in a movable peg world. Their fiscal and monetary policies were also better in the sense of being more restrained and flexible.

Maddison also asserts that Mexico differs from the East Asian countries by continuing to give top priority to economic growth over microeconomic efficiency. But it is my view that everyone in the South is pro-growth, has to be. The questions are rather how one goes about trying to achieve growth and what one does when things go temporarily wrong, as they inevitably do. For example, when the terms of trade deteriorate, does the government try to maintain growth artificially, substituting domestic purchasing power for foreign purchasing power, until it is finally forced into a return to controls and import substitution policies? Or, in the face of such adversity, does it de-emphasize quantity and let prices, interest rates and exchange rates adjust flexibly, as in the East Asian case?

Fundamentally, I agree with Maddison that the current debt crisis is but a manifestation of a deeper development crisis. But I disagree with his judgment that all was well for Mexico until about 1970. While I agree there was price stability between 1950 and 1970, along with a high growth rate and a fixed exchange rate, fundamental development problems were building up even then. These include: 1) an increasingly inefficient and heavily protected industrial sector, very narrowly focused on large scale industry; 2) a record of agricultural neglect with respect to ejido lands and small scale private agriculture -- in other words, all but the large scale capital intensive Northern tracts; 3) an increasing role for the public sector even in directly productive activities; and 4) a gradual decline in the country's overall and per capita export orientation. The export/GDP ratio in 1970 was one-half that of 1950, the growth rate during the 1960s was one-half that of the 1950s, and the income distribution pattern steadily deteriorated as well.

All in all, following a period of "natural" import substitution during the Great Depression and World War II, Mexico adopted an ever more severe version of the typical official import-substitution syndrome in the 1950s and 1960s. Thus, in my considered opinion, the populist spending policies of Echeverria and Lopez Portillo were not the major problem. It was only when both oil bonanzas and foreign bankers were no longer available to fuel an increasingly narrow and inefficient growth path that the economy finally collapsed.(1)

I find myself quite partial to Maddison's comparative historical approach, contrasting Latin American and Asian experiences. Moreover, I have little disagreement with him here except that I would argue that the lower level of Asian debt is not all due to their superior virtue. Especially the South Asians were much less attractive to the commercial banks that were brimming with OPEC deposits and touted countries like Mexico and Brazil as highly attractive investment opportunities.

Maddison's paper is provocative enough to prompt a host of questions about additional issues. For example, just how does Mexico's "social contract", which is due to expire in 1989 and will presumably have to be renegotiated, differ from the heterodox Brazil and Argentina versions to which Maddison refers? Mexico has in place a virtual freeze in the exchange rate, wages and prices, but unlike Argentina and Brazil, and more like Israel, it complements this strategy by tight monetary and fiscal policies. There nevertheless remains the question of the curtailment of inflation, which not even Israel has managed. Was this accomplished in Mexico by the availability of larger reserves initially and much more import liberalization? How much was due to more privatization, that is, a shrinking role for public enterprise and the financieras?

These are critical issues and also lead to the question of where Mexico goes from here. The crucial issue before this conference is whether the additional resources will be forthcoming to permit resumed investment and growth, now that Mexico has made very large and impressively courageous structural adjustments over the last few years. Also, what other domestic measures are required, if any, to convert Mexico to a fully participatory Latin American NIC closer to the Asian development model? By their own statements, most influential Mexican economists would probably include on any such list fiscal reform, decentralization of infrastructure and the encouragement of balanced growth between agriculture and rural non-agriculture.

Finally, though this topic is admittedly a bit far afield, it would have been interesting to have Maddison reflect on the political economy advantages of Mexico's particular sequence of adjustment and additional resources to restart growth. This process, I think, makes the Mexican structural adjustment story somewhat unique. In other words, instead of waiting for an IMF and/or World Bank mission to come in and preach the policies that needed to be adopted, this is rather more a case of the initiative being taken by the Mexicans in an effort to get a response from the international community to sustain the new policies that had actually been put in place. The matter of initiative is obviously a gray area heavily tinged with atmospherics, but here we encounter something slightly different from the usual procedure and probably politically more sensible and with a better chance for survival.

None of the above is, however, meant to detract one iota from what was said at the outset. I consider Maddison's paper to be a thoroughly enjoyable, intelligent and persuasive contribution of considerable value to anyone interested in the current international economic situation and its particular impact on the Third World.

NOTES

1. For a more extensive analysis and what was then viewed as a far-out prognostication of what was to come, see the author's "¿ Se Este Tormando Amargo el Milagro Mexicano?" ("Is the Mexican Miracle Turning Sour?"), Demografia y Economia, Vol. VIII, No. 1 (El Colegio de Mexico, 1974).

Social Impact of the Economic Crisis

Leopoldo Solis*
*Director, Lucas Alaman Institute of
Economic and Social Research*

The 1980s will go down in the history of Latin America as the "lost decade." Not only have countries ravaged by guerrilla movements, such as El Salvador and Nicaragua, lost ground, but even the regional leaders like Brazil, Argentina, Venezuela and Mexico will harbor bitter memories of these years. This paper focuses on some economic, political and social aspects of Mexico's unfortunate experience in the 1980s, but because the conditions all over Latin America are somewhat similar, the account should also be applicable at least in general terms to the region as a whole.

Since the financial crisis of 1981, the living standards of the Mexican people have deteriorated, as can be seen from the data in Table 1. The net transfer of financial resources abroad from both capital flight and payments on the foreign debt (see Table 2) and the general downward trend of prices for raw materials and other traditional exports, especially oil, have contributed to these problems, and the fall in GDP has affected every economic and social variable. Real wages, public sector revenues and spending on social welfare programs have all declined. Unemployment and underemployment have grown 3.9 percent and 10.3 percent, respectively, while the economically active population has decreased from 30.2 percent to 26.2 percent.

Every level of Mexican society has been affected by these changes, but in different ways. Many years will go by before Mexicans can return to the standards of living they enjoyed in 1981 and it is important to identify the groups

---

*I would like to thank Gabriel Vera for his kind collaboration on this document.

that have suffered most and to assess how much longer they can reasonably be expected to tolerate this stressful situation.

FUNCTIONAL DISTRIBUTION OF INCOME

The initial step in this analysis is to study the functional distribution of income. Table 3 presents some data on disposable income and illustrates the extent to which wages have dropped and real income has declined. Living standards today are well below those of 1981-1982; indeed, disposable real income per capita in 1987 was barely above 1977 levels, having fallen 60 percent from 1981 to 1987 as the pressure of population growth exacerbated the effects of the economic decline.(1)

The sixth column of Table 3 shows the steady decline from 40.3 percent to 28.4 percent in the ratio of wage income to GDP for the 1976-1986 period. The last column shows the evolution of the real annual minimum wage, which has also decreased steadily since 1976, with a cumulative decline of 45 percent. Such comparisons clearly show that the groups most affected by the crisis of the 1980s are wage earners. In order to prevent the 1990s from becoming another "tragic decade," the economic strategies Mexico pursues should be directed not only toward resumption of economic growth, but also toward a more even distribution of the burden of the crisis during the 1980s.

IDENTIFYING GROUPS AFFECTED BY THE CRISIS

It is important to remember that the crisis has probably affected the structure of income sources. Nevertheless, data from the period before the 1980s are necessary to identify the groups for which wages are the main source of income because the most recent information available on the structure of family income comes from the National Survey on Home Incomes and Expenditures for 1977.(2)

Table 5 indicates that the main components of family income in Mexico are wages and self-employment and that their relative importance depends upon family income level. For example, wages are relatively less important in decile I (37 percent), increasing successively to a maximum of 68 percent in decile X, with only one small decline in decile VIII. Self-employment income, on the other hand, is most important in decile I (35 percent), declining consistently through decile IX (15 percent), and then rising in decile X. I conclude that the families in income deciles V-IX have been most affected by the drop in real wages.

In 1981 close to 47 percent of Mexican families earned less than two minimum wages, while in 1987 the percentage was almost 60 percent.(3) The minimum wage, moreover, has fallen substantially in real terms. Clearly the consequences of Mexico's crisis have been concentrated on its poor; and reducing the living standards of the already poor implies that the social costs of the crisis are even more acute than they may first appear.

On the other hand, 50 percent of the population comprising the middle and upper income groups now command a smaller share of national income. A large group of people who in the previous decades had become accustomed to substantial economic advancement have now become relatively impoverished.

The underground economy, estimated at between 28 percent and 35 percent of the GDP in 1986, has provided an escape valve for this problem.(4) Drug trafficking is not included in this estimate of the underground economy, but its share has undoubtedly increased in part because of the economic crisis. The other escape valve is emigration. The number of emigrants is impossible to quantify exactly, but the estimated range is from 1 to 4 million Mexicans a year.

SOCIOECONOMIC PROFILE OF FAMILIES

In order to define these groupings more precisely, Table 4 indicates by income deciles some salient characteristics of the families most likely to have been affected by the crisis and highlights the importance of multiple earners for family income.

These data support the belief that families in which more than one member works to maintain their level of income have been hardest hit by the crisis and are the most sensitive to problems of unemployment and underemployment. In 1981, with an economically active population (EAP) of 23 million, unemployment was on the order of 4 percent, or 920,000 individuals. By 1986 estimates placed that number at 4 million, with an EAP of 26 million. Unemployment had skyrocketed by more than 400 percent, an increase that makes it easier to understand why the percentage of families with income below two minimum wages rose from 47 percent to almost 60 percent.

Table 6 completes the socioeconomic profile of family groups by showing the distribution of family expenditures. Spending on food and drink becomes less and less important as income increases, while most of the other expenditures become more important. Substantial changes in the distribution of family expenditures have therefore occurred during the crisis. Purchases of non-perishable or postponable consumer goods with positive income elasticities of demand have been reduced. The contraction in demand from those groups suffering the most severe consequences of the crisis has significantly affected the productive apparatus.

The situation for the group between deciles V-IX has been further aggravated by the fact that the rises in prices have not been homogeneous. Table 7 shows the average annual inflation rates for the period 1981-1987. While the cost of transportation has grown 92 percent a year, gross rent has increased only 67 percent, a differential of 25 percentage points in six years. The General Price Index, which is largely determined by changes in prices for food, beverages and tobacco, increased by 82 percent.

Another factor which has had a negative effect on the real disposable income of wage earners has been the treatment of payroll taxes, especially the adjustments made during 1987 and 1988. In real terms, tax rates were four times greater in 1988 than in 1987 and this change affects wage earners, who are captive taxpayers, more than recipients of other forms of income.

SOCIO-DEMOGRAPHIC FACTORS

Finally, examining some demographic factors will help in evaluating the magnitude of the social problems the economic crisis has caused for Mexico. Although the crisis has had a strong effect on fecundity and mortality, demographic inertia has been even more important, since the population structures that will determine social investment needs up to the year 2000 have already been set. For example, the individuals who will enter the labor force in the year 2000 have already been born. By the end of the present century Mexico will have a population of 105 million, of which 40 million will constitute the potential EAP. An estimated 1.5 million jobs must be created annually until the year 2000 in order to absorb the currently unemployed and to provide employment opportunities for the new entrants into the labor force. Such an increase in jobs is impossible without rapid and sustained growth in the economy, and this will require large amounts of public and private sector investment. Given the resources currently being sent abroad to cover the foreign debt, an adjustment in the pattern of international payments will be essential.

Another demographic phenomenon to be kept in mind is the accelerated urbanization occurring in Mexico and most other developing countries. For example, the proportion of Mexico's population living in urban areas rose from 14 percent in 1920 to 56 percent in 1985.(5) Projections for the year 2000 indicate that 75 percent of the population will live in urban areas.(6) Urban concentration will have significant effects on the supply and demand of goods and services. On the one hand, Mexico must encourage creation of jobs for a largely urban population by means of appropriate industrialization and educational policies. On the other hand, the process of the urbanization will have a strong effect on the demand for goods and services provided in whole or part by the government. Housing, education, health care, water, electricity, transportation and urban infrastructure in general will all require a large amount of public sector investment of a social nature. International organizations making loans for this type of infrastructure must play a key role in easing the financial limitations throughout Latin America.

Finally, internal and international migrations can have a definitive effect on economic, social and political variables. Almost 500,000 Guatemalans and Central Americans, the majority of whom are agriculturalists, have migrated to Mexico. At the same time, at least 1 million Mexicans have emigrated to the United States. Internally, the population growth of Mexico's three main metropolitan areas is irrational. Mexico City in particular, with 18 million inhabitants, shelters 20 percent of the country's population in an inhospitable location more than 2,400 meters above sea level with serious problems of pollution and water supply.

CONCLUSIONS

Although the entire society has felt the effects of Mexico's crisis, it has most seriously affected those in income deciles V-IX. This group includes approximately 50 percent of the population with the following profile: their incomes are derived principally from wages and salaries, with more than one family member in general employed; they are somewhat educated; and their expenditures are concentrated on food, beverages and housing.

The impact of measures meant to heal the domestic economy, such as devaluing the peso and eliminating the fiscal deficit, which raise the price of consumer goods and reduce real urban income, should be carefully weighed against other economic policy options. The political and social costs of devaluation and elimination of subsidies are high and eventually even the formidable patience of the Mexican people will wear thin.

As the reform measures of the Salinas administration begin to take hold, backing from the middle classes will need to be re-won. Mexico's situation remains unstable and perilous, and the economic challenge is enormous. Not only must the 4 million currently unemployed workers be absorbed, but 1.5 million more jobs must be created each year. Annual growth must average 1.8 percent just to provide these employment increases. And in order to recover the 1981 level of per capita income during the 1990s additional growth averaging more than 3 percent annually will be required.

The resources prospectively available to the government from internal and external sources are insufficient for this purpose. Priority should therefore be given to limiting the transfer of resources abroad and to reinforcing the domestic tax system so that the weight of the crisis setbacks can be borne more uniformly throughout society.

NOTES

1. We should remember that there was a substantial over-valuation of the peso vis-a-vis the dollar at the beginning of this period.
2. Instituto Nacional de Estadistica, Geografia e Informatica of the Secretaria de Programacion y Presupuesto. Families are grouped on the basis of income into 10 deciles, with decile I representing the lowest income group and decile X the highest.
3. Enrique Alducin A., "Los valores de los mexicanos," in Mexico: Entre la tradicion y la modernidad (Mexico: Fomento Cultural Banamex, 1981 and 1987).
4. Centro de Estudios del Sector Privado, La economia subterranea en Mexico (Mexico, 1986).
5. Alejandro Rodriguez, Del medio rural al medio urbano (Mexico: CONAPO, 1988).
6. Lorenzo Moreno and Leopoldo Nunez, Mexico: Proyecciones de poblacion urbana y rural, 1980-2010 (Mexico: AMDM).

TABLE 1. Real Income, Per Capita

	1981	1988	Percent Variation
Total GDP (Billions of 1980 Pesos)	4,862.22	4,749.01	-2.3
Total Population (Thousands)	71,250.	83,420.	17.1
Per Capita GDP (Thousands of 1980 Pesos)	68.24	56.93	-16.6

Source: Banco de Mexico, Indicadores Economicos.

TABLE 2. Net Transfer of Financial Resources Abroad
          (Millions of Dollars)

	1978-82	1983-88	1989-94
Net Revenues, Loans (A)	124,156	94,136	36,000[a]
Capital Repayments (B)	-66,112	-77,755	-44,893[b]
Net Indebtedness (A - B)	58,044	16,381	-8,893
Interest Payments	-38,298	-62,309	61,500[c]
Net Transfer	19,746	-45,928	-70,393

[a] Supposing credits averaging 6 billion dollars a year.
[b] According to figures from the Direccion General de Credito Publico of the Secretaria de Hacienda y Credito Publico, Cuaderno de informacion (May 31, 1988).
[c] At current interest rates.

Source: Banco de Mexico, Indicadores Economicos.

TABLE 3. Disposable Income

Year	Pop.[a] (1000)	Real Peso Income (1970 Prices)	Per Capita Real	Per Capita Dollar	Wages as % of GDP[b]	Real Annual Minimum Wage[c]
1976	61,978.4	635,831	10,259	685.5	40.3	33,848
1977	63,812.8	657,831	10,307	825.5	38.9	33,577
1978	65,658.3	711,983	10,844	1,020.7	37.9	32,602
1979	67,517.5	777,163	11,511	1,333.7	37.7	32,220
1980	69,392.0	841,855	12,132	1,819.8	36.0	30,024
1981	71,249.1	908,765	12,755	2,225.1	37.5	31,478
1982	73,122.3	903,839	12,361	627.8	35.2	27,908
1983	74,980.5	856,174	11,709	1,057.4	29.4	23,080
1984	76,885.9	903,839	12,054	1,398.7	28.7	21,838
1985	78,839.8	926,754	11,755	1,053.4	28.6	22,583
1986	80,843.3	892,123	11,035	861.6	28.4	19,665
1987	82,897.7	902,322	10,885	865.5	N.A.	18,587

[a]L. Moreno and L. Nunez, Proyecciones de poblacion de 1980 a 2010 (Mexico: AMIDM).
[b]Instituto Nacional de Estadistica, Geografia e Informatica, Sistema de cuentas nacionales (Mexico, 1988).
[c]Comision Nacional de Salarios Minimos, Salarios minimos: 1970–1987.

TABLE 4. Socioeconomic Profile of Families, by Decile

Family Decile	Residing in Home	Family Members	Members Working	Wage Earners	Head's Age	Head's Educ.
I	4.05	4.05	1.31	1.26	49.51	2.16
II	4.83	4.83	1.37	1.25	44.90	3.19
III	5.40	5.40	1.49	1.38	44.86	2.74
IV	5.66	5.66	1.50	1.41	43.03	3.52
V	5.73	5.73	1.55	1.46	42.43	4.63
VI	5.78	5.77	1.51	1.51	41.21	4.32
VII	5.93	5.92	1.61	1.59	41.36	4.92
VIII	6.09	6.07	1.72	1.70	43.14	5.61
IX	6.06	6.02	1.91	1.89	44.06	7.05
X	6.12	5.92	2.06	2.05	46.25	10.58

Source: Juan Diez-Canedo and Gabriel Vera, La distribucion del ingreso en Mexico, 1977 (Mexico: Banco de Mexico, 1981).

TABLE 5. Structure of Family Income, by Deciles (Percentages)

Family Decile	Wages	Self-Employ-ment	Income/ Interest/ Dividends	Rent Savings, Own Home	Self-Con-sump-tion	Family Trans-fers	Gifts Payment in Kind	Other Sources	Total
I	36.64	34.92	0.48	6.36	11.33	7.31	3.92	1.04	100
II	45.33	28.58	0.75	6.12	9.21	5.71	2.40	1.90	100
III	50.95	25.31	0.54	5.78	8.28	5.02	2.51	1.61	100
IV	54.43	23.04	0.46	6.10	5.67	5.37	2.16	2.77	100
V	64.47	18.55	0.95	5.86	3.23	2.67	1.93	2.34	100
VI	65.22	17.95	0.64	6.86	2.28	2.46	1.98	2.61	100
VII	67.03	17.80	0.76	6.18	1.28	2.60	1.93	2.42	100
VIII	66.88	16.09	1.02	7.11	1.08	2.89	1.97	2.96	100
IX	67.34	15.44	1.25	7.02	0.55	2.81	1.72	3.87	100
X	67.52	16.05	1.50	7.25	0.30	1.59	1.67	8.67	100

Source: Juan Diez-Canedo and Gabriel Vera, La distribucion del ingreso en Mexico, 1977 (Mexico: Banco de Mexico, 1981).

TABLE 6. Structure of Family Expenditures, by Decile (Percentage)

Family Decile	Food/Non-Alcoholic Beverages	Alcoholic Beverages	Clothing/Footwear	Gross Rent	Furniture/Accessories	Medical Services	Transportation	Education	Other Services	Total
I	77.27	2.16	5.86	2.56	1.07	3.59	2.86	1.21	3.42	100
II	76.22	2.89	6.99	2.78	1.07	3.05	2.39	1.11	3.50	100
III	73.29	2.29	8.27	3.23	1.53	3.39	3.33	1.73	2.94	100
IV	74.42	2.34	8.65	3.49	2.01	3.17	4.15	2.68	3.09	100
V	67.08	2.53	8.53	4.22	2.56	2.94	5.44	2.90	3.80	100
VI	62.47	2.01	9.96	4.81	3.55	3.20	6.09	4.34	3.58	100
VII	59.46	2.30	10.80	4.34	3.64	2.96	7.47	5.18	3.85	100
VIII	55.29	2.01	11.16	4.81	4.55	3.17	8.82	5.61	4.58	100
IX	49.47	2.15	12.36	4.57	4.06	3.16	11.40	6.68	6.15	100
X	32.72	1.40	11.35	3.91	4.47	4.39	22.23	9.81	9.72	100

Source: Juan Diez-Canedo and Gabriel Vera, La distribucion del ingreso en Mexico, 1977 (Mexico: Banco de Mexico, 1981).

TABLE 7. Average Annual Inflation Rates, 1981-1987 (Percentage)

General Price Index	Food Beverages/Tobacco	Clothing/Footwear	Gross Rent	Furniture/Accessories	Medical Services	Transportation	Education	Other Services
82	81	84	67	85	87	92	80	90

Source: Banco de Mexico, Indicadores Economicos.

Comments

Robert Pastor
Professor of Political Science and Director of the Latin American and Caribbean Program at the Carter Center, Emory University

The Latin American debt crisis of the 1980s has been reported largely as an endless series of negotiations between bankers and debtor governments. Sleek limousines carry dark-suited bankers and political officials from one meeting to another, where they negotiate an arrangement that keeps the debt payments coming. Each agreement is proclaimed a glorious solution to the problem, but few have lasted more than eighteen months.

From the onset of the debt crisis in 1982, the principal issue for the commercial bankers and creditor governments has been the solvency of the international banking system, while the debtor countries have been concerned with reducing their debt service to a level they can manage without default. The results have been jerry-built debt reschedulings that have enabled the international banks to reduce their exposure gradually while keeping some capital flowing to the debtor countries. The reschedulings have stretched out and sometimes reduced the debt by small amounts, but not enough to permit the countries to grow. The entire process has been biased toward a short-term financial view of the problem; the social, political and distributive consequences have been ignored.

The riots in Caracas in February of 1989 that left over 300 dead were the clearest signs of the cost of overlooking these consequences. To his credit, Leopoldo Solis shifts our attention from the negotiations between creditors and debtors to the social and economic pain of the people. He describes the 1980s as a "lost decade" for Mexico and Latin America, but the phrase is somewhat too felicitous as it suggests that the region was standing in place. In fact, Latin America and Mexico have fallen backwards; by 1988, their per capita gross domestic products were respectively 6.6 percent and 16.6 percent below what they had been in 1980.

In his analysis of the distributive impact of the debt crisis on Mexico, Solis reaches the rather startling conclusion that the largest share of the burden fell on the shoulders of the salaried, new middle class -- deciles V-IX. The political implications of this conclusion are significant.

Fifty years ago, in a comparative analysis of four revolutions, Crane Brinton argued that revolutions are most likely to occur at the end of an extended period of economic prosperity. If the standard of living of the new middle class then declines sharply and there is no prospect for peaceful political change, the children of this class lead the revolution.(1) This pattern, of course, is perfectly congruent with Mexico's recent history. After four decades of growth, the debt crisis has ushered in a period of declining living standards for Mexico's middle class. Moreover, the middle class face a relatively rigid political system, and, indeed, this might explain some of their support for the candidacy of Cuauhtemoc Cardenas. If Brinton's prediction holds, the continued disaffection of the middle class could imperil Mexico's political stability.

There is one important difference between contemporary Mexico and the countries previously wracked by revolution, and that difference was crystallized in a comment I overheard by a Mexico City taxicab driver in response to the ubiquitous question: "Will Mexico have a revolution?" "Mexico," he responded, "has already had a revolution, and we Mexicans have learned that revolutions do not improve life for anyone."

That simple remark captured a reality that many intellectuals extolling the benefits of revolution have persistently overlooked. A widespread myth is that Mexico's revolution began in 1910 and ended in 1940 when Avila Camacho replaced the last military President, Lazaro Cardenas. James Wilkie looked beneath the myth with a systematic statistical analysis of the data on federal expenditures and social changes in Mexico from 1910. He found that "social benefits for the masses as well as economic development came at a rapid rate only after 1940...Mexico experienced its most rapid social change for the masses between 1940 and 1960."(2) The real revolution according to Wilkie requires "political stability."(3) An awareness of the costs of violence and the burdens of past revolutions has led today's alienated and disillusioned Mexicans to choose either passivity or non-violent modes of change.

Nonetheless, I would agree with Solis that the system's limits are being tested by the most prolonged economic crisis since the 1930s, and that Mexican patience, while formidable, is not inexhaustible. Revolutions might be led by the middle class, but often the spark that sets them off is the product of political combustion, of rage; and a flame in Mexico would be much more difficult to cap than one in Venezuela. Because of its proximity to the United States the slightest sign of instability in Mexico would stimulate massive capital flight and large-scale migration that would make any solution to this problem much more difficult. All of this suggests that the U.S. government should take a broader perspective in attempting to forge a genuine, long-term solution to the debt crisis.

While I agree that the distributive consequences of the debt crisis are deadly serious for Mexico and also for the United States, I have some questions about Solis' methods in reaching his conclusion that the burden of the debt crisis has fallen hardest on the top half of the population.

He argues, correctly, that the relative decline in average and minimum wages in Mexico during the 1980s was greater than the decline in per capita gross domestic product. But without substantiation, he leaps beyond this assertion to conclude that the wage-earners -- the V-IX deciles -- have suffered the greatest. This conclusion disregards the effects of the crisis on the unemployed and underemployed -- those outside the wage-based indices.

Solis cites statistics indicating that unemployment and underemployment rose by 3.9 percent and 10.3 percent during the period and the economically active population declined from 30.2 percent to 26.2 percent. The World Bank judges these as very low estimates because Mexico considers a person employed if he or she works only one hour a week. "What is clear," according to the World Bank, "is that the main problem is not open unemployment but underemployment"; in considering the distributive effect of the crisis, "the relatively unskilled were more severely affected."(4) As the number of Mexicans below the poverty line increased, it is not unreasonable to conclude that they bore a larger share of the burden of adjustment than the fewer wage-based workers above the median.

Based on his extrapolations from a 1977 household survey, Solis' second conclusion is that the middle class has been harmed the most by the reduction in wages. To draw conclusions on the distributive impact of the debt crisis since 1982, however, one needs to compare the data in 1977 with a second set of data after the crisis. Without such a basis for comparison, one can speculate, but conclusions must be very tentative. Indeed, the 1977 survey data could just as easily be used as the basis for the opposite conclusion of

Solis': the poor were harmed a lot worse than the middle class.

According to the 1977 survey, the bottom 40 percent of the population had to spend about three-quarters of their income on food. A reduction in wages probably means less food, and indeed, a recent Mexican study demonstrated that per capita food consumption has declined since 1981 by 20 percent and that as much as 50 percent of the people living in rural areas suffer from malnutrition.(5) The 1977 survey also shows that the top 20 percent of the population spend less than half of their income on food, twice as much as the poorest 20 percent on clothing and four times as much on furniture. Undoubtedly, the richest would have to forego new clothes or furniture, but it is hard to argue that they will therefore become worse off than the poor who have less to eat.

A third point Solis makes is that since the top 50 percent of the population obtains a larger share of its income from wages, and since the prices of the goods that they purchase have tended to rise most rapidly because of inflation, then the top 50 percent have suffered more than the bottom 50 percent. This is a re-tread of the second point: it is quite true that the purchasing power of the top 50 percent might have declined the most statistically, but if their purchases can be postponed, then their sacrifice would seem less than for the poorest 40 percent living on the margin of life.

An underlying problem in interpreting these statistics is that the debt crisis has bent the economic system into new shapes. The modern sector has shrunk, and it is true that the wage-earners have suffered greatly. But during a depression, the people on the margin always suffer the most. In the 1980s the poor have been squeezed into the informal sector -- meaning that they have picked up work wherever they can find it, and many have returned to subsistence agriculture. This phenomenon is not unique to Mexico, but rather has been identified in all of the debt-crisis countries in Latin America.(6) What it demonstrates is the survival instincts of the poor in a declining economy.

In considering the long-term social and distributive effects of the debt crisis, however, the most significant statistics relate to government expenditures and public investment in health, nutrition and education. The long-term effects are best measured by the children whose bodies and minds are deformed by malnutrition, the students who drop out of school to support their families, and the graduates who cannot find work. Mexico's expenditures on health and social services as a percentage of gross domestic product declined by 80 percent from 1981 to 1984. Educational expenditures climbed from 1970 until reaching 3.6 percent of GDP in 1981. The debt crisis then caused them to plummet to 2.5 percent in 1984.(7) According to the World Bank, the levels of per capita food consumption and nutrition, "especially for the urban and rural poor, declined severely from 1982 to 1986."(8)

It is remarkable that after four decades of growth, the Mexican people have patiently and passively watched as their standard of living has fallen in the 1980s. Mexicans have coped. Some have returned to the rural areas; others have taken whatever work they could find. Many have left the country for the United States. According to U.S. census reports, the Mexican-origin population in the United States has increased by nearly three times since 1970, from 4.2 million in 1970 to 11.8 million people in 1987. This did not include the 1.5 million Mexicans who had entered the United States illegally and recently filed for amnesty. More importantly, the number of Mexicans who have decided to become U.S. citizens has increased dramatically in the 1980s.(9)

Those who believe that Mexico can grow by reducing government expenditures ignore the fact that it has shrunk by reducing investment in health and education. Only the state can invest in these areas. Moreover, the state has played an historically important role in stimulating development in Mexico, just as it has done in Japan, South Korea, and indeed, in the United States. It is true that the state overextended its reach into unproductive corporations during the last two decades, but under Presidents de la Madrid and Salinas, Mexico has privatized. To grow today, Mexico needs to invest more. The only way to do this is to reduce the debt.

Mexico has survived, but it has not grown, and its patience has limits. For these reasons, the United States and Mexico should join together to stop the middling, muddling process of adjusting to the past debt accumulation, and to start planning for the future by slicing the debt burden in half. The debt-reduction initiative proposed by Nicholas Brady, Secretary of the Treasury, in March of 1989 was first tested in the case of Mexico, but the agreement that followed between the banks and Mexico was inadequate. It was a positive step forward, but Mexico needed a great leap for economic, political and humanitarian reasons.(10)

Mexico has paid disproportionately for its profligate borrowing in the late 1970s. All Mexicans have been forced to pay, but as is usually the case, the Mexicans with the least have had to pay the most. The time has come for those with the most to relieve those with the least.

NOTES

1. Crane Brinton, The Anatomy of Revolutions (Englewood Cliffs: Prentice Hall, 1928). See also Chalmers Johnson, Revolutionary Change (Stanford: Stanford University Press, 1982).

2. James W. Wilkie, The Mexican Revolution: Federal Expenditure and Social Change Since 1910 (Berkeley: University of California Press, 1970), pp. 276-77.

3. Wilkie, p. 283.

4. World Bank, Mexico After the Oil Boom: Refashioning a Development Strategy (Washington, D.C., June 23, 1987), p. 82.

5. These Mexican reports are cited in David Bennett, "Starving Accounts," Mexico Journal (July 17, 1989), pp. 15-16.

6. United Nations Economic Commission for Latin America and the Caribbean, The Dynamics of Social Deterioration in Latin America and the Caribbean in the 1980s (San Jose, Costa Rica, LC/G.1557, May 3, 1989), pp. 6-10.

7. U.N. Economic Commission for Latin America and the Caribbean, The Dynamics of Social Deterioration, pp. 36, 38.

8. World Bank, Mexico After the Oil Boom, p. 83.

9. For the statistics, see Robert A. Pastor and Jorge Castaneda, Limits to Friendship: The United States and Mexico (New York: Alfred A. Knopf, 1988), pp. 5, 361, 364.

10. Editors' Note: This is one of two papers in this volume revised after the July 23, 1989 conclusion of Mexico's negotiations with the fifteen-member committee representing the country's approximately 500 commercial bank creditors.

Mexico's External Environment: Prospects for the 1990s

Raymond Vernon
Professor Emeritus of International Affairs and
International Business, Harvard University

Mexico's performance in the 1990s will depend to a considerable extent on forces that lie within the Mexican economy itself, such as its capacity to save and invest in ways that contribute to its continued growth. But some of the factors that will determine Mexico's future performance lie outside of Mexico, beyond the direct influence of its government and its people. In some cases, these factors suggest new opportunities for the Mexican economy; in others, they pose new threats. In any event, Mexican policymakers should take these external forces carefully into account in the formulation of national policies.

U.S. POLICIES AND PERFORMANCE

The most obvious factor in Mexico's external environment is its neighbor to the north, whose performance and policies continuously generate opportunities and threats for Mexico. Movements in U.S. output, prices, interest rates, and exchange rates, for instance, can have an enormous impact on Mexico's economy in the short run.

Despite the critical importance of U.S. economic performance to Mexico, I shall not pretend that I have anything fresh to offer on that subject. There is already widespread recognition in Mexico of the possibility that the United States may be entering into a period in which its policies will be predominantly anti-inflationary or even deflationary, as it attempts to reduce its trade and fiscal gaps and to offset the internal price effects of a cheap dollar. And it is well understood in Mexico that such U.S. efforts could prove to be bad news in the short run, reducing Mexican exports and attracting short-term capital from Mexico. These issues should be expressed in more detail by people with greater authority. What I want to explore here are the policies that the United States is likely to follow on issues of trade, debt, and investment. Although these policies, too, will be influenced in the short run by the performance of the U.S. economy, they will also respond to factors of a more durable and less uncertain kind.

The Underlying Forces

U.S. foreign economic policies have always appeared enigmatic and full of seeming reversals and contradictions to foreign observers. This is the country that produced the ultra-protectionist Smoot-Hawley tariff in 1930 and the remarkable Trade Agreements Act in 1934; the country that sponsored the tariff-reducing Kennedy Round in the 1960s along with the protectionist bilateral textile agreements of the same era; the country that ratified the radical U.S.-Canada Free Trade Agreement in 1988, while adopting a new trade law that measurably increased the power of protectionist groups. The illustrations carry an obvious moral: simple generalizations that purport to describe U.S. foreign economic policies, such as the view that special interests will always be served, are misleading. U.S. policies on foreign economic issues respond to a much more complex set of forces, generating results that must be described in more complex terms.

One cannot exclude the possibility that the United States may move in a highly protectionist direction over the next decade. But after an extended analysis, I conclude that although the United States will continue to make protectionist moves in selected commodities in response to the pressures of special interest groups, it is unlikely to move toward a protectionist policy on a broad front.(1) In fact, the United States will probably attempt some major steps in the direction of further liberalization, although not on the nondiscriminatory global basis that has been typical of such policies in the past. That prospect requires some words of elaboration.

In spite of the threatening character of recent U.S. trade legislation, the basic preference of its policymakers, whether in the executive branch or in the Congress, is for open markets. That preference rests on two factors, each of which counts heavily in the American political process. One is the strong tendency of the American public to limit the powers of government, especially powers that might increase the discretionary decisions of the bureaucracy. The second is the strong interest of the largest U.S. firms and banks in maintaining open international markets.

To be sure, the U.S. government has often imposed protectionist measures that appeared flatly at variance with these values. And in recent years, as the U.S. balance of trade has remained strongly negative, such measures have increased in frequency. To interpret the significance of these protectionist measures, however, one has to recognize that, in most cases, the measures have been initiated by individual interest groups rather than by the administration itself. Ironically, the provisions of U.S. law under which these groups have pressed their cases have reflected some of the same values that have led to favor open markets in general. Determined to limit the economic power of the executive branch and its bureaucracy, Congress has persistently widened the channels through which interest groups can press their cases for special treatment. And over the years those groups have organized themselves to exploit the existing channels with increasing effectiveness.

The conditions that the United States faces in world markets in the 1990s, however, seem to be pushing the new administration toward increasing resistance to the protectionist claims of interest groups. And under existing legislation the president probably still has enough discretionary power to be able to resist the bulk of these efforts if he has very strong reasons for doing so. The reasons for doing so appear especially strong in 1989.

One factor pushing in that direction is the increasing importance of exports in the economic well-being of the United States; the relatively buoyant performance of the U.S. economy in 1987 and 1988 is widely attributed to the unexpectedly strong showing of its export sector.

Another factor is the growing importance in American eyes of Europe's 1992 program. Anxious to hold down the margin of discrimination that U.S. exporters and investors might suffer in a tightly integrated European economy, the U.S. administration is already negotiating with the Europeans over the treatment of its exporters and investors in such a market. The outcome of wider negotiations, if they succeed, is likely to be a reciprocal commitment of the United States and Europe to keep their respective economies open to one another's exports and enterprises. While such negotiations are going on, the U.S. side has an added incentive to avoid having individual cases poison the negotiating atmosphere. The prospect of a relatively harmonious settlement of the U.S.-E.C. dispute over hormone-fed cattle is illustrative of the desire of the United States to take a restrained approach in such product-specific disputes.

Still a third factor pushing the United States toward trade barrier reduction is the pending GATT-sponsored negotiations over the liberalization of international trade in services. Scheduled for completion before June of 1993, when the powers of the U.S. negotiators run out, the negotiations will clearly also be of particular interest in Mexico. The United States has a considerable stake in the outcome of such negotiations, partly because its policy-makers see the increased export of services as important for the U.S. economy and partly because other countries regard the United States as the principal sponsor of these negotiations.

The negotiations promise to be especially arduous. Most developing countries will resist any significant commitments on the liberalization of services; such commitments as are negotiated will probably be limited to some relatively small groups of industrialized countries; and even these will crystallize slowly and painfully, as the negotiators approach the 1993 deadline.

If the negotiations do not break down altogether before 1993, the U.S. negotiators are likely to grow increasingly anxious to produce tangible results as they approach the statutory deadline. This concern should raise their determination not to muddy the waters with individual protectionist measures and increase their willingness to entertain proposals for liberalization -- however limited in scope and spread -- that can be touted as successes of the negotiating process. That state of mind could lead to more intense negotiations among a more limited group of countries, even including bilateral agreements. One could envisage the development among such smaller groups of improved dispute-settlement procedures or other innovations of the kind found in the U.S.-Canada Free Trade Agreement. But such relatively felicitous outcomes are far from certain.

LDC Debt

So much has been said and written about LDC debt that brevity at this stage is an obvious virtue. Until the Brady statement of March 1989 was issued, U.S. policy on this subject seemed stalled, hung up on the business-as-usual principles of the 1985 Baker plan. The Brady statement, with its acknowledgment of the need for debt reduction and its willingness to entertain the possibility of write-downs and guarantees by international agencies, set the stage for new policies and new measures.

The obstacles to framing a coherent long-term policy with respect to LDC debt stem partly from the complexity of the problem, including the fact that it covers several dozen debtor countries, a dozen or so creditor countries, hundreds of private banks, and several international agencies. There are other obstacles as well, notably the reluctance of the U.S. administration to entertain any proposal that might entail a new appropriation of funds and the reluctance of many congressmen to shift any of the losses from the lending banks to the U.S. taxpayers. Moreover, the Brady proposals leave large areas of uncertainty regarding critical dimensions of the U.S. proposals: the size of the commitments to be used for debt reduction; the nature of the conditionality attaching to new programs; the nature of the debt-reducing undertakings; the availability of fresh money for development; and so on.

Still, under the weight of a growing volume of such debt and of civil disturbances in Caracas and elsewhere, creditors and their governments now appear to believe that the political risks entailed in the muddle-through approach are quite high, taking the form of formal defaults, more civil disorder, and a slide back toward dictatorial governments in debtor countries.

Despite that growing realization, the technical and political difficulties of creating a long-term framework for debt relief still seem formidable. The special concern of the United States for the Mexican case may provide an added measure of security for Mexico. But the decision-making machinery of the United States, with its division of powers between Congress and the executive, always places projections as to the outcome of such issues at some considerable risk. Even the best-laid plans could founder over internal U.S. disputes regarding the appropriate distribution of costs between the public and the private sectors.

GLOBALIZATION OF INDUSTRY

While Mexico's future is likely to be heavily influenced by U.S. policies and U.S. performance, some of the factors that will affect Mexico profoundly are more general in character. One of these is the globalization of industry.

The multinational spread of large enterprises is a phenomenon with which Mexicans have long been familiar. Indeed, for many decades, a considerable part of Mexico's manufacturing output has been generated by enterprises that

were owned or managed by foreign firms. Until eight or ten
years ago, however, most of the output of those firms was
directed to Mexico's national market. Since then the orientation of the foreign-owned enterprises has shifted, as
exports have accounted for an increasing proportion of their
output.

Overlapping Jurisdictions

With the increasing emphasis on exports, the dependence
of Mexico's industry on the rest of the world economy has
undergone a considerable change. As long as foreign-owned
enterprises in Mexico were engaged in import substitution,
Mexico's dependence rested mainly on a need for foreign technology and capital. However, with the growth of exports,
including the growth of the maquila, Mexico's dependence on
the international marketing channels provided by these enterprises has grown as well.
Mexico's increased dependence on international marketing channels reflects a condition that is common not only to
other developing countries but also to the United States,
Canada and the countries of Europe. To an increasing
extent, final products are produced by networks that strad-
dle international borders. That trend has been evident not
only in developing countries but in industrialized countries
as well. Caterpillar's output in the United States, according to the New York Times, is dependent on "steel from Brazil, automated welders from Sweden, machine tools from West
Germany and Japan, and French-made steel castings..."(2)
Some of these foreign items come from independent foreign
producers but many are from Caterpillar affiliates.
The new interdependencies have implications that pose
difficult political problems for national governments. Governments ordinarily look to the enterprises in their jurisdiction as the means by which they carry out their basic
national policies, notably including policies aimed at security and growth. But increasingly the enterprises in their
jurisdiction are only units in logistical systems that
stretch outward into other countries. Increasingly, therefore, governments are discovering that economic problems
which they once regarded as of national concern alone
require cooperative action between governments. Problems in
taxation, competition, employment, and consumer safety,
among others, demand international action, as national measures become futile or self-defeating.
The problem is particularly important for Mexico
because of the inescapable fact that it sits so close to the

United States. Although the United States is not unaffected by the same trends toward increased interdependence, the initial disposition of U.S. administrations has been to deal with those issues through unilateral action. This reaction has been natural enough, given the relative size of the internal U.S. market and -- until very recently -- the relative unimportance of the country's foreign sector in the functioning of the national economy. But the habits and perceptions that relative invulnerability has generated in the United States present an added obstacle to easy cooperation with Mexico. It will take a considerable effort on both sides of the border, probably requiring some new institutional arrangements for consultation and response, for the two countries to deal cooperatively with issues that demand a joint response.

Shifts in Foreign Direct Investment

With the growing importance of multinational enterprises to the Mexican economy, that country's policymakers must be increasingly alert to possible shifts in the factors that determine the locational decisions of such enterprises.

The factors that have been most critical in encouraging the growth of multinational networks over the past forty years have been the improvement in quality and the decline in cost of international communication and transportation. During that forty-year span, the cost of transmitting voice signals over long distances dropped by over 90 percent, while the cost of transporting goods and people by air dropped by about two-thirds. In the same period the telex, the fax machine, the communications satellite, and the computer introduced a degree of speed and dependability to international communication that matched the expectations of science fiction.

As the costs of voice communication and the transmission of data and facsimiles have declined and the quality of such services has improved, the propensity of enterprises to establish subsidiaries and branches in foreign locations distant from their home base has persistently grown. In times past the difficulties of scanning distant places and of commanding and controlling distant subsidiaries had always figured strongly in the decisions of managers whether and where to set up such entities. Considerations such as these explain in part why U.S.-based enterprises in the early stages of developing a multinational network have historically favored Mexico; indeed, in an extensive study of the sequences by which U.S.-based enterprises set up their manufacturing facilities abroad, Mexico's attraction as a first or second site was exceeded only by Canada and the United Kingdom.(3)

Of course, pronounced shifts in currency values such as the depreciation of the Mexico peso and the U.S. dollar relative to Asian currencies also affected the timing and direction of foreign direct investment during the 1970s and 1980s; but the underlying regularities in the behavior of individual enterprises suggest strongly that exchange rate variations were important only in affecting the timing of investment rather than in determining the underlying trend.

The persistent shrinkage in cost and improvement in the quality of international communication promise to continue into the 1990s. And with the continuation of that trend, firms headquartered in other countries are likely to respond in complex ways to the possibility of establishing added production facilities in Mexico.

For example, with the improvement in transportation and communication, seasoned U.S. enterprises with well-established subsidiaries producing for export in Mexico could place a reduced value on the propinquity of a Mexican subsidiary, viewing locations in, say, Ecuador or Thailand as being almost as accessible as those in Mexico. In fact, the trend on the part of established U.S.-based multinational subsidiaries toward geographic dispersion of their foreign facilities has already been in evidence for some time.(4)

In response to the improvement in communication, however, enterprises headquartered in more distant places such as Japan or Italy appear increasingly amenable to considering a Mexican location as a possible production site. Once again, the data are already beginning to mirror these new trends. The persistent increase in the investments of Asian firms on North American soil in the past few years, although stimulated by the relative strength of their home currencies, probably received its basic push from the decline in communication barriers.

In summary, the incipient trends in foreign direct investment already visible in Mexico are likely to continue into the future. For established firms that already use Mexico as an export base, Mexico could find itself competing with more distant locations for added investment. Less experienced firms from the United States and firms from more distant countries, however, could provide an offset to the new sources of competition. How these disparate trends work themselves out could depend upon Mexican policies, including not only an understanding of the nature of the threat from the competition of other host countries but also an understanding of the character of the new opportunities.

TECHNOLOGICAL CHANGE

Improvements in communication are of critical importance in shaping Mexico's future, but technological developments can be expected to affect Mexico in other ways as
well.

Computer-Assisted Manufacturing

In particular, the movement of industry toward
computer-assisted processes is bound to have profound
effects. As usual, the estimates that were prevalent a
decade ago regarding that trend tended to exaggerate the
advantages and minimize the costs of the new computer-
assisted processes.(5) But the direction seems unmistak-
able, with complex implications for countries in Mexico's
position.

One implication is that, with the growth of computer-
assisted processes, competitive advantages that are based on
the relatively low costs of semi-skilled and unskilled labor
could decline. Such advantages have been critical for developing countries in a number of industries including sewing,
food processing, and steelmaking. Computer-based advances
are already evident in steel, where they account in part for
the sharp increases in productivity around the world.(6) The
pioneer efforts of a group of U.S. firms to use computer-
assisted processes for the sewing of sleeves in men's clothing presage much wider efforts in that direction.(7) To be
sure, the diffusion of such developments could prove a little slower than is commonly supposed; the introduction of
computer-assisted processes often requires changes in factory design and workforce so basic as to reduce the immediate cost advantages of making the shift. But over time the
trend is likely to be visible in many industries, wiping out
competitive advantages that once existed.

On the other hand, there are hints in Mexico's export
performance in recent years that firms located in Mexico
could learn to exploit the best of two worlds, by making
selective use of computer-assisted processes while retaining
some of the residual advantages of low-cost labor. In developing countries far removed from Europe, Japan, and North
American, computer-assisted processes often present some
high risks to the user, partly because of the dearth of technical personnel in the country and partly because of the distances from the foreign producers of the software and hard-
ware. But for Mexico such problems are much less acute. So
far at any rate, Mexico has managed to build up an

impressive core of technicians in spite of the risks of their being drawn to the United States by higher pay scales.

The spectacular increase in the export of manufactured products in Mexico since 1983 suggests the possible emergence of a new comparative advantage profile.(8) Plants in Mexico, drawing on the cadre of technical specialists in the national workforce as well as on the country's propinquity to the United States, may be able to capture the advantages of the computer-assisted processes while still employing low-cost labor where appropriate.(9) And with computer-assisted processes often providing better quality control and greater product flexibility and offering full-scale economies at reduced volumes of output, Mexico may be able to enlarge the advantages that it already displays in manufacturing and exporting relatively sophisticated products.

The Promise of Biotechnology

Speculating about the consequences of biotechnology development in the context of Mexico is a job for experts. Without the necessary credentials, I must confine myself to a few general observations.

As with computer-assisted manufacturing processes, biotechnology seems to present Mexico with both new opportunities and new threats. The new threats arise out of the likelihood that producers in the United States and elsewhere will be able to develop new types of livestock and plants that are capable of competing with those in which Mexico currently has a competitive advantage. The new opportunities stem from the possibility that Mexico may be able to monitor closely the developments in the United States, may repeat the extraordinary achievements of agricultural research conducted at Chapingo in a new cycle of innovation, and may develop new competitive strengths by coupling its relatively low-cost agricultural labor with new products.

In this case, again, Mexico's proximity to the United States could offer advantages. The history of Mexico's agricultural innovations suggests that such proximity can be used to good purpose, attracting technology and capital from the United States. As with manufacturing, however, the realization of these potentials could depend on early recognition and early response.

MINERALS AND PETROLEUM

The Market for Raw Materials

As in decades past, some long-term technological trends appear to be operating to reduce the real inputs of raw materials in the mix of goods and services demanded by modern economies.

For one thing, the rise in the role of services in the gross national product of most countries is contributing to that trend. Services such as health and education, for instance, derive most of their value from inputs other than raw materials. In industry, developments such as the computerized control of steel and chemical processing tend to increase substantially the efficiency with which raw materials are used in processing. Moreover, the increasing importance of pollution controls tends to discourage the use of products and processes that require extensive inputs of energy and metals, pushing manufacturers toward raw materials such as ceramics and composites and toward the recycling of used materials. In the case of steel, the rise in the use of scrap goes hand in hand with the growing importance of mini-mills and electric furnaces. Other scrap metals, notably including aluminum scrap, also are being drawn increasingly into the recycling process.

The decline in the relative use of raw materials is no sure guide to the future price of such materials or to the degree of profitability for producers; these depend not only on the nature of demand but also on supply conditions as well as on market structure. In some raw material industries, for instance, the reluctance of producers to make added investments in developing reserves and improving processing facilities could have the effect of shrinking supply, buoying up prices, and even maintaining unit profits. But even if profits and prices remain high, reduced volumes will mean that raw material production cannot be relied on to make its past contributions to employment and to foreign exchange earnings in developing countries.

Careful studies of individual commodities would be needed to determine more precisely how these factors are likely to affect Mexico's interests. But it would be surprising if such studies offered an optimistic view of the contribution these industries are likely to make in Mexico's future.

The Market for Oil

Needless to say, future developments in the market for oil are of particular importance for Mexico.

In the middle 1980s, after oil prices had suddenly slumped from over $30 to nearly $10 a barrel, the conventional wisdom had been that the slump was only transitional; prices might remain depressed for a few years, but by the 1990s the low oil prices of the 1980s would increase consumption everywhere, lifting prices and output. The developing world was expected to make a particularly strong contribution to the increase in oil consumption.

Moreover, it was widely supposed that by the latter 1990s, the relatively high-cost sources of oil that had been brought into the market by the elevated prices of the 1970s, such as the oil of the North Slope and the North Sea, would have been used up; and with such sources out of the way, that the Middle East would have reasserted its monopoly powers as the unchallenged source of the world's cheapest reserves.

That projection may still prove right. But it is threatened by various factors. Some have already been mentioned, including the long-term movement toward products and processes that conserve on the use of raw materials and energy; as a consequence of that trend, for instance, the energy consumption of OECD countries per unit of real output declined 25 percent between 1970 and 1987. Other factors that threaten the level of oil consumption in the future are more readily apparent, such as the possibility that economic growth in the next few decades may prove relatively slow, held down by governmental efforts to liquidate external debt and balance national budgets. In the 1990s, therefore, oil prices could fail to be increased by the buoyant factors that were foreseen a few years ago.

In any case, whatever the trend in the 1990s may prove to be, oil prices are likely to continue to register highly volatile movements both in the short and in the medium term. In the absence of a very strong set of control mechanisms, the economic characteristics of the product almost guarantee such patterns.

In the short term, price elasticities of demand are very low, impeding adjustments through a decline in consumption. On the supply side, as long as shut-in productions is being tapped, elasticities are relatively high; but when supply lines are suddenly called upon for higher volumes, bottlenecks can easily appear, producing sharp increases in prices. And storage is sufficiently expensive that oil

companies and oil users are loathe to build up large inven-
tories against an interruption of supply.

Over the longer term, it is true, the supply and demand
elasticities for oil are quite high. On the demand side,
they are eventually reflected in new designs for buildings,
products and processes, and on the supply side in new exploration and development projects. But these responses usually appear some years after the events that stimulated them.
As a result, when the responses actually occur, they often
generate new instabilities in the market rather than contributing to stability. The sharp increase in oil reserves
announced early in 1989 by Saudi Arabia and Venezuela, for
instance, probably represented a delayed announcement of
discoveries originally stimulated by the high prices of
1980. Nothing suggests that the future behavior of producers will be any less susceptible to the familiar "cobweb
pattern" than it was in the past.

Nor is the price instability inherent in this picture
likely to be reduced by the operation of the strategic oil
reserves of the United States and other countries. Those
reserves have created supplies that could be tapped to provide a month or two of the world's needs. But governments
that try to stabilize their oil markets in an emergency by
tapping such reserves are likely to encounter heavy resistance from their oil companies over what the companies are
sure to label as "premature" sales. The U.S. government,
for instance, is almost certain to delay any such sales in a
crisis until the inevitable internal political dispute over
the timing of such sales has dragged on.

A strong system of international control could conceiv-
ably reduce the level of instability in international oil
markets. And until the latter 1960s, the oil industry did
experience relatively high and stable prices as a result of
such a system. But the system included a complex web of
joint ventures and pricing conventions dominated by a hand-
ful of nationally integrated international oil companies and
supplemented by public production controls.

After 1973 OPEC's thirteen members attempted to take
over the control function, using nothing more than a series
of intergovernmental agreements as a means of implementing
their controls. A few years of extraordinarily high prices
created the widespread impression that their attempts to control the price of oil might be working.

Gradually, however, it began to be recognized that
although strong oligopoly elements were present in the oil
market and prevented prices from falling to marginal costs,
no effective mechanism was in place to temper the extreme

responses in price. The complex network of public and private controls that the international oil companies had developed between 1928 and 1950 was no longer in operation. The thirteen OPEC governments had such widely disparate national needs that it proved impossible for them to agree on common long-term objectives. Gradually, it became apparent that the extraordinarily high prices of the 1970s and early 1980s were created by fortuitous events, touched off by the Israeli-Egypt war and the fall of the Shah of Iran, rather than by an effective control system. New opportunities might well occur in the 1990s that could touch off another round of follow-the-leader price hikes; but agreements among the principal oil producers capable of producing stable prices over a period of years seem out of reach.

In recognition of their vulnerability to erratic changes in demand, some oil exporters have struck out on their own to reduce their risks through downstream integration. Kuwait, Saudi Arabia, and Venezuela among others have acquired downstream refining and distributing facilities in their principal foreign markets. Such investments have served to protect those countries from the risk that in times of glut their customers will shop around for lower crude prices, but they have failed to reduce the principal causes of such uncertainty. Because their refined products must still survive a market test, including the competition of refiners that acquire their oil in the open market, they remain exposed to the effects of changes in price and in aggregate demand. Moreover, with such vertical channels in place, the possibility that effective agreements over the price of crude oil may be reached through OPEC is reduced almost to the vanishing point.

Oil exporters, therefore, are likely to share a roller-coaster experience in the future as in the past. If differences exist, they are likely to stem from the fact that the price-depressing factors on the demand side would be stronger. For Mexico, prudence suggests that heavy reliance on oil exports is to be avoided even if boom times in the oil markets should briefly return.

CONCLUSION

As I look back on the factors summarized in these pages, they confirm the impression that we live in interesting times. For the immediate future, Mexico faces a series of fresh promises and fresh threats, emanating from factors that are largely external to the Mexican economy. Some lie beyond its influence to affect very much, such as the performance of the U.S. economy; but many do not. In those cases, appropriate Mexican policies could increase the opportunities and curb the threats that the changes presage. One development to which Mexico may be able to respond constructively is the likely decline in its historical reliance on large U.S. enterprises as its principal source of foreign direct investment. Another is an increase in the importance of computer-assisted manufacturing processes and biotechnology. Still another is the likely shrinkage in the relative importance of raw materials in world markets, possibly including oil.

All of these changes present major challenges for the Mexican economy. But some offer more promise than threat, provided that the appropriate policy responses are in place.

NOTES

1. The analysis appears in Raymond Vernon and Debora L. Spar, Beyond Globalism: Remaking American Foreign Economic Policy (New York: The Free Press, 1989).
2. New York Times (March 12, 1989), p. F-4.
3. The details of this study, based on an analysis of the multinational networks of 187 U.S.-based firms up to 1968, unfortunately went unpublished. The study, conducted by J. W. Vaupel, appears in his "Characteristics and Motivations of the U.S. Corporations That Manufacture Abroad" (May 3, 1971), Table 15A, prepared for the Multinational Enterprise Project of the Harvard Business School.
4. The tendency of U.S.-based firms to establish new product lines in more distant locations as their experience grows is seen in data presented in Raymond Vernon and W. H. Davidson, "Foreign Production of Technology-Intensive Products by U.S.-Based Multinational Enterprises," Table A-8, Report to the National Science Foundation, No. PB 80 148638 (Boston: January 1979).
5. For useful evaluations, see Herb Brody, "The Robot: Just Another Machine?" and Jeffrey Zygmont, "Flexible Manufacturing Systems: Curing the Cure-all," both in High Technology 6 (October, 1986), pp. 22-27 and 31-35; also Karl H. Ebel, "The Impact of Industrial Robots on the World of Work, International Labour Review 125 (January-February 1986), pp. 39-51.
6. George McManus, "Computers are Putting Steel Together," Iron Age 4 (June 1988), pp. 13-18.

7.   A summary of the project appears in "[TC]2 and the Apparel Industry," Harvard Business School Case 0-387-160 (Boston, 1987).

8.   Between 1983 and 1987, Mexico's exports of nontraditional manufactures rose from about $4 billion to about $11 billion.   See The Economist (July 4, 1987), pp. 65-66. Much of the increase was in motor vehicle parts.

9.   For illustrations elsewhere, see A. S. Bhalla and Dilmus James, eds., New Technologies and Development: Experiences in "Technology Blending" (Boulder, CO: Lynne Rienner, 1988).

Comments

Jesus Reyes Heroles
Coordinator of Advisers, Ministry of Foreign Affairs

It is a special privilege to comment on a paper by Professor Raymond Vernon. My remarks fall into two groups. The first set includes reactions to specific points, while the second contains general observations on the question of Mexico's future external environment.

COMMENTS ON SPECIFIC ASPECTS

1. I think it is useful to emphasize that the United States is a complex organization and that simple generalizations to describe its foreign policies are misleading. I only add that this message is also true for Mexico.

2. Vernon states that the United States will resist protectionist claims and move towards further liberalization, although not necessarily of a non-discriminatory nature. (Both country and product discrimination are possible.) I do not share that optimism, but I certainly hope he is right. I do, however, agree that the United States will establish additional bilateral trade agreements, which have to be interpreted as intermediate steps, or signs, of the global move towards further integration.

3. In my view the paper fails to point out what are the crucial issues surrounding LDC debt. On the one hand, the "debt problem" is a reflection of a broader and deeper international economic crisis that started in the early 1970s. The role of the

United States in that crisis has been very important; high fiscal and trade deficits absorbed an
enormous amount of resources from abroad, raising
real interest rates and reducing the availability
of funds for LDC's.

On the other hand, Vernon points out a factor
that, in my opinion, indicates why the solution to
the problem has taken so long: internal U.S. disputes regarding the appropriate distribution of
costs between the public and the private sector
have not been resolved. This distributional issue
is a fundamental aspect, probably the crucial
point.

Creditor countries must take four steps: (i)
recognizing that debtor countries cannot keep
absorbing by themselves the total costs of bad
past investments and of high real interest rates;
(ii) agreeing on the total loss that creditors
must absorb, as well as the place for doing so;
(iii) distributing this share among creditor countries and then between bank shareholders and taxpayers; and (iv) defining the operational mechanism to implement the corresponding distributions.
Current discussions about the debt problem seem to
concentrate on revising mechanisms used to deal
with the debt problem in the past. They do not
adequately address the steps outlined above, especially the third, which is the core problem. Until
creditor countries face openly and courageously
the need to reallocate the costs of LDC debt, the
problem will not be resolved.

4.   Vernon adequately stresses the role of modern communications in reshaping the flows of foreign
direct investment. There is no question about the
growing need for Mexico to compete with more distant locations for additional investment.

5.   I differ with Professor Vernon's view about the
impact of technological change on comparative
advantage. I think the argument that additional
robotization will reduce the comparative advantage
of labor-abundant countries like Mexico is not
clear. The central question concerns how far computer-assisted manufacturing will go; the answer
depends on the relative costs between labor and
robots. As usual, profit maximization criteria

will play the determining role, and it is unclear whether robotization will substantially reduce wage differentials (corrected by productivity) between Mexico and the developed economies.

6.   I think the paper misses a very important point: namely, that the future of labor cost differentials between Mexico and the rest of the world depends crucially on future labor mobility between Mexico and the United States.

7.   I will not comment on the oil market except to note that Vernon's remarks correctly stress the type of uncertainties and external shocks to which my country is subject. We only know that the price of oil is going to be volatile, and that "roller coaster" experiences still lie ahead. The future prospects, therefore, are quite grim.

GENERAL COMMENTS

8.   Mexico is on the verge of a new era of economic development. Its precise path and configuration will depend on how the Mexican economy adjusts to new internal and external environments.

9.   On the internal front much as been said. The country has undergone drastic changes in order to adjust to a new reality; and it is now poorer than before. Mexico lost income originating abroad equivalent to about 6 percent of GDP in the past seven years; at the same time it has to pay real interest rates that are about twice as high as historical averages. Those two facts are the core of the problem.

10.   On the external front, the country is dynamically adapting to a new environment, more global and more integrated in every respect. Mexico wants to take advantage of those changes. I agree with Vernon that a new concept of comparative advantage is emerging. What is the relevant definition for the twenty-first century?

11.   In speculating about these topics, one has to recognize that relative comparative advantages

will be reduced. Economies will have to operate on the edge of competitiveness. Any opportunity to develop specific activities, narrowly defined, must be taken. The concept of industrialization based on vertical integration will be obsolete.

12. For Mexico the new concept of comparative advantage has several implications. First is recognition of its unique geographical position, close to the North American market, between the Atlantic and the Pacific, close to Central America and the Caribbean, a market of more than 50 million people, and sharing various interests with South America. That reality cannot be overemphasized, and Mexico must therefore carry out a multidirectional international economic program.

13. On the other hand, the importance of "intangibles" in shaping relative comparative advantage should not be neglected. Language, solid institutions, political freedom, social peace, and so on play an important role in development.

14. Finally, what type of industrialization policy emerges from these considerations? First, it must recognize that the most important task is to establish a set of economic incentives conducive to efficient industrialization. Second, explicit policy actions must address specific economic issues like market imperfections, economies of scale, information problems and externalities. Third, the industrialization policy must help raise productivity and achieve the goals of regional development. Fourth, it should confine itself to these tasks, eliminating previous programs and regulations. Those guidelines configurate what can be called a "Zero Base Industrial Policy".(1)

NOTES

1. Jesus Reyes Heroles G.G., "Restructuracion industrial de Mexico: hacia una politica industrial de base cero," presented in a seminar organized by the University of California (Puerto Vallarta, Jalisco, October 1988).

Rebalancing Government Direction and Market Guidance

Pedro Noyola and Jaime Serra
Economic Adviser and Secretary, respectively,
Ministry of Trade and Industry

INTRODUCTION

Mexico's economic program has one main objective: to restore sustained and balanced growth. Since 1982, the Mexican economy has undergone a dramatic transformation as economic policies have reestablished the fundamental macroeconomic equilibrium. The social costs of the adjustments, however, have also been dramatic. Between 1982 and 1988 the minimum wage fell by 42 percent in real terms and real per capita income fell by 12 percent. Other measures also reflect the decline in the standards of living: real public spending on housing and health, for example, fell by 25 and 22 percent, respectively.

It is crucial for the economy to start growing steadily once again, for Mexicans are demanding from the government a bright economic horizon. During the next six years, the government's goal is for real GDP growth to be at least between 4 and 5 percent per year, or twice the expected average population growth rate for the period. Under the present conditions, foreign savings are unlikely to be the engine of economic growth. Instead, growth must be hinged on certain basic principles that provide internal consistency to the economic program. More precisely, two conditions must be met: government policies directed toward macroeconomic stability must be properly balanced and increased reliance must be placed on market forces for guidance of resource allocation.

This paper addresses these two issues. In the following section, we discuss the effects of government policy on macroeconomic stability, placing special emphasis on the achievements of the past six years. Next, we set forth the conditions for microeconomic efficiency and international competitiveness.   Finally, we interpret what "rebalancing government direction and market guidance" implies for the external sector.

GOVERNMENT DIRECTION OF MACROECONOMIC STABILIZATION

The period between 1983 and 1988 is characterized by notable, and in some ways unparalleled, macroeconomic adjustments.   This period followed a boom and bust saga, which was guided by ill-conceived policies that violated the basic intertemporal budget constraints of the economy.   The dynamic inconsistency of the policies adopted in the 1970s and early 1980s made the economy most vulnerable to external shocks, especially in the oil and foreign capital markets.

With the reduction of international oil prices and the outburst of the debt crisis in 1982, it became obvious that the time of economic reckoning had arrived.   Internal inefficiency and wasteful public spending could no longer be financed.   In 1983, the government started to rebuild the economy with programs that adjusted the basic macroeconomic accounts.   These adjustments are contained in three strategies: the fiscal correction, the trade policy reforms, and the stabilization program.

First, there has been a radical turnaround of the public finances.   For example, since 1983 the public sector's primary fiscal balance, which excludes interest payments, has shown a consistent surplus.   In fact, between 1982 and 1988 the fiscal correction, measured by the improvement in the primary balance, has amounted to 15 percent of GDP.

Over 70 percent of this correction, about 11 percent of GDP, is accounted for by expenditure cuts and additional revenues represent about 4 percent of GDP.   The effect of the internal revenue effort, which has included corrections of public prices, reform of the income tax code, changes in the formula through which the federal and state governments share revenues, and improvements in tax administration, more than offset the dramatic collapse of the international prices of oil during that period.

Another crucial element of the fiscal adjustment has been the reduction of public enterprises.   Between 1982 and 1988, over 700 enterprises were divested thereby increasing annual public savings by at least 0.3 percent of GDP.   This estimate includes the yearly return on asset sales and the reduction of subsidies.   From a fiscal standpoint it is more meaningful than the simple valuation of divested assets because it reflects the permanent effect of divestiture on the fiscal balance.

Second, the fiscal correction has been accompanied by far-reaching trade reforms. Between 1982 and 1988, and especially since 1985, the economy has opened up and protectionist import substitution programs have given way to export promotion.

In 1982 all imports were subject to quantitative restrictions and the maximum tariff was 100 percent. Evidently, average effective protection for some sectors had been very high, since intermediate inputs had substantially lower tariffs than final products. The elevated tariff dispersion distorted profitability across sectors and created "inefficiency havens".

In contrast, by 1988 less than 25 percent of imports were subject to control and the maximum tariff had decreased to 20 percent, 30 points lower than the level consolidated in the GATT. Average effective protection has decreased substantially, since intermediate inputs and final goods are subject to a compact tariff schedule. The reduction of tariff dispersion has decreased intersectoral profit distortions and enhanced more efficient resource allocation.

Third, the structural adjustment of these two fundamentals -- the fiscal balance and the trade regime -- has been complemented by the Pacto of 1988. This comprehensive stabilization program was designed to strengthen the basic macroeconomic accounts and simultaneously to rid the economy of the largest obstacle to sustained growth: high inflation.

The Pacto attacked every source of inflation in Mexico. On the one hand, the program's pillars were the fundamentals: it contained an additional fiscal correction and actions to continue opening up the economy. On the other hand, existing indexation schemes that perpetuated inflation were dismantled. As a result of the Pacto, monthly inflation rates dropped from an average of about 15 percent in January of 1988 to an average of about 1 percent for the second half of the year.

These three basic adjustments -- the fiscal correction, the trade reforms and the stabilization program -- have drastically altered Mexico's macroeconomic structure and the guidelines for government programs. Fiscal discipline is the norm, the arbitrage of international prices has given exporters the opportunity to compete in world markets, and internal inflation rates are drawing closer to international levels.

After the enormous internal effort of the last six years, the fundamentals have been corrected. It is now time to start an era of solid and sustained growth, based on the principles of macroeconomic stability and microeconomic efficiency. Above all, the growth oriented program requires that Mexico's inflation rates be similar to those of its principal trading partners. The Pacto must achieve sustainable low inflation rates to provide the relative price stability needed to increase the expected returns of productive investments.

Recent Mexican data show that high rates of growth have not coexisted with high inflation. In fact, between 1970 and 1988 growth and inflation exhibit a negative correlation for inflation rates above 30 percent and a positive correlation for inflation rates under 30 percent. High inflation adversely affects the expected return of productive investments and promotes financial speculation and unproductive hedging schemes as uncertainty and increased price volatility cloud economic decisions. Price volatility measured by the dispersion of inflation rates in a sample of sectors has been much higher in periods of high inflation than in periods of stability. This volatility has dampened considerably since the introduction of the Pacto. Relative price distortions have decreased and moderate misalignments can be accommodated for longer periods.

MARKET GUIDANCE FOR MICROECONOMIC EFFICIENCY

Price stability is a necessary, but not a sufficient condition for growth. A radical strategy to modernize the economy is an essential complement of the macroeconomic program in order to increase aggregate supply and improve overall market performance.

Modernization of the productive plant is necessary for the Mexican economy to compete effectively in international markets. All over the world, regardless of the ideological origins of their systems of government, economies are being reformed and adapted to the rules of global competition and interdependence.

Economic modernization requires the government to become an active promoter of growth so that competitive markets are able to function efficiently. The government's promotion oriented policies should be based on four pillars: internationalization of the domestic economy, technological innovation, internal deregulation and modernization of domestic commerce.

First, the economy must become "internationalized" to participate successfully in the global economy. For this purpose, adequate trade and investment policies are essential.

On the one hand, the trade reforms, which have made Mexico one of the most open economies in the world, must become permanent. Due to the reforms, producers are moving along the production frontiers, away from importable and toward exportable goods. They have access to inputs at competitive prices and consumers benefit from lower effective protection rates. Policy rollbacks should be avoided. In order to consolidate trade policy, non-tariff barriers should continue to be phased out and replaced with a compact tariff schedule.

On the other hand, the promotion of foreign investment is a natural complement to trade policy as a means to internationalize the domestic economy. In order to give certainty and confidence to investors, foreign investment requires above all consistent macroeconomic policies that are compatible with sustained price stability.

Moreover, effective tax rates in Mexico should be comparable to those in more developed countries. The recent modifications of the income tax code, which have included a reduction of tax rates and a permanent incentive to investment, have served this purpose. In particular, tax rates in Mexico are now comparable to average tax rates in the United States.

A major obstacle to foreign investment is the absence of clear and simple rules. The arbitrary characteristics of foreign investment authorizations should be replaced by neutral and transparent regulations.

The promotion of foreign investment through debt-to-equity swaps needs to be carefully analyzed. In addition to the adverse macroeconomic implications of swaps, the rationing schemes cause serious microeconomic distortions. Moreover, a swap should never be the main factor in the valuation of profitable investment projects, since a swap is a subsidy to capital and good projects, by definition, should not require subsidies.

Second, innovation must be promoted actively so that the economy can adopt the technologies best suited to the comparative advantage of each sector. Intellectual property rights should be protected to promote domestic innovation and the transfer of foreign technology. Domestic innovators will then be less likely to go abroad to patent a new process or product, and the Mexican markets will also be attractive to external innovators.

Historically, policies have emphasized only the supply of technological developments. This supply-side approach has severely limited the practical application of many innovations, which should be more closely linked to the productive plant. Technological policy should shift towards a demand-oriented approach; industries should work together with research centers so that a domestic market for innovation develops under the principles of competition and efficiency.

Third, the economy should undergo a deregulation process to eliminate the supply rigidities that raise transaction costs and seriously damage competitiveness. Excessive regulations are barriers to entry that create bottlenecks, promote monopolistic behavior and affect the ability of domestic producers to compete abroad. Moreover, regulations are fixed costs that affect small and medium-sized industries more intensely.

As long as the economy remains overregulated, it cannot reap the full benefits of trade liberalization. In fact, trade liberalization without complementary deregulation of the internal markets can be the worst of all possible worlds.

Because they are crucial to export promotion, the transportation and telecommunications sectors should receive special attention. For example, a rough estimate of the annual consumer loss due to the licensing requirements in the freight trucking sector is about 0.5 percent of GDP. This estimate is based on a 33 percent markup over marginal cost, which is the average markup reported in an informal survey of trucking companies made under the extreme assumptions of a pure monopoly. Quantitative precision requires a rigorous econometric study, but the main point here is a qualitative one: potential welfare gains associated with the internal deregulation of the economy are enormous.

Economic deregulation would alone substantially increase the competitiveness of exporters. They would no longer have to rely, as they did during the era of protectionism and macroeconomic instability, on the recurring adjustments of the nominal exchange rate to maintain a temporary competitive edge.

Internal deregulation also involves price liberalization. Under the Pacto nominal prices are set according to agreements among all the owners of factors of production. It is crucial, however, to devise a strategy to decontrol nominal prices gradually and allow relative prices to be adjusted by market forces. The mechanics should follow one basic principle: the decontrol of prices must be consistent with aggregate price stability.

Price liberalization should be sequenced according to a well-coordinated strategy. Proper sequencing is crucial to avoid unsustainable profit squeezes and the formation of

monopolistic market structures along the chains of production. Sectors with excess capacity are natural candidates
for price flexibility. Tradeable goods for which international prices already regulate the domestic market can also
be liberalized more rapidly. Liberalization in the non-
tradeables sector must be accompanied by market deregulation
to reduce cost pressures and promote competitive pricing.

Fourth, domestic commerce should be modernized. The
commercial sector currently has a regressive dual character.
On the one hand, modern establishments are efficient, benefit from scale economies and are able to sell at low prices.
On the other hand, traditional establishments are inefficient, work with low volumes and thus have to sell at higher
prices. The effect on income distribution is regressive
because traditional establishments usually serve the lower
income groups.

Commercial policy should increase the efficiency of traditional establishments. To reduce operating costs, for
example, the government should facilitate the formation of
co-operatives and credit unions for small establishments.
Moreover, adequate communication between suppliers and
clients should be promoted so that traditional establishments can obtain data on prices, market locations and other
relevant characteristics of the goods they supply.

In sum, the foundation of market guidance for microeconomic efficiency are these four pillars: internationalization of the domestic economy, technological innovation,
internal deregulation and modernization of domestic commerce. They provide the basic elements of policy for the
real sector of the economy. Tailor-made sectoral strategies
based on subsidies and protectionism are not compatible with
this model. In an open economy, each sector will find its
own market niche based on its comparative advantage and
international competitiveness.

IMPLICATIONS OF REBALANCING GOVERNMENT DIRECTION AND MARKET
GUIDANCE FOR THE EXTERNAL SECTOR

While consistent internal policies for macroeconomic
stability and microeconomic efficiency are necessary conditions for growth, they are still not sufficient. It is also
essential to address the main external constraints, particularly limitations on Mexico's access to export markets and
excessively burdensome net transfers abroad.

First, with regard to market access for Mexican
exports, it is essential to consolidate the structural

change that has taken place in Mexico's trade balance since 1982. About 70 percent of earnings then came from oil exports, whereas in 1988 about 70 percent were due to non-oil exports. This turnaround in the composition of exports is a result of the outward orientation of economic policy.

An effective export promotion strategy requires fair and permanent market access to non-oil exports. Mexico's objective in multilateral and bilateral trade negotiations is to guarantee such access. Policymakers of many countries may preach that protectionism is the cancer of global economic growth and that the principles of free trade should guide international trade relations, but they have been adopting extremely protectionist positions in multilateral and bilateral negotiations. This contradiction is disturbing.

On the multilateral front, Mexico should maintain its firm commitment to the principles of the GATT. It is necessary, however, to introduce a mechanism in the GATT that gives adequate recognition to unilateral liberalization. Since joining the GATT, Mexico has unilaterally opened up its economy. To date, the entire tariff schedule has been consolidated and non-tariff barriers have been substantially reduced, but the country has not benefited fully from this liberalization in the GATT negotiations.

The problem is that the existing rules do not give adequate recognition to unilateral actions to open up the economy. In fact, the system works in such a way that it punishes ex ante tariff and non-tariff barrier reductions, since unilateral liberalization actually reduces negotiating power. It would be difficult for the ablest game theorists to devise a set of incentives better suited for protectionism than the rules in the GATT. It is essential to change the rules and introduce adequate recognition through automatic external market access.

On the bilateral front, all negotiations should be consistent with agreements in the GATT. A crucial bilateral issue is trade bloc formation. When a trade bloc forms, at least in the short run, until enough trade creation takes place, average flows within the bloc will probably increase and average flows between bloc members and the rest of the world will probably decrease. Given the global tendency for trade bloc formation, Mexico must offset this effect through bilateral agreements that ensure export niches in common markets, based on the Mexican economy's comparative advantages.

Other bilateral agreements with specific countries should also be designed to protect Mexican access to foreign markets. Trade relations with the United States are of

special importance.   Bilateral negotiations cannot aim for
immediate comprehensive integration, as in the U.S.-Canada
treaty, since the Mexican and American economies exhibit
substantially different levels of development in many sectors.   Integration could be a realistic option in the medium
term, but in the contemporary context the most workable procedure is to strengthen specific accords within the recently
signed "Framework Agreement". In this agreement both governments stress the need to address bilateral trade issues in
the context of overall economic relations.   Trade negotiations are thus linked to foreign investment, intellectual
property rights and the external debt.

Second, it is essential to reduce net external transfers to a level that is compatible with the desired growth
path. Under the existing conditions, Mexico has to transfer
abroad the equivalent of its entire agricultural production
every year. This situation is clearly unsustainable.

Most of the outstanding debt was contracted during the
oil boom. Debtors and creditors together agreed on the projections of the basic economic variables.   Real interest
rate projections were low and oil price projections were
high.   Many projections for the steady state price of oil
varied between $30 and $50 per barrel. Of course, the financial evaluation of the loans depended crucially on these projections.

During the 1980s, real interest rates have been higher
than predicted because they have been used by the U.S. government to finance its deficit and control its inflation.
The mix of Mexican crude exports is selling at roughly a
third of the price projections of a decade ago.   Clearly,
the projections were wrong.

With an enormous internal effort Mexico's macroeconomic
accounts have now been adjusted to the new external scenario.   The external counterpart of this internal effort is an
adjustment in the terms of the debt that results in a permanent reduction of net transfers.

Such a reduction requires a multi-annual agreement to
give the economic program financial stability and certainty.
The agreement should free the resources necessary to finance
the current account balances that are compatible with growth
targets.   It should also lead to stable and decreasing debt-
output ratios.

Summing up, internal market guidance for microeconomic
efficiency requires adequate external market access to
exports, and rebalancing government direction for macroeconomic stability requires a permanent reduction of net
transfers abroad. A positive outcome on the external front

is essential not only for Mexico's growth prospects but also for the future of comprehensive liberalization strategies. The stakes are very high indeed and the policy options are limited. A solution must be found.

Comments

T. N. Srinivasan
Professor of Economics, Yale University

The paper by Messrs. Noyola and Serra is an extremely lucid presentation of both the phenomenal adjustment that the Mexican economy has gone through since 1982 and the policy reforms still needed to maintain internal and external balance while achieving sufficiently rapid growth to improve living standards and provide productive employment opportunities for a labor force that increases by about a million a year. The adjustment process has been carried out under external conditions that the World Bank once characterized as "unfavorable to a degree not witnessed since the depression of the 1930s." With the price of its major export, oil, experiencing a steep fall, with the real interest burden on its debt rising to unprecedented heights in the years after 1982, with voluntary lending virtually halted, the burden of adjustment was indeed tremendous. As the authors point out, between 1982 and 1988 the average net transfer of resources abroad from Mexico amounted to about 5 percent of GDP per year. Real minimum wages have declined by over 40 percent during the same period, and per capita real GDP in 1988 is perhaps no higher than it was a decade earlier.

While there can be no doubt about the fact that the Mexican economy has been put through a wringer between 1982 and 1988, it is important to recall that domestic policies pursued prior to 1982 are the major contributory causes of the crisis. As Professor Dornbusch has pointed out in a recent paper, although the second favorable oil shock in 1978–1979 increased Mexican oil export revenues from about $1 billion to $14 billion in 1981, spending increased far ahead of revenues. The non-interest budget deficit increased from 2 percent to more than 8 percent of GDP and the current-account deficit rose from 2.3 percent in 1977 to 5.8 percent of GDP in 1981. Large wage increases contributed to

accelerating inflation. It should hardly surprise anyone
that given the obviously unsustainable expansionary policy
of the government and with no evidence of any credible
change for the better, private Mexican investors took the
opportunity to invest their capital abroad. I am persuaded
that restrictions on capital movements are infeasible in the
Mexican case; and in any event, had they been in place, they
would have been evaded anyway given the policy environment.
It is worth recalling these aspects of the domestic economy,
if only to balance the tendency to associate the undoubted
hardships during adjustment with the policy of adjustment
rather than with the profligacy that created the need for
adjustment in the first place.

The authors point out, perhaps by way of explaining the
pre-1982 profligacy, that both Mexico and its creditors, particularly the private banks, projected the continuation of
the oil bonanza. Their forecast of future oil prices varied
between $30 and $50 a barrel. Apart from the fact that not
all analysts shared such a forecast, the history of commodity price booms should have warned against projecting an
indefinite continuation of a boom. True, oil is not like
any other commodity, particularly in the short run. But in
the medium and longer run it is like any other. Thus, there
is no excuse for the rosy projections given the information
available when they were made. In any case, since the
responsibility for these projections was shared by Mexico
and its private creditors, the cost of the mistake should
also be shared. In other words, the private bankers and
their Mexican borrowers should be free to decide how they
share these costs, without any intervention in the process
by the United States, other governments or multilateral
lending institutions acting as debt collection agencies for
private banks.

It is also evident that the long-standing, inward-
oriented development strategy that Mexico pursued prior to
the crisis reduced the flexibility with which Mexico could
respond to the crisis and thus added to the cost of adjustment and recovery. The authors, of course, are very much
aware of this problem and indeed the policy reforms that
they discuss address it. However, it is worth pointing out
that the development strategy was flawed and would have
needed reorientation even if there had been no crisis
whatsoever.

There is a view, held among others by the team that
directed the World Bank's research project on the sequencing
of liberalization, that countries endowed with natural
resources such as Mexico are more likely to persist with an

inward-oriented strategy long after it has outlived its use-fulness than are countries without such resources. While this argument has a certain surface plausibility, at a deeper level it is unconvincing. As economists we know that the reward to a factor that is inelastic in supply is a rent and by definition appropriating such rent has no effect on the supply of the factor. But the appropriated rents could be used for any purpose and not necessarily for financing the excesses of an inward-oriented strategy. Funds, as we all know, are fungible. Just because some governments derive a significant part of their revenues from natural-resource rents while others do not, does not mean that the former governments are driven to be profligate and the lat-ter governments to be frugal.

I agree entirely with the authors that both a sound macroeconomic management and a sound microeconomic incentive structure are essential for efficient, equitable and sustain-able development. One without the other is unlikely to suc-ceed. The authors rightly emphasize the need for encourag-ing Mexican producers to face international competition through the removal of trade barriers and to face increased internal competition through domestic deregulation. Above all, technological innovation should be encouraged, in par-ticular by easing counterproductive regulations on patents.

Let me now turn to the authors' suggestions for Mex-ico's negotiating positions in the Uruguay round as well as in the bilateral and regional fora. They complain that the GATT system does not give adequate recognition to Mexico's unilateral liberalization of its foreign trade. Three points are worth making in this regard. First of all, strange as it may seem, the notion of reciprocity enshrined in the GATT is quintessentially mercantilist -- after all, only a mercantilist would consider unilateral liberaliza-tion, which improves his own welfare, as a concession to his trading partner to be offered only in exchange for the part-ner liberalizing and thereby improving his welfare! Second, the negotiating power conferred by avoiding beneficial uni-lateral liberalization and liberalizing only in exchange for liberalization by others can be vastly exaggerated. The size of the coalitions that Mexico can promote to pursue par-ticular changes in the GATT and other rules governing inter-national trade are likely to be of greater significance in bargaining. The third point, which I owe to Professor Anne Krueger, is that Mexico would indeed have received recogni-tion for unilateral liberalization when becoming a signatory to the GATT, had Mexico agreed to bind the reduced tariffs, as the GATT requires.

The authors are rightly concerned about Mexico's trade relations with the United States, which has historically bypassed the multilateral institutions such as the GATT and taken the bilateral approach at its own choosing. A frightening example is the recently enacted omnibus trade bill aptly described as "ominous" by Professor Bhagwati.

It seems to me that there are three rogue elephants stomping the grounds of trade negotiations: the U.S., the E.C. and Japan. As the saying goes, when elephants fight, the grass gets trampled. Whether the rest of the trading world can offset these dominant players by forming coalitions, possibly of differing membership on different issues, is an open question. But what is clear, of course, is that oft-expressed sanctimonious concern of the United States about the "rule of law" being observed in trade matters is mostly rhetoric.

I would like to end with a query about the Pacto, on the continuation of which so much seems to depend. I hesitate to raise the question because my knowledge of Mexican political economy is virtually nil. But it is hard for me to believe that an agreement such as the Pacto can be sustained for very long unless it is not simply a short-term expedient to address inertial inflation but rather means acceptance by all parties of the implicit distribution of income. If it indeed means such acceptance, then enforcing it through non-market means should be unnecessary and may be detrimental. But if it is not, the fate of the Pacto may be no different from the late and not-so-lamented austral and cruzado plans.

Broader Perspectives on Development Problems

Victor Urquidi
Research Professor Emeritus, El Colegio de Mexico

For seven years Mexico has struggled with problems of economic stagnation and domestic adjustments while physical and human resources have suffered much damage. With new and adverse external shocks, more attempts at stabilization, debt reschedulings and debt service relief negotiation, Mexico now faces the task of not just resuming growth -- as is so glibly stated in many circles -- but becoming seriously concerned with the question of renewing development.

ECONOMIC POLICY CONSEQUENCES

The legacy of short-term policy adjustments includes a low rate of savings and investment, obsolete industrial plants, hampered initiative, vast open unemployment and the inability to absorb into the formal sectors the still high annual increment in the labor force. Population growth has abated over the past fifteen years to an annual rate of just under 2 percent, but lower fertility has not yet had an impact on labor force growth. Young entrants into the labor force and large numbers of those who have been displaced by the adjustment policies have created a "new" economic sector -- the urban underground economy -- which has served as a safety valve and a means of survival but hardly as a basis for future development. The alternative for the young labor force has continued to be part-time or temporary migration to segmented labor markets in the United States. The recent expansion of the tourist industry, the maquila operations along the northern border and other export-oriented activities have not offset the decline in employment opportunities associated with the domestic market. Moreover, as Leopoldo Solis has shown in his paper, the evidence is fairly clear that household income distribution has deteriorated and that the consumption of basic wage-goods has declined.

Policymakers must pay attention to immediate issues like preventing inflation from flaring up again after the successful reduction of the monthly consumer price index rate from 15 percent in January 1988 to about 1.5 to 2 percent recently. But Mexico must also pursue an active policy of restructuring to achieve industrial, agricultural and service efficiency. Such a policy has been clearly embraced since mid-1985 and particularly since Mexico's admission to GATT in 1986. It may, however, have gone too far in many respects, as I interpret judgmentally from the paper by Pedro Noyola and Jaime Serra; and this problem is compounded by the recent policy decision to freeze and then only very gently adjust the exchange rate thereby maintaining the currency on the edge of overvaluation.

The central aspect of industrial strategy is less simple than it might sound. Opening up the economy and lowering the customs barriers provides incentives for new investments and technological change to make Mexican industry internationally competitive. There have also been indications of a less rigid and closed attitude with respect to encouraging foreign direct investment, a steadily pursued effort at privatization of certain publicly owned corporations, a simplification of bureaucratic formalities and even the elimination of whole sections of the administration. Although export promotion policies and programs have also been pursued, they have been neither fully implemented nor sufficiently brought to the attention of potential exporters. The export growth of manufactures has occurred less as a consequence of the government's export promotion programs than a result of long-term strategies of transnational corporations operating in Mexico, the substantial lowering of real wages since 1983, and special agreements under which 100 percent foreign ownership was allowed in exchange for acceptance of export requirements.

On the other hand, while Mexican enterprises ready to seize the export opportunities have quickly modernized both their technology and their management, a substantial array of medium and small manufacturing industries that had been established and had expanded under past import substitution policies has not yet come to terms with the new trade policy. In other words, they have not been able to reconvert quickly enough to compete directly with imports coming in under the low tariff levels. Many of these industries have either closed down or had to operate under extremely disadvantageous conditions, including lack of access to financing at reasonable rates of interest (see below).

During the long period of domestic adjustment, public investment has declined severely in real terms. This decision has resulted in the leveling off of certain substantial investments in the oil industry, other sources of energy and petrochemicals. It has also implied neglected maintenance of crude oil productive capacity, highways and ports, urban infrastructure, and so on. Also unfortunate are delays in the expansion of communications, water supply and drainage, irrigation, feeder roads, urban transit and many other types of social capital necessary to maintain the generation of externalities for the economy as a whole and for the regions and smaller areas where some dynamic activity has taken place. Despite the requirements of the stabilization program, more attention should therefore have been paid to infrastructure development and to the efficient operation of basic public services.

Moreover, very little thought has been given in the last few years to the formulation of an employment-oriented strategy of development. Industrial restructuring and introduction of high technology do not necessarily create additional employment and plant closings have raised unemployment. Construction and public investment programs have been depressed and private investment is barely creeping along. Although the adjustment and realignment measures have been necessary, there are no signs that they have been conceived within a framework also allowing for the expansion of sectors using technologies that are not biased against employment. This neglect is particularly unfortunate for Mexico: notwithstanding significant declines in fertility, the momentum of past population growth rates is now revealed in the steady increase of the labor force at over 3 percent per year, a rate expected to continue for the next eight to ten years. It would require several years of a much higher rate of increase of GDP than now appears feasible to increase employment in the formal sector at the 3.7 percent annual rate recorded in 1970–1982, a period that includes years of more than average GDP expansion.

MATTERS OF FINANCE

Mexico must formulate a new financial strategy. Inflation has seriously eroded the domestic savings rate and stabilization has pushed up the real rate of interest so high that investment has become highly risky if not unprofitable. The high real rates of interest have been necessary in order to maintain liquidity within domestic financial institutions and to finance its global budget shortfall, but the impact on development prospects is quite perverse. Not only does this policy dissuade real investment, especially given other uncertainties about external debt reschedulings, debt relief and the exchange rate; but it also skews the distribution of savings by resulting in a massive <u>real</u> transfer of financial assets into the hands of the higher income groups and the large corporations. This is in part the cost of continuing the drastic stabilization and incomes policy program that began in early 1988, but at some point a serious reassessment must occur in order to set Mexico on a new growth and development path.

The complexity of this issue is also underlined by a point that has only recently been expressed by high government officials but has been clear all along to most economists. Since 1983 Mexico's policy on its external debt commitments has implied a real resource transfer to foreign and international creditors of some 5 to 6 percent of a GDP that has been stagnant. Current efforts to reduce this transfer to a more manageable 2 to 2.5 percent of GDP imply substantial debt reduction and/or new borrowing and inflows of new foreign direct investment. In all likelihood, Mexico will have to face the fact that over the medium term the external savings component for its annual investment needs will be quite limited. Augmentation of domestic savings will therefore be essential and the policy implications for trade, the balance of payments and exchange rates should not be ignored. While one should not be unduly pessimistic about further successes in raising the value of exports of manufactured goods, maquila operations and services such as tourism, international protectionism and other constraints must also be kept in mind, as Raymond Vernon has clearly pointed out in his paper.

SOCIAL CONDITIONS

Given the deterioration in social conditions to which Leopoldo Solis' paper has directed attention, Mexico must define more clearly the balance between socially directed expenditures and measures to achieve economic efficiency. The seven years of domestic readjustment have resulted in a decline in real outlays in the following areas: public education, public health programs, science and technology, low-cost housing, urban infrastructure and services, and rural welfare. Even population programs have tended to slow down. Meantime, rural-urban migration continues to add to the

growth of the central metropolitan area, large and medium-
sized towns, and certain local points of labor force attraction such as the northern border cities and some holiday
resorts. A combination of deteriorating public services and
the delay in meeting additional needs arising from high
rates of internal migration may bring about crisis conditions in many areas. Amelioration of these trends is not
just a question of allocating resources when they become
available, but also of better planning and increased efficiency. Policies favoring decentralization and democratiza-
tion at the local government levels are also inescapably
involved.

ECONOMIC AND POLITICAL RIGIDITIES

The Mexican economy is beset by rigidities. These are
not only of the basically structural and clearly identifi-
able sort involving the nature and quality of resources in
certain areas, the relative lack of adequate internal means
of communication, and the like. They are also cemented in
the political system, in outmoded legislation, in market
structures, and even in what I call "mindsets".

Mexican legislation dating back to the 1917 Constitu-
tion and its amendments tends today to inhibit rather than
to stimulate development. Amendments introduced in late 1982
have especially pointed in this direction. Not only is too
much regulation of economic activity on the books, but it
stems from a dirigiste approach that goes beyond the normally expected scope of a developmental State. The Mexican public sector does not fully regard the private sector as an
asset to development; and this attitude is not confined to
the treatment of foreign direct investment, where the policy
can be largely explained as defensive, but is equally applicable to relations with the domestic private sector, which
is seen as an "enemy".

On the other hand, and to some extent paradoxically,
Mexican policy on development has been paternalistic since
the 1930s. In the extreme case, it has actively supported
areas of non-market privilege, as in the detailed regulation
of business, labor, transport services, agriculture and land
tenure. If these policies enhanced productivity, competitiveness, creativity and income creation, the stage of regulation Mexico has experienced in past periods might be more
understandable. But the outcome has been to create monopo-
lies, rent-seeking groups, inefficiencies and even corruption. Perhaps it is remarkable that Mexico has developed to

the extent that it has under such a system. The winds of
change have been blowing for some time, however, and it now
appears that some of the privileged rent-seekers are being
forced into the market and that the economy may be moving
towards more efficient administration and operation.   It
remains to be seen, nevertheless, whether excessive subsidization, heavily controlled market structures, ingrained
inwardness and tolerance of waste and corruption in educational, health and other services can be quickly dissipated.

The issue of inequality in Mexico, not only of incomes
but in holdings of real property and financial and other
assets, should be seriously reviewed.   Sixty years of proclaimed egalitarian policies have certainly not had much visible result in reducing inequality and the recent stagnation
and inflation have made matters worse.   Apart from identifying the main structural and socio-political causes for this
general outcome, redefining a strategy to ensure that future
growth and development be directed more pointedly to reducing inequality seems essential.   This means not only action
through fiscal and other instruments but also attention to
the enhancement of human resource quality, market behavior
and the socio-political framework.

The whole question of agricultural organization also
looms large in Mexico's future.   The food deficit that is
met by close to $2 billion of imports each year is due in
part to past policies on farm prices and neglect of widespread basic improvements; it is also the consequence of
shifts in demand over a fairly long period as family incomes
rose in urban areas.   In view of price controls on consumer
goods, the massive devaluations of recent years have also
contributed to farm decapitalization.   Instead of dealing
forcefully with this problem, Mexico continues to manifest
indecision regarding the relative merits of the ejido system
of land tenure versus the small freeholder system.   Farm production and land tenure issues are excessively politicized
and ejidatarios and small freeholders are frequently pitted
against each other with unfortunate results.

The situation in the field of education is somewhat similar.   In the nineteenth century the liberals and the conser-
vatives were already fighting for the control of what little
education then existed.   The struggle continues in different
terms today -- leftist-inspired nationalists versus right-
wing reformers.   Educational enrollment has vastly increased
but the quality of education has visibly declined, higher
education has been relatively neglected and politization has
been introduced almost throughout.   Accordingly, Mexico is
failing to generate the quality of human resources that it

needs for future development. Seven years of steep decline
in the real wages of teachers and researchers and in allocations to R&D have only added to the divisive features of the
educational system and to its general deterioration. There
have been notable contributions in education from the private sector, but they cannot provide the solution on a large
scale.

CONCLUSION

    In sum, the complexity of Mexican development has
increased at a time when the resources available have contracted. The situation should not be evaluated in purely
economic terms, as some economists tend to do, but in socio-
political terms as well and in the framework of rapidly
evolving -- and as Professor Vernon has put it, "technology
driven" -- international conditions. Mexican development
strategy must be reframed in the context of both a more
interactive world economy and a more mutually beneficial
relationship with its major economic partner to the north.

PART II
MEXICAN–U.S. RELATIONS

Mexico, the United States and the World Economy

Hugo Margain
Senator from the Federal District

Every twelve years Mexico and the United States change their administrations at almost the same time. In Mexico President Carlos Salinas took office on December 1, 1988, and in the United States the new government headed by President Bush started on January 20, 1989. The new governments on both sides of the border have evidenced in an unprecedented manner the desire and determination to redefine the relationship between the two countries on the basis of mutual respect and commonality of interests. These interests coincide in large measure because of recognition that prosperity provides the best basis for peace both internally and internationally. Cooperation for development is therefore extremely important.

The following remarks are based in large part on my involvement during the past two and a half years in the work of the Bilateral Commission on the Future of United States-Mexican Relations, which culminated in a report presented to the heads of the two governments last December.(1) This has been an intensely enlightening and immensely satisfying experience for me and, I believe, for all of my associates in this endeavor as well. On this occasion I shall both summarize some of our principal findings and recommendations and elaborate on certain matters from my own personal point of view.

ECONOMICS: DEBT, TRADE AND INVESTMENT

Mexico has had a serious economic crisis since 1982. Inflation, which has been fought successfully in the past, has caused terrible distortions in the economy as it has increased from less than 5 percent annually to more than 130

percent in only a few years. The rate of exchange for the
dollar has gone up from 12.5 to almost 2,400. The purchasing power of wage earners is now half its pre-1982 level in
spite of nominal escalations every year. Because of the
lack of confidence, Mexico experienced capital flight to the
nations with strong economies and hard currencies. The last
six years have brought zero economic growth. Meanwhile population growth continues and the possibility of a social
upheaval becomes a major concern. Indeed, the elections of
July 6, 1988, were an expression of a broad-based attitude
of malaise and exhaustion stemming from the social costs of
prolonged economic crisis.

Mexico's social pressures are very serious due to the
painful fact that the standard of living has declined. During the past eight years there was no growth at all and
annual population increases of 2 percent exacerbate the problem. Mexico has been unable to create enough jobs for the
new generation of workers. Furthermore, Mexico's income distribution is heavily skewed: the top quarter of the population received 20 times the per capita income of the bottom
20 percent. In the United States the ratio is 9.5 to 1.
Mexico's challenge is to generate growth in a manner that
benefits all its people so that both employment opportunities and the distribution of income are improved.

Mexico is a large debtor and must sustain economic
growth by exporting in a time of protectionism. Notwithstanding the country's high deficit and indebtedness, new
investments and fresh financial support are essential for
Mexico's development.

Mexico's problem concerning debt is that very large
annual payments of money -- more than 6 percent of the GNP
-- are necessary for debt service. I believe that the ceiling on this service should be around 3.5 percent while
growth should be 6 percent annually.

The United States, the largest creditor nation in 1981,
shifted to being the largest debtor nation in 1985. When the
United States ceased to be a source of capital and instead
became a larger user of global capital, the cost of capital
was raised to all borrowers, including Mexico.

Mexico's external debt level and debt service burden
are simply too high in relation to the size of the economy
and the growth of export earnings. Total debt at the end of
1987 was 107 billion -- 76 percent of the GNP, and the debt
service burden alone is enough to stifle growth.

Capital flight has been in the tens of billions of dollars. These outflows have not only inflated the foreign
debt numbers, but also undercut productive investment. High

real interest rates must be maintained to minimize and ultimately reverse capital flight. But these high interest
rates also work to increase the domestic budget deficit and
otherwise contribute to inflationary pressures. Such pressures are extremely difficult to curb without recession, but
unless they are contained the economic and political underpinnings of structural reform will be destroyed.

The large creditor banks have so far not been willing
to allow Mexico to repurchase its public sector loans at the
discount established in the inter-bank market. If banks
realize losses, they receive tax credits which spread some
of the costs across the whole universe of taxpayers. These
tax credits should be translated into a reduction of service
payments for the debtor country.

It is essential to agree upon levels of debt payment
consistent with Mexico's capacity to pay under conditions of
growth. The "sovereign debt" problem must be addressed by
novel financial schemes that can lead to the reduction of
debt and debt service. The banks should remove contractual
obligations that restrict Mexico's ability to repurchase its
own debt. New loans are essential for viable investments
that conserve or generate foreign exchange. Another possibility is for the World Bank to establish a facility to purchase the foreign debt of Mexico at its market value and
pass on to the debtor the prevailing market discount thus
captured.

Mexico welcomed Secretary Nicholas Brady's new approach
when he suggested "voluntary" reductions in the rate of
interest and even in the capital owed as well in order to
facilitate growth in developing countries, to everyone's
benefit. This new approach will help Mexico and it is ready
to enter into negotiations with the bankers in order to
achieve a solution that might permit growth and public
investment in important areas like education, housing and
health. The minimum necessary rate of economic growth -- 6
percent per annum -- requires more financial support, and
borrowing fresh money is essential because the new investments must come from the most developed countries.

Mexico's industrialization began in the 1930s and
infant industries were protected by all sorts of prohibi-
tions, customs duties, import permissions, and the like.
Industrial development was successful, but over-protected.
With entry into the GATT, the openness of the economy is a
fact and custom duties have been eliminated. Many merchandise imports can now enter Mexico freely to compete with
Mexican products. Import permissions have been reduced substantially and in addition to the GATT a "framework

agreement" with the United States facilitates the settlement of many problems. It is still too difficult, however, for foreigners to invest in Mexico and rules should be clarified to provide an incentive for new investors. The establishment of an "early warning mechanism" is also required in order to know in advance about modifications in the dynamic spheres of trade and investment and thereby to prevent distortion of domestic markets.

The Canadian/United States/Mexico Common Market is in the minds of many people. The United States reached an agreement with Canada and the implications of that new policy will be watched carefully. The arrangements between the United States and Israel provide a possible model in this matter, but the asymmetry between the U.S. and Mexico make a United States/Mexico Common Market inappropriate at this time. Perhaps in the future a regional arrangement between the Northern Hemisphere of this continent will be a fact, but Mexico now supports the idea of a Latin American Common Market and would like to increase its commerce with Europe probably through Spain, a member of the European Common Market. Japan is also crucial. Mexico's eyes are on the Pacific. Asia, through the Philippines, was for centuries its trade partner, and Mexicans remember "La Nao de China". The influence of this trade from the Philippines to Acapulco was historically important. Silks, porcelain and specie formerly came from Asia to Mexico and there may now be another opportunity for trade with the Orient through countries like Korea, Taiwan and Japan.

The maquiladoras or in-bond industries on Mexico's borders have been an excellent program and many Mexicans can find employment with them instead of entering the United States illegally in search of jobs. It is possible for the maquiladoras not only to send their products to the U.S. market paying only the "added value" tax but also to send their manufactures to other continents, other markets in which the United States is losing competitiveness because of its high wage levels.

Growth is desirable not only per se but also to enable Mexico to meet its debt payments, and in order to grow it needs new investments and modern technology in industry and services. Mexico is concerned with the evidence that protectionism in the United States is gaining support. The two countries need each other. A good economic situation in the United States is good for Mexico, and the U.S. needs a strong neighbor to the south growing steadily, maintaining social stability and working in peace.

MIGRATION

The "push factor" increases with the Mexican economic crisis. Because Mexico is not producing the 1 million additional jobs required each year it is losing fine and aggressive young people who are going to the United States. The loss is tremendous for Mexico: good workers, healthy people, good minds. With the inflationary movement the migration increased because of the lure of dollars that in Mexico have a very high peso value. The push factor is working together strongly with the "pull factor" making ever more urgent the necessity for resuming economic growth. Mexico should increase its economical power and give them an opportunity to work in Mexico and to help increase the GNP.

THE DRUG PROBLEM

The most serious problem all over the world as well as for bilateral relations is the problem of drugs. The United States and Mexico are experiencing drug abuse in all levels of their social structures. Increasing numbers of rich people, middle class and poor people enter into the curse of illicit drugs. The profits of the illegal groups managing this criminal trade are truly enormous. Money laundering and bank secrecy, which protects all sorts of gangsterism, must be prevented.

In dealing with this problem it is necessary to separate two factors. Mexico and the United States are both against the production, traffic and consumption of illicit drugs. That is a point with which the two countries concur. But a conflict between the two governments and two peoples arises because of the unilateral "certification" or "decertification" of Mexico's conduct in this matter. Every year the executive branch of the American government unilaterally assesses Mexico's efforts to combat drug production and traffic, and may decide on decertification so that Mexico then loses the benefit of the "General Preferences" that were established in Geneva to help the countries in development. Another punishment is Mexico's loss of financial support. This unilateral system of certification or decertification is inappropriate. According to the Convention signed on December 20, 1988, in Vienna, the United Nations will be in charge of presenting to the General Assembly an annual report about the war against drugs in each nation. I hope this will replace the annual certification by the United States and thereby greatly improve bilateral relations.

Another unfortunate consequence of the problem of drugs is the presence in Mexico of the Drug Enforcement Agency, DEA, when incidences like the assassination of Camarena, an agent from the United States, and the apprehension of Cortez occur. When experts from the United Nations work in Mexico to combat drugs the bilateral clashes will disappear. With the support of the recent convention, the United Nations should now replace the DEA agents with experts from different nations, in accordance with the principles of "international cooperation" and "collective responsibility" with respect to production, traffic and consumption.

Another achievement in Vienna was to condemn as a criminal offense any publication that promotes by any means the consumption of illegal drugs. The International Court of Justice can now intervene to settle any future disputes regarding the bilateral campaign against drugs. In this matter "multilateralism" through the United Nations is much better than the "bilateralism" that has existed previously.

FOREIGN POLICY

Mexico and the United States have ideological discrepancies in foreign policy. The Mexican point of view regarding Central America favors peaceful settlement of the civil wars supported by the great powers, whose practice of sending weapons only assures death and destruction. Mexico has always been against the Contras, an army organized and trained by the United States in Honduras with the purpose of attacking the Sandinista regime in Nicaragua. Mexico's proposition was to negotiate peacefully and the Contadora Group was designed to pursue that goal: instead of weapons, development. Poverty and all its consequences have caused this civil war, and war never will achieve peace. Development is the only basis to achieve and ensure peace. One of the presidents of the Central American nations during the Esquipulas reunion said: "We are tired of the great powers supplying weapons while we deliver casualties."

If all the resources that went to the Central American conflict were utilized in developing the region instead of supplying weapons, changes in the infrastructure required for rapid growth would produce peace and tranquility. Disarmament is therefore an excellent idea. The amount of resources that the world has been investing in weapons instead of development and education is incredible. Olaf Palme caught the attention of the world by citing some statistics: the great powers were spending almost $900 billion in a year on weapons while the international organizations spent only $20 billion on education. It is necessary to reverse these figures -- and disarmament is the answer.

The economic distortion all over the world is caused by the armaments competition. A recent United Nations study reveals some astonishing facts about the consequences for developing countries. In peace development can proceed faster and resources devoted to arms can be channeled to development -- which is the only way to secure peace. Conversations between the two great powers about disarmament are encouraging.

All the problems discussed in this paper are interrelated. If impediments to economic growth can be removed, bilateral problems of migration will disappear and through education new generations can be prevented from abusing drugs. And in the global sphere there will be fewer tensions that produce civil wars and often contaminate international relations.

NOTES

1. Report of the Bilateral Commission on the Future of United States-Mexican Relations, The Challenge of Interdependence: Mexico and the United States (University Press of America, 1989).

Mexican members: Hugo B. Margain, co-chairman. Hector Aguilar Camin, Gilberto Borja, Juan Jose Bremer, Fernando Canales Clariond, Socorro Diaz, Ernesto Fernandez Hurtado, Carlos Fuentes, Mario Ojeda.

American members: William D. Rogers, co-chairman. Yvonne B. Burke, Henry Cisneros, Lawrence S. Eagleburger, Roger W. Heyns, Nancy L. Kassebaum, Robert S. McNamara, Charles W. Parry, Glenn E. Watts.

Staff directors: Rosario Green, Peter H. Smith.

Suggestions for Establishing a Special Bilateral Relationship

Anthony Solomon
Chairman, S. G. Warburg USA, Inc.

A sympathetic and friendly observer of the Mexican economy can't help feeling that Mexico has lost many years in the international race. Numerous countries throughout the world, both capitalist and socialist, have moved substantially toward freeing of domestic markets and opening of their economies to international competition while Mexico has lagged behind. Nevertheless, a strategy for rapid restructuring to openness and international competitiveness still makes the most sense for Mexico, and political developments in Mexico reinforce that compelling need.

Tougher international competition in the future plus the major and well-known setbacks to the Mexican economy in the 1980s lead me to conclude that Mexico needs a special assist that can come only from the United States, not for charitable reasons but for reasons of U.S. self-interest. The goal should be a unique and special bilateral relationship; and the recent U.S.-Mexican Bilateral Commission Report, in my opinion and with great respect to Hugo Margain, does not begin to go far enough toward that objective. Mexico may not need the assistance of a new and special bilateral relationship to resume minimally adequate growth, but it is in the best interest of both the United States and Mexico to foster a rapid return to economic dynamism in Mexico.

As I see it, there are two levels of problems in constructing the special bilateral relationship required to initiate and sustain Mexico's economic recovery. The first level is the general problem of mutual hypersensitivity and the associated problem of not speaking frankly to each other. The Bilateral Commission Report reflects that "walking on eggs" attitude: it contains, for example, not a word about Mexico's failure to pursue a vigorous curbing of population growth and says very little about the United State's irresponsible string of budget deficits that have forced up the interest rates Mexico must pay on its external debt. Aside from the Report there is a general pattern of unbalanced and sometimes misdirected lecturing, particularly from the United States. This is matched by a defensive hypersensitivity on the part of Mexico about its economic dependence on the United States but we have to face the world as it is.

(I can remember going to lunch a few years ago with Secretary of State, George Shultz, and the Foreign Ministers of Latin America when Secretary Shultz lectured the Latin Americans about the economic damage of governments' running excessive public sector deficits. I couldn't resist asking Shultz in an innocent voice when he returned to our table if he might have been referring to his own country -- and the Mexican Foreign Minister burst into laughter.)

There is a second, more substantive level of problems in constructing a special customized bilateral relationship between the two countries. I do not take lightly the postwar leadership role of the United States in the free world and the associated obligations to avoid discriminatory bilateral dealings. During the 1960s at the State Department, then in helping the House Ways & Means Committee write the 1974 Trade Act, later at the Treasury and finally at the Federal Reserve, I worked within and contributed to that framework of multilateral economic policies. But the severely troublesome situation in Mexico requires special measures by both countries, particularly in a world with rapidly growing trends toward regional trade groupings.

Now what would be the main thrust of a custom tailored bilateral treaty between Mexico and the United States? The options are many, but I offer here four suggestions.

1. In the trade area, the maquiladora zones at the border should be extended to other areas in Mexico but only for specified products. These would be products where foreign exporters such as the East Asian countries have market dominance in the United States. We know that Mexico, unlike others, will use any increased foreign exchange earnings to increase its import levels and will not run persistent trade surplus imbalances. Under Section 807 of the Customs Code, imports produced from U.S. materials pay U.S. customs duties only on the value added in the maquiladora zone. These arrangements are consistent with the GATT. Since

the value-added products that would be earmarked
for these additional zones are not products in
whose markets U.S. manufacturers can compete, U.S.
business, labor and consumers would not be harmed
by this increased competition to the East Asians
-- and would in fact benefit from the greater Mexican use of U.S. materials.

2. Also in the trade area, the bilateral treaty I
envision is not the negotiation one by one of particular sectoral free-trade areas. That is a formula for painfully drawn-out discussions and relatively little accomplishment in the end. A more
effective approach would be a framework that
assumes a sequence stretched out over, say, a 20
to 30 year period, of particular sectors becoming
free of trade restrictions in the enlarged U.S.-
Canadian market except where a tribunal of independent experts assessed the potential employment damage in either country as outweighing the advantage
to the consumers in the combined North American
market. Sufficiently lengthy periods of time for
adjustment and relocation would be provided in the
treaty framework to ensure that the trade-creating
effects would be greater than the trade-diverting
effects. The tribunal would have to publish the
relevant objective analyses of the costs to consumers, the employment changes, and the other consequences to the two economies of a move to free
trade in each sector. The legislative bodies of
the two countries might insist on retaining the
right of an overriding veto over freeing of trade
in particular sectors, but this kind of a treaty
framework would still expand trade relations more
successfully than a piecemeal approach.

3. In the investment area Mexico should set up a progressive time schedule for the sequential removal
of bureaucratic and other discriminatory obstacles
to foreign investment. The objective would be to
achieve an investment regime analogous to that in
the OECD economies.

4. In the debt area, I would envision that the bilateral treaty would provide -- aside from and in
addition to any IMF-World Bank enhancements under
the Brady program -- some carefully calculated,
partial guarantees by the U.S. government through
which Mexico could achieve a still greater reduction in its debt-service obligations. It is

clearly in the U.S. self-interest to add a carefully devised and partial government guarantee for
Mexico, and I believe that Congress would go along
with that view. Other OECD governments will very
likely add unilateral partial guarantees for those
countries where they have a particular political
or economic self-interest.

Other areas of bilateral importance such as drug and
immigration matters could, of course, be dealt with in the
treaty as well. Non-formalized understandings might be
appropriate for registering mutual recognition of such matters as the necessity for vigorous and effective Mexican
population policies and family planning programs for satisfactory economic growth.

In conclusion, the time has come when the varying "sen-
sitivities" and ideological constraints in both countries
must disappear (or be substantially lessened). The United
States' sensitivity about avoiding special -- or non-MFN --
bilateral trade arrangements should give way to a recognition that it is in our national interest to make an exception for Mexico. The Mexican sensitivity about increasing
its economic dependence on the United States should yield to
the understanding that the more rapid economic growth,
greater employment and higher real incomes are worth the
increasing interdependence. Canadians came to that conclusion; it's only a question of time, in my opinion, before
Mexicans do also. But why lose that time?

In the Eye of the Storm:
The State of U.S.-Mexican Relations

Cathryn Thorup
Senior Fellow and Director of U.S.-Mexico Project,
Overseas Development Council

The United States and Mexico are in the midst of a major realignment of their relationship. This shift is the result of both the growing strategic importance of Mexico to the United States and the spiralling complexity of their bilateral ties. It is particularly apparent in terms of the impact of domestic interest groups in both countries on the policymaking process. The discontinuities brought about by this transition affect U.S. policymaking toward Mexico and necessitate a reassessment of the state of the bilateral relationship.

THE POLITICAL LANDSCAPE

While Mexico has never experienced sustained high-level attention from the U.S. policymaking apparatus, the trajectory of U.S.-Mexican relations was particularly erratic during the 1980s. Though it received only sporadic attention from the U.S. government in the early years of the decade, by 1985 Mexico had become a top foreign policy priority. Unfortunately, however, its high profile at that time was the result of increasingly heated disagreements with the Reagan administration regarding Mexico's policies toward Central America, the pace and content of economic and political reform, drug trafficking and corruption.(1) By the time the frenzy of Mexico-bashing abated in mid-1986, U.S. relations with Mexico had been severely damaged. Perhaps of even greater long-term significance than the temporary deterioration in government-to-government relations were the negative impressions that lingered for the American public following this period.

Today the bilateral relationship is both stronger and more precarious than ever. On the one hand, there is a genuine rapport between the U.S. government and the new Mexican administration. The impressive electoral showing by the opposition in July of 1988 and the subsequent sagacity and skill Mexico's President Carlos Salinas has shown in rebuilding his political base and in further opening the Mexican economy seem to have convinced the Bush administration that Salinas is the best guarantor of U.S. interests in Mexico.

On the other hand, while these changes indicate an improving policy climate, serious problems remain. Despite graphic evidence in Venezuela and Argentina of the dangers of prolonged economic crisis, a long-term solution to Mexico's external debt problem remains elusive. President Salinas has stressed that the social and political costs of seven years of economic austerity have become unbearable and can only be alleviated through a return to economic growth. Recognizing that the viability of the Salinas administration is at stake, the Mexican government has adopted bold measures which signal its determination to push political and economic reform. These steps have included the arrest of several previously "untouchable" public figures (like the corrupt leader of the oil workers union), the release of some political prisoners, and a wide array of economic measures aimed at fostering growth through opening the Mexican economy. Mexico's foreign investment regulations, for example, were liberalized to permit 100 percent foreign ownership of enterprises in a variety of sectors.

Despite these dramatic adjustments, the Mexican government continues to battle a perception within U.S. public and private sectors that it is somehow "not doing enough." A growing sense of urgency -- even desperation -- among both Mexican policymakers and the general public regarding Mexico's economic situation contrasts sharply with the consistently hard-line posture that has characterized the U.S. commercial banks. Such was their intransigence that even U.S. policymakers were finally forced to press the banks to be more flexible and accommodating during the protracted debt negotiations in order to avoid unilateral action by Mexico.

Though Mexico is widely viewed within the U.S. government and the international financial community as a "model debtor" and one of the countries most deserving of immediate debt relief, the result of the 1989 negotiation fell far short of the debt reduction sought by the Mexican government. The outcome of the negotiation guaranteed the commercial banks a large margin of maneuver in terms of choosing whether to reduce debt or to loan fresh money to Mexico, and, as a result, is expected to provide only about $1.5 billion of debt service relief per year. Not only is this relief insufficient in terms of Mexico's needs, but it is unlikely to induce other debtors around the world to restructure their economies in hopes of securing

debt relief. The agreement may buy critical time for the
Salinas administration's attempts to turn the Mexican economy
around by bolstering investor confidence and promoting the
repatriation of flight capital, but in reality the plan
involves debt restructuring more than debt reduction.(2)

There is a tendency in Washington to announce a plan and
consider a problem resolved, as was the case with the 1986
Simpson—Rodino legislation on immigration. A similar attitude
may characterize reactions to Mexico's debt crisis. Excessive
focus on the debt per se has eclipsed concern for a return to
growth in Mexico which is the truly significant issue for both
countries. Underperformance of U.S. exports to Mexico in 1987
cost the United States $11.4 billion and over 300,000 jobs when
compared to what could have been achieved had the economic
trends of the 1970s continued.(3) The U.S. public, unfortunately, remains largely uninformed or misinformed about the way
in which long—term U.S. interests are directly affected by the
debt crisis in Mexico, tending instead to concentrate only on
the immediate costs of a "bail—out."

THE CHANGING PARAMETERS OF U.S.—MEXICAN RELATIONS

Two major trends over the past ten years help explain the
emerging realignment of this bilateral relationship. The first
shift is the growing strategic importance of Mexico to the
United States. From Mexico's oil wealth of the late 1970s to
today's debt crisis, Mexico's impact on the United States has
increased. This has produced rising concern in Washington
regarding the nature and direction of Mexico's economic and
political development and the details of its foreign policy,
and their potential impact on the United States.

The second major development over the last decade is the
spiralling complexity of the bilateral relationship, resulting
from the rising interaction of domestic and foreign policy, the
addition of a multitude of new bilateral actors and issues, and
more vigorous U.S. involvement in areas previously in the exclusive domain of the Mexican government. In addition to debt,
trade, immigration and narcotics, new issues —— such as the
environment, technology change and Mexico's political reform
process —— are entering the bilateral agenda.

In the trade and investment arena, for example, U.S. policymakers are paying close attention to growing Japanese
involvement in the Mexican economy as Mexico attempts to solid-
ify its trade and investment links with a variety of countries.
It is unclear whether Mexico will move towards a North American
economic alliance, a Pacific Basin arrangement or a revitalized

Latin American trading zone, or instead will choose to pursue a more independent path. Whatever the end result, Mexico's role as an emerging middle-range power will have a profound effect on the traditional parameters of its relationship with the United States.

These two major trends have affected as well the coherence of U.S. policymaking toward Mexico and have made the management of the bilateral relationship even more difficult.(4) At the federal level the number of executive branch agencies involved in U.S.-Mexican relations has expanded to include some whose traditional mandate has been strictly domestic so that the points of access to the policymaking process have increased. In responding to constituent interests, different agencies at times work at cross-purposes in their efforts to secure U.S. foreign policy objectives. For example, while the U.S. Treasury has struggled to ease Mexico's debt burden, U.S. trade policy has been relatively unresponsive to Mexico's economic restructuring. Similarly, the U.S. Congress has often reflected increased constituent concern for U.S. policy toward Mexico, at times acting as a useful counterweight to executive branch action (or inaction) on Mexico, but all too frequently -- for lack of a well-informed, broad perspective -- acting as a parochial spoiler.

DOMESTIC PUBLIC OPINION: CREATING A CLIMATE FOR CHANGE

Ten years ago there were no Washington-based programs dealing with Mexico, and interest in U.S. policymaking vis-a-vis Mexico was limited to a few specialized niches within the U.S. government. There was little interaction among the public and private sector actors who dealt with Mexico and their contacts with academics were rare. Today that situation is much improved with one glaring exception: the U.S. public at large.

The need for a broad-based effort to educate U.S. citizens about Mexico is made more pressing by the increasingly important role played in U.S.-Mexican relations by non-governmental actors, a development that stands out as likely to redefine the bilateral agenda in the 1990s. Today a key challenge for policymakers is how to incorporate the distinctive concerns of these groups into a broader framework of national interests.(5)

Throughout the United States, an astonishing number of domestic actors regularly voice their concerns -- through a wide variety of channels -- on an expanding number of issues directly or indirectly affecting Mexico. In Mexico as well, diversity of opinion is reshaping the political landscape. Efforts on the part of President Salinas to overhaul the traditional one-party system and to encourage increased civic involvement on the part of individual Mexican citizens combine with mounting pressure from new political actors to take that process further. Thus the emergence of civil society in Mexico is being propelled both from above and at the grassroots level.

In the United States, there is no consistent and widely held view of U.S. national interests regarding Mexico. The diversity of domestic constituencies inhibits consensus among U.S. officials and the public at large on appropriate policies toward Mexico and compounds the difficulty of achieving trade-offs on tough issues such as immigration and the maquila industry. Sporadic outbreaks of anti-Mexico sentiment in the United States could become the norm rather than the exception unless cooperative economic development and conflict management is more generally perceived as being in the joint interest of both nations.

New social actors in both countries must be drawn into national discussions regarding the bilateral relationship. These should include individuals and groups that are directly affected by decisions taken at the national level but do not generally share in that policymaking process. Union leaders, community organizers, Hispanic activists, environmentalists and others -- who through their daily activities help set the parameters of the bilateral relationship -- must take a more active role in policy debates about U.S.-Mexican relations.

Efforts to educate public opinion in both countries until now have been sporadic, underfunded and poorly conceptualized. Teachers and administrators must be better informed about Mexico, as well as those who produce textbooks and design courses of study. Educational and cultural exchange programs -- severely curtailed in the wake of the Mexican economic crisis -- must be strengthened. To do nothing is to risk losing an entire generation of Mexican scholars to the debt crisis.

A variety of other less traditional public educators -- such as professional associations of lawyers and scientists -- must be identified and U.S.-Mexican relations must be placed squarely on their agenda. Efforts should be undertaken to enable those in the print and electronic media who write, file, edit and produce the coverage of U.S.-Mexican relations better to inform their audiences. Finally, since popular culture acts as a powerful filter to new information and analysis, it is important to work with the creators of cultural images -- writers, artists and producers of cinema and television -- to sensitize them to the history and culture of these two countries.

CONCLUSION

U.S.-Mexican relations have entered the eye of the storm.
There is a strong sense of optimism and momentum in the bilateral relationship, but the new spirit of cooperation between
the two countries could easily be disturbed by an adverse turn
of events in the economic or foreign policy arenas. A somewhat
eerie sense of calm prevails, yet there is an undercurrent of
tension swirling around Mexico's still fragile processes of
economic and political opening. Any misstep -- real or perceived -- on either side of the border might mar the patina of
improved bilateral relations unless measures are taken in both
countries to create a domestic political climate conducive to
coherent, long-range planning on U.S.-Mexican relations long
after the initial glow of presidential "abrazos" has dimmed.

NOTES

1. For example, in May and June of 1986 Senator Jesse
Helms held a series of three subcommittee meetings that were
extremely critical of Mexico.
2. Editors' Note: This is the second of two papers in
this volume revised after the July 23, 1989 conclusion of Mexico's debt negotiations.
3. According to calculations by Stuart Tucker, trade
specialist and Fellow at the Overseas Development Council.
4. For more on this realignment in U.S.-Mexican relations and its impact on U.S. policymaking toward Mexico, see
Cathryn L. Thorup, "U.S. Policymaking Toward Mexico: Prospects
for Administrative Reform," Foreign Policy in U.S. Mexican Relations, Vol. 5, ed. by Rosario Green and Peter H. Smith (University of California at San Diego, San Diego, California: Bilateral Commission on the Future of United States-Mexican Relations, Summer 1989).
5. For more on the need for public education on U.S.-
Mexican relations see Prepared Statement of Cathryn L. Thorup,
in Hearings before the Subcommittee on Western Hemisphere
Affairs of the House Committee on Foreign Affairs, U.S. House
of Representatives, One Hundred and First Congress, First Ses-
sion, June 7, 1989, "Toward a Workable Partnership with Mexico:
Policy, Process, and Public Education" (Washington, D.C.: U.S.
Government Printing Office, 1989).

PART III
DEBT, TRADE AND GROWTH

Mexico: Foreign Debt and Economic Growth

Pedro Aspe
Secretary, Ministry of Finance and Public Credit

The debt crisis began in August of 1982 when Mexico experienced severe balance of payments problems which prevented it from servicing its foreign debt in accordance with originally agreed-upon terms. Today, having stabilized its economy and implemented one of the most novel and effective structural adjustment programs on record, Mexico is in the midst of foreign debt negotiations. An examination of the causes of the crisis, the way in which Mexico adjusted its economy, and the linkages between the debt negotiations and the economic adjust efforts is helpful in understanding the importance of these negotiations and their objective of combining further adjustments with a reduction in net external transfers that will allow the Mexican economy to resume a path of stable and sustained growth.

Before 1982 Mexican economic development was based on an import substitution strategy. Growth was attained by expanding the domestic market and covering balance of payments requirements through foreign borrowing and direct equity investment. Beginning in the late 1970s, a combination of factors allowed the Mexican economy to attain extraordinarily high rates of growth for more than four years. These included expansionary fiscal and monetary policies, availability of abundant financing in international capital markets (a consequence of the recycling of petro-dollars) and rapid development of the country's oil resources.

In 1981 the international economic scene started to change significantly. Worldwide economic activity slowed down, oil prices fell (from $37 per barrel in March of 1981 to $28 per barrel in December of 1982), and the anti-inflationary policies of the U.S. Federal Reserve pushed interest rates up to unprecedented levels (from 6 percent in 1977 to 18 percent in 1980). These events harmed the

Mexican economy as oil export revenues (which represented 72.5 percent of total exports in 1981) declined while interest payments on Mexico's foreign debt increased drastically.

Both the Mexican government and most international financiers thought that these economic shocks would be temporary and that oil prices and real interest rates would return to their previous levels. Economic policy was designed on the basis of these expectations and permanent adjustments were deemed unnecessary: foreign credit could be used in their stead to bridge the temporary external shock. It is important to emphasize that economic forecasts made by foreign commercial banks pointed in the same direction as those made by the Mexican government. Expansionary economic policies continued to be implemented, financed in the main by resources from foreign commercial banks granted under the expectation that oil prices would return to pre-1981 levels.

By August of 1982 it became evident that the oil price and interest rate shocks were not transitory, and that the Mexican economy had to abandon expansionary policies. Commercial bank lending ceased, and Mexico entered into a balance of payments crisis that prevented it from fulfilling its international financial obligations.

Mexico was not the only country with serious economic problems in the fall of 1982. Balance of payments problems were soon faced as well by a large number of countries (including Argentina, Brazil, Chile, and the Philippines) whose economies were deeply affected by the fall in raw materials prices, the drop in the pace of world economic activity and the increase in interest rates. Governments, banks and analysts considered the problem to be one of liquidity; and the inability of debtor countries to service their debts was perceived to be a temporary situation. Most adjustment programs implemented prior to 1987 were based on the premise that economic adjustment and adequate bridge financing would allow these economies to solve their balance of payments problems and regain voluntary access to international financial markets. Countries would adjust their economies and creditors would provide enough financing to keep them afloat. In most cases, the IMF acted as a catalyst for the adjustment programs designed by the debtor countries by coordinating financing negotiations between those countries and their creditors.

When the availability of foreign financing fell dramatically, the consequent domestic macroeconomic problems had to be attacked immediately. In Mexico's case, it was necessary to counteract internal disequilibria with economic policies that exacerbated the effects of the external shocks. Internal adjustment was necessary to absorb the decrease in revenues stemming from the fall in oil prices and the rationing of external credit and also to enhance the economy's ability to generate foreign exchange from other sources and eventually to promote growth.

Until 1982 -- when capital flows into the country were positive -- Mexico's overall expenditure on goods and services was larger than its national production. Current account deficits were the result of both the fiscal deficit and the excess of investment over savings.(1)

Mexico was forced to reduce its aggregate demand below the level of domestic output in order to meet the sudden cut in foreign financing, the abrupt fall in oil export revenues and the service requirements on its foreign debt. A second macroeconomic problem emerging from the external shocks was that the government required dollars and not pesos to service its debts. Mexico designed its economic adjustments so that it could regain growth under the new conditions and comply with short-term payment obligations. Public finances were a major source of both the disequilibria and the adjustment. Between 1977 and 1981, the public sector deficit had been a fundamental contributor to economic growth, increasing from 6.4 percent of GDP to 14.1 percent, but after 1981 it became a major cause of disequilibrium as the government budget had to be adjusted for the declines in both external financing and fiscal revenues from fossil fuel exports.

The adjustment of Mexican public finances undertaken during the past few years has no international precedent. Between 1981 and 1988, public expenditure, excluding interest payments on domestic and foreign debt, dropped by 10 percentage points of GDP, twice the amount that the fully enacted Gramm-Rudman legislation would produce. The adjustment aimed to concentrate scarce fiscal resources in high priority areas like education, health and housing, while eliminating socially unjustifiable subsidies. Public sector investment was cut from 12 to 5 percent of GDP during the same period. In 1987, Congress approved a fiscal reform that resulted in a substantial increase in non-oil revenues. As a result, total public sector revenues increased from 25.2 percent of GDP in 1982 to 29.2 percent in 1988 despite the drastic fall in oil prices. In addition, government enterprises producing goods and services that were not considered to be of strategic priority were sold, merged, closed or transferred to local governments. The number of state-owned enterprises in Mexico decreased from 1,155 in 1982 to only 433 in 1988. Complementary fiscal measures continued to be implemented in 1989 and Mexico's public finances have now been permanently restructured. Today the public sector is slimmer but more effective in reacting promptly to changing economic conditions.

As a result of the fiscal effort, the primary balance of the public sector, defined as the difference between total revenues and government expenditures (excluding interest payments on both domestic and foreign debt), has shifted from a deficit of 8 percent of GDP in 1981 to a surplus of 7.5 percent of GDP in 1988. This change in the primary balance has allowed the country to accommodate the drop in oil revenues and the lack of foreign financing, and has provided enough room to service its foreign debt. This adjustment has been accomplished in a manner that has allowed Mexico to maintain public investment at the minimum tolerable level.

The option of resorting to inflationary finance as an alternative to a serious and permanent fiscal adjustment was discarded from the very beginning because of the high social costs that it would ultimately imply. Some other countries facing a situation similar to Mexico's have followed the inflationary path and incurred these costs. The inflationary problem Mexico experienced was not caused by expanding aggregate demand, but rather by repeated external shocks and the inertia that developed therefrom. The Pact for Economic Growth and Stability (PECE), which followed the Pact of Economic Solidarity (PACTO) signed in December of 1987 to fight inflation, has also worked to curb inflation, and extension of PECE will further consolidate anti-inflationary gains.

Mexico has adjusted its trade balance to offset the fall in petroleum revenues and foreign financing by reducing domestic absorption. The 1982 devaluations -- along with complementary fiscal and monetary measures -- caused imports to fall dramatically, thereby reducing domestic absorption and generating the required trade balance surplus. The devaluations also significantly changed the relative profitability between the tradeable and non-tradeable production sectors, thereby promoting a rise of investment in the tradeable sector. The costs in foregone production were quite high, however, as the reduced absorption further reduced output through multiplier effects.

To complement the short-run macroeconomic measures, Mexico comprehensively liberalized its external trade system, transforming a highly protected economy into one of the most open in the world. Between 1983 and 1988, most quantitative restrictions on international trade were eliminated and replaced by a more efficient system based on tariff protection. In 1982, 100 percent of imports were subject to import permits. Today, only 6.1 percent of import value is protected by non-tariff barriers. In 1983, tariff levels ranged from 0 to 100 percent; today, the three tariff categories are limited to 10, 15 and 20 percent.

Opening up the economy has fostered the efficiency and competitiveness of the export sector by granting export industries access to intermediate inputs at international prices. So far, the results have been encouraging. In 1988 the value of non-oil exports almost reached $14 billion, compared to less than $6 billion in 1981. Mexico has diversified its foreign exchange sources so that oil exports now represent only 32.5 percent of total exports. Maquiladoras (in-bond industries) have also been extremely dynamic: employment in the maquiladoras has increased threefold in the past six years.

In sum, the Mexican economy is now much more solid. Its development potential is much greater today than it has been in recent years. Inflation has fallen substantially and the stabilization process is being consolidated. Public finances have been adjusted and state intervention in the economy is more effective. Non-oil exports are a fundamental source of dynamism in the economy and will continue to be an important impetus to the future development of the country.

But the economic adjustment of recent years has entailed significant costs as well. Over the past six years, GDP grew less than 2 percentage points. Given Mexico's increase in population, this rate of growth has meant a progressive fall in per capita income and consequently a substantial drop in the average standard of living.

In addition to making adjustments that enabled the economy to absorb the external shocks, since 1982 Mexico has been negotiating better terms for its foreign debt. Throughout the different phases of these negotiations, it has been able to lengthen amortization schedules, reduce interest costs and obtain fresh capital resources.

The structure of the economy has been stabilized and adjusted so that Mexico could attain growth without being excessively dependent on oil and foreign credit. Notwithstanding these adjustments, the debt service burden still represents an obstacle to continued growth. The question that naturally arises in this context concerns why the adjustment accomplished so far does not enable Mexico simultaneously to grow and service its debt. The answer is simple. In the past few years, as Mexico stabilized its economy and implemented structural adjustment measures, external economic factors worsened. In the summer of 1986, the price of Mexican oil plunged to $8 per barrel and the prices of most Mexican mineral and agricultural exports also decreased while international real interest rates remained at high levels. As a consequence, the country's terms of trade deteriorated by 40 percent, substantially reducing its ability to service its foreign debt. The debt problem turned out to be more than a liquidity problem.

In his inaugural address, President Salinas acknowledged the unfavorable situation caused by the worsening of Mexico's terms of trade and identified the conditions necessary for the economy to achieve sustained and stable growth. He also laid out four general guidelines for renegotiation of Mexico's foreign debt.

— First, external net transfers must be reduced to a level compatible with growth. The gap between debt service plus amortizations and new credits granted to Mexico has to be substantially narrowed. This objective should be attained through a combination of lower interest payments (via lower interest rates or principal reductions) and new credits under favorable terms.

In each of the past few years, the country has transferred abroad resources equivalent to 6 percent of what Mexican's produce. Decreasing these transfers to 2 percent of GDP will free resources necessary to finance the productive investment essential for economic growth, expanded employment opportunities and a better income distribution.

— Second, the reduced value of old debt must be recognized. In the renegotiation process, special attention will be given to loans contracted before 1988. When these credits were extended — especially in the case of credits obtained before 1982 — the prevailing economic conditions were substantially different from the situation today. Mexico has adjusted its economy in order to meet the challenge of new international conditions. Now it is the creditors' turn to share responsibility for having extended credits based on incorrect projections regarding oil prices and world economic activity.

In financial markets, the Mexican debt is traded at a discount, as investors recognize that the Mexican paper is worth less than its face value, given the deterioration in Mexico's ability to pay. In April of 1989, for example, the Mexican debt was worth roughly 50 cents per nominal dollar. The reduction of old debt will mean two things for Mexico. First, it is a mechanism for permanently decreasing transfers abroad. Second, it renders the national economy less vulnerable to sudden changes in international financial conditions. The fall in the value of the debt has the virtue of reducing the uncertainty that derives from the debt overhang. It is in fact this uncertainty that deters job-creating productive investment.

- Third, the necessary new credits must be made available on a long-term basis. In order to reduce transfers abroad, as proposed by President Salinas, new credits must complement the debt reduction instruments. The on-going negotiations are aimed at acquiring fresh capital in subsequent years in order to guarantee the availability of resources necessary to restore growth and to eliminate the uncertainty emerging from continuous and repeated negotiations.

- Fourth, the real value of the external debt and the debt/GDP ratio must be substantially diminished during the current administration. This goal will be attained once the above-mentioned reduction of transfers abroad induces a positive cycle of more investment and economic growth.

The Mexican foreign debt amounts to roughly $100 billion, 80 percent of which is owed by the public sector, 8 percent by Mexican banks, 6 percent by the private sector and 4 percent by Banco de Mexico. The public sector component of the foreign debt consists principally of credits from the Inter-American Development Bank and World Bank and credits from the international commercial bank community -- the latter constituting 72 percent of the total.

On the international scene, the way in which the debt problem is being approached has also changed. The launching of the Brady plan represents a major turning point from the approach followed since 1982 to solve the Third World debt problem. The conceptual basis of this plan is undeniably a major improvement over prior approaches to the debt problem. For the first time, it is officially recognized that a substantial degree of debt reduction is required in order for middle income, highly indebted countries to resume growth. This new approach to foreign debt calls for commercial bank debt reduction along with resumption of financial flows to debtor economies, channeled mainly through multilateral organizations. The plan also emphasizes implementation of the structural change strategies recommended in the Baker plan. The specific way in which the Brady plan will be put into practice is still being worked out.

The basic idea behind the Baker plan was a sound one. The plan was not successful, however, because it failed to recognize the uncertainty associated with excessive debt overhang. Policymakers believed that by granting new credits to indebted countries and implementing structural reforms and deregulation policies, growth would resume. The debt overhang, however, inhibited commercial banks from extending new credit.

The Brady plan is explicit about neither the timing nor the size of debt reduction a given country should obtain. There are strong arguments, however, to be made in favor of starting with a large debt relief operation involving all creditors rather than spreading operations over a long period of time. The latter approach is less likely to restore confidence in the Mexican economy and would generate serious free-rider problems. The short-term nature of rescheduling arrangements causes macroeconomic uncertainty. Investment and significant capital repatriation will resume only when investors perceive that real progress has been made in reducing the level of macroeconomic risk by eliminating the debt overhang. Medium- and long-term debt solutions are therefore appropriate and an up-front debt relief operation is a necessary condition for the success of the Brady plan.

One large debt reduction operation would require less use of enhancements on aggregate than a gradualist approach, since significant debt reduction is in itself the best credit enhancement. This is a principle recognized in all corporate restructurings. Troubled debtors need to eliminate excessive levels of debt in order to return to voluntary capital markets. However, mobilization of financial support is clearly more complicated for a single large debt reduction than for several operations spread over a longer period. The problem is figuring out how to concentrate into the immediate future the resources that would otherwise be available over a longer time span so that a country such as Mexico may begin a positive cycle of higher levels of confidence, investment and growth.

It is also apparent that the debt reduction scheme requires the involvement of all creditor banks, since the free-rider problem would otherwise jeopardize the entire strategy. It seems difficult to imagine a bank's joining a debt reduction operation if many of its competitors were still receiving full payment while neither participating in the operation nor providing new money. Obviously, this possibility provides a clear incentive to hold back and wait. This behavior, however, would result in a low volume and depth of the initial operations and therefore negligible relief. Creditor governments must be prepared to support debtor countries in their efforts to extract contributions from reluctant banks, even though they may be required to take unconventional actions.

To date, Mexico has renegotiated under the guidelines of the Brady plan 45 percent of its external debt. The renegotiation tackles the problems of each type of creditor in distinct and separate ways. In order to reduce net external transfers and to maintain the inflow of fresh resources, Mexico has requested contributions of net new money from international financial institutions and from official creditors. From commercial creditor banks Mexico is requesting some combination of providing fresh resources, reducing interest rates and/or reducing principal.

There are many signs of progress in the process of renegotiating Mexico's debt. The IMF has ratified the Mexican government's letter of intent and granted financial aid. Mexico has contracted a financial package with the World Bank and signed a multiannual agreement with the Paris Club. These institutions have all recognized the principle of reducing net transfers and the accumulated balance of the debt overhang.

The recent agreement entered into between Mexico and the IMF represents a fundamental advance in the external debt renegotiation process. IMF backing clearly strengthens Mexico's position in the impending negotiations with commercial banks. Moreover, the agreement guarantees access to IMF financial resources for at least three years, with a possible extension to four years if deemed convenient.

This agreement is extremely advantageous to Mexico and differs from every past IMF agreement. It necessitates no further recessionary adjustment of Mexico's economy and recognizes the scope and the importance of the structural adjustments carried out by Mexico in recent years. It also derives the amount of external resources required from the projected growth rate of the economy, instead of the other way around, as has been the case traditionally. Moreover, for the first time since the beginning of the debt crisis in 1982, the IMF recognizes that a real solution to the debt problem must encompass some form of debt reduction and a method of adjusting the debt to the country's capacity to pay so that the level of payments is compatible with economic growth. Finally, the IMF requires from Mexico no modification to its economic program. On the contrary, it has backed the economic measures Mexico has decided to implement within the PECE framework.

In the first days of June, the World Bank's board of directors decided to provide the necessary financing for various structural adjustment programs and to grant credits for projects totalling $1.96 billion. The funds, to be provided in three tranches of $500 million and one of $460 million, will be made available on a fast-disbursement basis. The Bank's financial package will support structural changes undertaken in the financial, industrial, commercial and parastatal sectors. A portion of these and the IMF funds will be available for use in debt reduction schemes, thus providing an important impetus to the renegotiation process.

Mexico has also concluded a multiannual agreement with the Paris Club, which includes the representatives of 16 industrialized nations. The Paris Club agreement provides for the rescheduling of $2.6 billion covering capital maturities and interest payments that were due before 1992. It is noteworthy that Mexico will retain assured access to credits for imports that originate in all of the Paris Club countries and are necessary to support sustained growth in the Mexican economy. The agreement with the Paris Club also recognizes the feasibility of Mexico's economic program, as the participation of all 16 creditor governments makes evident.

In recognition of the adjustments Mexico has accomplished so far, the international financial community has been extraordinarily supportive of Mexico during the phases of the foreign debt renegotiation process accomplished so far. The impending negotiations with the commercial banks constitute the last phase of the process. It is essential to remember that these banks share responsibility in the debt crisis. They channeled resources into Mexico with the expectation that the price of oil would reach a level of $50 per barrel by the end of the 1980s and that interest rates would remain near their historical levels. This scenario is clearly different from what has actually happened in recent years. Nonetheless, bankers have not shared in the costs of Mexico's adjustment to this miscalculation. While the debt/output ratio for debtor countries has increased significantly, the relative weight of Third World debt on banks' balance sheets has decreased significantly. Conditions are now appropriate for banks to accept some form of debt reduction. In contrast to 1982, debt reduction no longer endangers the stability of the international financial system.

Mexico has proposed a menu of options designed to facilitate negotiation of reduction in net transfers of resources abroad. The scheme consists of presenting equivalent options for principal reduction, interest rate reduction and/or automatic capitalization of interest payments or the provision of an equal amount of fresh money. Each bank may choose the combination best suited to its financial and legal environment and to its capital structure. The options are designed so that any combination of debt reduction (including official financing) results in net transfers abroad not exceeding 2 percent of GDP.

Mexico's bargaining position with respect to its creditor banks is quite favorable, given the support by the IMF, the World Bank and the creditor governments both to the country's economic program and to its strategy for reducing its net transfer of resources. But it is still worth stressing that the negotiation process with commercial banks will probably be a lengthy one -- as evidenced by prior experience. Since the other creditors have already relaxed their position, however, it is Mexico's hope that the commercial banks will agree to an acceptable deal soon. In light of the magnitude of the internal and external adjustment process followed during the past six years, Mexico will not alter its position vis-a-vis the commercial banks. Mexico must reduce its net transfer of resources so that it can assign savings to financing investment needed at home rather than to servicing its foreign debt. Only then will its capacity for economic growth be restored.

It is important to remember, however, that loosening the strangle hold foreign debt has on foreign exchange is a necessary but not sufficient condition for Mexico to attain its GDP growth objectives. Mexico must also maintain strict fiscal and monetary discipline in order to preserve the stable price climate without which productive investment will not resume. Similarly, the future growth of Mexico depends critically on the dynamism of its export sector. For this reason, current trade and exchange rate policies also must be continued in order to preserve the competitiveness of Mexico's industrial plant and to further integrate the country into the world economy.

Mexico's economic program -- based on macroeconomic and structural adjustment and on reduction of the net transfer of resources abroad -- forecasts only moderate economic growth for the coming years, picking up to about 6 percent around 1992. At this rate the economy could not only absorb the annual increases in the labor force but also improve the income distribution and raise the level of per capita income. Mexico really cannot settle for anything less. To do so would be to abandon the commitment of the Salinas administration to bring about the long overdue improvement in the economic circumstances of the Mexican people whose standard of living has been so drastically reduced.

NOTES

1.   Current account deficits are normal for a middle per capita income country, as indicated by the experiences of the United States (prior to 1910), Japan, Italy and Germany.   While these countries later became major net capital exporters, during the earlier stages of their development they complemented domestic resource availabilities with substantial amounts of foreign savings.

Comments

S. T. Beza
Director, Latin American Division,
International Monetary Fund

Because I agree with so much of what Secretary Aspe has written on Mexico's policies and their results, my task as a commentator is not an easy one. His presentation is so comprehensive that I have had to look into a few corners to find useful additions to his paper.

Aspe aptly characterizes Mexico's adjustments and reforms as far-reaching. They include the very large shift into a primary fiscal surplus, the major opening of the economy, the removal of domestic price distortions, the restructuring of public enterprises and the liberalization of the financial system. The blot on recent developments has been the behavior of domestic output, which has experienced very little growth since 1981. Indeed, adjusted for the terms of trade, the country's income has actually declined over the period.

Why has economic growth fared so poorly, given all the favorable adjustments and reforms? I gave part of the answer when I referred to the terms of trade. Since 1981 Mexico's terms of trade have deteriorated by some 45 percent, equivalent to an output loss of more than 8 percent over this period. The other part of the answer is that the curtailment of Mexico's access to international capital markets on a voluntary basis after 1981, together with the rise in real interest rates on foreign credits, left a very large gap. Domestic investment as a fraction of GDP (or in absolute terms) has not regained its pre-1982 levels, although the reforms carried out in the intervening period are undoubtedly making investment more efficient than it was some years ago.

Table 1 illustrates the problem faced by Mexico in the post-1982 period by comparing the five years just before the crisis with the last five years. The effects of the deterioration in the terms of trade, the curtailment of external credits and the increase in the real cost of servicing such credits showed up in the need to adjust "net exports" by more than 10 percentage points of GDP from 1977-1981 to 1984-1988. Domestic savings at constant prices rose by close to 2 percentage points of GDP, but over 8 percentage points of GDP still remained to be absorbed by cuts in domestic investment.

Aspe also mentions the goal of achieving substantial growth in per capita income by 1992. How can Mexico regain strong and sustained growth? In part, it should continue what it has been doing in recent years -- strengthening domestic savings, improving efficiency and assuring an adequate degree of international competitiveness. In addition, the Mexican authorities believe (and we on the IMF staff agree) that more external savings must become available to permit a faster growth of domestic investment. To the extent that these added resources can take the form of debt or debt service reduction, the flow of capital to Mexico will be encouraged as financial investors and direct investors perceive a reduction in risk as a result of the alleviation of the debt burden, and a favorable effect on real domestic interest rates also could be expected.

The other topic I wish to touch on briefly concerns the nature of the latest financial arrangement between Mexico and the IMF. Aspe says that this differs from every past arrangement because it necessitates no further recessionary adjustment to Mexico's economy, takes account of the scope and importance of the structural adjustment already carried out by Mexico, derives the necessary external resources from the projected growth rate of the economy, and recognizes that the debt must be reduced and adjusted to the country's capacity to pay so that the level of external debt service payments is compatible with economic growth. Change in the way problems are approached can be desirable, but perhaps I see more continuity and constancy in the IMF's relations with Mexico.

First, the arrangements developed between Mexico and the IMF in 1983-1985 and in 1986-1987 placed considerable emphasis on attracting external financing to support the economic program on a scale that would limit the pressures on domestic resources as Mexico adjusted to the cutback in voluntary credits, particularly from the foreign banking community. The intent was therefore to contain recessionary forces, although, to be sure, the gap to be filled after 1981 was a very large one and in 1986 a new shock came as oil prices fell sharply.

Second, the willingness of the IMF to accept Mexico's latest economic program as presented reflects, of course, the major adjustments and reforms already carried out by Mexico in the past seven years and attests to the quality of the program developed by the Mexican authorities. It goes without saying that an economic program is less likely to be successful if it is not the creation of the country itself. But it must also be recognized that the IMF's support of a program depends on whether it offers the prospect of clear progress toward durable economic growth in the context of domestic price stability and external balance. Mexico's current program does offer that prospect.

Third, economic programs supported by the IMF seek to blend domestic and external savings in the effort to achieve growth objectives, and in that sense the external resources needed are derived in part from the growth rate desired for the economy. This commitment is not open-ended, however, in that it cannot be any growth rate or any volume of external resources. The contribution to growth made by domestic resources (savings) and domestic conditions (the efficiency with which resources are used) is crucial -- indeed, for all practical purposes the domestic policy component is the decisively important one. The contribution to growth made by external resources, particularly those that involve the creation of external debt, must take account of their cost, repayment terms and other factors that can affect a country's external vulnerability when it relies on external saving to promote its development. In the specific case of Mexico, the program's required flow of external savings fell within a range that seemed entirely reasonable.

Fourth, there is the question of the evolution of thinking on the role of debt reduction in dealing with the debt problem. When the debt crisis erupted in the middle of 1982 it was far from clear how long it would take to re-establish voluntary capital flows, although it was fully clear that such flows could not (and ought not) regain the importance they had prior to 1982 and that substantial domestic adjustment was therefore necessary. Indeed, in the wake of the balance of payments successes of major debtor countries in 1983 and 1984, the conclusion drawn by the authorities of a number of debtor countries was that the debt problem was amenable to treatment through the negotiation of long-term restructuring agreements with lengthy grace periods for the repayment of external debt.

These agreements alone were insufficient, however, because international interest rates continued to be high in real terms, further external shocks occurred like the drop

in oil prices in 1986, and a number of instances demonstrated that the weight of the external debt was high in
relation to the adjustments the debtor countries were able
to perform. (In the case of Mexico, if oil prices were as
high in relation to prices in general as they were in 1981,
oil export earnings would be some $15 billion, around 7-8
percent of GDP, higher than at present.) These factors
together with the growing reluctance of foreign commercial
banks to provide external financing, owing in part to their
evaluation that many countries had such large external debts
that they were difficult to service, have now made debt
reduction seem a reasonable option in dealing with the debt
problem.

The outcome of the negotiations underway between Mexico
and representatives of its commercial bank creditors will
provide important information on how banks view the options
and on the role to be played by debt reduction. As Aspe
points out, however, a positive result in this area is not
the sole condition for Mexico to attain its growth objectives. Although a favorable solution for the balance of payments problems would be welcome per se as well as for bringing in its wake voluntary capital inflows from Mexican residents and foreigners, it still leaves much to be done by
domestic policies.

Secretary Aspe appropriately stresses the importance of
maintaining strict fiscal and monetary discipline and pursuing trade and exchange rate policies that assure an adequate
degree of external competitiveness as Mexico continues to
integrate itself with the world economy. These are wise
words, and I agree with them wholeheartedly.

TABLE 1. An Economic Comparison Before and After the Crisis

	1977–81	1984–88
	(In percent of GDP in real terms)	
Domestic Expenditure	101.0	90.9
Consumption	75.9	74.1
Investment	25.1	16.8
Domestic Saving	24.1	25.9
National Saving	20.6	22.9
External Saving	4.5	-6.1
Net Exports (Resource Gap)	-1.0	9.1
Net Factor Payments Plus Transfers	-3.5	-3.0
	(In percent)	
Interest Rates on Foreign Credits (in US$ terms)	9.2	9.3
Real Interest Rates (based on U.S. Inflation)	-0.6	5.6
	(Average Annual Percentage Changes)	
Real GDP	7.5	1.0
Exports (in US$)	40.3	1.5
Non–Oil Exports (in US$)	13.6	19.1
Terms of Trade	1.9	-6.1

Mexican Debt

Rudiger Dornbusch
Professor of International Economics,
Massachusetts Institute of Technology

This paper reviews the role of Mexican debt in the macroeconomics of stabilization. The main point is that the overhang of debt service creates uncertainty about the sustainability of the exchange rate. The government can deal with this problem in two ways. First, it can adopt a highly depreciated real exchange rate, thereby assuring the external transfer but threatening domestic political and economic stability and undermining the chances for a resumption of social progress. Second, it can set real interest rates so high that ultimately the internal debt becomes a source of fiscal instability. The credible, medium-term reduction of external transfers is therefore an essential condition for achieving macroeconomic stability and growth.

THE BACKGROUND

The macroeconomic performance of the past few decades is shown in Table 1. Note that until the early 1970s Mexico was a low inflation country. In fact, the exchange rate relative to the U.S. dollar was kept fixed, with unrestricted convertibility, for the entire period from 1954 to 1976. In 1976-1987 inflation increased sharply, rising to nearly 200 percent in 1986-1987. That was far less than the inflation experience of Brazil or Argentina. But for Mexico, with the U.S. proximity, and with a very low inflation experience in the postwar period, inflation became the #1 problem, even dominating the stark decline in the standard of living.

Per capita growth in Mexico between 1900 and 1940 averaged only 0.7 percent. In fact, in 1940 real per capita income was at the same level as it had been in 1910! But in

the next four decades, between 1940 and 1980, per capita
income growth amounted to an impressive 3.1 percent, just
slightly below that of Brazil.   This high per capita income
growth occurred even though population growth over the four
decades averaged 3.2 percent per year.

Mexico had accumulated significant debt in the period
prior to World War I.   From 1913 until 1942 the country was
in debt moratorium, even though there were occasional negotiations and agreements with the creditors, as for example
in the 1920s.   In this period the secondary market price of
Mexican bonds fell from 95 cents on the dollar to only a few
cents as shown in Figure 1.   An agreement was made in 1942
for public debt (and in 1946 for railroad debt) which
restructured the public external debt.   The face value of
the debt was reduced by approximately 80 percent, arrears
were cancelled and payments of the reduced principal were
rescheduled at a very low rate.(1)   This restructuring set
the beginning for Mexico's return to the international capital market.

The early borrowing was from the Ex-Im bank.   As Bazant
(1968) notes, Ex-Im bank loans started in 1942.   Soon commercial bank loans also resumed.   Long-term public borrowing
abroad of $166 million in 1945-1950 paid nearly the full
amount of interest and amortization on the external debt of
$196 million.(2)   The ratio of interest payments (public and
private) to current foreign exchange earnings in 1945-1950
averaged only 10.5 percent; the 1942 debt settlement had
assured that the debt was written down to a manageable size.

Bank lending increased significantly in the 1950s and
the first public bond issue occurred in 1960, following the
repurchase of the remaining amounts of the renegotiated
bonds at about 20 percent of their original face value.   At
the time the New York Times noted:(3)

    Mexico is closing a checkered page in financial his-
    tory, a story of default and rebirth that goes back to
    the misty era of international promise that preceded
    World War I...The turn of the century investors had
    vision but were off in their timing...How were they to
    know that the bonds they bought would stop paying
    interest and remain in bad standing for a quarter of a
    century...
        With most of the old bonds sucked out of the mar-
    ket by the redemption call last week [at 20 cents on
    the dollar of initial face value], most of this linger-
    ing public evidence of Mexico's long struggle to live
    down the old debt default has been wiped out for good.

Throughout the 1960s and early 1970s the extent of external borrowing remained moderate. The non-interest current account deficit remained below 1 percent of GDP. In the early 1970s the ratio of external debt to GDP was still under 20 percent and even in 1980 the external debt ratio was only 30 percent.

The large run-up in the external debt occurred in the period 1980-1982. From December 1980 to December 1982 Mexican debt increased from $40 to $91 billion. Bank lending came to a halt in the first half of 1982, the last credit being a $2.5 billion jumbo loan that was unusually hard to place. The moratorium was announced in August 1982. As in all previous episodes, the sudden rationing of credits made it impossible to pay interest on old loans by contracting new debt. This sudden credit rationing that put an end to a rapid debt accumulation proved devastating, thus vindicating the bankers' adage: "It is not speed that kills, it is the sudden stop."

THE DEBT PROBLEM

If the borrowing has not been applied productively, debt becomes a severe burden on the external balance and on the budget, and causes as a consequence inflation, reduced standards of living and investment that is much too low.

The debt crisis involves an involuntary, premature and costly transfer of resources from the debtor to the creditors, as measured by a substantial non-interest current account (NICA), shown in Figure 2. Generating the budget resources and the trade surplus required to effect this transfer adversely affects macroeconomic performance. The worsening of financial stability in turn generates capital flight, which imposes a further transfer burden.

Inflation

The financial instability that comes from strained budgets, high and rising inflation and frequent depreciation has proved a powerful incentive to capital flight. Attempts to stem capital flight by high interest rates have brought about bankruptcy and budget problems. Sharply undervalued exchange rates which might stem capital flight in turn risk promoting political instability as a result of the very low real wages implied by this policy.

A major acceleration of inflation was experienced not only in Mexico but throughout the debtor economies in the last few years. Inflation rates have increased because the attempt to gain competitiveness through depreciation could not effectively be prevented from also affecting domestic wages and prices. In many cases debt service was financed by outright money creation. The result of high, rising and uncertain inflation has been a very unfavorable climate for private markets. Financial considerations, not productive investment, are now in the forefront and capital flight has become pervasive.

Investment

The attempt to find resources for debt service has come to a large extent at the expense of investment. Investment has been depressed because the government has found it easier to cut investment budgets than to raise taxes or reduce spending programs. The lack of growth, or outright contraction, and the disturbed financial conditions have also depressed private investment, as shown in Table 2.

The sharp decline of investment may reflect in part an artificial inflation of investment levels in 1975-1984. But a countervailing argument is that with a labor force growth of more than 3.5 percent, failure to invest at a rapid rate implies a growing, acute imbalance between the actual capital stock and the level that would sustain high employment. Bottlenecks in infrastructure are certainly an additional consideration.

The lack of investment has serious long-term implications. Low public sector investment builds up dangerous bottlenecks to an ultimate resumption of growth. Combined with the lack of private sector investment, an imbalance develops between the rapidly growing labor force and the ability of the economy to create employment at current, already depressed standards of living.

Public Finance

The debt crisis shows up not only in inflation and a deterioration of public sector investment but also in rapid growth of the domestic debt. To the extent that domestic borrowing finances the payment of external interest, stabilization of the growth of external debt comes at the expense of a more rapidly rising domestic debt. Table 3 shows this debt growth.(4)

The tendency for high domestic debt growth resulting from the financing of external debt service is reinforced by very high real interest rates in the most recent period, as shown in Figure 3. These high rates are required to avoid reserve losses, thus leaving reserves for debt service, or even to attract capital inflows with which to finance debt service and debt reduction.

CURRENT STATE

By 1989 Mexico's external debt amounted to $1220 per capita. The external debt/GDP ratio that had been 49 percent in 1982 now was 58 percent.(5)

The Adjustment Effort

The adjustment efforts in 1982-1988 show up in a large shift of the non-interest current account (NICA) toward a surplus. A large real depreciation (see Figure 4) and no growth of the Mexican economy were the means to swing the trade balance toward a surplus. Much of the fluctuation in the external balance reflects movements in the world oil price. (See Table 4 and Figure 5.) Movements in the current account reflect the movements in the NICA as well as changes in the London inter-bank overnight rate, Libor.

The rules of thumb about the impact of oil and interest rates are as follows:

- Every percentage point increase in interest rates raises debt service by $1 billion or one half percent of GDP.

- Every $1 increase in oil raises export revenue by $500 million or one-quarter of a percent of GDP.

From a macroeconomic point of view the non-interest current account (NICA), the measure of resource transfer, receives central attention. An important factor in worsening the NICA is the liberalization of imports which took place in 1988 in particular as an effort to enlist increased import competition in the anti-inflation fight. Imports increased within a single year by nearly 50 percent even though the economy was stagnant. Real appreciation (see Figure 4) may also have helped. The liberalization of imports has as a counterweight the impressive growth of non-oil exports. But even so, the latter did not grow sufficiently to maintain the NICA in the face of reduced oil prices.

The financing of the external balance is shown in Table 6. The non-interest current balance financed approximately half of the net interest due. External borrowing or reserve losses had to finance not only the remaining half, but also capital flight and amortization.

The financing of the external balance in 1988 high-lights all the problems: debt reduction in the private and public sector and a current account deficit all constitute demand for foreign exchange; reserve decumulation is used to provide the financing. The dramatic decline in reserves, first fully justified by very high reserve levels, has become outright precarious and cannot continue. Nor can the domestic policies of extremely high real interest rates and related stagnation that have so far contained the trade deficit and caused some return of flight capital.

The External Environment

Three U.S. scenarios are possible for the immediate future, each with different implications for Mexico. First, the increase in U.S. interest rates over the 1988-1989 period is expected to lead to a U.S. slowdown and then to a sharp decline in short-term interest rates and the dollar in 1989-1990. The slowdown may hurt Mexican export prospects, but much lower interest rates and the drop in the dollar are bound to be highly beneficial.

Second is a scenario less favorable for Mexico. The U.S. expansion continues strongly through the end of 1989 and brings about substantially higher inflationary pressure. The Federal Reserve responds by yet another dose of tighten-ing. As a result the slowdown becomes a recession. Because interest rates increase significantly more, this scenario is strongly adverse for debtor countries. The early high inter-est rates would create a dramatic shortage of foreign exchange.

Third is a very optimistic scenario, with a very small probability of occurring. As part of a major fiscal pack-age, the budget is progressively cut and the Federal Reserve accommodates by reducing interest rates in order to maintain full employment. The improved policy mix would almost cer-tainly bring with it a significant fall of the dollar in international currency markets and that in turn would help raise oil prices in dollars. This scenario would be excep-tionally beneficial for Mexico, but it is not likely to occur in 1989 or perhaps for several years thereafter.

Financing Requirements

The question now is to find an external financing program that allows a resumption of growth on a sustained basis. Moreover, the financing should assure that growth can continue with a reduction in the extreme real interest rates and a build-up of reserves, but without a major real depreciation or an undoing of import liberalization. Finally, this combination of objectives and constraints, which can add substantially to a major foreign exchange requirement, should ideally be met without an unsustainable increase in indebtedness. Any solution that can accomplish these objectives while satisfying the constraints must involve a significant reduction of debt or debt service.

A projection of the external balance with financing in the form of new money or debt reduction on the order of $6-7 billion a year is shown in Table 7.

There are three major uncertainties in this outlook. First, will the current account deteriorate significantly further in a situation where demand grows at 3-4 percent per year? If it involves a return of private investment, such an expansion may result in a much larger deficit. Following the import liberalization, the spillover of growth into the external balance is certain to be much more substantial both for capital goods and for consumer goods.

Second, if interest rates are reduced significantly, will the risk of further capital flight be increased? This risk arises especially in conjunction with a current account deterioration brought about by growth which raises the possibility of depreciation.

Third, what are the potential sources of external financing? There are, of course, significant resources to be had from the IMF and from the World Bank, but they are likely to be a major front-end financing of perhaps $5 billion for 1989-1990 rather than a continuing flow at a multibillion dollar level. Moreover, at least for IMF loans the maturity is relatively short so that these resources cannot provide a basis for sustained financing.

There are, of course, two optimistic views. First, as already noted above, there could be a major realignment of the U.S. policy mix resulting in lower interest rates and a much lower dollar. The other possibility involves radically good news: a return of flight capital if a major debt initiative helps call off the bank run on Mexico. It is difficult to know the size of external holdings, but $60 billion is certainly a low estimate, so once capital heads home the upside potential is substantial.

The remainder of this paper discusses different approaches to debt in order to evaluate which mechanisms might be most suitable to help consolidate Mexican financial stability and growth.

MECHANISMS FOR DEBT REDUCTION

Three developments have come together to change radically the outlook for debt. First, contrary to past rhetoric, debtor countries are falling behind rather than getting ahead. Even countries like Mexico which have made all conceivable adjustment efforts have not become better credit risks. The hard choices in the public sector have not improved external balances. Second, the politics of debt are worsening. The most striking evidence is the growing appeal of populism and the tragic events in Venezuela. Politics clearly make it impossible to squeeze economies further for the purpose of external debt service. Third, the U.S. banks have achieved solvency. After years of building up reserves most of them are now in a position to face a serious debt reduction. Table 8 indicates their exposure to Latin America in general and to Mexico in particular.

Secretary of Treasury Brady has drawn the lesson from these developments, in the manner Senator Aiken had suggested in the context of Vietnam: "Declare victory and get out!"

Predictably, the retreat will be messy. Lacking a strategy and resisting a major public intervention, the Secretary's speech of March 10, 1989, begged several questions. It is not clear at this time how many resources will be committed to debt guarantees, to whom they will be made available and under what conditions. It is also not clear what change in regulatory treatment (carrots or sticks) commercial bank creditors will receive.

1)   Market-Related Mechanisms(6)

Over the past few years an active secondary market for developing country debt has emerged. In this market debts trade at significant discounts. These discounts have elicited interest in the variety of ways in which investors and/ or debtor countries could take advantage of this market for debt reduction and profit opportunities. Two possibilities in particular are debt-equity swaps and buybacks.

Debt-Equity Swaps. In a debt-equity swap a commercial bank sells debt to a private investor who presents the claim to the debtor government for payment in local currency, with the proceeds to be used for investment.

The attractiveness of debt-equity swaps for debtor countries depends on a variety of features in any individual case. In the extreme, debt-equity swaps may merely replace investment that would have occurred anyway, leaving the authorities without any significant share in the discount while requiring the financing of the local currency payment by money creation or expensive domestic debt finance.(7) At the other extreme, the discount may be the leverage that provides foreign investment with the required return, while the authorities share in the discount to an extent that reduces interest payments.

There is some illusion about the balance of payments effects of debt-equity programs. Since they give rise to future profit remittances, some way down the road, the balance of payments effect is a reduced outflow of interest payments but an increased outflow of profit remittances. There is no presumption that the net effect should be favorable. Moreover, it appears now that in Brazil, for example, debt-equity swaps have become basically a borrowing operation where "side letters" arrange for external interest payments dressed up as profit remittances. A major shift in this direction may well deteriorate the regulatory climate for bona fide investment.

Mexican policymakers are aware of the potential difficulties. They have started judging debt-equity swaps more accurately in terms of the costs and benefits, thus dampening some of the early enthusiasm, but perhaps also clearing the way for them to become a more productive, albeit smaller, part of long-term debt solutions.

Buybacks. In the 1930s and 1940s defaulted debt of Latin America traded at large discounts and part of it was ultimately "repatriated" by buybacks on the part of debtor governments. At the time debt holders' Protective Councils severely protested this practice. They argued that resources not used for interest payments could not be applied to buy back bonds at deep discounts, when these discounts reflect primarily an unwillingness to pay.

Today the sharing clauses in commercial bank debt contracts proscribe buybacks, but the idea that debtor countries could achieve important debt reduction through this route is widely accepted. Several countries, including Mexico on a significant scale, have used the secondary market to buy back private debts. So far, apparently, public debts have not been returned on any scale. The only major attempt was the Mexico-Morgan attempt to use a zero coupon bond to collateralize principal and exchange the new instrument at a discount for old debt. The plan, not unexpectedly, failed to convince investors since the major portion of the new instrument was the unsecured interest rather than the distant, safe principal. (8) In the meantime the secondary market price has been steadily declining.

The scope for buybacks is intrinsically limited: to be able to buy back on a large scale the debtor needs resources which, if they are available and will be used, would mean that the claim does not trade at a large discount. Only when information is very imperfect, creditors are very impatient, or regulatory and tax considerations create asymmetries will a constellation exist where debtors can retire debt advantageously. But even then the amounts will tend to be minor.

One reason to expect some scope for buybacks is if commercial banks feel, rightly or wrongly, that one piece of Latin American debt is as bad as another, regardless of the debtor country. In that event, because of the contamination effect, there is room for the relatively better placed countries to take advantage of the across-the-board discount for a refinancing operation.

Another reason is that resources may be made available by creditor governments or multilateral institutions strictly and exclusively for buybacks. In this case there is, of course, every interest in using them. Table 10 sets out a scheme for assessing the benefits.

This table highlights the fact that buybacks require resources with possible alternative uses. Specifically, if the resources could be committed to defending exchange rate stability and reduced real interest rates, they might be worth more in that use than in reducing the face value of debts. Using domestic resources, at the potential cost of macroeconomic instability and capital flight, may involve net losses. Moreover, the benefits from debt reduction must be identified. In many cases reduced debt may imply increased macroeconomic stability, but it may simply mean that in very favorable circumstances less interest needs to be paid.

The table indicates that when donors make available resources earmarked for debt reduction there is no question about the desirability of debt reduction. But it is not clear that free resources (like World Bank loans) should be used that way. It certainly is entirely clear that using scarce reserves is outright counterproductive.

In principle buybacks might help repatriate private capital flight or reduce debt service. Allowing residents to participate in the external purchase of debts to be converted by the central bank into domestic interest-bearing liabilities is a means of capturing the external discount and splitting it between residents and the central bank. Such a conversion has, in fact, been done with some success in Chile. But once again, it will be particularly attractive only when interest rates in the debtor country are not far in excess of rates on external debt and if foreign exchange is plentiful. Such a combination would be rare. Accordingly, the scope for market-related debt reduction schemes, while potentially present, is in fact limited. This point was amply demonstrated by the very limited success of the Morgan-Mexico attempt.

Beyond the issues raised so far, there is also the question of how to do a large buyback. It would appear that the only effective way is with a once-and-for-all, all-or-nothing offer. This could solve the free-riding problem and achieve debt reduction. Other schemes are likely to be dissipated by secondary market price increases that limit debt reduction. The Mexican agreement of 1942 remains an attractive example.

2) Recycling of Interest Payments

Until recently Mexico was paying all the interest it owed. The decline in investment and the depressed economic conditions made meeting this obligation possible. But it is clear that a resumption of growth, and of public sector investment, would very quickly worsen the external balance and make it impossible.

This problem is best addressed by a fundamental restructuring of debt service to take care of the major part of interest payments due. Actual payments in dollars would be reduced to servicing trade credit and the loans of multilateral organizations. A large share of the remaining interest payments would in part be capitalized, thus freeing resources for much needed public sector investment, and in part be made in local currency. Creditors who received the local currency payments could use them for unrestricted investment in the debtor countries' economies. The only limitation on the use of funds would be that they could not be transferred abroad. The claims to these payments could, however, be sold.

Recycling amounts to a debt-equity swap applied to interest payments rather than to principal. It amounts to a recycling of interest payments to finance reconstruction and development.(9)

Advantages. It will help to see the mechanics of a recycling scheme by focusing on the national income accounting identities relating investment on one side and the resource availability for investment on the other side:(10)

$$\text{Investment} = \text{Saving} + \begin{array}{l}\text{Non-interest Current}\\\text{Account Deficit}\end{array}$$

Today the budget correction has raised the national saving rate and reduced the rate of investment because of reduced public-sector investment spending. As a counterpart of higher saving and reduced investment, a large external surplus finances the payment of interest and even debt retirement. A recycling would not reduce the national saving rate -- the government would maintain fiscal austerity, thus freeing resources for investment. But the external surplus would be replaced by an increase in the rate of investment. The surplus would decline because firms would divert sales from exports to the home market and investment goods imports would sharply rise.

The advantages of the interest recycling are many:

- The transfer abroad of resources is suspended. Rather than running trade surpluses debtor countries have resources freed that can be devoted to investment. Of course, serious budget action is required to assure that in fact the resources go into investment rather than consumption. The shift of resources toward investment implies an expansion in capacity, thereby sustaining job creation. This issue is central in an economy where labor force growth rates in excess of 3 percent have created major imbalances between labor supply and demand. The expansion in capacity removes the bottlenecks which today stand in the way of growth. Growth in turn translates into more stable public finance via a broadened tax base.(11)

- The scheme creates a more stable and prosperous business environment. With the current strategy a foreign exchange bottleneck is always around the corner and the reaction is invariably contraction of demand and exchange depreciation. This reality

153

has led to a lack of interest in productive investment and extensive capital flight. The center of
gravity has shifted to financial markets, far away
from productive activity. By removing the need
for immediate debt service the debtor economy can
resume a more balanced position with an emphasis
on long-term investment and growth. The best
lever for returning capital flight is a restoration of business confidence and an end of exchange
pressure. Recycling also offers two further advantages to creditor countries: it avoids outright
debt relief (or debt default) and hence avoids
involvement of creditor country tax payers on a
large scale. Furthermore, by providing debtors
with room for growth there is every expectation of
increased exports to debtor countries and a reduction in the currently high levels of imports.

- There is a third, once-and-for-all gain. In the
present situation the need to maintain substantially depreciated real exchange rates translates
into inflationary pressures and low demand in the
debtors' domestic markets. The removal of external constraints allows some real appreciation and
hence provides a breathing space for stabilization
of inflation. Inflation stabilization is, of
course, an essential quid pro quo in a restoration
of normal business conditions.

- Interest recycling, by removing exchange rate
uncertainty, creates an essential precondition for
a return of capital flight.

- Creditor countries benefit from the reversal of
trade surpluses; exports from developing countries
will decline and imports, especially of capital
goods, will rise. Thus recycling provides the
financial underpinnings for solving at least a
part of the U.S. trade imbalance.

As a counterpart for acceptance of interest recycling
by creditors (or to make it less offensive, in the case of
unilateral action) Mexico would have to sustain the budget
improvement and to liberalize the scope for foreign direct
investment. Dissipating the resources into a restoration of
consumption might be tempting after so many years of depriva-
tion. But that would be unacceptable. Tough-minded fiscal

measures and broad-based liberalization of investment opportunities are the quid pro quo for the suspension of resource transfers.

It is worthwhile asking how banks would deal with a recycling situation. The immediate reaction of banks to a recycling proposal is entirely negative, but the concerns are largely exaggerated and lie mostly in the accounting area. Of course, compared to a bailout by the World Bank recycling is thoroughly unattractive, but it is strictly preferred to default by all of Latin America.

Individual banks would take one of three steps. A first group might manage directly their receivables in local currency. This strategy is clearly the route for banks that are now in the debt-equity swap business for their own account or have sought possibilities for expanding their activities in debtor countries. Rather than funding themselves by deposit taking they would use their own capital in the form of local currency interest payments. A second group of banks might use their local currency receivables by having them managed by major host country financial institutions -- banks, money-market funds or funds that invest in real assets. A third group, typically small banks, would try to sell off their claims to investment funds to avoid high transactions costs. These funds (like the Korea Fund or the Brazil Fund that was just offered on the New York Stock Exchange) sell shares to the broad public and use the proceeds to buy assets in the debtor country. Buying claims from banks, possibly at a discount, would be a natural way of increasing the return to their shareholders.

Consideration of the details of how banks would use the recycling funds makes it clear that short-term, illiquid debt is basically transformed into long-term investment. This is an essential step in strengthening the possibilities of long-term growth in debtor countries, avoiding the recurrent bouts of rescheduling with the attendant, massive capital flight.

Such a scheme would be similar to reconstruction programs like those administered after World War I or World War II. It would extend over a decade or so. Ultimately creditors would be able to recover their principal and accumulated earnings with a guarantee of no frivolous exchange losses.

Capital Flight. Return of flight capital would almost certainly be one of the favorable consequences of a recycling proposal. On the resource side financial stability would be enhanced and one reason for capital flight removed.

Additionally, the sharp reduction in foreign exchange requirements for debt service would open the way for the large flow of imports required to sustain growth.

The extent of capital flight from Mexico in the past decade cannot be determined with certainty. A number of estimates, using different methodologies, are reported in Table 11.

Investors have an option to postpone the return of flight capital and they will wait until the frontloading of returns is sufficient to compensate for the risk of relinquishing the liquidity option of a wait-and-see position. This is the case even when interest rates are high and rewarding. Moreover, when capital does return it stays highly liquid, sitting so to speak in the parking lot (or on the tarmac), with the engine running. There is definitely little commitment to a rapid resumption of real investment due to residual uncertainty concerning the sustainability of stabilization.

But how can governments reassure investors? The common answer is to bring about a "credible" stabilization. In practice it comes down to high interest rates and a real exchange rate so competitive that expected further real depreciation is unlikely. But high interest rates are counterproductive from a growth perspective because they lead to holding paper assets rather than real investment. A low real exchange rate cuts the standard of living and thus reduces domestic demand and profitability for all investments except in the traded goods sector.

But if real depreciation is not sufficient to bring about investment the government faces a very awkward position: income is being redistributed from labor to capital, but because the real depreciation is not sufficient, the increased profits are taken out as capital flight. Labor will obviously insist then that the policy be reversed. This uncertainty is important in understanding the relationship between the real exchange rate and capital flight as well as the post-stabilization difficulties in developing countries and the stabilization experience of the 1920s.

Today asset holders must wonder whether growth and debt service will be reconciled. As a result they hang on to their dollar positions even in the presence of extraordinarily high real interest rates. Resolution of the uncertainty would accelerate the reflow. Paradoxically, if debt service can be recycled Mexico may well have enough of a private capital inflow so that it can actually pay creditors a major part of debt service in dollars. Conversely, if creditors are adamant in their opposition to recycling, private capital will stay abroad and, in the end, they risk getting nothing. Just as deposit insurance stabilizes banks, so does recycling stabilize the macroeconomy in a situation where there are two equilibria, one with capital moving out and the economy deteriorating, the other with capital flowing in and the economy returning to growth and financial stability.

Bank Runs. The capital flight problem can be thought of like a bank run. If the public is concerned about the value of their assets they stage a run on the (central) bank and force depreciation. The belief that everybody else will do the same reinforces each individual investor's belief that he must move out of domestic assets because the general exodus will, inevitably, force depreciation. Hence the "run". But if the external balance constraint is suspended, via recycling, then there is no concern with exchange depreciation. On the contrary, the bank is safe and flight capital will return.

The chief mode of operation of the recycling proposal is not to reduce the present value of obligations. The interest of debtors and creditors alike is to return the economy to a situation where growth and financial stability make debt service plausible. To do so the external drain must be temporarily suspended. But because private capital cannot be controlled effectively, convertibility for the organized creditors must also be suspended.

Suspension of convertibility for creditors could be effected by a moratorium on interest payments or by paying interest in frozen accounts. These schemes inevitably are far more detrimental to creditors, and hence less acceptable, than recycling would be after even a brief period. If, as expected, recycling leads after a few years to a significant reflow of capital the means will exist to open the bank and allow withdrawals on a more stable basis.

CONCLUDING REMARKS

A resumption of growth and anything near full debt service are generally recognized today to be incompatible. Even moderate proposals such as Feldstein (1986) recognize that at most a portion of debt service can be transferred without prejudicing the opportunities for growth. How, then, should the rest of debt service be handled? One answer is that international financial institutions must assume an increasing role. This is indeed the banks' position as they ask for guarantees on any new money to be committed. Of course, increasing the commitments by international agencies raises questions about equity. Why, for example, bail out banks and Latin America rather than provide poverty relief in Africa?(12) Discussion of these issues is going around in circles. In the meantime a debtor country like Mexico, having taken the first step toward growth in the form of fiscal stabilization, must move on or else face the risk of sliding back.

Mexican officials have always insisted that Mexico does not want confrontation on the debt. This position was expressed once again by the Mexican debt negotiator, Jose Angel Gurria (1988), in his presentation to the PRI's committee on international issues. But this time the official message went further: it insisted that Mexico grow at 5-6 percent per annum over the course of this sexennio in order to avoid still more unemployment. Financing this growth path requires a significant increase in domestic saving and, as a complementary condition, the elimination of external transfers. Over the next few months, Gurria noted, every step would be undertaken to explore market-based, voluntary debt alternatives. On assuming office, President Salinas stressed the need for debt reduction and now Secretary Brady has joined the ranks even though it remains to be seen what he intends to do.

Mexico needs to accomplish two things at this stage. First, it must achieve a credible multi-year financing of the external balance, including provisions for shortfalls. Second, it must work on the return of capital flight. Debt reduction and guarantees will be forthcoming, but it now appears that they will be rather small and can accomplish reductions in interest payments of no more than $1-2 billion. A major part of the financing therefore remains open. In view of the need to bring back flight capital the recycling option seems especially attractive.

NOTES

1.   See Council of Foreign Bond Holders, Annual Report (1961), p. 110; Wynne (1951), pp. 96-99; and Bazant (1968), pp. 215-225.
2.   See Ortiz Mena, et al. (1953), p. 138.
3.   New York Times, July 3, 1960.
4.   Calculations of the foreign debt ratio are exceedingly sensitive to the real exchange rate and to inflation. The decline in the external debt ratio reflects in a large

measure the constancy of the nominal exchange rate and the real appreciation of the peso in 1988.

    5.   Note that the debt/GDP ratio increases not only as a result of debt accumulation but also when a real depreciation reduces the dollar value of GDP.

    6.   The following sections draw on Dornbusch (1988) and my background paper in Taskforce (1989).

    7.   The large investment by Nissan in Mexico is typically given as an example of an operation that had already been planned and was about to be implemented when debt equity swaps emerged and were used as a financial vehicle for the operation.

    8.   See Bulow and Rogoff (1988) for an analysis of buybacks. See, too, the comments by Dornbusch (1988a).

    9.   The recycling option is strictly different from payment in "script" or in "blocked pesos". The point of the recommendation is to reduce interference with creditors while capturing growth benefits for the debtor. The recommendation is unattractive to Mexico compared to a situation where nothing is paid and attractive only by comparison with paying everything in dollars. I understand that Victor Urquidi is an early advocate of recycling.

    10.   The government sector is included in saving and investment.

    11.   The argument must be qualified. As Ize (1988) and Carliner (1989) observe, Mexican tax collection as a fraction of GDP is significantly lower than that of other countries at the same income level.

    12.   See Buiter and Srinavasan (1987) on this issue.

REFERENCES

Bazant, J. Historia de La Deuda Exterior de Mexico. Mexico, DF: El Colegio de Mexico, 1968.

Buiter, W., and T. N. Srinivasan. "Rewarding the Profligate and Punishing the Prudent and Poor: Some Recent Proposals for Debt Relief," World Development, Vol. 15, No. 3 (1987), pp. 411-417.

Bulow, J., and K. Rogoff. "The Debt Buyback Boondoggle," Brookings Papers on Economic Activity, 2 (1988).

Cardoso, E., and S. Levy. "Mexico." In The Open Economy, ed. by R. Dornbusch and L. Helmers, Washington, D.C.: Oxford University Press, 1988.

Carliner, G. "Comments on Ramos," NBER, unpublished (1989).

Cohen, D. "External and Domestic Debt Constraints of LDCs: A Theory with Numerical Applications to Brazil and

Mexico." In Global Macroeconomics, ed. by R. Bryant and R. Portes. London: Macmillan, 1987.

Cuddington, J. "Macroeconomic Determinants of Capital Flight: An Econometric Investigation." In Capital Flight and Third World Debt, ed. by D. Lessard and J. Williamson. Washington, D.C.: Institute for International Economics, 1987.

Cumby, R., and R. Levich. "Capital Flight: Definitions and Magnitudes." In Capital Flight and Third World Debt, ed. by D. Lessard and J. Williamson. Washington, D.C.: Institute for International Economics, 1987.

Deppler, M., and M. Williamson. "Capital Flight: Concepts, Measurement and Issues," IMF Staff Studies for the World Economic Outlook. Washington, D.C: International Monetary Fund, 1987.

Dornbusch, R. "Mexico: Stabilization, Debt and Growth," Economic Policy, 1 (1988).

_____. "Comments on Bulow-Rogoff," Brookings Papers on Economic Activity, 2 (1988a).

_____, and F. Modigliani. "Easing the Mexican Interest Burden," Wall Street Journal (January 3, 1989).

Feldstein, M. "International Debt Service and Economic Growth: Some Simple Analytics," NBER Working Paper No. 2076 (1986)

Gil Diaz, F. "Inflation and Inflation Stabilization: Lessons From Mexico." In Stopping High Inflation, ed. by M. Bruno, et al. Cambridge, MA: MIT Press, forthcoming.

_____. "Mexico's Debt Burden," Mimeo, Banco de Mexico, 1988.

Gurria, J. A. "Politica de Deuda y Financiamento Externo," Mimeo, Ministry of Finance, Mexico, 1988.

Ize, A. "Savings, Investment and Growth in Mexico: Five Years After The Crisis," Mimeo, International Monetary Fund, 1988.

_____, and G. Ortiz. "Fiscal Rigidities, Public Debt and Asset Substitution: The Case of Mexico," IMF Staff Papers, Vol. 31, No. 2 (1987), pp. 311-332.

_____. "The Exchange Rate and Stabilization Policies in Mexico: 1983-1985," paper prepared for the Conference on Exchange Rate and Inflation, Jerusalem, 1985b.

Lessard, D., and J. Williamson (eds.). Capital Flight and Third World Debt. Washington, D.C.: Institute for International Economics, 1987.

Ortiz, G., and J. Serra Puche. "A Note on the Burden of the Mexican Foreign Debt," Journal of Development Economics, 21 (1986), pp. 111-129.

Ortiz Mena, A., et al. The Economic Development of Mexico. Baltimore: Johns Hopkins University Press, 1953.

Reynoso, A. "Capital Flight: The Case of Missing Markets," Mimeo, MIT, March, 1988.

Rubio, L., and F. Gil Diaz. A Mexican Response. New York: Twentieth Century Fund, 1987.

Solis, L. Economic Policy Reform in Mexico: A Case Study for Developing Countries. New York: Pergamon, 1981.

_____, and E. Zedillo. "The Foreign Debt of Mexico." In International Debt and the Developing Countries, ed. by Smith and Cuddington. Washington, D.C.: The World Bank, 1985.

Taskforce of the Twentieth Century Fund on Debt. The Road to Recovery. New York: Twentieth Century Fund, 1989.

Tellez Kuenzler, L. "Essays of an Open Economy: The Case of Mexico," unpublished dissertation, Cambridge, MA: Massachusetts Institute of Technology, 1986.

Turlington, E. Mexico and Her Foreign Creditors. New York: Columbia University Press, 1930.

Wionczek, M. (ed.). LDC External Debt and the World Economy. Mexico: El Colegio de Mexico, 1978.

Wynne, W. State Insolvency and Foreign Bond Holders, II. New Haven: Yale University Press, 1951. (Reprinted by Garland, New York, 1983).

Zedillo, E. "The Mexican External Debt: The Last Decade." In Politics and Economics of the External Debt Crisis, ed. by M. Wionczek. Boulder: Westview Press, 1985.

_____. "Case Studies: Mexico." In Capital Flight and Third World Debt, ed. by D. Lessard and J. Williamson. Washington, D.C.: Institute for International Economics, 1987.

TABLE 1.   Long-Run Performance of the Mexican Economy
           (Average annual percentage change, except as noted)

	Per Capita Growth	Inflation	Transfer Abroad[a]	Real Wage[b]
1955–72	3.3	5	-0.7	3.7
1973–81	2.6	22	-1.3	3.1
1982–88	-2.2	83	6.7	-8.3

[a] Percent of GDP.
[b] Purchasing power of wages.

TABLE 2.   Gross Investment as a Share of GDP

	Total	Public	Private
1970–74	19.2	6.5	12.8
1975–79	21.3	8.9	12.4
1980–84	21.5	9.5	12.0
1985	16.9	6.0	10.9
1986	15.5	5.2	10.3
1987	15.3	5.1	10.2
1988	16.5	5.3	11.2

Source: Banco de Mexico and, for 1985–87, Hacienda,
Mexico: Economic and Financial Statistics, November 1987.

TABLE 3.   Mexico: Public Debt Ratios (Percent of GDP)

	External Debt	Domestic Debt
1980	13.7	7.0
1981	20.0	11.2
1982	39.8	15.4
1983	39.8	17.6
1984	35.3	18.1
1985	41.7	17.7
1986	60.5	20.9
1987	60.1	21.4
1988	43.4	18.3

Note: The debt ratios are calculated by taking the average (in pesos) of debt at year end and the end of the preceding year.

Source: Banco de Mexico, Informe Anual, various issues.

TABLE 4.   Mexico's External Balance

	1984	1985	1986	1987	1988
Current Acct.[a]	4.2	1.2	-1.7	4.0	-2.9
NICA[a]	13.8	9.6	5.1	11.2	4.8
Trade Balance[a]	12.9	8.5	4.6	8.4	1.8
Oil Price ($US/brl)	26.8	25.4	17.1	16.1	12.1
Libor (%)	10.9	8.4	6.9	7.2	8.0
Real Exchange Rate[b]	82	91	65	67	80
Terms of Trade (1980=100)	76	72	52	57	52

[a]Billion $US.
[b]Morgan Guaranty, 1980-82=100.

Source: Banco de Mexico, IMF and Morgan Guaranty.

TABLE 5.   The Non-Interest Balance and Net Interest
           (Billion $US)

	1985	1986	1987	1988[a]
NICA	9.6	5.1	11.2	4.8
Exports	21.7	16.0	20.7	20.7
Oil	14.7	6.3	8.6	6.7
Non-oil	7.0	9.7	12.2	148.9
Imports	13.2	11.4	12.2	18.6
Nonfactor Exports (Net)	0.7	0.9	2.0	2.3
Net Interest	8.4	6.8	6.2	6.6

[a]Estimate.

Source: Banco de Mexico.

TABLE 6.   Financing 1985-1988 (Billion $US)

	1985	1986	1987	1988
Current Account	1.2	-1.6	3.9	-2.7
Private Capital	2.7	0.2	-2.0	-3.7
Direct Investment	0.5	1.5	3.0	3.7
Public Capital	0.6	0.9	2.8	-4.1
Errors and Omissions	2.1	0.4	0.9	0.6
Net Reserve Change	3.0	-0.1	5.5	-9.9
Memo:				
Gross Reserves[a]	4.9	5.7	12.5	5.3
External Debt[a]	97.3	101.0	107.4	105.5[b]

[a]End of period.
[b]March 1988.

Source: Secretaria de Hacienda and IMF.

TABLE 7. The External Balance Projection

	1988	1989	1990	1991
Current Account	-2.6	-5.6	-6.5	-6.2
Capital Account	-7.8	6.7	7.6	7.3
Public Capital	-4.1	7.0	7.3	6.6
Private Capital	-3.7	-0.3	0.3	0.7
Errors & Omissions	0.6	0	0	0
Reserve Changes	-9.9	1.1	1.0	1.1

TABLE 8. U.S. Bank Claims on Latin America: September 1988
          (Billion $ and Percent of Capital)

| | Latin America | | Mexico | |
	Bill. $	%	Bill. $	%
All U.S. Banks	65.4	48.1	19.3	14.2
9 Money Center Banks	45.5	83.9	12.2	22.5
13 Other Large Banks	11.0	42.8	3.3	12.8
All Other Banks	8.9	15.9	3.9	7.0

Note: % denotes percent of capital and reserves.

Source: Federal Deposit Institution Examination Council.

TABLE 9. The Secondary Market Price of Mexican Debt

7/85	7/86	7/87	7/88	3/89	5/89
80	56	54	51	33	41

Source: Salomon Brothers.

TABLE 10.   Should A Country Buy Back Debt?

	Special Gain in Efficiency	
	Yes	No
Earmarked Resources	Yes!	Yes
Alternative Uses	?	No!

TABLE 11.   Estimates of Capital Flight
            ($ Billion cumulative flow)

	1976–82	1983–87
World Bank	25.3	35.3
Erbe	36.1	35.1
Morgan Guaranty	36.6	33.9
Cuddington	29.4	16.0
Zedillo	21.3	n.a.

Source: See Lessard and Williamson (1987) updated by the author, and Zedillo (1987).

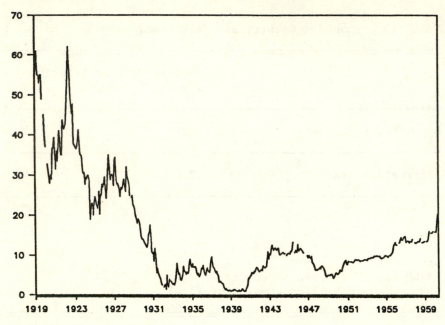

Figure 1.   Mexican Bond Price in New York (Cents per dollar)

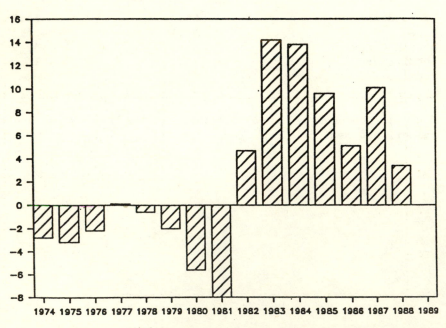

Figure 2.   Mexico: The NICA (Billion $US)

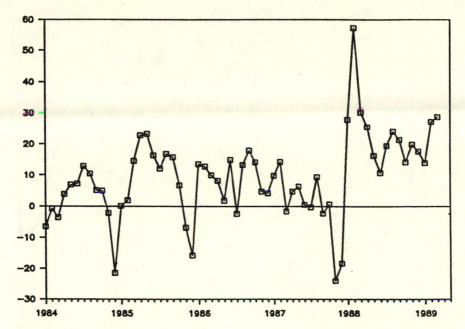

Figure 3. Mexico: The Real Interest Rate (Percent per Month)

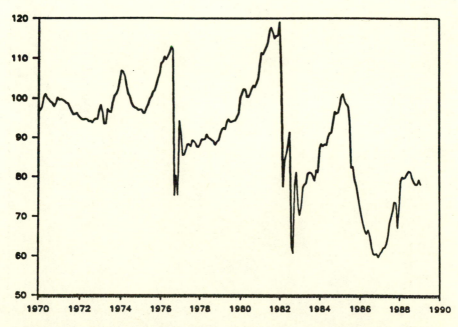

Figure 4. The Mexican Real Exchange Rate (Index 1980-82=100)

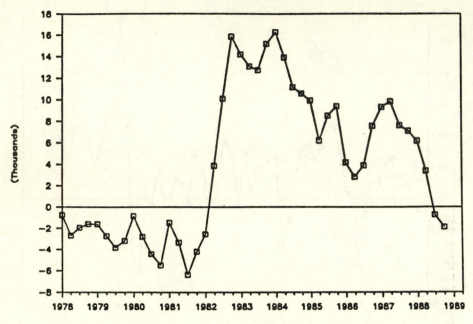

Figure 5.   Mexico: The Trade Balance
(Million $US, at Annual Rates)

APPENDIX I.   HISTORICAL STATISTICS

Table A-1.   Key Macroeconomic Data

Year	Growth	Invest.	Budget Deficit	Current Total	Acct. Nica	Real Ex.Rate	Real Wage	Infla- tion
1970	6.9	18.1	1.4	−1.9	−1.7	100	79	5.2
1971	4.1	18.8	0.8	−1.1	−0.8	99	87	5.2
1972	8.4	19.4	3.0	−0.6	−0.8	95	92	5.0
1973	8.4	20.6	4.0	−1.0	−1.4	99	90	12.0
1974	6.1	20.9	3.8	−2.7	−2.7	101	90	23.7
1975	5.6	21.6	4.9	−3.3	−2.9	101	93	15.1
1976	4.2	20.9	4.7	−2.1	−2.9	100	100	15.7
1977	3.4	18.8	5.4	0.2	0.1	89	102	28.9
1978	8.2	20.0	5.5	−0.8	−0.8	90	100	17.5
1979	9.1	22.0	6.3	−2.4	−1.6	94	99	18.2
1980	8.3	23.4	6.8	−4.5	−1.8	103	96	26.3
1981	7.9	24.9	13.6	−5.1	−2.7	115	99	27.9
1982	−0.5	21.0	16.2	0.1	2.6	83	100	63.0
1983	−5.2	16.0	10.8	5.8	10.3	79	77	101.8
1984	3.6	16.3	8.8	5.6	8.4	82	72	65.4
1985	2.7	16.9	9.5	4.3	5.7	91	71	57.7
1986	−3.8	16.4	17.4	1.0	4.7	65	65	86.2
1987	1.4	16.1	18.6	4.0	7.1	67	61	131.8
1988*	1.1	16.9	10.7	−2.9	4.8	80	53	114.2

*Estimate.

Note: Growth as percent per year, real wage index 1978=100, real exchange rate index 1980–82=100, inflation as percent per year, December–December. All other variables as percent of GDP.   The term NICA denotes the non-interest current account deficit expressed as a fraction of GDP. The budget is not adjusted for the inflationary component of interest payments. The real wage series reports the minimum wage deflated by the consumer price index.

Source: Banco de Mexico, Secretaria de Hacienda and Morgan Guaranty.

Comments

Angel Gurria
Undersecretary for International Financial Affairs,
Ministry of Finance and Public Credit

Professor Dornbusch has presented a lucid overview of the history of Mexican debt in the first half of the twentieth century. I think it is especially noteworthy and relevant in today's context that Mexico's return to capital markets occurred only <u>after</u> the debt overhang of the first half of the century disappeared. Dornbusch's description of the external debt problem Mexico currently faces is generally accurate: in particular, the balance of payments, budgetary and resource transfer (NICA) problems are well represented. The high domestic real interest rates that are a consequence of these problems are an important obstacle to investment and sound public finances. I believe, however, that Dornbusch's estimates are very much on the high side for both capital flight and domestic debt. For the latter, the true ratio is 20-25 percent of GDP, not the over 50 percent indicated in the paper. Nonetheless, the fact remains that financing negative net external transfers has put a heavy strain on domestic financial markets.

The paper failed to discuss several of the main contributors to the crisis -- like a deterioration in Mexico's terms of trade and, especially, high real interest rates abroad. The ratio between oil prices and real interest rates (a key measure in evaluating Mexico's debt-servicing capacity) decreased from 30:1 in the late 1970s to just 3:1 currently. Until recently, Mexico has borne the full burden of adjustment to this change. In this respect, fiscal and monetary policies in the United States are crucial for improving external macroeconomic conditions for Mexico, as Dornbusch has rightly pointed out. In fact, a reduction in the U.S. primary fiscal deficit in proportion to GDP of even one-quarter the magnitude of the one actually undertaken by Mexico would go a long way toward resolving Mexico's problem of excessively high foreign real interest rates.

Dornbusch's analysis of debt reduction instruments is basically correct with respect to their limited effectiveness. Debt-equity swaps and buybacks are both debt prepayments. Each causes important financing problems for Mexico, the first because of extremely high domestic real interest rates and the second because of the negative impact on foreign reserves. Moreover, since swaps have to be rationed due to their monetary impact, they inhibit investment. Investors tend to delay their investments in anticipation of receiving the subsidies that are implicit in swaps regardless of whether they are necessary for a project to have a positive net present value. Debt-for-debt exchanges, on the other hand, require fewer resources but are less attractive to banks, since a large portion of the risk is still Mexican (as seen in the Morgan/Mexico deal). All of these instruments were important conceptual developments in their time; however, today a more comprehensive solution is required.

Dornbusch suggests one such solution: interest capitalization for an extended period of time. Given the high real interest rates that prevail currently and the volatility in Mexico's terms of trade, this solution is, however, quite risky. The argument that banks would rather capitalize most of their interest payments than grant debt reduction is not in general corroborated by actual private sector debt restructurings. For the case of Mexico in particular, Dornbusch's solution poses other problems. If the capitalized interest were lent to the private sector, as has been suggested, the government would in effect have to finance these loans by issuing domestic debt at real rates so high that the cost would eventually wipe out the benefits. Equivalent to a debt-equity swap without a discount, this is not a very attractive proposition. In addition, since Mexico has no general foreign exchange controls, it would be extremely difficult to control relending to prevent resource outflows.

It is not clear that all banks will accept recycling in exchange for fiscal efforts and trade liberalization. Banks look out for their own interests -- which they basically see as collecting as much as possible as fast as possible from a problem debtor. Trade liberalization, for example, is not really in their short-term benefit (in fact, some see it as being against their interest) and would not, in any case, be "tradeable" for debt reduction.

A more fundamental problem relating to interest capitalization as opposed to debt reduction is its effects on private sector confidence and capital repatriation. Capitalization increases the stock of debt exponentially and is likely to create the expectation of even bigger external and fiscal problems in the future. Under this scenario, private investors will be less likely to invest and repatriate flight capital. In this respect, debt reduction is a superior alternative because it dispels any doubts about the future overhang.

On the other hand, Dornbusch's conclusion regarding debt reduction as an all-or-nothing situation is probably right. Competitive dynamics in the banking industry point to the conclusion that a bank would be extremely reluctant to take a large hit on its capital without its competitors doing the same -- hence pari passu clauses in loan contracts. A recent example is the case of the Bolivian debt buyback, where some of the banks leading the debt reduction effort did not willingly participate at the last moment. From a single bank's perspective, the best solution is clearly for all other banks to participate, leaving an enhanced asset for the remaining bank. To avoid this free-riding, debt reduction has to be an all-or-nothing solution for all banks concerned.

Front-loading is an important feature of debt reduction from a debtor's perspective. Debt reduction spread over many small operations does not lead to the required relief financially, nor does it generate the swing in confidence caused by one large, front-loaded operation. The way to induce banks to enter into such an operation is to offer enhancement (like collateralized principal and partial interest guarantees) on the new debt, making its acceptance attractive to banks within a framework of free choice. However, the debt exchange would be offered only once.

Dornbusch observes that "Today asset holders must wonder whether growth and debt service will be reconciled. As a result they hang on to their dollar positions even in the presence of extraordinarily high real interest rates." After seven years of crisis, these asset holders don't wonder -- they know! Until the debt overhang is eliminated and the possibility of sustained growth in a low-inflation environment is assured, investors will hold only short-term, speculative financial assets and not real assets. Lack of growth and astronomical real interest rates will persist until the debt overhang is eliminated and debt service reduced to sustainable levels. It is in the interests of all parties concerned that this solution be effected as soon as possible.

Trade Liberalization and Macroeconomic Adjustment

Jaime Zabludovsky*
*General Director of External Commercial Policy,
Ministry of Trade and Industry*

1.   INTRODUCTION

During the period 1983-1988 the Mexican economy has undergone deep structural changes, including important reforms in the protectionist trade regime which dominated its economic activity for three decades. This paper provides an historical review of Mexico's trade policy in its macroeconomic context and with special emphasis on the reform program in place since 1983.

The paper is organized as follows. Sections 2 and 3 discuss respectively the macroeconomic policies from 1958 to 1982 and the import substitution regime established in this context. Macroeconomic adjustment and trade reform during 1983-1988 are then taken up in Section 4 and the process of trade liberalization is analyzed according to three chronological stages. The outcomes of trade liberalization are briefly surveyed in Section 5 before Section 6 presents some tentative conclusions.

2.   OVERVIEW OF MACROECONOMIC PERFORMANCE: 1958-1982

There were two distinct phases in Mexico's macroeconomic performance over this twenty-five year period:

---

*The opinions of this paper are those of the author alone and should not be interpreted as representing official views of the Mexican Government. The assistance and extensive comments of Jorge Miranda, Florencia Lopez de Silanes, Dorothy Avery, Humberto Jasso, Francisco Rueda and Laura Carrera are gratefully acknowledged.

"Stabilizing Development" during 1958-1970 and "Shared Development" during the oil boom period of 1971-1982. Each was characterized by different macroeconomic management strategies, but their trade regimes were essentially identical. The overview of this period will be brief, since the literature on these topics is already extensive.(1)

2.1 Stabilizing Development: 1958-1970

The term "Stabilizing Development" was coined by Antonio Ortiz-Mena, Secretary of Finance during 1958-1970, and refers to a combination of rapid output growth and stable prices and exchange rates. This period contrasts markedly with the 1940-1954 years, when growth was accompanied by sporadic inflation and recurrent devaluations. According to Gil-Diaz (1985), the essential elements of Stabilizing Development were low and stable ratios of public deficits and external debt to GDP, domestic inflation at international levels, positive real interest rates for asset-holders and a fixed nominal exchange rate.

Because money growth was pegged to expected output growth, inflation was kept at a minimum and real interest rates were positive, so that financial savings grew notably. The ratio of financial savings to GDP grew from 10 percent in 1956-1960 to 25 percent in 1966-1970 (Gil-Diaz 1985, p. 357), thus enabling the government to fund its deficit through the banking system with few monetary or foreign debt effects. Moreover, the fiscal deficit was kept at the manageable average level of 1.6 percent of GDP during 1961-1970, as indicated by Table 1. In addition, the Central Bank followed a monetarist policy with respect to the balance of payments under a fixed nominal exchange rate. Incipient reserve losses were viewed as indicative of excessive money growth, which was remedied by a contractionary monetary policy.

The Stabilizing Development strategy was implemented within the framework of an import substitution policy involving the redistribution of resources towards the production of goods in which Mexico did not have a comparative advantage and which did not make intensive use of factor inputs abundant locally. Output growth was therefore heavily biased against labor and serious employment and distributional problems followed.

2.2   Shared Development and the Oil Boom: 1971-1982

The Echeverria administration took office in late 1970.
Its economic policy of Shared Development aimed at increasing employment and improving income distribution by means of
large increments in public spending.   Fiscal restraint was
abandoned.   Public expenditures on both consumption and
investment rose dramatically without concomitant increases
in fiscal revenues.   A rising public deficit resulted,
excessive spending pushed up inflation, and as inflation
increased, both real interest rates and financial savings
declined.   Since the public deficit could not be entirely
financed through the banking system, it began to be monetized.   Moreover, the government resorted to foreign debt
issues to supplement public revenues.   The public deficit
problem worsened as the extensive price control programs of
the Stabilizing Development era were continued in spite of
mounting inflationary pressures.
The Echeverria administration changed only the macroeconomic aspects of Stabilizing Development leaving the
microeconomics in general and trade policy in particular the
same.   A trade regime reform gearing production towards
labor intensive goods would have provided employment and distributional gains.   Commercial policy should have changed,
but it did not.
By the end of 1976, the government confronted a situation of little output growth, rapid inflation and a major
balance of payments problem.   The peso was devalued and the
next administration, led by Lopez-Portillo, was forced to
enter into a standby agreement with the IMF and to implement
a major macroeconomic adjustment program.
At first the public sector deficit was substantially
reduced, dropping from 9.9 percent of GDP in 1976 to 6.7 percent in 1977.(2)   At the same time, the annual output growth
rate fell to 3.4 percent, the lowest since 1959.   Mexico
then experienced a brief growth bubble fueled by income from
oil exports.   Public spending increased again and from 1977
to 1981 the share of government expenditures in GDP rose
from 30 to roughly 40 percent.   Non-oil exports were penalized by the policy of fixing the nominal exchange rate while
inflation was rising so that the real exchange rate appreciated at an average annual rate of 8 percent over 1977-1981.
The price of Mexican oil then began to slide downwards
and by late 1982 it had dropped roughly 25 percent from
early 1981.   Faced with huge fiscal revenue losses, the
Lopez-Portillo administration chose not to curtail public
expenditures, but rather to borrow its way out of the crisis

by monetization and massive accumulation of foreign debt.
Thus, in 1981 alone the Mexican external debt rose by some
$20 billion. Exclusive of increments in nominal interest
payments due to inflation, (3) the public deficit increased
from 8.3 percent of GDP in 1980 to 11.6 percent in 1981 and
15.4 percent in 1982.

3.   OVERVIEW OF THE TRADE REGIME: 1958-1982

     Because the history of trade policy in Mexico has been
the topic of numerous academic papers, the following summary
will be brief.(4) A discussion of available protection estimates and an analysis of the effects of the import substitution trade regime in place during 1958-1982 will then follow.

3.1 Import Substitution

     Mexico began to implement import substitution policies
in the early 1940s, but the inward-oriented model did not
become firmly established until the Stabilizing Development
period.   This model was consistent with the philosophy of
"export elasticity pessimism", which dominated academic
thought in the post-war period.   According to the then-
leading exponents of development theory, the domestic market
represented a stronger and more stable basis for growth than
the international market, as the latter had become increasingly unfavorable for developing countries. Outward-oriented
growth was therefore dismissed and trade policy was directed
towards protecting local producers and stimulating import
substitution.
     The effects of the anti-export bias produced by the
import substitution model are illustrated by a shift in output composition away from exports.   Merchandise and service
exports fell as a percentage of GDP from 10.6 percent in
1960 to 7.7 percent in 1970.   During Stabilizing Development
merchandise exports grew in real terms at an average annual
rate of 1.6 percent, down from 4.0 percent in the 1936-1956
period.   (See Zabludovsky, 1987, p. 12).   In addition, since
the import substitution model was "import intensive", to use
Diaz-Alejandro terminology, high growth rates raised import
demand and increased trade deficits.   Indeed, with the existing output-employment elasticities, growth high enough to
absorb employment was inconsistent with balance of payments
equilibrium.

In spite of the import substitution trade regime, however, one sector of the economy operated under conditions
akin to free trade. Rather than buying over-priced domestic
inputs, maquiladoras (in-bond plants located in the border
areas) could purchase their inputs abroad in order to compete in world markets successfully. Over the period 1970-
1982, maquiladora output grew at a annual rate of 6.7 percent, compared to a rate of 3.4 percent for manufacturing as
a whole.(5)

Under Mexico's import substitution trade regime protection was provided to local producers through a variety of
instruments: tariffs, official import reference prices and,
most importantly, import licenses. Import licensing was significantly increased from the late 1950s to the early 1960s.
Thus, in 1956-1957 the percentage of import value subject to
licenses jumped from 18 to 35 percent and by 1958-1959 it
had increased to over 43 percent. By 1961 it had gone up to
54 percent and by 1963 it was over 60 percent. The percentage of import value subject to permits remained roughly at
this level into the early 1970s but during the Shared Development period balance of payments disequilibria were offset
by further licensing of imports rather than by absorption
cuts, and the percentage of import value subject to permits
increased to 82 percent in 1974 and 90 percent in 1977. The
causal relationship between spending and import licensing is
illustrated by Graphs 1 and 2, where spending is proxied by
the public deficit.

In 1978, however, a modest program of trade liberalization began. The percentage of import value subject to
licensing dropped to 76 percent in 1978, 70 percent in 1979
and 60 percent in 1980. Although the program simply brought
import licensing back to the levels prior to the onset of
the balance of payments disequilibria in 1974, its effects
on the number of import categories subject to licensing was
more extensive. The percentage went from 77 percent in 1977
to 43 percent in 1978, 31 percent in 1979 and approximately
25 percent in 1980-1981.

This episode of mild liberalization did not, however,
take place under a compatible macroeconomic framework. During 1978-1980, the public deficit rose from 5.1 percent of
GDP to 8.3 percent. By 1981, the balance of payments disequilibria resulting from excessive spending and oil revenue
losses were met again by import licensing instead of absorption cuts, and this trade liberalization episode was
aborted. The percentage of import value subject to licensing went up to 85 percent in 1981, and 100 percent in 1982.
(See, again, Graphs 1 and 2.)

3.2   Estimates of Protection: 1958-1981

Due to the extent of import licensing in Mexico during 1958-1981, protection cannot be properly estimated through average tariff rates alone. Import licenses and official import reference prices allow the prices of domestic trade-ables to deviate from international prices over and above what would be indicated by tariff rates alone. The compilation of protection estimates over the years 1958-1982 accordingly includes estimates that refer only to implicit protection, that is, price differentials incorporating the effects of all protection instruments, in both nominal and effective terms.

Based on industrial sectors, estimates of implicit nominal and effective protection rates are available for 1960 (Bueno), 1970 (Ten Kate et al.), 1975 (Cavazos), and 1979-1981 (Ten Kate and De Mateo)(6).   Because they are not strictly comparable over time due to the differences in methodologies employed and because the relevance of effective protection in a general equilibrium framework may be limited, the following comments are brief and general in nature.

Effective protection rates noticeably increased from 1960 to 1981 although those for the primary sector were far below those for manufacturing. In particular, capital and durable consumer goods had the highest rates of effective protection. In agriculture, both nominal and effective protection rates fell in 1970 and then rose significantly in 1980-1981.   This increase is probably attributable to the price support system established under the Mexican Food-stuffs Program (SAM) during the late 1970s. The mining sector, meantime, had negative nominal and effective protection rates during 1979-1981; exports from this sector were therefore taxed by the policy.

The degree of effective protection significantly shifted the structure of the economy towards importables and non-tradeables. While in 1951-1955 non-tradeables accounted for 54 percent of GDP, from 1966 throughout the 1970s non-tradeables represented some 60 percent.   Importables increased from about 12 percent of GDP in 1951-1955 to roughly 15 percent in 1966-1970 and 17 percent in the late 1970s. Conversely, exportables dropped from 31 percent of GDP in 1951-1955 to about 23 percent in 1966-1970 and 20 percent in the late 1970s (see Gil-Diaz 1985, p. 362).

4.   MACRO AND TRADE POLICIES UNDER DE LA MADRID: 1983-1988

4.1 Macro Adjustment During 1983-1988

As noted above, the Mexican economy experienced a severe crisis in 1982, when the output growth rate deceased from roughly 8 percent in 1981 to -0.6 percent, while inflation increased from about 28 percent to close to 60 percent.

The task of adjusting the economy fell to the de la Madrid administration, which took office in late 1982. The public sector deficit was cut by two-thirds in 1983, from 15 to 6 percent of GDP, and then further reduced to 2-3 percent of GDP in 1984 and 1985. As a result of this severe adjustment program, output fell by 5.3 percent in 1983. Growth then recommended at the moderate rates of 3.7 in 1984 and 2.5 in 1985. In addition, inflation dropped from about 100 percent in 1983 to 58 percent in 1985.

This macro adjustment program was then thrown off course by a series of exogenous shocks: the 1985 earthquake and major decreases in the price of oil exports during 1986 and 1988. In 1986 the price of Mexican oil exports fell some 50 percent from its 1985 levels. As a result of the ensuing revenue losses, the public deficit rose to 6.4 percent of GDP in 1986 but was again reduced to 4.9 percent in 1987. The economy contracted by 3.7 percent in 1986 but then grew slightly by 1.5 percent in 1987.

The severe macro adjustment programs in effect since 1983 cut domestic absorption of current production significantly. The ratio of absorption to GDP averaged 101 percent during 1978-1981, compared to 91 percent during 1983-1987. The absorption cuts hit investment the hardest: the ratio of investment to GDP decreased from 29 percent in 1981 to 17 percent in 1983 and 16 percent in 1987. Such cuts in investment curtail future output growth and are clearly unsustainable.

The 1982 crisis is a landmark in Mexican economic history because it revealed the structural deficiencies inherent in the import substitution model. Maintaining this regime involved a high cost in terms of both lower output and employment. Mexico could no longer rely on oil exports to lead growth; and as oil export revenues fell from $16.5 billion in 1982 to roughly $6 billion in 1986 and 1988, increasing non-oil exports to avoid further reductions in domestic absorption became imperative. As the servicing requirements of mounting foreign debt soared from $5.5 billion to $12.2 billion during 1981-1982, the growth of non-oil exports also became obligatory from a policy standpoint. Increasing exports of manufactures would also yield employment and distributional gains because their production is typically labor intensive.

4.2 Trade Liberalization During 1983-1988

The liberalization program put into place by the de la Madrid administration can be divided chronologically into two stages: the first from early 1983 to June of 1985 and the second from July of 1985 to November of 1988. A third stage of trade liberalization is currently being implemented to consolidate and extend the reforms. Each of these stages is described in some detail below.

Reforms in export trade policies are not included in the discussion because they have been rather limited: indeed, the percentage of export value subject to licensing actually increased from 10.1 percent in 1983 to 14.6 percent in 1987. The ability to remove export licenses is constrained by their often having been established either to stay within export quotas set by international agreements (as in the case of oil, coffee and cocoa) or to comply with import quotas imposed on Mexico by its trading partners (as in the case of textiles and steel).

4.2.1 First Stage of Trade Liberalization: Early 1983 to June of 1985

The Lopez-Portillo administration avoided cutting absorption to deal with the 1981-1982 balance of payments crisis. Instead, it required all imports to be licensed. The trade liberalization program initiated by the de la Madrid administration began in 1983 by reducing import tariffs but maintaining licensing requirements. Thus, 42 percent of import value was exempted from tariffs in 1983, as compared to 21 percent in 1982. In addition, the percentage of dutiable imports subject to tariffs above 25 percent was reduced from almost 20 percent in 1981 to 7 percent in 1983.

After the nominal exchange rate was freed in 1982, it appreciated over 100 percent, from 56 to 120 pesos per dollar in 1983.(7) With the benefit of hindsight, it appears that the government missed an excellent opportunity to launch a more aggressive and extensive trade reform because exchange rate protection could have been a substitute for import licensing.

The trade liberalization program began to remove import licensing requirements in 1984 and the percentage of import value subject to permits dropped to 83 percent. The amount

of imported capital goods subject to licensing was reduced
from 31 percent in 1982 to 19 percent of the licensed import
bundle. However, as import licensing was being phased out,
tariffs were increased to provide a roughly equivalent
amount of protection. The percentage of import value exempt
from tariffs declined to 36 percent in 1984 and tariffs
rates of 10, 15 and 25 percent were applied to most imports.

4.2.2 Second Stage of Trade Liberalization: July 1985 to November 1988

July 1985 Reforms.   The trade liberalization program
advanced at full speed beginning in mid-1985. By then it
had become clear to the de la Madrid policy-making team that
the economy needed to increase non-oil exports in order to
restore high growth rates. This point was underscored by a
12 percent decline in manufactured exports (in value terms)
from $5,691 billion in 1984 to $4,978 billion in 1985. This
decrease stood in sharp contrast to the growth rates
attained in 1983 and 1984, when manufactured exports
increased by 51 and 24 percent. To make matters worse, oil
export revenues also fell by 11 percent in 1985 due more to
a decrease in volume than to declining price.

In response to this deteriorating export performance,
the de la Madrid team quickened the pace of trade reform.
There was a consensus that protection taxed exporters and
that as a consequence the growth of non-oil exports was
being constrained by the heavy protection that still
remained. On July 25, 1985, an Executive Decree removed the
import licensing requirements from 3,064 of the 5,219 tariff
categories. The percentage of imports subject to licensing
dropped from 64.7 percent in 1984 to 10.4 percent by the end
of 1985. More importantly, the percentage of import value
subject to licensing decreased from 83 percent to 37 percent
-- nearly 50 percentage points. As indicated above, the
removal of import licensing was offset by specific tariff
hikes. Thus, in 1985 the percentage of dutiable import
value subject to tariff rates of 25 percent went up from 8
to 19 percent, whereas the percentage of dutiable import
value subject to tariff rates of 40 percent went up from 3
to 14 percent. The removal of import licensing significantly affected capital goods imports. In 1985 they fell from
19 to 10 percent of the licensed import bundle.

Trade liberalization continued as the percentage of
import value subject to licensing was reduced from 37 percent in 1985 to about 31 percent in 1986. The tariff structure was also compacted so that about 90 percent of the

dutiable import bundle was subject to three rates -- 10, 22.5 and 37 percent. In 1986 the nominal exchange rate increased by more than 100 percent over 1985, from 257 to 612 pesos per dollar. The elimination of commercial protection was accordingly replaced somewhat by exchange rate protection.

All in all, a remarkable degree of trade liberalization had occurred by 1986. But as a non-member, Mexico was unable to take advantage of the system of reciprocal concessions available to members of the GATT. An entry agreement was therefore negotiated and signed in July of 1986. Mexico was obligated to continue import license removal and tariff reductions, but was allowed to establish a system to assess anti-dumping and countervailing duties(8). Since by mid-1986 Mexico had already undertaken major reforms affecting tariffs, official import reference prices and import licenses, most of the adjustment costs of joining the GATT had already been met, at least for the immediate future. Indeed, in 1985, the year before the GATT agreement, only 5 percent of dutiable imports was subject to tariff rates of 50 percent or above. Official import reference prices applied mainly to intermediate goods comprising less than 10 percent of the dutiable import bundle. Joining the GATT in 1986 therefore involved a low marginal cost and brought not only the benefits of membership but also immediate gains in credibility. GATT membership was a signal to domestic producers that trade reform had become permanent.

Another strong signal was the continuation of trade liberalization in 1986 in the face of a 50 percent decrease in the price of oil exports from their 1985 levels, the huge loss of oil revenue that followed and almost a 4 percent fall in GDP. This provided clear evidence that trade liberalization was not a circumstantial policy but rather would be pursued despite seriously adverse exogenous shocks and was a sharp contrast to 1979 when Mexico had refused to enter the GATT even though world prices for oil exports were on the rise.

Further Liberalization during 1987-1988. As noted above, the macroeconomic adjustment program put into effect by the de la Madrid administration was set off course by exogenous shocks in 1985 and 1986. As a result output growth decreased from 2.5 percent in 1985 to -3.7 percent in 1986 and 1.5 percent in 1987, while inflation increased from 58 percent in 1985 to 86 percent in 1986 and 132 percent in 1987. A major macroeconomic adjustment program was clearly necessary to bring inflation under control and return to rapid output growth. This stabilization program was launched in December of 1987 and came to be known as the "Economic Solidarity Plan". Acknowledging that inflation was influenced by inertial factors, it placed controls on nominal wages, prices and the exchange rate. These controls were intended to dampen inflationary expectations while absorption cuts reduced fundamental inflationary pressures.

Under the Economic Solidarity Plan the dispersion of tariffs was compacted to the 0-20 percent range, with only five rate categories of 0, 5, 10, 15, and 20 percent. As a result tariff dispersion was halved from 14 percent in 1986 to 7 percent by the end of 1987 (see Table 2). By this time, the unweighted average tariff and the import-weighted average had also declined to 10 percent and 5.6 percent, respectively. In sharp contrast, the tariff structure in 1982 involved an unweighted average tariff of 27 percent, an import-weighted average tariff of 16 percent, tariff dispersion of 25 percent, and 16 tariff levels within a 0-100 percent range. The average production-weighted import tariff fell from 23 percent in 1980 to 12 percent in December of 1987.

The tariff reforms executed within the Economic Solidarity Pact were continued in 1988 by eliminating the 5 percent import surcharge (which had been introduced in stages since 1985) and by abolishing the remaining official import prices. Moreover, the percentage of import value subject to licensing dropped from 31 percent in 1986 to 20 percent in 1988.

4.2.3   Third Stage of Trade Liberalization: December 1988 Onwards

The Salinas administration took office in late 1988 and proceeded to institute a macro adjustment package of its own. This program is formally known as the "Stabilization and Economic Growth Plan" and is similar to the Economic Solidarity Plan in that it aims to reduce inflation by addressing both expectations and fundamentals. However, it differs from the latter plan in its goal to speed up adjustment so that growth can be restored as quickly as possible.

In order to provide general tariff protection without discriminating among sectors, the trade reform package of the Salinas administration has made effective protection rates significantly more uniform by closing the dispersion in nominal tariffs. Thus, in January and March of 1989 two Executive Decrees raised tariff rates for most goods previously exempt from import taxes or subject to only a 5 percent rate(9). As a result of these tariff increments, by March of 1989 the unweighted average tariff rate rose to 13 percent, the import-weighted average tariff increased to 10 percent and tariff dispersion dropped to 4.3 percent (see Table 2).

The economic sectors that remain protected under an import licensing regime consist mainly of agriculture and industries like automobiles, pharmaceuticals and electronics that are the focus of development programs.(10) These sectors account for approximately one-fourth of tradeable output and according to the terms of the GATT agreement they are permitted to retain licensing protection temporarily.(11)

4.3 Export Incentives

The trade reform program implemented since 1983 has removed some of the anti-export bias in Mexico's commercial regime by reducing the profitability of producing import substitutes. Moreover, Mexico has countered the remaining anti-export bias with export incentives. The neutrality of most of these export incentives is important to emphasize: they merely offset existing trade distortions. Firms eligible for export incentives can import intermediate and capital goods without obtaining import licenses or paying import taxes. Thus, the export incentive scheme allows local firms access to tradeable factor inputs at world prices distorted by neither tariffs nor quotas.(12)

5. EFFECTS OF TRADE LIBERALIZATION

5.1 Export Performance

From 1983 to 1988, total non-oil exports and manufactured exports grew in value terms at an average rate of roughly 20 percent and 25 percent, respectively. These high growth rates are mainly attributable to volume rather than price increases. Combined with decreases in the price of oil exports, this growth has radically changed the composition of exports as a whole in value terms from that observed prior to the trade reforms. While in 1982 non-oil exports represented 28 percent of merchandise exports, by 1988 they had increased roughly 68 percent. Most of this change is attributed to relative growth in manufactured exports. In 1982 manufactured goods comprised 20 percent of merchandise exports as compared to 56 percent in 1988.

The effects of the trade liberalization program on
export growth can also be illustrated by firm-level data.
According to surveys that include most major exporting
firms, export shares in total sales have risen considerably
in the trade liberalization years.(13) It is not clear, however, to what extent rapid growth in non-oil exports is
traceable to changes in relative output prices brought about
by trade liberalization and to what extent it reflects deep
absorption cuts from macro adjustments at unchanged relative
output prices. Prima facie, the record points both ways as
discussed below.

5.2 Effects of Trade Liberalization on Employment, Output and Prices

Because research findings on these issues are scarce
and relevant data are often biased and incomplete, it is too
early to assess properly the effects of trade liberalization
on employment, output and prices. Nevertheless, Mexico probably stands to benefit in all three of these ways.

5.2.1 Employment and Output Effects

As noted above, the trade liberalization program undertaken since 1983 has shifted the composition of merchandise
exports from oil to non-oil exports, particularly manufactures. To the extent that Mexico's manufactured exports are
labor intensive, trade liberalization is bound to result in
employment gains and a rise in the relative price of labor.
(In the short run, of course, changes in the relative price
of labor will be smaller than in the long run; see Neary,
1978.) In contrast output growth during 1958-1982 had an
anti-labor bias, since it was fueled by either import substitution or oil exports, both of which are typically capital
and/or natural resource intensive.

Employment gains are somewhat difficult to identify,
however, since the trade liberalization program was implemented in the midst of high inflation and an ensuing macro
adjustment plan which almost certainly caused most of the
observed increase in unemployment.(14) Any employment
losses attributable to the trade liberalization program per
se should be measured in net terms because the purpose of
such a program is to redistribute productive resources. As
a result of trade reform, import substitution sectors will
contract, while sectors producing exportables will expand.
If the former are capital and natural resource intensive and
the latter are labor intensive, trade reform will raise

employment in net terms. The argument that gearing production towards labor intensive goods raises employment growth
is supported by the record of the Southeast Asian trading
economies. Manufacturing employment in Korea, for example,
grew by 8.5 percent over 1965-1987 (IMF, 1988).

5.2.2   Input Prices and "Price Discipline"

Trade liberalization has increased the access of producers of exportables to tradeable factor inputs at international prices so that they can compete in world markets.
The remarkable performance of non-oil exports and the experience of maquiladoras indicates how quickly industries can
grow if provided with competitively priced factor inputs.

Because many industries in Mexico are heavily concentrated, there is also ample room for trade reform to encourage internationally competitive behavior (see De Melo and
Urata, 1984), and the liberalization program has probably
imposed price discipline upon domestic oligopolies engaged
in production of tradeable goods. All the complaints inves-
tigated so far by Mexico's anti-dumping authority involve
oligopolistic or monopolistic industries -- especially chemi-
cals, although recent complaints also include electrical
equipment, steel products and plastics.(15)

The recent performance of the maquiladoras indicates
how trade liberalization can enforce price discipline and
reduce anti-export bias. Not only does it force factor
input producers to price competitively, but it also induces
them to sell to exporters, since selling to producers of
import substitutes and non-tradeables is less profitable.
On the one hand, some maquiladoras in both border and non-
border areas have greatly increased their use of domestic
factor inputs (see Table 3). Border firms producing food-
stuffs increased domestic factor input use from 13 to 21 percent of total factor inputs from 1980 to 1987. For non-
border firms producing electrical and electronic goods,
these figures are 2 and 10 percent, respectively. In Nuevo
Leon State, home to much of Mexico's industry, domestic factor inputs account for roughly 26 percent of total factor
inputs. On the other hand, maquiladoras are locating increasingly in non-border areas. While in 1980 only 12 percent of
the maquiladoras were located in non-border areas, by October of 1988 this figure had increased to 22 percent.(16)
This shift in location suggests that the price incentives to
remain in the border areas have decreased.

5.3   Literature on the Effects of Trade Reform

Few empirical exercises currently exist on the effects of trade liberalization in Mexico.   One such study is by Cervantes and Tapia (1988), who use an econometric model to show that trade reform has improved the trade balance, raised industrial output and lowered inflation.   A more sophisticated exercise by Quintanilla (1988) uses a general equilibrium model to predict that relaxing tariffs and other distortions on goods and factor inputs would increase trade-able value added by roughly 11 percent.

6.   CONCLUSIONS

This paper has provided a detailed account of Mexico's trade reforms since 1983, emphasizing the relationship of trade liberalization to the concurrent process of macroeconomic adjustment.   Liberalization continued in 1986 in spite of huge export revenue losses due to falling oil prices. The trade reform strategy had a slow start, but picked up speed by mid-1985, when extensive import license removal took place.   Tariff dispersion was also significantly narrowed in late 1987.   By early 1989 licensing applied to only some 20 percent of the import bundle, official import reference prices were eliminated and the import-weighted average tariff rate was roughly 10 percent.   Current attempts to close the existing nominal tariff dispersion even further are designed to make effective tariff protection rates increasingly uniform.

Trade liberalization involves factor reallocation and if the expanding sectors are more labor intensive than the declining sectors, total employment will increase.   Trade liberalization also serves to enforce price discipline on oligopolies, as well as allowing access to tradeable inputs at world prices.   In short, it appears that Mexico stands to benefit in terms of employment creation, output growth and price stabilization.   Some empirical evidence supports these conclusions, but more detailed study of the specific issues is required.

During 1978-1981 Mexico pursued trade reform without making the necessary macroeconomic adjustments.   The failure of this initiative can therefore be attributed to an incompatible macroeconomic framework.   In important contrast, from 1983 to 1988 trade liberalization and macro adjustments have been implemented concurrently so that the macro environment has not hampered the micro reforms.   However, undertaking stabilization and liberalization programs simultaneously has posed difficult challenges to policymakers. In particular, fully reaping the benefits of trade reform necessitates widespread investments in infrastructure. Such investments, however, currently appear out of reach since the macro adjustment program has cut absorption to minimum levels. In this context the increment in economic efficiency that trade liberalization may produce is greatly restricted by the investment constraints imposed by macro stabilization. Hence, fuller realization of the efficiency gains potentially available from trade liberalization will require some relaxation of the current limitations on infrastructure investments.

Finally, trade reform in Mexico has yet to be accompanied by a program of domestic industrial deregulation, and numerous legal barriers still hamper export activities. These limitations continue to curtail the benefits from trade liberalization.(17)

NOTES

1. Readers interested in more detailed analysis may consult Ortiz and Solis (1979), Thompson (1979), Solis (1981), Gomez Oliver (1981), Garcia Alba and Serra (1984), Gil Diaz (1985 and 1987), Zedillo (1985), Ortiz (1985), Ize and Ortiz (1985), Cordoba (1986), Hierro and Sangines (1987), Cardoso and Levy (1988), and Gil-Diaz and Ramos (1988).

2. Editors' Note: This and the many other factual assertions throughout this paper are amply corroborated by data contained in the 16 tables submitted with the original version. Constraints imposed on the length of this conference volume and problems of legibility exacerbated by the necessity for reducing print size forced us reluctantly to eliminate 9 text tables and all 4 of the tables included in the original appendix. Many contain data made publicly available in their entirety for the first time; the interested researcher should consult the author.

3. As long as asset holders re-lend their inflation-ballooned interest payments to the government, the public debt does not increase in real terms. Public deficit figures cited in the text henceforth refer to the "adjusted operational deficit" and were taken from Banco de Mexico sources (1987 and 1988).

4. Readers interested in a more detailed historical description of trade policy in Mexico should consult Izquierdo (1964), Reynolds (1967, 1970), King (1970), Bueno

(1971), Cavazos (1977), Aspra (1977), Ten Kate, et al. (1979), Balassa (1983), World Bank (1986 and 1988), Bucay and Perez Motta (1987, 1988), Ten Kate and De Mateo (1988), and De Mateo (1988). Zabludovsky (1987) takes up both macro-economic and trade regime issues.

5.   See Banamex, et al. (1988), Appendix Table 1.

6.   While the Bueno, Ten Kate and Cavazos estimates were constructed according to the industrial classification employed in the 1960 input—output matrix, the Ten Kate and De Mateo estimates were constructed according to the indus-trial categories currently used in the national accounts. Nevertheless, the two classification systems can be recon-ciled since the national accounts differ from the 1960 input—output matrix by incorporating on occasion a more detailed industrial breakdown.

7.   Nominal exchange rates refer to yearly averages and not year—end quotations.

8.   The specifics of the GATT agreement consist mainly of (i) tariff concessions on about 16 percent of the 1985 import bundle, (ii) a reduction in the maximum tariff to 50 percent, (iii) elimination of official import reference prices and (iv) the right temporarily to exclude from license removal both agriculture and industries that are the focus of promotion programs.

9.   These decrees left unchanged the tariff rates applicable to goods under a 10, 15 or 20 percent regime. The group of goods affected by tariff increases included mainly raw materials and intermediates, whereas the group whose tariff rates remained unchanged included mostly final goods.

10.   Import licensing has already been removed from some agricultural sectors. For example, since July of 1985 hogs and pork meats have no longer required import permits.

11.   Although the literature on the rationale and sequencing of trade reforms is extensive, the practical prob-lems faced by the policymaker when implementing trade reform have not received much attention. An effort to articulate these problems for Mexico is presented in Zabludovsky (1989).

12.   The trade reform package includes several programs involving neutral export incentives. The main ones are PITEX (Programa de Importacion Temporal para la Produccion de Articulos de Exportacion), DIMEX (Derechos de Importacion para la Exportacion) and ALTEX (Empresas Altamente Exporta-dora). The PITEX program was set up in May of 1985 and exempts firms from paying tariffs on imports of intermediate and capital goods. Entrance to the PITEX program has not been hindered by regulations: to join PITEX, a firm must

show only that it exports at least 10 percent of its output. It does not have to meet regulations concerning local-origin contents, imports volume, geographical location or ownership provisions. Such regulations vitiated the trade schemes that preceded PITEX and have been typical of industrial development programs in Mexico. The impact of the PITEX program on merchandise imports is notable. Thus, while in 1985 "temporary" imports accounted for 9.6 percent of merchandise imports, in 1988 they accounted for roughly 21 percent. The implied average annual growth rate is about 46 percent and the fastest growth is for temporary imports of intermediate goods.

The DIMEX program exempts exporting firms from import licenses on inputs, while the ALTEX program essentially simplifies import-export regulations for member firms. These firms, for example, do not have to employ chartered customs agents to process import-export paperwork, and imports can be inspected by customs at the business address of member firms rather than at the port of entry.

13. See "Las 200 Exportadoras," Expansion (Mexico), several issues. The reason for increases in export share might be a fall in total sales, of course, but this is by no means very common.

14. According to Banco de Mexico data, although manufacturing employment dropped by -3.2 percent on average over 1983-1987, employment losses were heaviest before the trade reform program took full force in 1985. Manufacturing employment dropped at an average rate of -5.4 percent over 1983-1984, compared to -1.7 over 1985-1987.

15. From October of 1987 to April of 1989, the antidumping authority received 76 complaints, 37 of which were dismissed early on for lack of supporting evidence. Of the 24 cases that have been accepted and resolved, dumping practices were found in only 7. The remaining 17 resulted in no action, due to insufficient evidence. In these instances, it would seem that oligopolies were in fact confronting competitively priced, and not dumped, imports.

16. These data come from the Planning and Budgeting Ministry.

17. Editors' Note: Please see the "General Comments" by Anne Krueger, pp. 251-253, as well as the "Comments" by Koichi Hamada and Juan Enriquez that immediately follow this paper for a further discussion of some of Zabludovsky's points.

REFERENCES

Aspra, A. "Import Substitution in Mexico: Past and Present," World Development, 5 (January-February 1977), pp. 111-123.

Balassa, B. "Trade Policy in Mexico," World Development, 11, No. 9 (1983), pp. 795-811.

Banamex, et al. (eds.). In-Bond Industry. Mexico City: Administracion y Servicios Internacionales, S.A, 1988.

Banco de Mexico. Indicadores Economicos. Several Issues.

Banco de Mexico. Informe Anual, 1987, 1988.

Bucay, N. and E. Perez Motta. "Mexico's Trade." In Dealing with the North, ed. by J. Whalley. CSIER Research Monograph. London, Ontario: The University of Western Ontario, 1987.

_____. "Trade Negotiation Strategy for Mexico." In The Small Among the Big, ed. by J. Whalley. CSIER Research Monograph. London, Ontario: The University of Western Ontario, 1988.

Bueno, G. "The Structure of Protection in Mexico." In The Structure of Protection in Developing Countries, ed. by B. Balassa. Baltimore, Maryland: The Johns Hopkins University Press, 1971.

Cardoso, E. and S. Levy. "Mexico." In The Open Economy, ed. by R. Dornbusch and F. L. Helmers. New York: Oxford University Press, 1988.

Cavazos, M. "Evolucion del Proteccionismo en Mexico," Comercio y Desarrollo (Nov.-Dic. 1977), pp. 28-42.

Cervantes, J. and J. Tapia. "Mexico - Un Modelo Econometrico del Impacto de la Apertura Comercial en la Balanza Comercial," Actividad Economica y Precios. Documento No. 40. Direccion de Organismos y Acuerdos Internacionales. Mexico City: Banco de Mexico, 1988.

Cordoba, J. "El Programa Mexicano de Reordenacion Economica, 1983-1984." In El FMI, el Banco Mundial y la Crisis Latinoamericana, ed. by SELA. Mexico City: Siglo XXI Editores, 1986.

De Mateo, F. "La Politica Comercial de Mexico y el GATT," El Trimestre Economico, 55 (enero-marzo 1988), pp. 175-216.

De Melo, J. and S. Urata. "Market Structure and Performance: The Role of International Factors in a Trade Liberalization." Discussion Paper No. 71, Development Research Department. Washington, D.C.: World Bank, 1984.

Expansion. Las 200 Exportadoras. Mexico. Several Issues.

192

Garcia Alba, P. and J. Serra. Causas y Efectos de la Crisis en Mexico. Jornadas 104. Mexico City: El Colegio de Mexico, 1984.

Gil Diaz, F. "Mexico's Path from Stability to Inflation." In World Economic Growth, ed. by A. C. Harberger. San Francisco: Institute for Contemporany Studies, 1985.

_____. "Macroeconomic Policies, Adjustment and Growth in the Long-Run." Paper prepared for the World Bank Conference on Macroeconomic Policy and Growth. Madrid, Spain, June, 1987.

Gil Diaz, F. and R. Ramos. "Lecciones desde Mexico." In Inflacion y Estabilizacion, ed. by M. Bruno, G. Di Tella, R. Dornbusch and S. Fisher. Mexico City: Fondo de Cultura Economica, 1988.

Gomez Oliver, A. Politicas Monetaria y Fiscal de Mexico: La Experiencia desde la Posguerra. Mexico City: Fondo de Cultura Economica, 1981.

Hierro J. and A. Sangines. "Public Sector Behavior in Mexico: 1970-1985," Mimeo, 1987.

IMF. International Financial Statistics Yearbook, 1988.

Ize, A. and G. Ortiz. "The Exchange Rate and Stabilization Policies in Mexico, 1983-1985." Paper prepared for the Conference on Exchange Rate and Inflation. Jerusalem, 1985.

Izquierdo, R. "Protectionism in Mexico." In Public Policy and Private Enterprise in Mexico, ed. by R. Vernon. Cambridge, MA: Harvard University Press, 1964.

King, T. Mexico: Industrialization and Trade Policies Since 1940. London: Oxford University Press, 1970.

Neary, J. P. "Short-Run Capital Specificity and the Pure Theory of International Trade," The Economic Journal, 88 (September 1978), pp. 488-510.

Ortiz, G. "Economic Expansion, Crisis and Adjustment in Mexico (1977-1983)." In The Economics of the Caribbean Basin, ed. by M. Connolly and J. McDermott. New York: Praeger, 1985.

Ortiz, G. and L. Solis. "Financial Structure and Exchange Rate Experience," Journal of Development Economics, 6 (December 1979), pp. 515-548.

Quintanilla, R. "Trade, Distortions and Employment in Mexico," unpublished Ph.D. Thesis. University of Minnesota, 1988.

Reynolds, C. W. Changing Trade Patterns and Trade Policy in Mexico: Some Lessons for Developing Countries. Research Memorandum No. 17. Center for Development Economics. Williamstown, MA: Williams College, 1967.

_____. The Mexican Economy: Twentieth Century Struc-
ture and Growth. Berkeley: University of California
Press, 1970.

Solis, L. Economic Policy Reform in Mexico. New York:
Pergamon Press, 1981.

Ten Kate, A., et al. La Politica de Proteccion en el
Desarrollo Economico de Mexico. Mexico City: Fondo de
Cultura Economica, 1979.

Ten Kate, A. and F. De Mateo. "Apertura Comercial y
Estructura de la Proteccion en Mexico en los Anos
Ochenta," Mimeo, 1988.

Thompson, J. K. Mexican Financial Policy: The Origins of
Economic Development with Price Stability. Greenwich,
Connecticut: JAI Press, 1979.

World Bank. "Trade Policy, Industrial Performance and
Adjustment." Report No. 6215a-ME. Washington, D.C.,
1986

_____. "Trade Policy Reform and Economic Adjust-
ment." Report No. 7314-ME. Washington, D.C., 1988.

Zabludovsky, J. "Panorama a Largo Plazo de la Economia
Mexicana." Mexico City: Committee of Economic Advisors
to the President, Mimeo, 1987.

_____. "Problems of Implementing Trade Liberaliza-
tion: The Mexican Case." Paper prepared for the World
Bank Workshop on Trade Liberalization. Annapolis,
Maryland, May 8-10, 1989.

Zedillo, E. "Mexicos's Recent Balance of Payments Experience and Prospects for Growth." UNDP/UNCTAD, Mimeo,
1985.

TABLE 1. Mexico's Macroeconomic Performance: 1960-1988

	1961-1970	1971-1982	1983-1988
GDP (% change)	7.02	6.10	-0.09
CPI (% change)	2.73	20.54	91.10
REAL EXCHANGE RATE (% change)	n.a.	108.58	136.20
FINANCIAL DEFICIT / GDP	1.56	8.46	13.02[a]
ADJUSTED OPERATIONAL DEFICIT / GDP	n.a.	9.4[b]	4.03
DOMESTIC ABSORPTION / GDP	97.81	99.05	90.59[c]
PRIVATE CONSUMPTION / GDP	71.03	66.11	62.30[c]
PUBLIC CONSUMPTION / GDP	8.05	9.72	11.58[c]
INVESTMENT / GDP	18.73	23.22	16.71[c]
CURRENT ACCOUNT / GDP	-2.08	-3.54	1.23

Source: International Financial Statistics, unless otherwise indicated. For 1985-88, GDP, CPI and current account ratios to GDP are from Banco de Mexico. Financial deficit data are from Gomez-Oliver (1981) for 1961-64, and Gil-Diaz and Ramos (1988) for 1965-86. Operational deficit and absorption data are from Banco de Mexico.

n.a. Not Available.
[a]1973-1987.
[b]1978-1982.
[c]1983-1987.

TABLE 2. Import Tariff Structure 1982-1989[a]

YEARS	TARIFF MEAN	DISPERSION	TRADE-WEIGHTED AVERAGE	NUMBER OF TARIFF RATES
1982	27.0	24.8	16.4	16
1983	23.8	23.5	8.2	13
1984	23.3	22.5	8.6	10
1985	25.5	18.8	13.3	10
1986	22.6	14.1	13.1	11
1987	10.0	6.9	5.6	5
1988	10.4	7.1	6.1[c]	5
1989[b]	13.1	4.3	9.8[c]	5

Source: Direccion General de Politica de Comercio Exterior. SECOFI.

[a]Data are end-of-year.
[b]Includes all modifications in the tariff structure up to March 9, 1989.
[c]Under the harmonized tariff system, trade data are now available only for July-November of 1988. Thus, the trade-weighted average tariff incorporates changes in tariff rates but uses weights corresponding to the 1982-1989 period.

TABLE 3. Domestic Input Content of the Maquiladora Industry by Region and Type of Industry: 1980, 1987

REGION AND TYPE OF INDUSTRY	DOMESTIC INPUT CONTENT (percentages)	
	1980	1987
NATIONAL AVERAGE	1.70	1.50
BORDER AREA	0.82	0.80
FOODSTUFFS	12.94	21.30
TEXTILE INDUSTRY	0.19	0.40
LEATHER PRODUCTS AND FOOTWEAR	8.57	2.50
FURNITURE	9.53	3.80
CHEMICAL PRODUCTS	3.00	3.90
TRANSPORTATION	0.26	0.60
ELECTRICAL MACHINERY & EQUIPMENT	0.05	0.10
NON ELECTRICAL MACHINERY & EQUIPMENT	0.17	0.70
ELECTRICAL AND ELECTRONIC ACCESSORIES	0.28	0.60
SPORTING GOODS AND TOYS	0.90	0.20
OTHER MANUFACTURING INDUSTRIES	0.72	0.10
SERVICES	11.35	1.50
INTERIOR AREA	9.95	6.90
TEXTILE INDUSTRY	5.94	2.90
LEATHER PRODUCTS AND FOOTWEAR	82.00	5.80
FURNITURE	3.33	n.a.
CHEMICAL PRODUCTS	n.a.	77.20
TRANSPORTATION	0.15	2.40
ELECTRICAL-ELECTRONIC MACHI. & EQUIP.	1.55	9.80
ELECTRICAL AND ELECTRONIC ACCESSORIES	5.17	1.00
OTHER MANUFACTURING INDUSTRIES	77.29	17.60
SERVICES	65.61	20.30

Source: Direccion General de Estadistica. INEGI.-SPP.

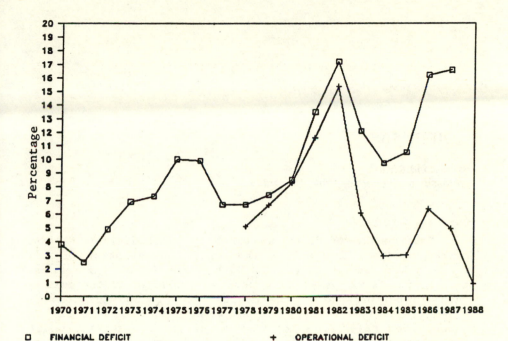

FINANCIAL DEFICIT   +   OPERATIONAL DEFICIT

Graph 1. Financial and Operational Deficits (As a percentage
          of GDP)

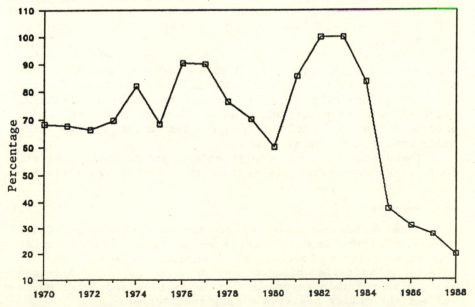

Graph 2. Controlled Import Value (As a percentage of total
          imports)

Comments

Koichi Hamada*
Professor of Economics, Yale University

Zabludovsky provides an excellent introduction to the Mexican economy in general and to the development of its trade policy in particular. With the help of informative tables, he first presents a concise overview of the macroeconomic performance of the Mexican economy and its remarkable volatility in desirable as well as undesirable directions. For example, a long period of price stability under fixed exchange rates until 1972 was followed by steady inflation and then high inflation combined with sizable declines of output. Total absorption, which surpassed 100 percent in 1975 and in 1980–1981, became less than 90 percent in 1988. This decline indicates courageous steps taken by Mexican officials to adjust the economy to the excessive external debt burden.

Even more remarkable is the process of trade deregulation and liberalization. I wish Zabludovsky had explained how this radical process of trade liberalization was at all feasible politically -- that account would be an exciting piece of work in political economy. But in any case, it is amazing to see so rapid a deregulation in an economy once under such strong import control.

Three points in particular attract my attention. First, Zabludovsky repeatedly claims that the highly protectionist

*The author is indebted to Masaaki Kuroyanagi, Chief Economist at the Export-Import Bank of Japan, who is now in the International Development Economics Program (IDE) at Yale, for valuable discussions on this paper. Opinions along with possible errors are strictly mine and by no means reflect the policy position of any institution.

policy of import substitution has anti-export biases. His point is certainly well taken, but as a theorist I wonder whether the underlying explanation is something like the Lerner symmetry theorem that import tariffs are equivalent to export taxes.

Second, the role of maquiladoras (in-bond plants) is extremely interesting. Do all of them function as full-fledged de jure duty-free zones, or are there some informal de facto elements as well? How do the legal and informal aspects interact? What is the importance of maquiladoras in total trade and what kinds of effects (including distortions) do they have on Mexico's industrial structure? These are fascinating questions to explore in further detail from a theoretical as well as a policy perspective.

Third is Zabludovsky's explanation for not addressing export trade reform:

> The ability to remove export licenses is constrained by their often having been established either to stay within export quotas set by international agreements (as in the case of oil, coffee and cocoa) or to comply with import quotas imposed on Mexico by its trading partners (as in the case of textiles and steel).

This is a typical example of how formal and informal trade restricting arrangements might eventually erode the free trade system itself (see Jagdish Bhagwati, Protectionism (MIT Press, 1988)).

In sum, I learned much from this paper about macroeconomic development and particularly the process of trade liberalization in Mexico. My major criticism of -- or perhaps frustration with -- the paper is as follows.

First, the discussions of trade liberalization and macroeconomic adjustment are given more or less independently. Trade liberalization generally reduces distortion in resource allocation, but at the same time it has a strong impact on macroeconomic performance. The real (and accordingly nominal) exchange rate appropriate for a highly protected regime will not be desirable for one that has been liberated. Reduction of tariff revenue will also affect the government budget. A proper combination of fiscal, monetary and exchange rate policies is essential for the success of trade liberalization policy, and yet the linkage is studied hardly at all in this paper.

Second, the reasons for trade liberalization's becoming the top agenda in the 1980s are not well explained. Why did Mexico bother to join in the GATT, which can be regarded as a club of industrialized countries, instead of enjoying the position of free rider? Was international political pressure from the IMF or the World Bank one of the reasons? Were there sufficient economic rationales -- aside from the benefits of free trade in general -- that suddenly became important at this particular moment? I wish Zabludovsky gave some explanation. (Also, weren't some modern projects like Sicartsa hurt by the uniform cut in government expenditures due to the austerity measures accompanying liberalization?)

Third, the discussion of total absorption is interesting but lacks the perspective of intertemporal consumption choice. Mexico has suffered from a "Dutch disease" and the prospect of oil surpluses encouraged consumption. Can the decline in total absorption be explained by the pessimistic outlook for future oil exports? What was the role of terms of trade in the spurt of non-oil exports? I am also curious about these questions.

Fourth, the effect of deregulation on rent-seeking processes is yet another important aspect of trade liberalization policy neglected in this paper. Wherever government regulation exists, there is potential for rent-seeking lobbying activities, which in turn may lead to bureaucratic as well as political corruption. Why didn't vested interests have sufficient clout to resist deregulation? How did deregulation affect these often unproductive activities?

Finally, I shall deviate from the paper a little to give my general observations on the debt relief issue for Mexico in particular and the world as a whole.

Suppose we were living in an environment where all the conventional assumptions of neoclassical economics were valid. In such a world it would be very difficult to make a case for foreign aid and debt relief except on humanistic and distributional grounds because problems of indivisibilities, increasing returns to scale and external economies would not exist. I am strongly aware that these concerns are of crucial importance in considering development issues -- without them economics would become a really cold, dismal science. But the objective fact is that without them, unless the above assumptions are invalidated, it is hard to make a case for foreign assistance and debt relief.

Consider two examples to illuminate this point. First, in the Solow type of growth model, the world economy would eventually reach balanced growth. If savings behavior were by individual rational calculation, the resulting stage would be Pareto optimal and hence would provide no economic justification for assistance or relief. Second, in a sophisticated dynamic game setting with reputation effects considered, the debt crisis would be viewed as the consequence of miscalculation by careless lenders and undisciplined borrowers. In order not to repeat this crisis, the best solution would be a cold turkey policy of penalizing those participants.

The question is whether we live in a world resembling such a neoclassical economic environment. Recent studies by Lucas and Romer suggest that increasing returns and external economies play an important role in economic development. Studies of the willingness to delay consumption imply that people do not save when they are extremely poor and that saving functions are non-linear. Population dynamics also involve non-linear responses or the mixture of differential and difference equations. All of these findings point to non-linear dynamics, which are more difficult to manipulate technically but at the same time provide the space for more dreams or visions than water-tight equilibrium analysis.

In my recent work with Kyoji Fukao of Hitotsubashi University on the long-run consequence of non-linear saving behavior, we found a case for foreign aid and debt relief purely on economic grounds. There is a watershed line beyond which a developing country's economy may be trapped in a subsistence-minimum equilibrium. If the fates are unkind and push the economy beyond this point to the perpetual destiny of subsistence, why do we not appeal to an angelic touch to pull it back to the side that leads to an harmonious equilibrium among nations?

In general it seems that there are many questions in economics in which non-linear behavior and evolutionary paths are important. Such questions about the economic development process as when people start working diligently, when they start substantial savings, when Marshallian external economies start working, and where and under what circumstances markets start functioning could be analyzed more properly by an approach that is itself evolutionary and non-linear.

The careful quantitative analysis underlying this paper is certainly a starting point for addressing such questions. The rich statistical data have made me wonder not only how this remarkably rapid deregulation was at all feasible, but also how it will change the qualitative behavior pattern of the Mexican people, especially those who engage in trade-related activities.

Comments

Juan Enriquez*
General Director of Metropolitan Services, Federal District

Close to 60 percent of the world's commerce takes place among the 600 million people who live in Japan, Europe and the United States. Most of the other 4 billion live on the outskirts, with limited access to technology and markets and little hope of a sustained rise from poverty. Those who live and prosper in modern economies are not business geniuses or super laborers. And in almost every case, they or their parents have from time to time allowed their country to go broke and be ravaged by war.

Nor are they doing everything right and manifesting competitive superiority in every area now. To take but one example, Japan's agricultural sector is so inefficient and pre-modern that consumers are forced to pay several times the world price for their daily staple, rice. The nation's distribution network is also grossly outdated and reportedly less than 13 percent of the work force is involved in activities that are internationally competitive. Nevertheless, the Japanese have focused carefully and worked very hard to produce, among many other things, 95 percent of the world's VCRs, 80 percent of the single lens reflex cameras and 68 percent of all motorcycles.(1)

As international trade continues to be dominated by the economic giants, Mexico's decision to enter into the global competition leads to some serious concerns. Zabludovsky's emphasis on the importance of a compatible macroeconomic framework is well placed, but I would like to raise some other key issues as well.

---

*The author wishes to thank Mary Schneider and Tito Vidaurri for their useful remarks on this paper.

Most of the jobs being created in export markets are in areas that either require a great deal of capital investment or are involved with the provision of services. Lack of adequate capitalization makes it evermore difficult for Mexico to improve its standard of living by using cheap labor as a strategic weapon. The second option, development of service industries, is an area Mexico has traditionally neglected.

Some indication of the results of trade liberalization can be obtained from examining those activities that are already working and competing directly in global markets, the maquiladoras (in-bond industries). Although this sector accounts for only 1.5 percent of Mexico's GDP, it has grown rapidly, particularly relative to the rest of the economy. Between January of 1986 and August of 1988, the number of people insured by the Social Security Institute in manufacturing and electronics increased by 256,000. This figure provides a rough indication of the formal nationwide job creation rate in these sectors. During this same period, the maquila program alone created 137,000 new jobs (53.7 percent of the total in these sectors).(2)

Nevertheless, dramatically reducing trade barriers in Mexico without first retraining our workers so that they can better face the new competition has been very costly. Cheap labor has not yet translated into a wave of national inputs that could make our manufacturing world competitive. Of the 14 billion pesos the maquilas exported from January through October of last year, Mexico provided only a billion pesos in value added. Wages and salaries comprise 45 percent of the value added by the maquilas and the sale of Mexican materials or packaging account for only 1.5 percent of the foreign exchange inflow. Thus, what Mexico mainly offers so far in this new competition is poor people who are willing to work long hours. The export-oriented industries, moreover, are highly localized: 93 percent of these jobs are in border states and 52 percent of them are in three municipalities.(3)

If labor were an increasingly important, or even stable, component of manufacturing costs, the maquila strategy might be successful. Many Mexicans will work for less than $4 per day while Americans get paid close to $30. Unfortunately, a cheap labor strategy in manufacturing is not viable in the long term. For the average businessman in the world economy, labor costs are less important in terms of total product cost than are transport and insurance. A substantial part of Mexico's new jobs are therefore being created from and depend on an input, low-cost labor, which is shrinking in global importance and is likely to generate less and less wealth.

Moreover, as tastes and production become international, the ability to introduce products quickly and widely becomes crucial. This requires an integrated business system that starts with technology and product design, passes through manufacturing and finishes with marketing, distribution, sales and service. Each step a nation completes competitively is likely to increase wealth. But Mexico has cut research and development drastically on one side of the chain, and few companies have the cash and knowledge to carry out marketing and distribution on the other.

Finally, the way the rules are established for the international trading system is particularly important. Most of the world's discretional income is now concentrated in Japan, Europe and the United States. Those suppliers who lose access to these areas are unlikely to find other markets rich enough to support their aspirations for export-led growth.

What, then, should Mexico's economic strategy be? In its search for a growing global niche Mexico must solve several basic problems and address such concerns as financing, the importance of services, the role of government, and international relations.

Financing is an area of increasing concern for Mexico. From the 1880s through 1950, for the most part we maintained a favorable trade balance. Then import substitution led to increasing deficits that became critical when Mexico started borrowing to finance its current account. Since 1981 the country has lost its ability to attract external credits from the international capital market. We are suffering the consequences of having enjoyed for a time a standard of living that we did not earn but rather borrowed. (An interesting parallel can be found in this respect with the current U.S. economic situation.)

If we are to grow, two financial decisions become critical. First is investment in basic infrastructure like roads, communications and knowledge processing. Second is a willingness to maintain a positive trade balance while working to make other options available. In this regard, the $5 billion drop in foreign exchange reserves from 1987 to 1988 (January through October) is very worrisome, particularly given current negative outflows. Even a very favorable solution to the current debt negotiations is unlikely to result in large and sustained flows of fresh debt financing from abroad. Investment and growth will therefore continue to be

constrained unless increases in direct foreign equity investment become a more significant part of Mexico's effort to
grow into foreign markets.

Given Mexico's large pool of high-level professionals,
trained and untrained workers, there should be far more
debate over why we are fighting for increasingly small
niches in world manufacturing while only 4 percent of the
maquiladora output is in the service area. This is, after
all, an area that represents over 70 percent of the U.S.
economy and in which labor remains a key cost component.
Some interesting experiments in services have ranged from
coupon and check processing to architectural draftsmanship.
Still, Mexican businesses remain focused mainly on manufacturing.

The Mexican government can be neither totally in charge
nor totally laissez-faire. Many bureaucrats must face a
harsh transition from their roles as powerful regulators
within a protected economy to those as outmoded government
employees in search of a justification for their salaries.
The PRI party is no longer winning every election. Tariffs
and discretionary policies no longer shackle the economy,
and 700 state enterprises have been sold, transferred or
closed while others struggle for profits. The result is a
shifting and risky political environment that rewards entrepreneurs and tends to diminish traditional forms of discipline and machine politics.

The international economic arena is also shifting and
risky, and even with domestic economic miracles, Mexico can
still be hurt by global recessions. Current U.S. economic
policies are eroding both the credit lines and the credibility we need to face a global financial crisis. If our
growth strategy depends increasingly on international openness, what happens to our standard of living if the major
trading blocs suffer an economic decline?

Mexico is not ready to become part of a common market,
but it can and should find areas of mutual benefit on a
company-by-company and sector-by-sector basis. This strategy requires supporting a large-scale effort to integrate
more closely with parts of the three major economic blocs, a
task far more ambitious than the current maquila process.

Mexico's traditional focus on friendly countries with
small economies must now be complemented by a pragmatic
business approach to Japan, Europe and the United States.
Aside from staying out of wars and maintaining our
independence, the key foreign policy priority must be
raising the economic welfare of our citizens. An important
step in this direction is maintaining access to global

trading blocs, an effort requiring a far more sophisticated lobbying, promotion and communications strategy.

Failure to communicate a clear image has confused and disconcerted other nations. To cite only one example, Mexico's favorable image in the United States has dropped 17 percent from 1976 to 1989. During this same period, the Soviet Union has improved its image by 95 percent.(4) Now, like Gorbachev, President Salinas has started to attack this problem by initiating much needed and spectacular reforms. We must be secure enough in our own culture and values that we do not fear competing and interacting with others. And we must also recognize that while trade liberalization has certainly made Mexico more open it has not necessarily made us more competitive.

NOTES

1.   Kenicht Ohmae, Triad Power, The Coming Shape of Global Competition (New York: Free Press, 1985).

2.   Instituto Nacional de Estadistica, Geografia e Informatica, Cuaderno de Informacion Oportuna No. 187, (Mexico, Octubre 1989); and Avance de Informacion Economica, Industria Maquiladora de Exportacion (Mexico, Diciembre 1988).

3.   Ibid.

4.   George Gallup, The Gallup Poll (Princeton, N.J., April 6, 1989).

Growth, External Debt and the Real Exchange Rate

Sweder van Wijnbergen*
Lead Economist, Mexico Department, World Bank

I. INTRODUCTION

Mexico's growth rate averaged 6.6 percent between 1950 and 1974, but between 1982 and 1987 there was no growth at all. This stark contrast sets the agenda for the next six years. Restoration of growth to rates that offer some hope of improvement in per capita income should be the predominant economic concern in the coming sexennio.

Of course, Mexico's growth in the more recent past was even better than 6.6 percent. Between 1978 and 1982 the economy grew at no less than an average annual rate of 8.7 percent. However, over the same period external debt tripled, from $29 to $86 billion. The ratio of external debt to GDP therefore jumped from 28 to 52 percent, the high growth rate notwithstanding. This period was brought to a crashing halt by the debt crisis of mid-1982. The 1978-1982 episode highlights the constraints under which the economy should operate even if not externally imposed; growth accompanied by unsustainable debt accumulation leads to later losses that more than offset the earlier gains. The Mexican agenda, therefore, is not just restoration of economic growth, but renewed growth within the limits set by creditworthiness.

---

*The opinions in this paper are the author's own and do not necessarily coincide with those of the institutions with which he is affiliated. The author thanks Willem Buiter, Rudiger Dornbusch, Reuben Lamdany, Alejandro Reynoso, Marcelo Selowsky and his colleagues in the Mexico Department in the World Bank for helpful comments and discussions. He is also indebted to Sergio Pena for excellent assistance with data collection and estimation.

Recent economic history has taught another lesson. The
outburst of spending in the late 1970s and the subsequent
decline in oil prices and increases in real interest rates
payable on the external debt caused serious public finance
problems. These in turn triggered a high rate of inflation
not seen earlier in Mexico's economic history. International evidence clearly demonstrates that high inflation rates
are accompanied by high relative price variability even when
underlying supply and demand factors show no such variability. It also adds fears of recessionary-causing stabilization programs. High inflation therefore precludes efficient
private sector investment at levels necessary for satisfactory output growth. Since economic stability is accordingly
a precondition for efficient economic growth, the agenda are
further restricted: to the external constraint are added the
fiscal constraints dictated by the requirement of low and
predictable inflation rates.

In sum, Mexico's economic circumstances raise the following questions. Can external restraint and internal balance be reconciled at levels of savings and investment that
allow satisfactory output growth? What is the role of fiscal policy, interest rates and exchange rates in bringing
such a configuration about? Should an attempt be made further to increase borrowing? What are the implications for
the future burden of the debt? To what extent do the
answers to all these questions depend on external events
such as oil price or interest rate shocks?

The remainder of the paper is organized as follows.
Section II sets the stage by providing a brief historical
overview of the developments leading up to the current situation. Section III assesses the limits on fiscal policy
imposed by the macroeconomic targets embedded in the stabilization program. Section IV provides a quantitative framework for discussing the possibility of achieving satisfactory output growth within these constraints without jeopar-
dizing external balance. It also considers the role of
exchange rates and fiscal policy, and traces the impact of
external developments on growth and external debt in Mexico.
Section V concludes the paper.

II. STABILITY, EXPANSION AND COLLAPSE: A BRIEF REVIEW OF THE PAST

Between 1950 and 1974, Mexico enjoyed a remarkable period of high growth, low inflation and moderate external debt accumulation. Real growth averaged 6.4 percent and inflation was in single digits throughout the period. This era of fiscal conservatism came to an abrupt end in the early 1970s. Rapidly expanding government involvement in the economy pushed up the rate of economic growth. However, increasing government expenditure was not matched by rising public sector revenues. At the same time, as real interest rates turned sharply downwards, a decline in the incentive to save prevented a matching increase in private savings. As a result, the inflation tax and external debt became increasingly important sources of finance. The period of single-digit inflation ended in 1973, the real exchange rate started to appreciate and thereafter growth in external debt accelerated beyond that in GDP.

Sharp adjustment measures in 1976 were not followed by a major crisis because significant oil discoveries and subsequent oil price increases provided relief from both fiscal and external problems. In fact the subsequent period was characterized by both rapidly expanding government revenue and vastly increased public sector borrowing. Measured by its share in value added, the government sector grew by almost one-third over this period. Government investment increased its share in total investment from 33.5 percent over the period 1970-1975 to substantially over 40 percent in later years. Not surprisingly, the real exchange rate once again started to appreciate, eroding the gains of the 1976 devaluation. This expansion was fueled largely from abroad: between 1975 and 1982 Mexico's external debt increased from $16 billion to $86 billion, but a rapidly appreciating real exchange rate masked this increase when measured as a share of GDP.

In 1982 rising world interest rates and falling oil prices put an end to the increasingly expansionary policies of the Lopez-Portillo administration. The subsequent cutoff from external capital markets left no option but fiscal retrenchment. After having run non-interest current account deficits in each of the preceding thirty years, Mexico suddenly needed to achieve surpluses in that account every following year. Nevertheless, the ratio of external debt to GDP shot up under the influence of rising interest rates and falling growth rates. The gap between real interest rates on external debt and real GDP growth went from -6.3 percent in 1980–1981 to a full +10.5 percent in 1983. Differences of this magnitude mean that the burden of debt will increase rapidly even without deficits on the non-interest current account, simply through the compounding of interest on debt inherited from the past. In addition, substantial capital losses on external debt resulted from the real exchange rate depreciation that was unavoidable given the major decline in oil revenues and the rise in real interest obligations. This added no less than 30 percentage points to the ratio of external debt to GDP during the period 1982–1987.

The counterpart to the non-interest current account improvement was a fiscal adjustment effort that is probably unmatched on a sustained basis by any other country. A primary fiscal deficit of 7.1 percent of GDP before the crisis was converted into an astounding surplus of 5.3 percent in 1987 and an estimated 7.6 percent in 1988. This turnabout occurred even as revenues from oil exports fell by more than 7 percent of GDP between 1983 and 1988 and GDP growth declined dramatically. Non-interest government expenditure was reduced from 34 percent of GDP in 1982 to about 25 percent in 1987. The public enterprise divestiture program was successful in closing or selling roughly 600 smaller entities, from a total of about 1200 at the beginning of the period, with additional negotiations initiated or scheduled to begin for a few larger enterprises. Mexico has also undertaken structural reforms at an accelerating pace over this period.

In 1983 a stabilization effort supported by the IMF halved the fiscal deficit, recovered international reserves and reduced inflation. However, some fiscal expansion and monetary relaxation occurred in 1984 and 1985, and on top of these policies came the earthquake late in 1985 and a major deterioration in the terms of trade in 1986 due to falling oil prices. In response, the authorities adopted a new stabilization program in July of 1986. In return for renewed monetary and fiscal austerity, this program also called for a concerted financing effort by Mexico's creditors.

The 1986 policy package included reforms designed to eliminate structural rigidities in the economy. The most significant change was a major reorientation towards exploiting the benefits of international trade. Spurred by a 42 percent real depreciation from July of 1985 to December of 1987, exports of manufactures overtook oil exports and more than compensated for the $7 billion loss in oil revenue over the same period. The trade liberalization process has gained momentum since 1985. Quantitative restrictions have been more than halved, tariffs reduced sharply and quantitative controls on non-oil exports almost eliminated.

The fiscal retrenchment was clearly unavoidable given the sudden lack of access to international capital markets and the series of adverse shocks to the terms of trade. As a by-product, the severe fiscal cutbacks have greatly increased the efficiency of many of the remaining government operations. But cutting the public sector investment budget from almost 10 percent of GDP in 1982 to an estimated 3.0 percent of GDP in 1989 clearly has its costs: government investment has a role to play in the social sectors and in areas that complement private investment. Moreover, private investment has not compensated for the decrease; indeed, it is surprising that the volatile macroeconomic situation has not led to a larger decline in private investment, which is now more or less at the level of 11 to 12 percent of GDP attained before the oil boom.

With lower investment on the one hand and restrictive demand management on the other, no real growth occurred between 1982 and 1988 and per capita income therefore declined severely. Rather than slowing down, inflation accelerated towards the end of the period, partially in response to a sharp nominal devaluation. This devaluation had become necessary because of the abrupt oil price decline in 1986. The subsequent de facto targeting of the real exchange rate, together with an increase in the frequency of wage and cost adjustments, introduced into the system an element of inherent instability that became fully apparent towards the end of 1987. The stock market plunge and a temporary opportunity for private debt buybacks evolving from the 1987 debt rescheduling triggered a run on the peso. This resulted in reserve losses and eventually a further 37 percent devaluation, again fueling inflation and expectations of further exchange rate depreciations. Mexico responded with the Pacto de Solidaridad, a concerted effort to bring down inflation that was now running well into triple digits.

The original Pacto and its revised successor, the PECE, have clearly been successful to date. Inflation was around 1 percent a month most of the second half of 1988. The March 1989 rate is back in this range, so a brief increase in December and January appears to have been temporary. Nevertheless, sustainability fears are not yet allayed: domestic interest rates are still over 50 percent when compounded on an annual basis, and slightly over 30 percent in real terms if the inflation target of 20 percent is met. These high rates are clearly related to worries about the public finance and exchange rate impact of the external debt situation.

III. CONSISTENCY OF FISCAL POLICY

A fiscal stance that does not conflict with sustained low inflation, even in the event of unfavorable external developments and continued high real interest rates, is clearly necessary, although possibly not sufficient, to allay inflationary fears. Only if the inflation compatible with public finance requirements is also compatible with the inflation rate implied by the fixed exchange rate regime, will the latter, which is the cornerstone of the Pacto, be sustainable. Because violating medium-term consistency requirements gives a signal that greatly complicates short-term macro-management, restrictions on both the overall deficit and its mode of financing are essential.

Revenues obtained from the regular tax system can be supplemented by three sources of financing for public sector expenditure: external borrowing, monetization and issuing of domestic interest-bearing debt. The amount that can be derived from each source will depend on other macroeconomic targets like inflation, output growth and interest rates. The revenue from these three sources can be combined into the calculation of a "financeable deficit". This is defined as the deficit that does not require more financing than is compatible with available external lending, existing targets for inflation and output growth, and a sustainable internal debt policy. If the actual deficit equals this "financeable deficit", fiscal policy is consistent with the macroeconomic assumptions and the targets lying behind the calculation.(1)

The framework suggested for this calculation is a model describing private portfolio choice as a function of inflation, output and interest rates.(2) The model indicates the amount of currency, demand deposits and time deposits the private sector is willing to hold given output, inflation and the level and structure of interest rates. This can be coupled with a simple financial sector model incorporating reserve requirements and other bank regulatory policies to derive the demand for reserves by commercial banks, which is then added to the demand for currency to estimate the total demand for base money. Total revenue from monetization, net of interest payments on reserves, can then be derived for different output growth rates, interest and inflation rates and regulatory policies. With the addition of the revenue the government can expect from external and internal debt issue, given its external borrowing policies and debt management approach, the financeable deficit can then be calculated.

The difference between the actual deficit in 1988 and this financeable deficit is the "required deficit reduction," RDR. A deficit cut equal to RDR will restore consistency with other macroeconomic targets. The results of such an exercise for Mexico are summarized in Table 1, which also indicates the effects of various assumptions about other macroeconomic variables.

Underlying the calculations presented in Table 1 is the assumption that the issue of interest-bearing domestic debt is low enough to keep the real value of the domestic debt constant. A faster rate of domestic debt issue is not allowed because of the high interest rate it currently carries: at around 30 percent per year (almost 40 percent by year end), it is well above the real growth rate of the economy and debt service would therefore escalate as a percentage of GDP if used more extensively to finance the deficit. Different options are explored for foreign financing. The first row of Table 1 assumes that the nominal value of the foreign debt stays constant (CAD=0). The second row looks at the consequences of changing that option either to a constant real value of the debt or to a constant debt/output ratio.

With no increase in net foreign debt, the 1988 operational deficit (4.4 percent of GDP) is seriously out of line with inflation targets, as the first row demonstrates. Either the actual deficit in 1988 needs to be cut by 4.4 percent of GDP for compatibility with an inflation target of 15 percent, or the entire operational deficit needs to disappear. These results reflect the fact that Mexico receives very little from the inflation tax and seigniorage, because of low growth and the practice of paying interest on reserves. Even for a 50 percent inflation target, the RDR still amounts to a hefty 3.3 percent of GDP.

Of course more liberal access to foreign financing changes all these results. The second row shows that the current deficit is compatible with an inflation target of 15 percent if enough foreign financing is available to maintain a constant debt/output ratio. A less liberal target would be constancy of the real value of the debt, which implies a 3 percent current account deficit, or refinancing of about half of the interest payments, with a correspondingly higher need to cut back on the fiscal deficit.

The third row of Table 1 shows how fiscal leeway increases with output growth given a constant debt/output ratio target for foreign borrowing. The RDR falls from 1.5 percent of GDP at a zero growth rate to -1.3 RDR at a 4 percent real growth rate for GDP.

Fiscal Implications of Debt Management

With real interest rate differentials at their current high levels, debt management takes on a great fiscal importance. Consider, for example, a debt-equity swap where $10 billion is retired by issuing a corresponding amount of public sector domestic debt to acquire the private equity used in the swap. With a staggering real interest rate differential of 25 percentage points, this operation would increase the real interest rate burden by no less than 1.5 percent of GDP, raising the required deficit reduction for a given inflation target correspondingly. The impact on the operational deficit would be 1.2 percent. The effect is smaller because the operational deficit, somewhat inconsistently, includes nominal interest charges on foreign debt, rather than real foreign interest payments as it does in the case of domestic debt. The whole operation would have a major impact on equilibrium inflation: at current interest rate differentials, even as small a debt-equity swap as the $10 billion considered here would raise equilibrium inflation by no less than 50 percentage points. (See van Wijnbergen, et al. (1988) for the methods used to arrive at this claim.) The large numbers are due to Mexico's very low base for the inflation tax: as mentioned above, commercial bank reserves carry essentially market rates, so the inflation tax base is only currency in hands of the public, an almost negligible amount.

These figures lead to the general question of domestic debt. At 1.5 percent real growth and no net increase in foreign nominal debt, the fiscal gap is 3.1 percent of GDP for 15 percent inflation. What if this gap were filled by issuing internal debt rather than foreign debt? Since interest rates on internal debt exceed the real growth rate by such a margin, this funding policy would solve current fiscal problems at the cost of substantially more serious ones in the future. It would raise the required deficit reduction for a 15 percent inflation rate from 4.4 percent to 5.3 percent of GDP within one year. If continued for six years, the debt/output ratio would have risen from 19 percent to 52 percent of GDP. Mexico should clearly avoid at almost any cost issuing internal debt during the current situation.

The final exercise demonstrates the extent to which high real interest rates are at the root of Mexico's current fiscal problems. Table 2 shows the equilibrium inflation rate, that is, the inflation rate requiring no fiscal adjustment, for various real interest rates on Mexico's internal debt. It assumes that no net increase in the nominal value

of the foreign debt is allowed, so that the external current
account deficit for the public sector is zero.

At the current interest rate, the required deficit
reduction is 4.4 percent of GDP; alternatively, an inflation
rate of 150 percent is needed to cover this amount through
an inflation tax. At a more reasonable 15 real interest
rate, the equilibrium inflation rate falls to 22 percent;
and at a real interest rate of 10 percent, it becomes zero.
As inflation rises, the elasticity of money demand
increases. Accordingly, additional revenue from the inflation tax falls, so that ever larger increases in inflation
are necessary to cover a given increment in the operational
deficit.

IV. MACROECONOMIC STABILITY, EXTERNAL BALANCE AND GROWTH: CAN THEY BE RECONCILED?

1. A Quantitative Framework

A. <u>Purpose and Structure of the Model</u>. The model
sheds light on the following key questions. Can the objectives of external balance and satisfactory output growth be
reconciled? What is the role of fiscal policy in this
trade-off? Which real exchange rate path is compatible with
the various policy scenarios and growth requirements? What
is the relationship between exchange rates and external balance? The model is used in an empirical investigation of
the role relative prices have to play in the trade-off
between output growth and external balance.

Real interest rates are an important variable in the
model. High rates depress private investment and consumption, thereby allowing larger fiscal deficits for any given
external balance target. At the same time, they complicate
fiscal management by raising the cost of servicing the domestic part of the public debt. The sensitivity of private savings and investment with respect to the real interest rate
are crucial parameters and receive detailed attention in the
empirical section below.

A second channel between fiscal policy, output growth
and external debt depends less on the relationship of aggregate fiscal deficits, real interest rates and the current
account than on the composition of the public sector expenditure program. A substantial part of aggregate investment
in Mexico has traditionally been undertaken by the public
sector. As a consequence, the government's allocation of
its total expenditure between consumption and investment is

an important determinant of output growth for any given aggregate expenditure level and time path of the real interest rate.

Another important relative price endogenized in the model is the real exchange rate. It affects the allocation of expenditures on different goods at a given moment of time, much as the real interest rate influences intertemporal expenditures for a given intratemporal allocation. (See van Wijnbergen (1989) for a detailed exposition of the theory underlying this model.) This approach differs from most other empirical models, where the real exchange rate, if endogenized at all, is often derived from current account considerations. In this setup, the real exchange rate also influences the current account, but in a rather complicated manner, through its impact on aggregate supply and investment behavior. No empirical evidence could be found to support the Laursen-Metzler notion that the real exchange rate also influences consumption expenditure.

It is in fact more natural to think of the real exchange rate as the relative price clearing the market for "Mexican" goods. Its equilibrium value is thus derived not from current account considerations, but from commodity market clearing conditions. The level of external transfers, the composition of government expenditure over home and foreign goods, and commercial policy all have an important impact on the real exchange rate in this approach. Explicit nominal exchange rate policies targeting the real exchange rate may, if successful, cause persistent commodity market disequilibrium (see van Wijnbergen (1989)).

The next subsection provides a simplified exposition of the analytical structure of the model. This is followed by discussion of the empirical application to Mexican data.

1)   Real Interest Rates, Fiscal Policy and Output Growth.   As long as domestic interest rates are not completely linked to foreign interest rates (plus exchange rate depreciation) there is an additional degree of freedom in macroeconomic policy. Changes in domestic real interest rates can then resolve potential discrepancies between fiscal deficits and external targets through their impact on the net private savings surplus, which equals private saving minus private investment. In the process, private investment and hence output growth will be affected. This is one of the more important links between fiscal policy and output growth embedded in the model. The mechanism is shown in Figure 1. Underlying this depiction is the following identity

derived from the national accounts, but with behavioral content built into private savings and investment functions:

$$CAS = FS + NPS(r)$$
$$= FS + PS(r) - PI(r)$$

The private sector's surplus of savings over investment, NPS=PS-PI, is shown as a function of the real rate of interest. A higher real interest rate will slow down private sector investment and increase private savings, thus increasing NPS, as represented by the upward-sloping line "NPS" in Figure 1. Empirical evidence on these effects is presented in Section IV.B.1.

The sum of NPS and the fiscal surplus (FS), or minus the deficit, equals the external deficit that is compatible with given real interest rates and FS. The external deficit is represented by the line CA in Figure 1. The horizontal line TCA is the target value for the current account. The real interest rate at which the current account target TCA equals the current account CA is the real rate at which fiscal policy and current account targets are in line.

An increase in the fiscal deficit represents a decline in the fiscal surplus and hence a downward shift in the current account line CA. To continue meeting the same current account target, the interest rate must rise to call forth the required extra surplus of private savings over private investment (r shifts from rA to rB). A cut in fiscal deficits will thus allow lower real interest rates for given current account targets, and hence higher private investment.

The analysis so far has focused on the impact of the fiscal deficit on private investment; but output growth depends on total, not just private, investment. Clearly, the impact of changes in fiscal deficits on output growth depends on whether the underlying adjustment is made from public investment or public consumption. The model therefore considers these components as well as their sum.

Of course, interest rate arbitrage between domestic and foreign rates may eliminate any leeway for the domestic real interest rate to reconcile fiscal deficits with current account targets so that another degree of freedom is lost. For any given rate of real depreciation, the link between fiscal deficits and the current account is direct if real interest rates at home and abroad cannot diverge more than the expected real rate of depreciation. The remarkably close link between the fiscal deficit and the current account in Mexico (see Figure 2) suggests that interest arbitrage is in fact taking place in Mexico; the no-arbitrage version of the model, with real rates reconciling fiscal deficits and external balance, thus seems too extreme. The model therefore fixes real interest rates instead of the fiscal deficit. The real exchange rate is not fixed in the real world, of course; nor is its rate of change exogenously given. Policy measures will have a direct or indirect impact on both the level and the rate of change of the real exchange rate. An analysis of these effects therefore follows.

2) <u>Commodity Market Clearing and the Real Exchange Rate</u>. The presentation until now has focused on the current account, fiscal deficits and the real rate of interest. But what about the real exchange rate? Popular discussions of the current account invariably involve this variable. Its inclusion stems from the days when the current account was analyzed using partial equilibrium trade-flow equations, with little attention to the underlying macroeconomic and intertemporal aspects. In modern theory the real exchange rate has an impact on the current account, but in a much more ambiguous and indirect manner than in the standard open economy models inherited from the 1950s and 1960s. The approach of this paper thus starts from the simple observation that the real exchange rate can be viewed as the relative price of Mexican (non-oil) goods in terms of foreign goods. (The "non-oil" qualification will be omitted in the remainder of this section.) The "market" cleared by the real exchange rate (possibly only after periods of disequilibrium) is the one for Mexican goods. The real exchange rate is thus a static relative price, measuring the rate at which two different (aggregate) commodities can be exchanged at a given moment of time. The real interest rate measures the rate at which commodities can be exchanged at different moments of time, through savings or investment processes; it is thus an intertemporal relative price.

Figure 3 provides a diagrammatical elaboration of the determinants of aggregate demand (see Edwards and van Wijnbergen (1988) for a similar approach in a static framework). One component of this demand comes from Mexican consumers and investors. At a more appreciated real exchange rate (de < 0, since e is defined as foreign over domestic prices, or the inverse of the relative price of home goods), Mexicans will tend to allocate their aggregate expenditure towards foreign goods rather than towards Mexican goods. Similarly, an appreciated real exchange rate will, ceteris paribus, cause lower export sales as foreign demand falls off. This effect is represented by the upward-sloping curve A_d in Figure 3.

Aggregate supply of Mexican goods is likely to increase when the real exchange rate appreciates (again, de < 0), if only because intermediate imports will then become cheaper in terms of Mexican goods (see the econometric evidence presented below). The aggregate supply curve A_s therefore slopes down in Figure 3. The equilibrium exchange rate equates the aggregate supply of Mexican goods with its demand -- at the intersection of A_s and A_d in Figure 3. Above that intersection, excess demand exists for home goods and output will be supply determined: the exchange rate is undervalued (excessively depreciated). Below the intersection, supply exceeds demand and output is demand determined; the real exchange rate is overvalued and there is Keynesian unemployment.

An increase in government expenditure on home goods would shift the A_d curve down, reducing excess supply and Keynesian unemployment problems. As a consequence, the equilibrium real exchange rate that clears the commodity market would fall.

3) <u>The Real Exchange Rate, Interest Rates and the Current Account</u>. What about the current account? The real exchange rate that equilibrates the aggregate demand for Mexican goods with their aggregate supply can do so at any level of the external deficit. An external deficit indicates that aggregate expenditure, by Mexicans but on both foreign and domestic goods, exceeds aggregate income. It provides no indication, however, that the aggregate demand, by Mexicans and by foreigners, but now for Mexican goods alone, is greater than the aggregate supply of Mexican goods at the going real exchange rate.

This ambiguity does not mean that the real exchange rate and the current account are entirely unrelated. Figure 4.A draws on the preceding figures and demonstrates how the current account, the real interest rate and the real exchange rate interact. Consider first commodity market equilibrium, GM, no longer in "e-A" space, but with the real exchange rate and interest rate on the axes. Assume that commodity market equilibrium obtains at E. A movement to the left (the exchange rate appreciates, de < 0), creates excess supply. This effect was also demonstrated by Figure 3. To restore equilibrium, demand must be curtailed. Because raising real interest rates lowers the demand for all consumption and investment goods (see the empirical evidence presented below), it also dampens demand for domestic goods, and the locus for commodity market equilibrium accordingly slopes upward in r-e space.

Consider next the combinations of r and e that will achieve a particular current account target for given fiscal policy. If that target is achieved at E, moving up (to a higher r) will lead to overachievement: higher real interest rates will, ceteris paribus, reduce private consumption and investment and thus lead to a CA improvement. Which way must the exchange rate move to bring the CA back in line with its target? As theory suggests, and the empirical analysis presented below confirms, the answer is sometimes unclear. Theory suggests that for a constant rate of time preference the exchange rate has no effect on the private consumption (see Razin and Svensson (1983)). The empirical analysis presented below supports this theory in the case of Mexico. Investment, however, will be affected negatively, mostly because of the impact of a devaluation on intermediate import prices. Because it is assumed that this effect shows up only after a lag of one year, in the short run the only influence in play is the negative impact of a real depreciation on aggregate supply. Thus in the short run a real devaluation is in fact likely to deteriorate the current account. However, in the longer run the negative effect on investment will reverse this impact, as in the standard J-curve analysis although through a different mechanism. Accordingly, a depreciation is necessary to restore the CA to its target in the short run (the CA curve also slopes upward, like the GM curve; see Figure 4.B), but in the longer run an appreciation will be necessary (CA slopes downward in Figure 4.A). Since this analysis has a medium-run focus, it concentrates on the case where the slope is negative.

What does this analysis suggest will happen if the real exchange becomes overvalued, say because of inertial inflation and a fixed nominal exchange rate? This situation is represented by the move from E to D in Figure 4.A. First of all, there will be excess supply of domestic goods and hence falling exports, declining capacity utilization and Keynesian unemployment. The effect on the current account depends upon whether the CA curve slopes up or down: if the latter, it deteriorates when moving from E to D; if the former, it actually improves. If the two effects net out, the current account is unaffected. In the medium run, however, a deterioration is more likely according to the empirical analysis presented below.

If the government responds to the rising unemployment and falling capacity utilization by raising government purchases of domestic goods rather than by devaluing, the GM curve shifts to the left and the commodity market problem is resolved. However, especially if this fiscal expansion is not matched by increased revenues, the CA will deteriorate and the CA curve shifts up so that the original CA target becomes increasingly unattainable. Thus an overvalued exchange rate will lead to unemployment and possibly to a deteriorating CA as time goes by, or to no unemployment but a real CA problem if fiscal policy is used to offset the employment effects of the overvalued exchange rate. In the latter case the appropriate policy response to falling exports and sluggish capacity utilization is in fact a real depreciation, to which a nominal depreciation may contribute.

Of course, as in the preceding subsection, interest rate arbitrage takes away one degree of freedom: the real interest rate, for given RATE of depreciation, confines the economy to the line at $r^* + \hat{e}$. It will also pin down the growth rate for any given public investment program, as illustrated in the left quadrant of Figures 4.A and 4.B.

B.   Empirical Results

1.   Aggregate Supply and Aggregate Demand. Consider aggregate expenditure first. Government expenditure on both consumption and capital goods is considered a policy instrument. Consumption expenditure depends upon estimates of permanent and temporary income and the after-tax real rate of interest. The measure of permanent income is based on a simple trend regression of real disposable income on time, with a trend break from 1984 onwards (so that the decline in 1983 is interpreted as a surprise). The results of this regression are:

(1) $\log(y_{DR,t}) = 2.19 + (0.063 - \text{D83PLUS}*0.017)*t$
          (64.9)   (21.3)   (7.21)

   $R^2 = 0.96$, DW = 1.58, 1965-1987

Inflationary expectations are derived from a four-year weighted average of actual CPI inflation rates. The predicted value of this weighting procedure is used in the calculation of real after-tax interest rates. The nominal rate is the nominal after-tax time deposit rate series presented in Gil-Diaz (1988) for 1965-1986 and the three-month after-tax time deposit rate for 1987. With these definitions of temporary and permanent income and the real interest rate, the econometric results for private consumption are:

(2) $\log(C_{pr,t}) = 5.18 - 0.44 \log(1+rr_{TD,t})$
       $\quad\quad\quad\quad(25.6)\ \ (1.83)$

$\quad\quad\quad\quad\quad + 0.70*\log(Y_{DR,T}) + 0.86*\log(Y_{DR,T})$
$\quad\quad\quad\quad\quad\ \ (4.41)\quad\quad\quad\quad\ \ (12.2)$

$R^2 = 0.97$, DW = 1.14, 1970-1987

The results are promising. The coefficient with respect to permanent income is highly significant, but not significantly different from one; the coefficient on temporary income is significantly lower than the coefficient on permanent income; and the coefficient on the real after-tax deposit rate is significant (at the 10 percent level) and negative. However, the low value of the DW coefficient indicates some remaining specification error. The regression results deteriorated significantly when the real exchange rate was included; its coefficients were never significant and it was therefore omitted. This finding has important consequences for the assessment of the impact of a real devaluation on the current account.

The second interest-sensitive component of aggregate expenditure is private investment (fixed capital formation). Private investment depends upon real interest rates, the relative price of intermediate inputs and the output/capital ratio as a proxy of capacity utilization, for which no data are available before 1980. The real interest rate is based on the pre-tax nominal interest rate reported in Gil-Diaz (1988); this rate is converted into a real rate using a GNP deflator on its own past values going back three years, plus a constant term. The predicted values of this equation are used as a proxy for inflationary expectations; this proxy, in turn, is used to derive the real interest rate, rr_{GNP}. The measure of intermediate imports prices is the dollar-based unit-value of intermediate imports deflated by the dollar-based Mexican GNP deflator. The results are:

(3) $\log(I_{pr,t}) = 0.75 - (0.60*\log(1+rr_{GNP}(-1)))$
       $\quad\quad\quad\quad(0.80)\quad\ (2.64)$

$\quad\quad\quad\quad - 0.26*\log(1+rrr_{GNP}(-2)) + 1.59*\log(y_t/K_t)$
$\quad\quad\quad\quad\ \ (1.05)\quad\quad\quad\quad\quad\quad\quad\quad(7.18)$

$\quad\quad\quad\quad - 0.30*\log(P_{Mint}(-1))/P_{GNP}(-1))$
$\quad\quad\quad\quad\ \ (2.12)$

$R^2 = 0.95$, DW = 1.23, 1970-1987

The results show a strong negative dependence of private fixed capital formation on real interest rates and on the relative price of intermediate imports in terms of final goods. Both enter with a lag, as should be expected: I_{pr} is actual investment expenditure, not orders.

Private investment and consumption expenditure plus total government expenditure and inventory accumulation (considered exogenous in the current version of the model) comprise aggregate expenditure. Aggregate supply of non-oil Mexican goods depends on the beginning-of-period capital stock, the relative price of intermediate imports and the relative price of final Mexican goods in terms of an index of the prices of foreign competitors abroad. This index is measured as an aggregate of the dollar-based WPI of Mexico's main trading partners, with 1980 export weights.

(4) $\log(y_t/K_t) = -2.02 + 0.39 * \log(P_{GNP}/P_f)$
                      (2.15) (5.51)

$+ 0.18 * \log(P_{GNP}(-1)/P_f(-1))$
  (2.95)

$- 0.13 * PDL(\log(P_{Mint}(-1)/P_{GNP}(-1))$
  (1.64)

$R^2 = 0.96$, DW = 1.38, 1974-1987

The equation shows a strong positive response to the (inverse of the) real exchange rate: a real appreciation increases aggregate supply. Both an increase in the relative price of intermediate imports and a decrease in the capital stock lower aggregate supply.

Aggregate employment, N_t, depends on the real product wage and on aggregate non-oil output:

(5) $\log(N_t)-\log(N_{t-1}) = 0.006$
                            (0.11)

$- 0.13 * (\log(W/P_{GNP}) - \log(W(-1)/P_{GNP}(-1))$
  (1.87)

$+ 0.54 * (\log(y_t)-\log(y_{t-1}))$
  (5.22)

$R^2 = 0.67$, DW = 1.74, 1966-1987

The elasticity of real wages is small, negative and significant at a 10 percent level; and the income elasticity is substantially below 1.

Next year's capital stock depends on this year's stock and on total fixed capital formation:

(6) $K_{t+1} = (1-0.04)*K_t + (I_{pr,t}+I_{G,t})$

The assumption of a 4 percent depreciation rate is based on SPP data with some correction for the national accounts' likely understatement of true depreciation during inflationary periods due to historical-cost accounting practices.

The current account identity rounds out the intertemporal part of the model:

(7) $CA = y_t + X_{oil}*P_{oil}/P_{GNP}$

$$- i^*B_f e_t - C_{pr,t} - I_{pr,t} - G_t$$

2) Allocation of Expenditure and the Real Exchange Rate. The part of the model presented in the previous section focused mostly on intertemporal trade. It thus dealt with the allocation of current production and expenditure over the present and future periods, rather than over domestic and foreign goods. In line with that focus, the most important relative price variable was the real interest rate. In this section, the focus is intratemporal trade, or allocation of expenditure over current Mexican versus current foreign goods, and the relevant relative price variable is the real exchange rate.

Consider first the allocation of domestic expenditure over foreign and domestic goods by explicitly estimating import demand equations for the different import categories. The volume of imported capital goods, Mcap, depends on their price relative to investment goods in general (the GNP deflator for investment) and on aggregate investment:

(8) $\log(Mcap) = 14.11 - 1.12*\log(P_{mcap}/P_{INV})$
          (5.93) (5.63)

$$- 0.74*\log(P_{mcap}(-1)/P_{INV}(-1))$$
          (2.72)

$$+ 0.71*\log(I_{pr}+I_g) - 0.88*MQUSH(-1)$$
          (5.77)   (4.52)

$R^2 = 0.94$, DW = 1.40, 1970-1987

The variable MQUSH is the fraction of imports covered by quantitative restrictions; it is included in an admittedly crude attempt to capture the many changes in Mexico's trade regime during the sample period. The results show relatively high elasticities, all estimated with great precision as indicated by high t-statistics. The trade regime variable seems to pick up the degree of the policy's repressiveness: it enters with a strong negative sign.

Consider next imports of consumption goods, Mcon:

$$
(9) \quad \log(\text{Mcon}) = \underset{(0.94)}{2.34} - \underset{(4.85)}{2.12} * \log(P_{mcon}/P_{CPI})
$$

$$
- \underset{(2.7)}{1.23} * \log(P_{mcon}(-1)/P_{CPI}(-1))
$$

$$
+ \underset{(4.15)}{1.31} * \log(C_{pr}) - \underset{(2.54)}{0.96} * \text{MQUSH}(-1)
$$

$$
R^2 = 0.82, \ DW = 1.54, \ 1970\text{–}1987
$$

Once again price elasticities are high and significant and the impact of the proxy for trade intervention is strong and negative.

Finally, consider the demand for intermediate imports, Mint:

$$
(10) \quad \log(\text{Mint}) = -\underset{(2.20)}{18.7} - \underset{(5.29)}{0.64} * \log(P_{Mint}/P_{GNP})
$$

$$
+ \underset{(10.2)}{2.84} * \log(y_t) - \underset{(1.34)}{0.96} * \text{MQUSH}(-1)
$$

$$
R^2 = 0.91, \ DW = 1.40, \ 1970\text{–}1987
$$

This equation shows a somewhat lower, although still highly significant price elasticity and an unusually high income elasticity.

The total demand for Mexican goods by domestic residents in any given period can be deduced by combining the import demand equations with the equations for aggregate domestic expenditure, and scaling by the relevant relative prices. However, completing the analysis of commodity market equilibrium in the market for (non-oil) Mexican goods requires an additional element: foreign demand for Mexican goods, or export demand.

The specification of the export demand equation assumed that Mexican exporters compete not so much with domestic producers in Mexico's export markets, but with other exporters to the same markets. This is a reasonable assumption, given that Mexico's two main export markets are the United States and the EEC. Empirical analysis for other developing countries tends to confirm this view (see Kharas (1988), van Wijnbergen and Arslan (1989)). The relevant activity variable is therefore aggregate imports into Mexico's export markets (weighted by their share in Mexico's total exports), and the relevant relative price variable is the ratio of Mexico's export price over the aggregate price index of imports into Mexico's export markets. The regression then yields:

$$(11) \quad \log(XD_{noil}/XD_{noil}(-1)) = 1.55$$
$$(0.96)$$

$$- 0.95 * \log(RPXPF/RPXPF(-1))$$
$$(2.79)$$

$$- 0.12 * \log(RPXPF(-1)/RPXPF(-2))$$
$$(0.40)$$

$$+ 1.50 * \log(MF/MF(-1))$$
$$(3.38)$$

$$R^2 = 0.59, \quad DW = 2.56, \quad 1968\text{-}1987$$

$RPXPF = (P_X/P_{MF})$ is the dollar price of Mexican non-oil exports over the aggregate dollar-based price index of imports into Mexico's export markets. MF is the volume of imports into those markets, weighted again by each country's share in Mexico's total non-oil exports. Analysis of the error structure suggested estimation in terms of rates of change rather than (log) levels. The equation performs reasonably well: it has significant price elasticities and a high, significant "income" elasticity. However, distinguishing different export markets would probably be useful.

The model is completed by an equation for the commodity market clearing of current Mexican non-oil goods:

$$(12) \quad y_t = C_{pr,d} + I_{pr,d} + G_d + XD_{noil}$$

In this set-up, the relative price of exports in terms of aggregate home goods, $RPXPF = (P_X/P_{MF})$, is considered exogenous. This assumption is relaxed in the next section.

3) **An Extension: Export Supply Considered Explicitly.**
The analysis presented so far made no explicit distinction
between the supplies of home goods for domestic versus foreign markets.   Hence there was only one domestic output
price.   In practice, however, it is more than likely that
such an explicit distinction does exist, either because of
product differentiation or because of non-competitive market
structure and different degrees of competition in home and
foreign markets.   A shorthand way of capturing this difference would be to endogenize the relative price of exports
versus goods sold at home and estimate an explicit export-
supply function, where firms choose to sell at home or
abroad depending on that relative price.   Commodity market
equilibrium would then involve two separate equations, one
for goods sold at home and one for goods sold abroad.   The
latter estimation, with $RPXY = P_X/P_{GNP}$, follows.

(13) $\log(XS_{noil}/y_t) - \log(XS_{noil}(-1)/y_t(-1))$

$$= 0.12 + 0.12*\log(RPXY/RPXY(-1))$$
$$(0.41) \quad (0.63)$$

$$+ 0.51*\log(RPXY(-1)/RPXY(-2))$$
$$(2.76)$$

$R^2 = 0.31$, DW = 1.97, 1966-1987

The R^2 is low, as is to be expected for an equation estimated in rates of change; but supply elasticity with respect
to price is significant and has the "right" sign.   In this
set-up, equation (12) is replaced by commodity market clearing for goods sold at home and for goods sold abroad:

(12a) $y_t - XS_{noil} = C_{pr,d} + I_{pr,d} + G_d$

(12b) $XS_{noil} = XD_{noil}$

The extra relative price variable is RPXY.

2.   **The Framework Applied: Mexico's Outlook for Growth**

A.   **Private Savings, Investment and the Current
Account: Is There Room for Growth?**   The base case begins
with an assumption of moderate (2 percent of GDP) current
account deficits over the next two years.   It generates less

than half of the interest due and at projected world inflation rates would result in a fall in the real value of the
debt. From 1992 onwards, a slight widening of the CA deficit to 3 percent of GDP is assumed. This scenario is roughly compatible with a constant real value of the external
debt and a falling debt/output ratio, since by that time
growth will be gathering steam.

Given projected private savings and investment developments, what does this target imply for fiscal deficits? The
model runs suggest that the non-interest budget surplus
would have to average around 7 percent for most of the
period, down from 7.6 percent in 1986. This is below the
consistency requirements derived in Section III in the first
two years when real interest rates are likely to stay high.
But it is above what is necessary towards the end of the
sexennio when, if all goes well, real rates should drop to a
more reasonable risk premium over foreign real rates. Real
rates are assumed to stay at 30 percent in 1989 and then to
fall to 20 percent in 1991 and 10 percent from 1992 onwards.
The operational surplus would thus recover from its likely 3
percentage deficit in 1988 and a projected deterioration in
1989 to approximate balance by the end of the sexennio.

Private consumption as a share of GDP is projected to
slow down somewhat next year and to recover the lost ground
later in the sexennio. Public investment is assumed to fall
slightly in 1989 due to budgetary restraint, but to recover
gradually thereafter, becoming 5 percent of GDP in 1990 and
climbing to 6.5 percent at the end of the sexennio. Total
investment and thus output growth depend on private investment behavior, which in turn depends on real interest rates
and the tax policy followed. Without any tax credit, investment is projected to slow down under the impact of continuing high real interest rates, falling almost 2 percentage
points of GDP in 1990 compared to 1988. As a consequence,
total investment, which was 15.4 percent of GDP in 1988,
would fall by 1 percentage point in 1989, gradually recover-
ing thereafter to reach 18.5 percent of GDP towards the end
of the sexennio.

This investment behavior would lead to a resumption of
growth, but in a rather unspectacular manner (see the solid
line in Figure 5.A). After a projected growth of 1.5 percent in 1989, output growth would slowly climb from 2 percent in 1990 to 3.7 percent in 1993 and 3.9 percent in 1994.
Under the influence of lower real interest rates, private
investment, after dropping initially, would have recovered
by then its 1988 value of around 12 percent of GDP (see the
solid line in Figure 5.B). The main impetus would in fact

come from government investment, which would rise by between 2 and 3 percent of GDP over the sexennio.

An investment tax credit along the lines of the one that has been on the books since 1988 would have a significant impact, especially in the early years where real interest rates are high, because the scheme has been constructed to give bigger credits for higher real interest rates. Rather than dropping by a full percentage point in each of the first two years of the sexennio, private investment would now hardly fall at all in 1989 (down to 11.9 percent from 12.1 percent of GDP in 1988, as indicated by the dotted line in Figure 5.B). A strong recovery would then follow as the tax credit reached its full impact. Private investment would rise to a peak of 14.1 percent of GDP in 1992, after which it would taper off slightly as the declining value of the tax credit more than offset the impact of falling real interest rates. The end result would be a still respectable 13.5 percent of GDP by 1994.

Since public investment would not be affected by the tax credit, total investment would increase in line with private investment, to reach around 20 percent in the last three years of the sexennio. As a consequence, real growth would accelerate; as indicated by the dotted line in Figure 5.A, because of the tax credit it would reach 4 percent in 1992 rather than in 1994. In the last two years of the sexennio, this scenario projects growth at a healthy 4.7 percent a year.

Stronger investment performance under the same current account target of course requires higher private and/or public sector savings to maintain the same current account performance. The econometric model runs suggest that under this high-growth scenario, private consumption would grow faster than before, but less than GDP. As a consequence, private savings would increase to provide extra leeway of between 0.5 and 1 percentage point of GDP towards the end of the sexennio. Fiscal improvement would have to make up the remaining difference. An initial improvement of between 1 and 1.5 percent of GDP in the non-interest surplus would be necessary to accommodate the increased investment by the private sector. Reforms in tax administration and the structure of personal income and property taxation take on an added importance in this context, and international comparisons of personal income taxes suggest that such an improvement in public sector revenue is not infeasible.

What about debt and the exchange rate under all these scenarios? Under both scenarios, net external debt would decrease as a percentage of GDP, but it would fall faster under the high-growth scenario. Without the investment tax credit, net external debt would decline from 67 percent of GDP in 1988 to 56 percent at the end of the sexennio. Under the high-growth scenario it would actually decrease to 54 percent of GNP by 1994.

The model was run assuming a constant real exchange rate throughout both periods. Accordingly, a potential imbalance exists between the aggregate demand for and supply of Mexican (non-oil) goods. The ratio of the total demand for (non-oil) Mexican goods by foreigners (export demand) and by domestic residents to the aggregate supply of Mexican goods can thus be interpreted as an indicator of exchange-rate misalignment. A decline below 1 suggests exchange rate overvaluation (see Figure 6.A). The model run suggests that exchange rates may in fact become a problem early in the sexennio. The ratio is projected to drop from 89 percent in 1988 to 86 percent in 1989. The situation would then improve as increasing investment raised the demand for domestic goods. Under the scenario of no tax credits, the ratio improves rapidly after 1989 and actually reaches 1 by 1993. Growth in 1989 could therefore actually be restricted because of low aggregate demand for Mexican goods at the current relative price (the real exchange rate). A real devaluation would help avoid this problem by shifting domestic and foreign expenditure towards Mexican goods; at issue, however, is whether a real devaluation can in fact be achieved under the Pacto.

Some comments on employment complete this section. The real wage was assumed to rise at 4 percent per annum. According to the econometric analysis, this increase would just offset the autonomous rise in the demand for labor for given GDP. However, with a modest 0.64 estimated labor demand elasticity with respect to GDP, employment growth would be only 0.7 percent for the first two years, then rising gradually to 2 percent at the end of the sexennio. It is not clear that the projected increase in the labor force can be absorbed into productive employment under these circumstances.

B. External Financing, Output Growth and the Public Sector. The scenario has assumed so far that the foreign financing necessary to cover a current account deficit of between 2 and 3 percent of GDP would indeed be forthcoming. Additional financing would therefore be required because Mexico has just entered a period of substantially increased repayment obligations. The implicit assumption is that these can be refinanced, and that additional funds will be

available to allow a current account deficit of 2 percent of
GDP initially and 3 percent later on.   Alternatively, debt
relief could provide the necessary room, in which case the
necessary decline in the non-interest current account could
be reached without a deterioration in the current account
and less new money. Of course, in the current external environment it is conceivable that more funds cannot be raised.

    This section considers two additional scenarios.   The
first allows Mexico to run the same current account deficit
as before, but involves a major debt reduction of about 20
percent of 1988 GDP early in 1989 so that the value of the
outstanding commercially held debt is halved.   The second
alternative outlines what is likely to happen when no debt
reduction takes place and the only new money that comes in
is rolled-over principal.   In this case Mexico would have to
run a zero current account deficit.   If the government
attempts to maintain its stabilization effort, it is highly
unlikely that domestic interest rates will come down.   Under
this latter run, therefore, domestic real interest rates
would stay at their current 30 percent level.

    Consider first the case of neither new money nor debt
relief.   Mexico would simply run a current account balance
of zero, fully paying interest but rolling over principal.
The macroeconomic consequences would clearly depend on how
the internal adjustment to this external shock took place.
Would the fiscal sector adjust one for one?   If so, would
the adjustment be through cuts in government consumption or
cuts in public sector investment?   By assumption, public
investment would be cut back in line with the decline of
"allowable" external net borrowing and private investment
would also fall because of higher real interest rates.

    The external shock would reduce GDP by 2 percent ini-
tially, and by 3 percent from 1993 onwards.   Public investment would fall to an absurdly low 0.9 percent of GDP initially, never regaining the 3 percent level assumed for 1989
in the base case.   It would hover instead around 2.7 percent
of GDP for the rest of the sexennio.

    This investment behavior would clearly have a major
impact on growth (see Figure 6.B, line "YGROCAOHR").   Output
growth would slow down by 1 percentage point initially; as
time went by the fall in growth would deepen to more than 2
percent by the end of the sexennio as private and public
investment declined.   On average over the next six years,
growth would fall by almost 2 percent of GDP, to reach only
2 percent at the end of the sexennio and less than that
before.   The slowdown in growth would have a perverse multiplier effect on the need for public sector adjustment.

Slower growth would lead to a decline in private sector savings, so that a larger fiscal adjustment would become necessary. Because of higher domestic real interest rates, however, private investment would also fall and create more room for public sector deficits given the CA constraint.

Employment growth would slow down as well, exceeding 1 percent in no year of the sexennio. Finally, the exchange rate misalignment indicator would also drop, never coming close to 1 (see Figure 6.A). Under this scenario, exchange rate misalignment would be a continuing problem. The conclusion is that without access to external funds a real devaluation is unavoidable. This is of course the main channel through which uncertainty on the external debt situation influences domestic real interest rates.

The debt-relief scenario paints a substantially rosier picture. Figure 6.B shows that with a 2 percent CA deficit increasing to 3 percent in 1992 and a 50 percent reduction in commercially held debt, output growth would probably come earlier and go farther than in the base case. Moreover, the problem of exchange rate misalignment, while still present in 1989, would disappear towards the second half of the sexennio.

The message of this section is clear: unless debt relief or long-term new money is provided on a scale allowing private investment to recover, growth of both output and employment is not possible. Renewed output growth is incompatible with full service of the existing debt.

C. External Shocks: Oil Prices and World Interest Rates. A simple rule of thumb already indicates Mexico's sensitivity to changes in world interest rates and oil prices. One dollar less per barrel of oil costs Mexico annually approximately $0.5 billion, and 1 percentage point in the world interest rate adds $1 billion to the servicing burden of its external debt. Thus the recent rise in world interest rates (over 2 percentage points since March of 1988) costs Mexico roughly 1 percentage point of GDP, or half of the "low case" scenario explored in the last section.

However, interest rates in particular have an impact that goes beyond their income effect. Interest arbitrage would almost certainly lead to higher interest rates in Mexico if world interest rates rose. A further negative impact on output growth would therefore probably occur through a decline in private investment. Figure 7 shows the net effects.

Once its impact on public and private investment were fully incorporated, the recent rise in interest rates would lead to a fall in the growth rate of almost 1 percentage point towards the end of the sexennio. This underscores the extent to which Mexico's problems are by now mostly foreign-made. According to some estimates, a $150 billion cut in U.S. deficits (the Gramm-Rudman target) would lower real interest rates by 3 percentage points (van Wijnbergen (1985)). The U.S. fiscal deficit can thus be blamed for a 1.5 percentage point drop in Mexico's growth rate in each year it is in effect.

V.   CONCLUSIONS

Without renewed access to foreign capital markets, Mexico faces a grim fiscal situation. Unless the net nominal foreign debt increases, a 15 percent inflation target requires for fiscal consistency no less than a 3 percent increase in the non-interest surplus, up from the already extraordinarily high 7.6 percent primary surplus in 1988. Put in perspective, it would amount to a wholesale scrapping of the entire public sector investment program. In fact, the fiscal effort should be even larger: at unchanged policies the operational deficit is likely to worsen in 1989 unless there is a substantial turn-around in the international price of oil. Measures to offset this increase would come in addition to the 3 percent.

An adjustment this large would clearly be a very difficult task after the massive fiscal retrenchment of the past few years. Issue of indexed domestic debt could alleviate the fiscal problem caused by high domestic real interest rates; but another conclusion seems inevitable. As long as internal interest rates remain as high as they are, Mexico's fiscal problems are intractable without renewed access to foreign capital markets. The analysis suggests that roll-over of half or two-thirds of foreign interest payments, in addition to principal payments, would bring a solution within reach. The paper also demonstrates that service of the face value of the current debt without substantial amounts of new money is incompatible with renewed output growth and accordingly is not in any group's real interest.

An important issue is the macroeconomic impact of the particular approach taken to debt relief. The paper demonstrates that swaps of public debt for private equity would raise the equilibrium inflation rate substantially if implemented on a scale that is interesting from a macroeconomic point of view.

But without access to foreign capital markets in one form or another, output growth would be compromised, as the simulations have shown. Moreover, low growth would immensely complicate the funding policies of the public sector. In addition, with low growth and a high resource transfer to foreigners, the real exchange rate would need to be devalued much more than would be necessary with a smaller resource transfer out of Mexico. Low growth because of insufficient access to foreign capital markets would thus also jeopardize the short-term stability sought under the Pacto. Renewed access to foreign capital markets is therefore not only imperative for restoration of medium-term growth, but also essential for the success of the current short-term stabilization effort.

The increase in external debt implied by renewed access to international capital markets does not really threaten Mexico's credit-worthiness. Even a current account deficit of 3 percent of GDP (about $5 billion) per annum, with a corresponding increase in external debt, would simply keep the external debt constant in real terms. Thus the debt/output ratio would in fact decline even at moderate rates of growth. On the other hand, a cut-off from external capital markets, with the attendant short-term stabilization problems and likely medium-term slow down in output growth, would compromise Mexico's ability to service even its current debt. Thus, paradoxically, lending to Mexico would very likely increase, not decrease, the expected net repayment in discounted value terms, the increased up-front borrowing notwithstanding.

This analysis depends crucially on developments in world commodity and capital markets. The income effects of a percentage point increase in the world interest rate is roughly equal to the income effect of a $2 decrease in the price of oil. Both cause Mexico to lose almost $1 billion a year. But higher world real interest rates are likely to create at least equivalent increases in real interest rates in Mexico, and possibly more if they lead to expectations of devaluation. They thus have a stronger impact on economic growth than oil price changes with equivalent income effects. As an example, the paper demonstrates that the effect of an increase of 2 percentage points in world interest rates between March of 1988 and March of 1989 slowed down Mexico's growth by an estimated 1 percentage point. The lesson seems to be that any external debt arrangement should include contingency clauses conditional on oil price and foreign interest rates. Otherwise it might be difficult to maintain stable growth amidst the vagaries of international developments.

With foreign financing in place and the internal reform program continued and deepened beyond the considerable progress already made, a cautiously optimistic prognosis seems justified. The analysis presented suggests that a recovery of growth is then likely to begin by the end of 1989, with positive per capita growth expected thereafter. Moreover, Mexico's debt indicators are projected to decline substantially in spite of the additional funding required from abroad. With a continuation of the government's reform program, investing in Mexico promises a high pay-off.

NOTES

1.   This should be interpreted with care. Consistency with macroeconomic targets is no guarantee of possible or actual achievement of these targets. Indeed, the latter may require other measures, possibly including fiscal retrenchment beyond what is required for consistency as defined here.

2.   A simple version of this framework was first used in Anand and van Wijnbergen (1989). The current version incorporates external debt considerations and implications of the financial structure for inflation tax revenues (van Wijnbergen and Anand (1988)).

REFERENCES

Anand, R., and S. van Wijnbergen. "Inflation and the Financing of Government Expenditure in Turkey." World Bank Economic Review (1989).

Dornbusch, R. "Mexico: Stabilization, Debt and Growth." Economic Policy, Vol. 7, Issue 1 (1988).

Gil Diaz, F. "Macroeconomic Policies, Crisis and Growth in the Long Run: Mexico Country Study." Mimeo, World Bank (1988).

Ize, A. "Savings, Investment and Growth in Mexico: 5 Years after the Crisis." Working Paper No. 89-19, Fiscal Affairs Department, IMF (1989).

van Wijnbergen, S. "Real Exchange Rate Rules, Employment and the Current Account." Mimeo, World Bank (1989).

van Wijnbergen, S., and R. Anand. "Inflation, External Debt and Financial Sector Reform: a Quantitative Approach to Consistent Fiscal Policy." NBER Working Paper No. 2170 (1988).

TABLE 1.   Required Deficit Reduction (RDR) for Consistency
With Various Macroeconomic Targets (as percent of
GDP)

1.   No Real Exch. Depreciation; CAD=0; Output Growth 1.5%

Inflation Targets	p:	0	5	15	50
	RDR:	5.1	4.8	4.4	3.3

2.   No Real Exch. Depreciation; Inflation 15%; Output
Growth 1.5%

For. Borrowing	CAD:	0	3.1[a]	4.0[b]
	RDR:	4.4	1.3	0.4

3.   No Real Exch. Depreciation; Inflation 15%; Const. B*/Y
Ratio

Output Growth Targets	n:	0	1.5	4	5
	RDR:	1.5	0.4	-1.3	-1.9

4.   Inflation 15%; Output Growth 1.5%; Const. B*/Y Ratio

Real Exch. Rate	c:	0	5	10
Depreciation	RDR:	0.4	3.0	5.7

[a]Constant real debt case
[b]Constant debt/GDP case

c   : Rate of depreciation of the real exchange rate
CAD : Current account deficit
n   : Growth rate of real GDP
p   : Inflation rates
RDR : Required cut in fiscal deficit compared with 1988
      (operational) deficit
B*,B: Foreign, domestic debt
Y   : GDP

TABLE 2.   Equilibrium Inflation and the Real Interest Rate
on Internal Debt

No Real Exch. Depreciation; CAD=0; Output Growth 1.5%

Real Int. Rate on Dom. Debt	R:	30	15	10
Equilibrium Inflation	p:	150	22	0

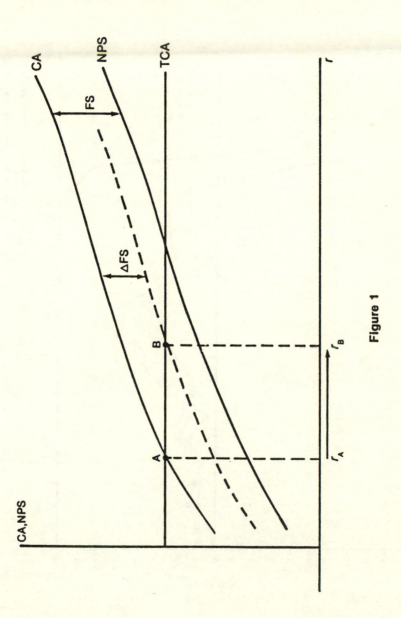

Figure 1

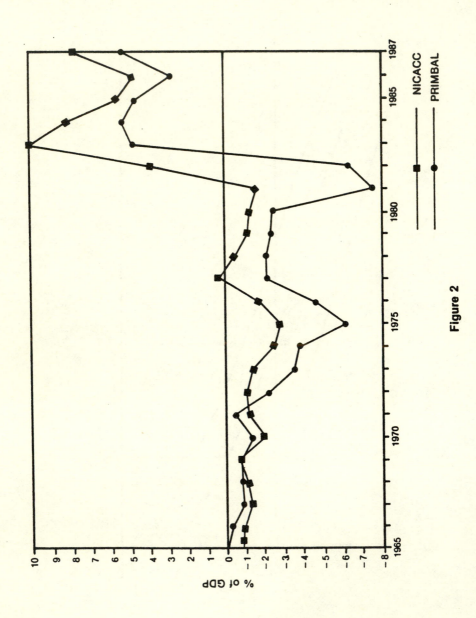

Figure 2

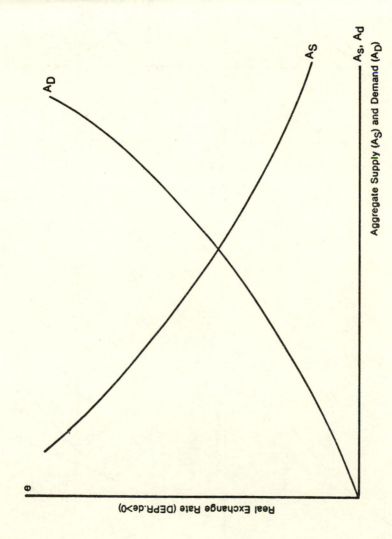

239

Figure 3

240

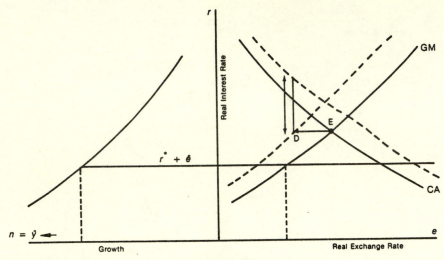

Figure 4.A

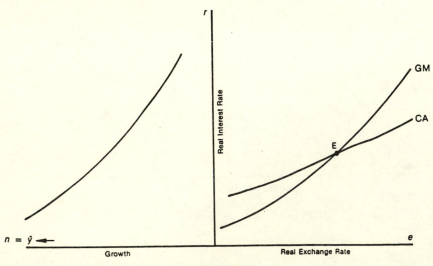

Figure 4.B

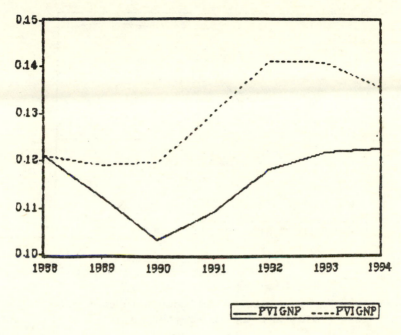

Figure 5A.   Base case private investment with and without
accelerated depreciation.

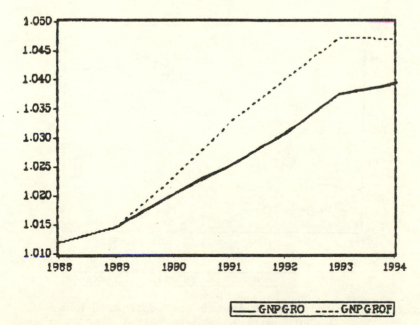

Figure 5B.   Base case output growth with and without
accelerated depreciation.

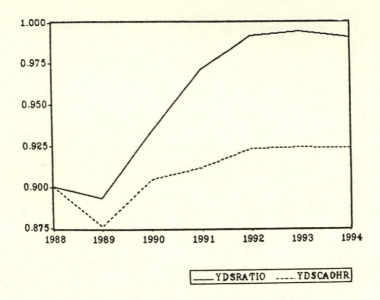

Figure 6A. Exchange rate misalignment in base case
            (YDSRATIO) and in no-debt-solution case (YDSCAOHR).

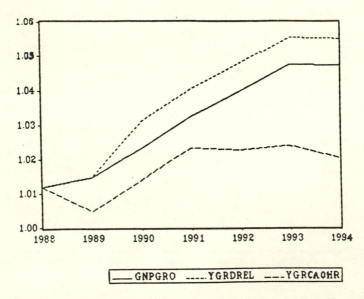

Figure 6B. Output growth in the base case with new money
            (GNPGRO), with more debt relief (YGRDREL) and
            without any debt solution (YGRCAOHR).

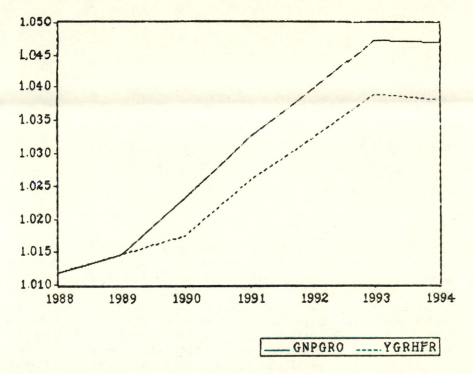

Figure 7. The impact of 2 percent points higher world
interest rates on output growth.

Comments

Willem Buiter
Professor of Economics, Yale University

This is an interesting and in some ways a brave paper. It starts out with a well-informed narrative of the Mexican macroeconomic experience since the early 1970s. This is followed by the exposition of an intertemporal accounting framework augmented by a minimal set of explicit behavioral relations and used to evaluate the consistency of fiscal plans and inflation objectives, with important application to Mexico. A small econometric model of the Mexican economy then focuses on the equilibrating responses of a few key static and interpretable relative prices.

THE HISTORICAL NARRATIVE

Mexico's collapse of fiscal control in the early 1970s stands out in the historical context of several decades of solid fiscal conservatism. Equally striking is the fact that the major oil discoveries of 1976 and the subsequent increase in world oil prices associated with OPEC II did not improve the fiscal balance after the first public spending splurge in 1973-1974. While government revenues from oil expanded rapidly, public expenditure grew even more swiftly. It is hard to come up with a set of reasonable forecasts of future oil revenues (given the information generally available at the time) that would make this kind of behavior consistent with the maintenance of government solvency without the need for major future spending cuts or increases in nonoil revenues. This episode suggests, to the not inconsiderable discomfort of those who try to make a living by conventional economic theory, that receiving a large windfall, far from being a boon, can be a considerable handicap for a country.

Sudden increases in world real interest rates, declining oil prices and worsening market prospects for non-oil exports (all reflections of a recession in the industrial countries brought about by tight monetary policies) caused the retrenchment of commercial banks, which had become the major creditors of the semi-industrial countries. This brought about the debt crisis, first in Eastern Europe and then in Mexico and the rest of Latin America.

The subsequent story for Mexico is one of major fiscal retrenchment and structural reform. The fiscal turnaround figures given by van Wijnbergen are truly staggering: the government converted from a primary (non-interest) general fiscal deficit of 7.1 percent of GDP in 1982 into a primary surplus of 5.3 percent of GDP in 1987 and an estimated 7.6 percent of GDP in 1988. This adjustment occurred while revenues from oil exports declined by more than 7 percent of GDP between 1983 and 1988 and real GDP growth also fell dramatically.

I must admit that my first response was that the figures couldn't possibly be correct. There had to be major "off-budget" fiddles of the kind now popular in the United States in connection with the socialization of the bankrupt savings and loan industry. Even though van Wijnbergen has assured me that the turnaround is real rather than cosmetic, I still have some uneasy feelings. Why didn't Mexico erupt in flames if Venezuela and Argentina exploded when rather more modest fiscal cutbacks were attempted?

Mexico's structural adjustment measures are also wide-ranging and thorough. A major liberalization effort, symbolized in the field of international trade by Mexico joining the GATT, has resulted in a significant reorientation of production towards export markets and a very rapid growth of non-oil exports. Privatization of publicly owned enterprises has also been undertaken in earnest.

The key political economy question in connection with this dramatic stabilization effort and structural reform concerns its durability. What are the pressures on the government to raise expenditure (social, public consumption and infrastructure investment) and to avoid a long overdue widening of its revenue base though more efficient and equitable forms of taxation? How strong are the forces calling for protection and import substitution against the thrust of comparative advantage? How powerful are the industrial and union interests in the newly privatized enterprises? If and when the logic of the market calls for further cutbacks in production and employment or even for the wholesale abandonment of certain kinds of economic activity that were previously sheltered by the public sector's willingness to underwrite losses, will the public purse remain tightly shut despite the undoubtedly intense lobbying efforts by those adversely affected? How much longer can the hard-handed social contract that supported the Mexican (de facto) one-party state for more than seventy years survive this kind of strain? If the old political system collapses, what will take its place, ungovernability Argentine style or Pinochet-style repression? What would be the fiscal and the wider economic consequences of such changes in the political system?

THE CONSISTENCY OF INFLATION TARGETS AND FISCAL POLICY

Van Wijnbergen applies to Mexico a "shorthand consistency check" on the government's fiscal, financial and monetary strategy. From the projected fiscal deficit are subtracted the amounts that can be borrowed internally and externally. The remainder has to be covered through domestic credit expansion. Given the government's target for (or constraint on) the decumulation of international reserves, this determines the amount of high-powered or base money the government must issue. A demand function for base money and an inflation equation then determine the rate of inflation (which need not be unique if there is a "seigniorage Laffer curve") implied by the current and projected fiscal stance. If this implied rate of inflation is different from the target rate of inflation (which will typically have been an input into the projections for the deficit and other variables that generated the implied rate of inflation), either the fiscal stance or the inflation target or both will have to be changed to ensure consistency.(1)

One of the striking conclusions of the analysis is that the Mexican government does not raise "serious money" through seigniorage. There does not appear to be a compelling revenue argument for recourse to the expected inflation tax. Of course there may be additional gains (or losses) from unanticipated inflation through its effect on the real rate of return on non-indexed public debt of finite maturity and denominated in the domestic currency. For Mexico such effects are probably minor. Finally, both expected and unexpected inflation will affect the primary public deficit. I don't know of any estimates of the magnitude or even the sign of this Tanzi effect (Tanzi [1978]) for the Mexican economy.

As I emphasized in Buiter [1989b], the "consistency check" approach carries with it the danger that one might infer, on a casual reading, that the only requirements for engaging in macroeconomic policy evaluation are estimates of a base money demand function and an inflation equation. (Of course even these two involve non-trivial theoretical and econometric issues.) In fact, in order to do the exercise, a considerable amount of (implicit or explicit) economic and econometric modeling is required to generate the projections of public sector deficits, internal and external borrowing opportunities and so on, that produce the inflation rate implied by the fiscal stance. Indeed the kind of econometric model developed later in van Wijnbergen's paper would seem to be an indispensable ingredient of the fiscal consistency checks, which require projections of domestic and foreign interest rates, the exchange rate, the relative price of domestic and foreign goods and the level of economic activity. There is no royal road to policy evaluation that can short cut the painful process of estimating and testing key econometric relationships.

THE ECONOMETRIC MODEL

Central to van Wijnbergen's small macroeconomic model of the Mexican economy is the role of the real exchange rate (the relative price of Mexican non-oil goods and foreign non-oil goods) and the real interest rate. It is not strictly correct to assign a particular price to a particular market or equilibrium condition (in principle, since recursive structures are rare, all prices are determined simultaneously by all equilibrium conditions). Nevertheless, it is helpful to think of the real exchange rate as clearing the market for Mexican non-oil goods while the domestic real interest rate either assures internal-external portfolio balance or (if there is no international capital mobility) equates national saving and domestic capital formation. Nominal variables (such as the general price level, the nominal exchange rate and the nominal rate of interest) can be incorporated by adding a monetary sector, although this addition was not attempted in the present version of the paper.

The simulations rely on a strong negative effect of the domestic real interest rate on domestic capital formation and a strong positive effect on private saving. I used to think that Michael Boskin was the only economist who believed he had identified a significant effect of the real interest rate on private saving, so I turned to the empirical consumption function estimates with considerable anticipation. What I found was a statistically insignificant real-interest elasticity of private consumption as well as strong evidence of dynamic misspecification of the consumption equation. A statistically significant real interest elasticity of private capital formation was found, but again the equation suffered from obvious dynamic misspecification. The inclusion of current-dated endogenous variables as regressors (such as the real interest rate in the consumption function and the investment function, economic activity in the investment function and in the intermediate import function, the real wage in the employment function and the real exchange rate in the three import functions) raises fears of simultaneity bias. It also isn't clear whether the import functions are to be interpreted as demand functions, supply functions or reduced form equations.

It is striking that no wealth terms enter the consumption function or the import functions (if the latter are import demand functions). External debt therefore does not have any negative effect on domestic absorption and a potential equilibrating mechanism is excluded. Foreign factor income and foreign debt have no behavioral consequences, although foreign factor income is an item in the current account identity.

In further developments of the econometric model one would hope to find a decomposition of total public spending into consumption and capital formation and into spending on domestic goods and on foreign goods. The key issue of the productivity of public sector capital formation, which cannot be dealt with in the current version of the model, can then be evaluated.

At the moment, the real interest rate is not endogenized. While one symphathizes with the author in view of the well-known problems of modeling interest rates empirically, the consequence is that there is no way of knowing whether his view of the nature of the transmission mechanism can account for the data. One would also expect that in an economy like the Mexican, credit rationing would play a key role, both on the demand side and on the supply side (through the working capital channel). Commodity rationing shows up in the import demand equations through a quantitative restrictions dummy. I would expect to see significant credit rationing effects on private capital formation and the demand for consumer durables and perhaps on aggregate non-oil supply as well.

Van Wijnbergen deserves credit for trying to impose the discipline of a formal quantitative model on what must be a set of very recalcitrant data. I am looking forward to further developments of his method and model.

CONCLUSION

After reading this rich paper, some key questions remain. First, why does Mexico have these ridiculously high real interest rates of over 30 percent? Who pays these rates? Are they truly the after-tax cost of capital? If uncovered interest parity holds, these levels make sense only if the market expects a major depreciation of the nominal and real exchange rates. If the market's perception of a massive overvaluation is correct, the viability of the whole economic strategy is put into question, since the real exchange rate realignment that is anticipated will involve a significant real income loss and a further serious erosion of real wages. In addition, any repatriation of flight capital will have to wait until the realignment in question has taken place.

If the excess of Mexico's domestic real rate of interest over the world real rate reflects a risk premium, what is the risk in question? What policy measures can be taken to bring it down?

The second question concerns the importance of debt management when internal and external rates of return differ as much as they do in the case of Mexico. Debt-equity swaps have to be undertaken on terms that are prima facie very favorable to Mexico if they are to be worthwhile for the country.

Finally, how can Mexico widen its revenue base to raise more revenue in a less distortionary and more equitable manner? This is not primarily a technical economic question but a political one. Do the middle and upper classes now have the political will to tax themselves to the extent required to support the levels of public expenditure needed for economic growth and efficiency and for minimal social justice? Nothing suggests that one can be optimistic about this matter. Mexico is still ruled by the same party, by the same political institutions and often by the same personalities that failed to tackle this key issue before, and it still has the same neighbor to the north.

NOTES

1.   This approach is based on the work of Anand and van Wijnbergen [1987], Knight [1986] and Coutinho [1986, 1988] in the World Bank and is closely related to some recent work of mine (Buiter [1983a,b; 1985; 1987; 1989a,b]).

REFERENCES

Anand, R., and S. van Wijnbergen. "Inflation and the Financing of Government Expenditures in Turkey: an Introductory Analysis," Mimeo, World Bank (revised June 1987).

Buiter, W. H. "Measurement of the Public Sector Deficit and Its Implications for Policy Evaluation and Design," IMF Staff Papers, 30 (June 1983a), pp. 306–349.

_____. "The Theory of Optimum Deficits and Debt." In The Economics of Large Government Deficits, Federal Reserve Bank of Boston, Conference Series No. 27, October 1983b, pp. 4–69.

_____. "A Guide to Public Debt and Deficits." Economic Policy, 1 (November 1985), pp. 14–61.

_____. "The Current Global Economic Situation, Outlook and Policy Options with Special Emphasis on Fiscal Policy Issues," Centre for Economic Policy Research, Discussion Paper 210 (November 1987).

_____. "Can Public Spending Cuts be Inflationary?" Chapter 13 in W. H. Buiter, Principles of Budgetary and Financial Policy, Harvester-Wheatsheaf, 1989a.

_____. "Some Thoughts on the Role of Fiscal Policy in Stabilization and Structural Adjustment in Developing Countries." Chapter 14 in W. H. Buiter, Principles of Budgetary and Financial Policy, Harvester-Wheatsheaf, 1989b.

Countinho, R. "Public Sector Deficits and Crowding Out: a Consistency Model for Brazil," Mimeo, World Bank (December 1986).

_____. "Public Deficits, Financeable Deficits and Stabilization," Mimeo, World Bank (February 1988).

Knight, P. "Brazil, Structural Adjustment, Stabilization and Growth," 1986 Country Economic Memorandum, World Bank, 1986.

Tanzi, V. "Inflation, Real Tax Revenue and the Case for Inflationary Finance: Theory with an Application to Argentina," IMF Staff Papers, 25 (September 1978).

General Comments*

Anne Krueger
Professor of Economics, Duke University

Although many of these papers differ in their focus, many of their concerns are held in common. Perhaps even more interesting, however, is the degree of agreement about what we do not know.

There are, I think, two major sources of this uncertainty. The first is the unreliability of conventional policy prescriptions and implies that policymakers are groping to find more adequate policies; the second is lack of factual knowledge and implies a strong need for research. I am struck by how closely interrelated are these two deficiencies.

Recall Maddison's classification of Mexico's "five" problems: negative real growth per capita, inflation, debt, the public sector deficit and inefficient resource allocation. Then consider the focus of van Wijnbergen's paper on inflation, debt and the public sector deficit and his investigation of whether investment could increase enough to stimulate growth within acceptable inflation and debt servicing scenarios. Zabludovsky's examination of trade regime liberalization focused on one of the major sources of microeconomic inefficiency, and while the analysis is certainly relevant to issues of growth and debt servicing it is not easily linked to a macro policy model.

As these papers illustrate, there are a number of sources of policy uncertainty facing the Mexican authorities. First, there is uncertainty about the trajectory of

---

*Editors' Note: Professor Krueger's comments refer explicitly to three papers (Maddison, van Wijnbergen and Zabludovsky) because of her responsibilities as chairperson for one of the actual Yale/Mexico Conference plenary sessions.

the international economy. The key parameters for Mexico in this regard are interest rates, oil prices and the openness of the international economy. As was pointed out by van Wijnbergen, the interest rate paid on Mexican external debt is crucial; a 1 percent point increase in the interest rate internationally adds almost $1 billion to its annual interest obligations. The oil price is also important: a $2 change in the oil price is equivalent to a move of about 1 percentage point in the interest rate. Second, the trade policies of the major participants in the international economy are clearly critical to the success of Mexican trade liberalization and exchange rate policy. Uncertainties in this area pose major questions about how much growth Mexico can expect to generate by achieving financial stabilization and by removing sources of microeconomic inefficiencies, as well as about how soon these gains might start being realized. And, third, the political degrees of freedom open to policymakers is not all clear.

In a sense, the first and third sources of policy uncertainty are inherent in the policymaking process. There are numerous forecasts of the future path of interest rates, oil prices and the rate of expansion of the international economy and in the short run, very little can be done to reduce that uncertainty. Over the longer run, perhaps the Mexican authorities should consider indexing to oil prices or other schemes that might hedge some of these sources of uncertainty. Institutional arrangements to build up foreign exchange reserves during periods of high oil prices and then use them during periods of low prices might also help, but putting such schemes in place is difficult when the underlying determinants of price are related to political structures within OPEC and not simply to market forces. The third source of uncertainty -- the amount of political latitude available -- is obviously one that the politicians must evaluate. But even in that regard, there is a sense in which the lack of knowledge about the second set of issues is the real problem. If we had better knowledge and predictive ability with regard to the payoffs from macro and micro policy changes, politicians would be better able to explain their programs and promise future delivery in return for present sacrifices.

As it is, we know, or think we know, that trade liberalization has a payoff, but we remain uncertain about its timing and magnitude. Equally fundamental are questions about whether the current real exchange rate is appropriate and whether potential nontraditional exporters will find the new policies credible in light of the present tendency toward appreciation of the real exchange rate.

Likewise, we know, or think we know, something about the measures necessary to bring down inflation. However, we do not understand why real internal interest rates are so high. Is it the lack of credibility of the current real exchange rate? Or is this due to expectations that the "primary" fiscal deficit will once again increase? Or is there a genuine scarcity of loanable funds? The explanation matters a great deal for both exchange rate and fiscal policies. If, for example, the lack of credibility of exchange rate policy is significantly deterring exporters while simultaneously resulting in the very high real domestic interest rate, adopting a crawling peg exchange rate system might be anti-inflationary. Currently, policymakers apparently believe that the exchange rate should be used as an anti-inflationary weapon, and are permitting some real appreciation. Is that policy in the right, or in the wrong, direction?

Finally, we do not really have a good understanding of the relationships between Mexico's (or any other country's) macroeconomic policy problems and underlying microeconomic inefficiencies. The van Wijnbergen model is built, in accordance with best practice, on the presumption that more investment will mean more growth. Yet Mexico had more investment in the 1970s than the 1960s, and grew more slowly! If microeconomic reforms are truly effective, the incremental capital/output ratio should fall, as it did in Korea in the 1960s and Turkey in the early 1980s, and the growth rate attainable with any given rate of investment will be higher. Finding an appropriate framework within which to analyze the links between macroeconomic and microeconomic reforms is perhaps one of the most pressing challenges for researchers in the years ahead. Greater understanding of these linkages would not make policymaking simple, but it would certainly reduce the degree of uncertainty with which policymakers are faced.

Private Sector Net Exports and the Real Exchange Rate

Everardo Elizondo
Director, Economia Aplicada, S.A.

INTRODUCTION

This paper discusses very briefly some salient features of Mexico's balance of trade in the last two decades. In particular, it focuses on the recent evolution of private sector net exports and relates this evolution to the real exchange rate, the domestic wage in dollar terms and an index of competitiveness.

MEXICAN FOREIGN TRADE IN THE 1980S

It is useful first to review the external trade data for the 1980s (see Table 1) and to discuss some general features that seem to apply as well to other countries of Latin America. Mexico's trade balance shifted from a deficit of $7.4 billion in 1980 to a hefty surplus of almost $13.8 billion only three years later. This change was due to an increase of almost $10 billion in exports and a decline of almost equal magnitude in imports. Thereafter through 1988 total exports stagnated at about the same level of 1981. In sharp contrast, imports more than doubled between 1983 and 1988 -- a surge which served only to regain their 1980 levels. Although Mexico's trade balance has been favorable for seven years in a row, the 1988 surplus of $1.7 billion was the lowest for this period and the balance was negative in the last months of the year. The $6.7 billion reduction in the surplus, about 80 percent of the robust $8.4 billion level attained a year earlier, was almost exactly the same amount by which oil exports fell.

The consensus among observers is that a combination of several factors explain what happened in 1988. First is the negative impact of falling oil revenues, which were offset almost to the dollar by increasing non-oil exports. Among non-oil exports, the growth of manufactures has been very impressive, and has been attributed to both the wide advantage of the low price of labor(1) and the positive effects of the liberalization process which have allowed local producers to buy inputs at competitive world prices. The growth of imports, in turn, was determined by the progressive dismantling of quantitative restrictions, the falling margin of "undervaluation" of the peso, the positive -- though weakening -- rate of economic activity and a wave of speculative buying at the end of 1988, motivated by fears of another round of tariff increases and devaluations.

With the reduction of the trade surplus, the overall current account showed the biggest deficit of the last six years. Given the lack of private capital inflows, this condition indicated a substantial degree of external imbalance.(2)

Several analysts of the Mexican foreign sector have suggested the existence of a close relationship in the last twenty-five years between the inflation adjusted operational balance(3) of the public sector and the current account balance. In 1987 the former had a surplus of 1.4 percent of GDP and the latter had a surplus of 3 percent of GDP. In 1988 the operational balance showed a deficit of perhaps 3 percent of GDP, while the deficit on current account was about 2 percent of GDP. The Mexican research institution, CEESP, concluded: "...the operational deficit deteriorated ...putting pressure on domestic demand and reflecting itself in the current account deficit."(4)

During the first months of 1989 the condition of the public finances has improved very significantly as a result of higher oil income, improved tax revenues and an additional spending adjustment. Hence, it can be assumed that the external accounts also will register some improvement. As yet, it is not clear, however, that the changes will be enduring.

FOREIGN TRADE AND THE PRIVATE SECTOR

External shocks aside, the overall balance of trade moves in close relationship with the net exports of the private sector. In 1987 the private sector balance of trade had a surplus of $1 billion and in 1988 it had a deficit of $2.7 billion. It is important to examine in detail the evolution of this item, paying some attention in the process to the real exchange rate and some related concepts. The essential points can best be made with reference to the graphical representations at the end of this paper.

In Figure 1, the scale on the right measures the net exports of the private sector in 1980 dollars. The scale on the left shows the real exchange rate, operationally defined to be the nominal exchange rate (pesos per dollar) divided by the Mexican National Consumer Price Index, and multiplied by the U.S. Wholesale Price Index.(5) There appears to have been a close relationship between the real exchange rate and the private trade deficit for almost two decades: the deficit grows when the dollar cheapens. This relationship was evident in the changes between 1987 and 1988 when the trade balance went from surplus to deficit precisely when the peso appreciated against the dollar.

Alternatively, it can be shown that the domestic wage level expressed in dollar terms is a good explanatory variable.(6) When the wage rate decreases, exports tend to grow and imports to fall. The declining cost of labor implies increasing competitiveness for the domestic producers, reduced purchasing power for the population and therefore an inverse relationship between the wage in dollars and the net exports of the private sector. And that is what Figure 2 shows for all but one of the nineteen years considered. This relationship held in 1988 as well when the dollarized wage increased and the balance of trade deteriorated.

Taken one by one, the components of the overall balance react in general as expected.(7) Exports from the private sector are directly related to the real exchange rate (see Figure 3) and inversely related to dollar-equivalent wages (see Figure 4).

However, exports increased in 1988 (albeit at a decreasing rate) in spite of rises in the real exchange rate and wage levels. This increase suggests that other factors must have been at work -- like the extraordinary expansion of the U.S. economy, Mexico's liberalization of imports or a lagged response to the abnormal increases in the world price of some manufactured goods.

Imports behaved roughly in accordance with the assumed pattern: they were inversely related to the real exchange rate (see Figure 5). This relationship was particularly strong in the last two years when the lowering of protection coincided with the devaluation of the peso. The result has been an explosion of imports, although 1988 imports remained lower than the peak in 1981 associated with the oil boom.

Another perspective on the question is provided by the "home spun" index of competitiveness shown in Figure 6. This index is simply labor costs in the manufacturing sector of

Mexico (that is, wages, salaries and fringe benefits per unit of output) in terms of dollars, divided by unit labor costs in the manufacturing sector of the United States. When the index increases, Mexico's ability to compete declines.

Figure 6 shows the quarterly trajectory of the index against the net exports of the private sector in the last eight years. As was expected, the relationship is clearly an inverse one. The explanation is simple: the loss of competitiveness encourages imports and deters exports.

Figure 6 also lends support to some worries currently being expressed by the private sector in Mexico. While net exports were the highest at the same time (end of 1986) that this index of competitiveness was its lowest, since then the index rose and private sector exports deteriorated. The new Pacto (effective in January of 1989) implies that these trends are likely to continue.

CONCLUSION

Mexico had an increasingly significant external imbalance in 1988 reflected in a rapid reduction of foreign exchange reserves. One of the factors behind this development was the contraction of the private sector trade balance associated, inter alia, with appreciation of the real exchange rate.

The economic policy of the present administration is premised on the assumption of a moderate but persistent deficit in the current account over the next several years. The administration has not yet solved the question of how to finance the deficit, however, and it is hoped that the answer will be forthcoming shortly.

NOTES

1. Centro de Estudios Economicos del Sector Privado, A.C. (CEESP), Actividad Economica, #130 (1988).

2. W. M. Corden, Inflation, Exchange Rates and the World Economy, 2nd ed. (The University of Chicago Press, 1981), p. 8.

3. The operational balance "...is the concept to use if one wishes to measure the real change in government debt. It is also the concept to apply if one wants to look at the real excess demand the government is applying to the economy." F. Gil Diaz and R. Ramos Tercero, "Lessons from Mexico," in Inflation Stabilization, ed. by M. Bruno, G.

DiTella, R. Dornbusch and S. Fischer (The MIT Press, 1988),
p. 389.

    4.   CEESP, op. cit.

    5.   S. Edwards, Exchange Rate Misalignment in Develop-
ing Countries, Occasional Paper #2, New Series (The World
Bank, 1988), p. 4.

    6.   "The real exchange rate is thus simply the wage in
dollars." R. Dornbusch, "Overvaluation and Trade Balance,"
in The Open Economy, ed. by R. Dornbusch and F. Leslie C.H.
Helmers (Oxford University Press, 1988), p. 87.

    7.   This result coincides with some econometric estima-
tions, including my own. For example, a model recently
developed by analysts of Banco de Mexico includes the following equation for the exports of the private sector:

$$X_t = 0.0868\ TCR_t + 1.048\ Y_t + 0.0039\ AC_t$$
$$- 0.024\ AP_t + 0.0559\ X_{t-1}$$

where TCR is the real exchange rate, and is positively
related to X, the exports of the private sector in real
terms; R^2 = 0.90. J. Tapia Maruri and J. Cervantes,
"Mexico, Un Modelo Econometrico del Impacto de la Apertura
Comercial en la Balanza Comercial, Actividad Economica y
Precios," Boletin de Economia Internactional (Banco de
Mexico, Oct.-Dec. 1988), p. 7.

TABLE 1. Trade Balance of Mexico ($ US Billions)

	Exports	Imports	Balance
1980	11,511.8	18,896.6	-7,384.9
1981	20,102.1	23,948.4	-3,846.3
1982	21,229.7	14,437.0	6,792.7
1983	22,312.0	8,550.9	13,761.1
1984	24,196.0	11,254.3	12,941.3
1985	21,663.8	13,212.2	8,451.6
1986	16,031.0	11,432.4	4,598.6
1987	20,656.2	12,222.9	8,433.3
1988[a]	20,657.0	18,903.0	1,754.0

[a]Preliminary
Source: Banco de Mexico and INEGI

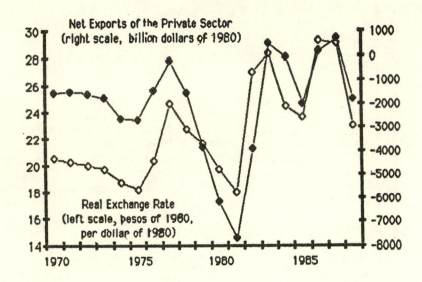

Figure 1

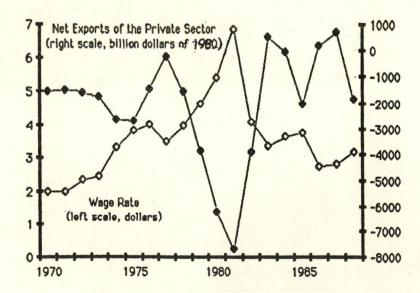

Figure 2

Figure 3

Figure 4

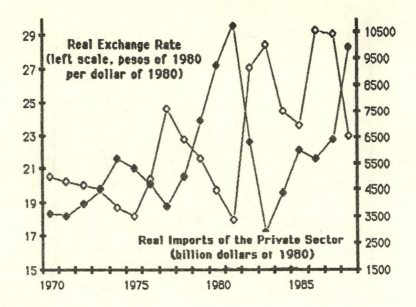

Figure 5

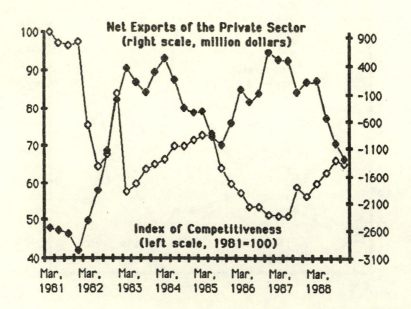

Figure 6

Comments

Enrique Espinoza
Vice President, Banco Nacional de Mexico, S.N.C.

Most thoughtful observers including the principal international financial institutions agree that the private sector must play a major role in any recovery of the Mexican economy. This view has also become an established feature in the official discourse of Mexico's economic authorities, who have openly acknowledged the need for more market-oriented policies in such important areas as external trade, financial intermediation and public enterprise. I am therefore rather surprised by how little has been said at this conference about the performance of Mexico's private sector in the recent past and its capacity to play the role it is being called on to assume in the future.

An exception to this remark is Everardo Elizondo's paper which commendably focuses on an important aspect of private enterprise in Mexico: its contribution to the country's external trade balance. After all, private sector exports grew at an average annual rate of 24 percent between 1982 and 1988, while private imports expanded at an annual pace of only 9 percent. As a result, the share of private businesses in total exports has grown from 16 percent in 1982 to 61 percent in 1988, a far more dramatic change than the increase in their share of imports from 63 percent in 1982 to 81 percent in 1988. The evidence presented by Elizondo clearly shows that a highly depreciated real exchange rate has played a major role in the underlying process: he finds a close association between the private trade balance, the exchange rate and other key variables. On the basis of these findings, Elizondo is skeptical about the continuing use of the nominal exchange rate as the main anchor for the stabilization program. To the extent that this policy implies a real exchange rate appreciation, the result could well be gradual discouragement of private enterprises from exporting.

The import-export data for the private sector since the beginning of the current stabilization program certainly warrant concern. The monthly balance implied by these figures show a surplus in all but three months of 1987, but during 1988 trade deficits occurred almost every month, with a substantial overall deficit for the year (see Table 1). However, private exports still showed a healthy increase of 20.4 percent in 1988, only 5 points lower than the previous year. It is the behavior of imports that largely explains the shift from a surplus to a deficit position: their rate of growth jumped from 16.2 percent in 1987 to 62.0 percent in 1988.

The growth pattern of privately imported producer goods (both non-factorial inputs and capital goods) resembles that of private exports much more closely in 1988 than in 1987. In contrast, there is an increasing divergence between imported producer goods and industrial output (see Figure 1). This evidence is not inconsistent with the notion that trade liberalization, which became truly widespread within the Mexican economy only in 1988, finally allowed firms to reap the benefits from using inputs of international quality and price and induced them to modernize their plant and equipment. Increases in the importation of producer goods in the immediate aftermath of trade liberalization are to be expected, as the experiences of Taiwan in the late 1950s and South Korea in the mid-1960s suggest.

These remarks provide a framework within which to discuss two related issues. The first concerns the wisdom of sticking to a pre-announced crawling exchange rate policy as a means for keeping inflationary pressures under control. As I have tried to show above, it is far from clear that the strength of private exports in Mexico was seriously undermined by a fixed exchange rate through most of 1988. Foreign sales continued to grow and did so at a fairly steady pace. Private exporters understandably complain about the effect of a gradually appreciating real exchange rate on the profitability of their sales abroad, but the real issue is one of the relative profitability between domestic and foreign sales.

Reliable data to measure this relationship are difficult to obtain, but based on extensive conversation with some of the major private exporters in the country, my best guess is that this comparison remains favorable towards exports. Moreover, firms that got off to an early start in their efforts to penetrate foreign markets have invested not only time but quite sizable amounts of financial resources in pursuing their goals. They are unlikely to let this accumulated investment and experience go to waste, even if their export profits fall from the truly extraordinary heights frequently registered before 1988 to levels more comparable to international standards. The well-known profit cuts taken by Japanese firms to offset the disadvantages of a rising yen vis-a-vis the dollar clearly support this suggestion.

The Mexican government is being urged by some business interests to use its exchange rate policy as a shelter for "infant exporters" that may never find it convenient to attain the size and efficiency required for true international competitiveness. Given the costs of protecting them on a steady basis -- high inflation, real wage erosion and implicit subsidization of foreign consumers, among others -- I believe such a policy to be as unacceptable as the now-rejected notion that domestic producers in an underdeveloped economy must be protected indefinitely from international competition.

The second issue that must be addressed is whether or not a nominal devaluation is an appropriate course of action if the real exchange rate becomes excessively appreciated. The methodological problems in determining exchange rate equilibria with reasonable accuracy are well known. Here I emphasize the fact that the level of any real variable can be affected in the long term only by changes in other related real variables, not by simple nominal adjustments. Sooner or later, a devaluation of the national currency tends to affect the domestic price level and in the Mexican case there is every reason to believe that such feedback would occur in a matter of weeks, or even days. Prices of real estate in Mexico are often quoted openly in dollars already, despite the fact that this is the ultimate example of a non-tradeable good.

Mexican authorities have learned since 1982 that the key to preventing domestic demand from overwhelming exports, thereby inducing excessive imports and fostering speculation in the foreign exchange market, lies in fiscal and monetary restraint. However, the burden of debt service has made this lesson increasingly difficult to apply in practice. An agreement with Mexico's creditors that closes the gap between the current external payments schedule and the country's true capacity to pay is therefore a necessary condition to keep in place the enormous real adjustments the Mexican economy has already undergone.

TABLE 1. Mexico: Balance of Trade for the Private Sector,
1987-1988

Date:	EXPORTS	IMPORTS	BALANCE	EXPORTS	IMPORTS
	(Thousands of dollars)			(Yearly growth rates)	
Jan 87	758.8	554.9	203.9	6.0%	-26.1%
Feb	754.2	603.9	150.3	18.7%	-11.4%
Mar	907.6	750.3	157.3	30.0%	18.4%
Apr	861.5	758.7	102.8	18.7%	-2.4%
May	891.5	717.5	174.0	29.0%	-8.3%
Jun	961.7	760.9	200.8	60.0%	10.8%
Jul	844.4	863.5	-19.1	37.8%	15.2%
Aug	776.0	821.9	-45.9	32.0%	28.5%
Sep	862.7	860.5	2.2	28.8%	50.2%
Oct	935.8	972.1	-36.3	23.6%	46.8%
Nov	906.9	882.3	24.6	14.5%	54.6%
Dec	1030.7	896.1	134.6	15.2%	54.3%
Jan 88	949.8	887.5	62.3	25.2%	59.9%
Feb	1078.9	966.6	112.3	43.1%	60.1%
Mar	1122.2	1163.1	-40.9	23.6%	55.0%
Apr	1040.0	1185.7	-145.7	20.7%	56.3%
May	1132.6	1249.1	-116.5	27.0%	74.1%
Jun	1085.2	1358.3	-273.1	12.8%	78.5%
Jul	1007.2	1284.8	-277.6	19.3%	48.8%
Aug	1111.0	1423.8	-312.8	43.2%	73.2%
Sep	945.1	1355.3	-410.2	9.6%	57.5%
Oct	960.2	1397.5	-437.3	2.6%	43.8%
Nov	1158.5	1584.6	-426.1	27.7%	79.6%
Dec	1045.1	1495.9	-450.8	1.4%	66.9%
1987	10491.8	9442.6	1049.2	25.2%	16.7%
1988	12635.8	15352.2	-2716.4	20.4%	62.6%

Source: Department of Economic Studies (BANAMEX), based on
data produced by Banco de Mexico.

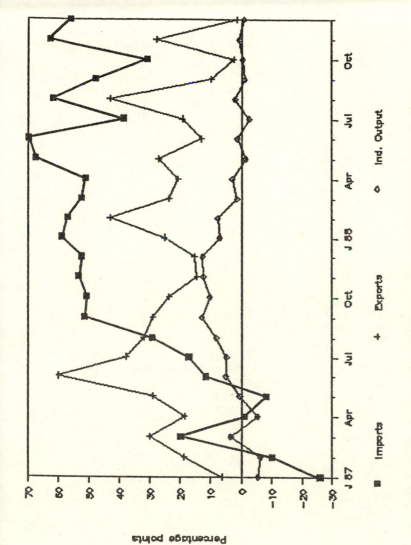

Source: Department of Economic Studies (BANAMEX), based on data produced by Banco de México.

Figure 1. Private Imports of Producer Goods (Annual growth rates, in percent)

PART IV
FINANCIAL SECTOR REFORM

Financial Sector Planning and Mexico's New Development Strategy

Dwight Brothers
Research Fellow, Economic Growth Center, Yale University

BACKGROUND

During 1987 and 1988 a Financial Sector Studies Program (FSSP) was conducted under auspices of the Secretaria de Hacienda y Credito Publico (SHCP) and in liaison with the World Bank, for which I served as principal consultant. A "final report" on the results of this activity was submitted to the new leadership of SHCP in January of 1989, and this paper is based on pertinent sections of that document.(1)

Since the time the FSSP was initially commissioned in late 1986 it had been intended that the findings would serve in due course as a basis for discussions between SHCP and the Bank regarding financial sector reforms that might be mutually agreeable as an adjunct of the larger structural adjustment lending program. Such discussions were initiated in October of 1988, and the ensuing negotiation of terms and conditions for a $500 million financial sector structural adjustment loan (F-SAL) were successfully concluded in May of 1989.(2)

FINANCIAL SECTOR PLANNING IN MEXICO

It is established practice for each presidential administration to formulate at an early stage a national development plan which sets forth in a wide-ranging and indicative manner the principal objectives and strategies for the upcoming sexennio. The Plan Nacional de Desarrollo (PND) for 1983-1988 devised during the first year of the de la Madrid Administration reflected the unprecedented financial crisis and the associated political dangers then confronting the country, and consequently was a program more for guiding crisis management and maintaining social cohesion than for promoting economic development. The basic objectives enunciated were "to overcome the crisis, to recover the capacity for growth, and to initiate the qualitative changes required for economic and social restructuring". But, understandably under the circumstances, the document lacked much specificity with regard to the strategic guidelines and policy directions to be followed by the governmental authorities in pursuing these general objectives.

Because of the highly unsettled circumstances and the related necessity for maintaining a relatively short-term focus on the task of crisis containment and abatement, provision was made for reformulation of the government's financial management policies on a year-to-year basis. The framework employed for doing so was the Programa Nacional de Financiamiento del Desarrollo (PRONAFIDE) which, among other things, called for a series of Programas Operativos Anuales de Financiamiento (POAFs) intended to provide annually revised guidelines for the policies to be followed by SHCP and other governmental agencies centrally involved in the country's financial affairs. Not only was this scheme a novel and demanding extension of indicative planning as traditionally practiced, but its implementation was complicated by the successive budgetary and balance-of-payments crunches resulting from gyrations in the international petroleum market and the episodic negotiations with external creditors -- as well as by the lingering shock waves generated by the bank nationalization action taken in the final days of the preceding administration.

SHCP had primary responsibility for performance of the financial planning function as mandated by the PRONAFIDE-POAF conception, and the actual operational burden was assigned to the Planeacion Hacendaria division of the Ministry. The objectives established for guiding the planning of financial policies were promotion of domestic savings and efficiency in resource allocation, consolidation of financial system institutions, and re-ordering of external financial relationships. As means to facilitate pursuit of these objectives separate directorates were established within SHCP to supervise operations of the newly nationalized commercial banks, the established national development banks, and the various types of non-bank financial institutions.

In retrospect it appears that these sub-sector directorates tended to fall into administrative limbo between the budget planning and management responsibilities exercised jointly by SHCP and SPP,(3) the supervisory and regulatory roles performed by CNByS(4) and CNdV,(5) and the monetary and credit control functions conducted under Banco de Mexico auspices. In any case, the role for the Planeacion Hacendaria division of SHCP in planning, directing and monitoring financial sector activities has been significantly curtailed by the new administration, with the likely result that these responsibilities will revert in substantial degree to the traditional trilateral institutional framework.

It would be presumptuous to predict at this time either the procedural arrangements or the substantive characteristics of financial sector planning and policy implementation during the Salinas administration. While the national development plan for 1989-1994 published on May 31, 1989,(6) contains a good deal more emphasis than did the preceding document on financial sector problems and policy issues, the composition of the financial sector reform agenda is yet to be revealed in full detail. All that is clear at this stage is that the new government intends to carry out a program of "financial modernization".

PURPOSE OF THIS PAPER

The intention here is not to propose objectives and procedures for the upcoming stage of financial sector planning. Rather it is to engage in some forward-looking speculation regarding how financial sector policy and reforms might best be formulated to link with the new development strategy which the Salinas Administration is still struggling to formulate and make operational (publication of the latest PND notwithstanding).

In other words, the purpose is to propose some conceptual guidelines that appear to warrant consideration as the government proceeds to devise its plan of action with respect to the financial sector for the coming few years. Some of the findings and conclusions contained in the FSSP report are utilized as the basis for these proposals, but without repeating much of the theoretical analysis and empirical evidence. While that wider-ranging study of contemporary problem areas and policy issues in the financial sector of the economy was not intended to provide a basis for financial sector planning, nevertheless extension of the line of argument in this direction seems to be appropriate.

The speculative nature of this paper warrants emphasis. As indicated above, even though the traditional national development plan has now been presented, certain key aspects of the government's strategy remain unclear -- largely because of continuing uncertainties about the external financial parameters relating to on-going negotiations with foreign creditors. But even if the basic numerical parameters were known there would remain a number of theoretical and political imponderables to complicate prognostication of the critical linkages between the macroeconomic variables around which the stabilization and structural adjustment processes must be molded and the more mundane financial sector policy and institutional adjustments that would be most consistent with these processes.

Nevertheless, in spite of these limitations, an attempt to formulate a prospective scenario for the near-term restructuring and longer-term development of Mexico's financial system during this interim period of macroeconomic strategy deliberations appears to be worthwhile. If nothing more, the exercise might serve to anticipate and clarify certain of the policy issues in the financial sector that will need to be addressed in due course. And, if the suggestions offered are sufficiently realistic and convincing, they might stimulate more detailed exploration of the pertinent considerations by Mexican officials charged with responsibility for the charting and piloting of financial sector reform and modernization initiatives during the months and years ahead.

ALTERNATIVE DEVELOPMENT STRATEGY SCENARIOS

The place to begin the discussion, however, is not with consideration of the specific financial sector policies and institutions that appear to be candidates for remodeling, but rather with an articulation of basic assumptions regarding the macroeconomic and macrofinancial framework that seems most likely during the coming period. It will be sufficient for present purposes to devise a hypothetical forecast of the future in this regard in the broadest and most general terms.

Two basic macro scenarios warrant consideration. First, suppose that the current line of policy endeavors directed toward stabilization, structural adjustment and growth resumption within the context of widened scope for private sector activities and less restrictive regulation of international trade and foreign investment should fail to produce the desired results for one reason or another. In this case the Mexican economy would continue to stagnate and soon to deteriorate further, the policies currently being followed would be discredited and eventually abandoned, and there would be little point in bothering to think expansively about possibilities for financial sector reform in such an inhospitable environment. Therefore, such a scenario must be rejected for present purposes on the grounds that it is too horrible to contemplate and also uninteresting as a basis for projecting possibilities for bringing about improvements in financial sector performance.

The alternative macro scenario supposition which is more optimistic (and also, one hopes, more realistic) would be based on contrary assumptions regarding the course of events. In this scenario the missing pieces in the macroeconomic stabilization/structural adjustment/growth resumption puzzle soon will be found and fitted into place in proper coordination with the related macrofinancial fiscal/ monetary/debt management elements. Accordingly, the Mexican economy would gradually recover and become progressively revitalized, the policies currently being pursued would be vindicated and further extended along similar lines, and there would be a good deal of merit in thinking ahead about how to protect and augment momentum toward development objectives by means of supportive financial sector reforms. This, therefore, is the only acceptable scenario for present purposes -- recognizing, of course, that optimism should not be allowed to overwhelm realism and prevent recognition of the substantial risk that things could go wrong yet again, whether temporarily or for an extended period.

Financial sector policy issues warrant considerable priority within the context of the optimistic scenario because at various stages in the implementation of a sound development strategy flaws in the support system afforded by processes conducted in the financial sector tend to become sources of constraints that, if not properly addressed in a thoughtful and timely manner, would work to undermine the sequential recovery processes. There are numerous recent examples of this vulnerability in contexts not unlike the optimistic scenario being assumed for Mexico. On the other hand, there is also considerable evidence of both a theoretical and an empirical nature to indicate that careful attention to correction of policy and structural deficiencies pertaining to activities conducted within the financial sectors of national economies can serve not only to forestall problems that might otherwise arise but also to reinforce successful implementation of development strategies.

THEORY OF FINANCIAL LIBERALIZATION

The financial management aspects of macroeconomic stabilization and structural adjustment programs have been the subject of a good deal of theoretical speculation and empirical investigation during the past two decades. The path-breaking works of Shaw and McKinnon(7) have been instrumental in definition of the pertinent concepts and issues, and in formulation of the research agenda as advanced by numerous contributors.

The essential elements of the Shaw-McKinnon model can be formulated diagrammatically as shown in Figure 1. As depicted, saving (S) and investment (I) are functions of the real rate of interest (R), which in turn is a function of the degree of financial repression, FR. Saving and the rate of economic growth (g) are also functionally related. Financial repression (assumed for simplicity to be reflected in the level and structure of interest rates), holds the average real interest rate below its free-market equilibrium level (R_2), and works to limit the amount of saving and investment and, thereby, the rate of economic growth.

This diagrammatic formulation can be utilized to illustrate the following points, each of which is pertinent to appraisal of Mexico's recent experience and contemporary problems:

1. If an administered interest rate ceiling of R_0 is applied only to savers' deposits, and the lending rate is left to be freely determined in the market for loanable funds, banks and other intermediary institutions profit unduly from the administered spread between deposit and lending rates $(R_3 - R_0)$. As a consequence the level of saving and investment is curtailed, and the rate of economic growth is retarded.

2. If ceilings are imposed administratively on both deposit and loan rates (as in most financially repressed economies), the profitability of intermediation is constrained and non-price rationing of loanable funds occurs. This situation works to discourage risk-taking on the part of financial institutions (since risk premia cannot be charged under uniformly binding loan rate ceilings), to ration out most potentially high-yielding investments (since lending institutions will tend to seek out the safest lending opportunities), and to

cause the investments that do qualify for loan financing to be those yielding returns only marginally above the ceiling lending rate.

3. If administered interest rate ceilings are raised (that is, the degree of financial repression is reduced by shifting FR to FR'), saving and investment and growth increase, lower yielding investments are rationed out, and average investment efficiency increases. However, to the extent that the real interest rate R_1 associated with FR' is lower than the equilibrium rate R_2, the level of saving and investment as well as the rate of economic growth continue to be retarded.

The central point illustrated by the diagram, therefore, is that a relatively high and ideally unrepressed real rate of interest is the key to realization of optimal levels of saving and investment, greater investment efficiency, and a higher rate of economic growth.

The principal hypotheses underlying empirical research relating to the Shaw-McKinnon model can be summarized as follows:

1. There is a pronounced tendency in most developing countries for governments to repress the financial sectors of their economies. This repression increases vulnerability to macroeconomic instability and retards economic growth.

2. Governments are motivated to impose restrictions on financial sector activities principally by the desire to command at lower interest rates than would otherwise be possible a larger share of domestic resources both for the public sector and for selected activities in the social or private sectors deemed to warrant high priority.

3. The techniques employed for this purpose include interest rate ceilings, high bank reserve requirements, preferential credit regimes, foreign exchange controls, and other interventions in the money and capital markets.

4. In situations characterized by large fiscal deficits and balance-of-payments disequilibria, and by high and unpredictable rates of inflation and

devaluation, government policies mandating substantially negative real rates of interest and allocation of bank credit to favored borrowers at preferential interest rates have a number of adverse
consequences. These include:

a. lowering the demand for money and other
    liquid assets as a percentage of GDP;
b. decreasing the ratio of domestic savings to
    GDP;
c. reducing the ability of banks to attract
    deposits vis-a-vis non-bank financial insti-
    tutions;
d. fostering disintermediation from the banking
    system and financial institutions generally;
e. fragmenting financial markets, raising the
    real costs of financial processes;
f. lowering both the quantity and quality of
    capital formation;
g. allocating financial resources to speculative
    inflation/devaluation hedges (including capi-
    tal flight); and
h. undermining socially desirable regulation of
    financial processes directed toward mainten-
    ance of efficiency, safety and probity.

The large and continually growing body of literature
devoted to extension and testing of these hypotheses generally confirms the disadvantageous consequences of financial
repression. The numerous studies also have served to make
clear the main policy implications derived from the theory
of financial liberalization, which are the following:

1. Regulations enabling government to absorb an undue
    proportion of total credit availabilities, to allo-
    cate credit arbitrarily to preferred borrowers
    through interest rate subsidies or other means,
    and to segment financial markets artificially
    should be modified in ways that minimize the
    degree of administrative repression of the finan-
    cial system.

2. Uniformly high real rates of interest within com-
    parable deposit and loan categories should be
    established -- by raising administered nominal
    rates, reducing the rate of inflation or abolish-
    ing interest rate ceilings altogether.

3. Fiscal and monetary measures not involving repres-
    sion of the financial system should be relied on
    to stabilize the domestic price level; and trade
    and exchange rate policies also not involving
    repression of the financial system should be
    relied on to bring about equilibrium in the bal-
    ance of payments.

4. Liberalization of regulations governing financial
    activities is generally required as an adjunct to
    successful macroeconomic stabilization and struc-
    tural adjustment programs.

REASSESSMENT OF EMPIRICAL EVIDENCE

Indications of uncertainty about the universal applicability of the policy implications of the theory of financial
liberalization as summarized above have surfaced recently in
the literature -- particularly regarding the role of financial liberalization in the process of macroeconomic stabilization. The series of domestic financial crises in the
Southern Cone of Latin America have been an important stimu-
lus to reassessment of these matters. More specifically,
the similar experiences of Argentina, Chile and Uruguay during the late 1970s and early 1980s in attempting to pursue
simultaneously financial stabilization and financial liberalization policies culminated in widespread insolvency of
enterprises and banks which, in turn, contributed to the
failures of the stabilization programs.

While some observers have blamed the failure of the
Southern Cone financial liberalization experiments on a combination of unfortunate external shocks and poorly conceived
stabilization programs, perhaps the most judicious appraisal
of the implications of these experiences for financial liberalization theory has been offered recently by Professor
McKinnon himself. While continuing to hold steadfastly to
the basic principles regarding the disadvantages of financial repression and the merits of financial liberalization,
he has acknowledged that:

The general case favoring financial liberalization has
been called into question by a series of bank panics
and collapses in the Southern Cone of Latin America...
Without retreating to the older view which elevates
repressive financial measures to being potentially
desirable instruments of public policy, we now

recognize that our knowledge of how best to achieve financial liberalization remains seriously incomplete. The order in which the monetary system is stabilized in comparison to the pace of deregulation of banks and other financial institutions must be more carefully considered than had previously been thought.

...There are limits to which real rates of interest can be raised in immature bank-based capital markets without incurring undue adverse risk selection...among industrial and agricultural borrowers. Furthermore, when...the banks' deposit base is, implicitly or explicitly, insured by the government, macroeconomic instability could well induce considerable moral hazards in the banks themselves. Thus macroeconomic instability reduces the socially desirable level of real interest rates in the banking sector, and makes financial liberalization more difficult.

* * * * * *

Sustained stability in the domestic price level is a necessary condition for achieving high real financial growth without undue risk of some major financial panic and collapse. When general macroeconomic and price level instability is pronounced, the use of extremely high nominal rates of interest to offset anticipated inflation, and balance the supply and demand for loanable funds in the capital market, becomes very risky -- although perhaps necessary.

(Source: Ronald I. McKinnon, "Financial Liberalization in Retrospect: Interest Rate Policies in LDCs," 25th Anniversary Symposium, Economic Growth Center, Yale University, Mimeo, April 1986, pp. 3-4, 17-18.

Although there are conflicting appraisals of the lessons to be learned from the Southern Cone experiences, most commentators appear to agree on the following points:

1. Substantial progress toward establishment of macroeconomic stabilization is a prerequisite for commencement of the financial liberalization process.

2. Significant risks are entailed in financial liberalization initiatives undertaken within an unstable macroeconomic environment. These risks

should be carefully weighed at each juncture against benefits potentially available from liberalization (including beneficial stimuli to the stabilization and structural adjustment processes).

3. Proper coordination of financial liberalization initiatives with stabilization policies is essential for the success of either.

Mexican officials, of course, are aware of the results of financial liberalization experiments elsewhere as well as of the revisionism underway in the literature concerned with financial aspects of development, and currently are attempting to make the correct inferences in formulating their own macroeconomic policy and financial sector reform agendas. Given the prolonged economic crisis, and the associated political pressures this situation has generated, Mexico's leaders are principally concerned to establish a credible macroeconomic stabilization program consistent with near-term recovery and longer-term growth -- while minimizing risks of further setbacks. They are, therefore, inclined to proceed cautiously in deciding how best to reformulate policies governing financial sector activities, paying particular attention to the question of what constitutes proper ordering or coordination of macroeconomic stabilization initiatives and financial sector reforms.

POLICY COORDINATION PROBLEM

Underlying the caution that has been manifested by Mexican authorities with respect to financial sector reforms is the fact that the policy problem is multi-dimensional and therefore fairly complicated. It is necessary not only to diagnose deficiencies in the operation of the financial system but also to prescribe corrective measures that are not inconsistent with and ideally are supportive of the government's larger macroeconomic strategies. Furthermore, it is recognized that corrective measures must be ordered sequentially with reference to the dynamics of the situation, and particularly to the sensitivity of the stabilization process to inappropriately timed disruptive changes in financial sector operations. Considerable care must be exercised to avoid actions that might have unwanted effects on the economic, psychological or political parameters governing successful pursuit of the stabilization objective.

It is largely because of the sequential ordering dimension of the problem that the theory of financial liberalization and related analytical techniques are not very helpful as guides to policy decision-making in the contemporary Mexican circumstances. Nevertheless, somehow the Mexican authorities must deal with this complication, whether by means of some form of sequential policy analysis, reliance on intuitive judgment -- or most likely, a combination of the two. In any case, it is important for the financial sector problems being addressed and the policy alternatives being considered to be structured within an appropriate conceptual framework.

The essential elements of such a framework are illustrated in the schematic diagram shown in Figure 2. The main points intended to be conveyed by this condensed guide to planning of financial sector reforms are summarized in the following paragraphs.

First, the basic differences between policies oriented toward macroeconomic stabilization and structural adjustment on the one hand, and those oriented toward financial sector efficiency and soundness on the other hand, need to be clarified. The principal distinctions are as follows:

1. Stabilization policies are intended to induce movement in the near term toward equilibrium in markets for factors of production, goods and services, and financial claims within a context of acceptable levels of employment and capacity utilization. Such policies are essentially concerned with aggregate demand management; are conducted principally by means of monetary and fiscal policy instruments; and are appraised primarily with reference to their impact on the rates of inflation and devaluation.

2. Structural adjustment policies are intended to promote longer-term economic growth by facilitating increased productive efficiency and international competitiveness. Such policies are essentially concerned with management of supply-side parameters; are conducted primarily by manipulation of relative prices, investment incentives and competitive pressures; and are appraised primarily with reference to the rate of economic growth and the strength of the balance of payments.

3. Financial sector policies are mostly oriented toward intermediate-term optimization of financial intermediation processes as related to savings mobilization, credit and investment allocation, and management of the national wealth portfolio held in the form of financial claims. Such policies are essentially concerned with the functional efficiency and systemic soundness of banking and other intermediary institutions; are conducted largely by means of modifications in governmental regulations exercised over the activities of these institutions; and are appraised with reference both to the level and structure of real interest rates and to consistency with macroeconomic stabilization and structural adjustment objectives.

The second point intended to be illustrated by the schematic diagram is that interest and exchange rate management policies impinge strongly on each of the three distinguishable areas of policy enumerated in the preceding paragraph. Because of the centrality of interest and exchange rates, governmental management of these variables principally by means of central banking techniques should be considered as adjuncts to or extensions of each of the other areas of policy endeavor. For present purposes, however, it is useful to conceive of interest and exchange rate management as a distinct function which serves to link together, and in large measure to determine the success of, stabilization, structural adjustment and financial sector policies. It should be emphasized, however, that there are severe limitations on governmental ability to control the level and structure of interest rates as well as rates of exchange with other currencies because of the pervasive influences of both domestic and external market forces.

The third point which the diagram is intended to illustrate is an inherent intertemporal overlapping between policies directed toward stabilization objectives and those directed toward structural adjustment objectives. Likewise, there is a corresponding but less clearly defined intertemporal overlapping between financial sector reforms and stabilization policies on the one side and structural adjustment policies on the other side. The proper timing or sequential ordering of financial sector initiatives varies with the particular type of measure concerned as well as with the larger macroeconomic circumstances. It is this third issue regarding the ordering or coordination of financial sector reforms with other types of policy endeavor that is the principal concern of this discussion.

Finally, there are three additional conceptual distinctions illustrated in the diagram which need to be taken into
account when planning a financial sector reform agenda for
Mexico. These can be briefly stated as follows:

1. Proper coordination of financial sector reforms
    with stabilization and structural adjustment poli-
    cies requires attention to simultaneous integra-
    tion as well as sequential ordering.

2. Planning of financial sector reforms should be
    premised on differentiation between the two main
    types of such reforms, namely:

    a. reforms directed toward revision of the exist-
        ing structure of financial repression and
        oriented toward controlled resource realloca-
        tion and provision of necessary protections
        from financial market forces, and

    b. reforms directed toward liberalization of
        financial institutions and orientation of mar-
        kets toward stimulation of efficiency through
        competition and innovation.

    Revision of previously installed repressive finan-
    cial policies (for example, curtailment of prefer-
    ential credit schemes) in most instances should
    precede liberalization initiatives (like relaxa-
    tion of regulatory regimes).

3. Financial sector reforms should be distinguished
    from changes in programs devised for financing
    activities in other sectors (such as agricultural
    credit and housing finance), and linkages between
    the two should be taken into account in planning
    the financial sector reform agenda.

The foregoing conceptualization of how financial sector
reforms fit into the larger macroeconomic policy picture,
and of what are the principal categories of financial sector
reforms, is utilized as the basis for the following appraisal of Mexico's near-term financial sector reform agenda.
Underlying the discussion is recognition that it is the
soundness of the macro strategy -- and the appropriateness
of the underlying policies, tactics and maneuvers -- that
will be the primary determinants of the government's success

in bringing about revitalization of the Mexican economy.
Financial sector reforms cannot salvage an inadequate overall strategy; such reforms should rather be thought of as
means for assisting occupation and defense of ground captured by macro initiatives and thereafter for taking fullest
advantage of a propitious environment for economic growth
and development.

NEAR—TERM FINANCIAL SECTOR REFORM AGENDA

As a result of the pervasive influence of theories pro-
pounded by Shaw, McKinnon, Fry and others regarding relationships between macroeconomic and financial sector policy
issues in developing countries, it has become conventional
wisdom to presume that desirable financial sector reforms
are generally liberalization measures. The term "liberalization" as used in this context means freeing financial institutions and markets from governmental regulations and manipu-
lations that work to repress forces of supply and demand.
Without wishing to question the significance of the contributions of liberalization proponents to the larger body of
relevant financial theory, I believe that the immediate priority for Mexico is not so much freeing financial institutions and markets from governmental "repression" as it is
revising existing policies impinging on these institutions
and markets in ways that are consistent with and supportive
of macro policies directed sequentially toward stabilization, structural adjustment and growth.
While the longer—run objective of financial sector
reforms should clearly be reduction of counterproductive distortions in financial processes (vis-a-vis the optimality
criteria indicated by competitive market models), the more
immediate objective in badly disrupted circumstances such as
those currently prevailing in Mexico should be progressive
revision of the various forms of governmental intervention
in ways that will facilitate adjustment of financial institutions and markets in proper coordination with macro—policy
successes. Put in terms of the military strategy analogy
employed earlier, the initial task in the financial sector
policy area is to secure the ground captured on the macro
policy front or, in other words, to create defenses that
minimize the risks of setbacks brought about by gross mal-
functioning of the financial system. Optimization of financial sector processes should be considered as a second—stage
operation to be carried out in a gradual and systematic manner when success of the macro campaign is less vulnerable to

erosion from inadequate governmental supervision and guidance of financial sector activities.

The central point is that coordination (or sequential
ordering) is required between implementation of the over-
arching strategy and the subsidiary financial sector reform
agenda. And the corollary point is that distinction is
required between types of financial sector reforms warrant-
ing priority attention during the successive stages of
advance in the macro arena. The main distinction to be made
in this latter regard is between "revised repression" and
"progressive liberalization", as already indicated and as
explained further below.

INITIAL PRIORITY: REVISION OF REPRESSION

Several sorts of interventionist policies currently
being followed in the financial sector of the Mexican economy need reform during the near term in order to facilitate
the government's stabilization and structural adjustment
initiatives. First, the existing array of preferential
credit schemes requires further revision beyond that already
made during the past year or two. Second, the government
needs to reduce the risk of a widespread domestic financial
crisis by dealing systematically and on a case-by-case basis
with the many distressed debtor-creditor relationships still
remaining to be resolved. Third, the standards and procedures for conducting prudential supervision and regulation
need to be further strengthened with respect to both management of financial institutions and operations conducted in
financial markets. And, finally, a number of problem banks,
both commercial and development, require renewed governmental attention with regard to the specifics of the individual
cases as well as to standardized criteria for gauging operational efficiency and systemic soundness.

As indicated more fully in the following paragraphs,
each of these items is integrally linked to the larger macro
strategy but has little direct connection with the theory of
financial liberalization. It should be noted, furthermore,
that a number of actions have been taken during the past two
years in each of the areas listed above, but without fully
correcting the problems. The initial priority agenda for
governmental actions therefore can be considered as items of
unfinished business.

Preferential Credit Regime

Mexico has long employed preferential credit schemes and associated interest subsidies to pursue a variety of economic, social and outright political objectives. The original, innovative rationale for this policy has become obscured in recent years by the overwhelming pressures of the public sector borrowing requirement on the one hand and by the proliferation of separate preference schemes on the other. The government and other preferred deficit spending units have commanded credit well in excess of what the financial system could provide without resorting to inflationary measures, and the preferential credit regime has become a major source of resource misallocation.

While estimation of the subsidies and related inefficiencies involved in the various schemes is a problematic exercise, the measurement procedure agreed upon by SHCP and the World Bank indicates that the aggregate interest subsidies dispensed by the development banks and the numerous associated "trust funds" established for this purpose amounted to an average of nearly 4 percent of GDP during the 1982-1986 period (see Table 1). To put this into perspective, these credit subsidies were equal to about one-third of the government's cumulative financial deficit -- and also to about the same proportion of funds mobilized by financial sector institutions from private sector sources. These estimates would be even more shocking if made by measurement methodologies which included credit subsidies administered through the commercial banking system.

While it is virtually impossible to trace accurately the incidences on ultimate beneficiaries and providers, it is reasonably clear nevertheless that many of the individual interest subsidization schemes are not justifiable on the basis of benefit-cost appraisals. More specifically, the burden imposed on the federal budget and the drain on the capitalization of financial sector institutions, when combined with the real costs in terms of resource misallocation and administrative superstructures, outweigh substantially the economic and social dividends derived from the preferential credit regime.

It is noteworthy, however, that the aggregate level of interest subsidies conveyed through development finance institutions was sharply curtailed in 1987 (to an estimated 1.8 percent of GDP) and perhaps further during 1988 and 1989. Also, most of the major preferential credit schemes are now more clearly targeted than before on priority development objectives and disadvantaged social groupings whose

requirements for governmental assistance cannot be readily
met by other means. Nevertheless, the conclusion remains
inescapable that this is an area in which further reforms
are clearly desirable -- both at the level of overall policy
and with respect to the numerous individual schemes in need
of substantial rationalization if not outright termination.

Distressed Debtor-Creditor Relationships

As a result of the prolonged turmoil in Mexico's domestic financial affairs, and particularly of erratic inflation
and related discontinuities in interest and exchange rates,
severe distress in domestic debtor-creditor relationships
has inevitably occurred. The government has been forced on
numerous occasions to intervene in these situations, usually
in an ad hoc manner but in two notable instances with quite
imaginative policies and related institutional innovations
-- namely, creation of FICORA(8) and FONAPRE(9) in 1983 and
1986, respectively. Moreover, restructuring in the public
enterprise and banking sectors has been motivated to a large
extent by the necessity for dealing with unsustainable
debtor-creditor stresses.

While statistical evidence of the degree of financial
distress is doubtless clouded by the common propensity of
debtor enterprises, creditor institutions and regulatory
authorities to mask their problems from one another and the
general public, nevertheless it is noteworthy that both the
commercial and development banks have clearly experienced
substantial decapitalization as a result of bad debt losses.
For the nationalized commercial banks as a group, the reported ratio of capitalization (excluding asset revaluations) to
total credit was reduced from 3.9 percent to 3.5 percent
between 1982 and 1987 (see Table 2). The corresponding figures for the development banks are 2.5 percent and 1.3 percent, respectively (see Table 3). Furthermore, during this
period the aggregated accounts for commercial banks show
ratios of non-performing loans to total capitalization ranging from nearly 80 percent in 1983 to about 8 percent in
1987, and financial losses actually realized ranged from 10
percent of capitalization to about 5 percent over the same
period. For the development banks, non-performing loans as
a percentage of total capital also reportedly decreased
between 1982 and 1987 from 35 percent to 23 percent; but the
corresponding ratio of realized financial losses increased
from slightly over 1 percent in 1982 to a shocking 36 percent in 1987. These aggregated data, of course, conceal a
wide range of differences in the circumstances of individual
institutions.

Comparable data on provisions for additional future realizations of bad debt losses are not available. But other evidence suggests that while neither the commercial nor the development banks (nor, for that matter, the regulatory authorities) observe particularly high prudential standards in this regard, the development banks are especially vulnerable to severe distress in the near future -- due both to under-provisioning and to inadequate capitalization.

The basic point is that in spite of the initiatives already taken by the government a high level of distress in domestic debtor-creditor relationships continues to exist. This is doubtless compounded by the extraordinarily high real interest rates brought about by the current strenuous stabilization efforts. These distressed situations will, in many instances, lead to further impasses and bad debt losses -- beyond those already suspended in the system while awaiting the inevitable recognition, allocation and absorption. In addition to the dangers posed to individual debtor enterprises and creditor institutions there is the larger risk that if debtor-creditor stresses are allowed to become too intense and widespread the success of the stabilization program could be imperiled.

While much has already been accomplished under difficult circumstances to defuse the potential explosiveness of distressed debtor-creditor relationships in the domestic context, some unfinished business still remains -- particularly with reference to loan portfolios of the development banks. Considerable ingenuity and forcefulness will be required to facilitate further restructuring of financially distressed situations in consistency with the government's new development strategy.

Prudential Regulation

The existing institutional arrangements for supervision and regulation of financial sector activities appear to be rationally structured and adequately extensive. Nevertheless, there are some significant deficiencies in the operational effectiveness of the two key agencies -- namely CNByS and CNdV. These deficiencies are largely attributable to excessive centralization of the evidence-weighing and decision-taking functions, as well as ultimate executive authority, within SHCP. Conflict of interest is inherent in this situation because SHCP is also the agency with ultimate responsibility for direction and utilization of the country's financial institutions for the government's purposes, be they developmental or political.

Furthermore, there is a worrisome disparity in the way the two supervisory agencies focus their energies and resources. CNByS appears to be much more concerned to monitor and appraise the operations of the commercial banks than those of the development banks. Similarly, the CNdV appears to focus principally on behavior of the money and capital markets rather than on the deportment of the players -- which, in the case of the casas de bolsa, has been left until quite recently largely to self-supervision by the industry association. Not only are there dangers inherent in these disparities but also they tend to create inequities in the competitive capabilities of the various types of financial institutions.

Numerous statutory changes have been made during the past six years, largely in response to the bank nationalization action in 1982 and the stock market "crack" in 1987, but further substantial upgrading of prudential supervision and regulation is clearly required. Modifications should be in the general directions of more uniform application of performance standards to all types of financial institutions, more adequate and timely public disclosure of activities and results, and substantial devolution of responsibility and authority from SHCP to truly autonomous regulatory agencies.

Institutional Restructuring

Since the commercial banks were nationalized in 1982 a total of 41 had been terminated by means of merger or liquidation by the end of 1988, leaving only 19 separate institutions. Although Banco de Mexico has actively assisted the remaining commercial banks in dealing with their liquidity and solvency problems, at least 6 of the 19 were in serious difficulties during 1988, as evidenced by their forced reliance on the "preventive assistance" afforded by the FONAPRE instrumentality. In spite of the reconfiguration that has already occurred, it appears therefore that the period of commercial bank restructuring is far from completed.

The situation of the development banks is even more tenuous, largely because relatively little of the necessary restructuring has been accomplished. As previously indicated, the development banks have realized substantial bad debt losses in recent years and the prospect is for further erosion of their already badly depleted aggregate capitalization. The situation may actually be much worse than indicated by the available accounting data, but even more worrisome is the fact that at least some development banks will continue to be cut off from their traditional sources of external and budgetary funding for the indefinite future. In short, the development banks and associated trust funds operating under their administrative jurisdiction are over-due for a major structural overhaul.

Each of the priority items listed above is integrally related to development bank operations. Therefore, it could be argued that a program of radical restructuring of develop-ment banking, addressed to the whole range of problems in this important sub-sector of the banking system, is the sin-gle most important item of unfinished business on the finan-cial sector reform agenda. There have been some encouraging signs recently to indicate that the new administration is also leaning toward this conclusion.

SECONDARY AGENDA: PROGRESSIVE LIBERALIZATION

The distinction between the priority reform agenda and the secondary agenda for progressive liberalization is based on appraisals of relative urgency and sequential timing vis-a-vis the pace of progress likely to be achieved in the area of macro policy implementation. It is not possible to be precise about these matters, however, because judgments regarding the urgency and timing requirements in particular instances may be governed by a variety of considerations including political feasibility. For example, it may be decided that certain liberalizing reform actions can conven-iently be taken before some of the more necessary but diffi-cult revisions in repressive policies can be effectively implemented. Nevertheless it is useful for present purposes to maintain the distinction.

Many specific financial sector policy measures of a liberalizing nature can be differentiated, but three categor-izations of such measures appear to be particularly perti-nent to Mexico's prospective circumstances. These are indi-cated and briefly discussed in the following paragraphs.

Promotion of Inter-Institutional Competition

Competition among financial institutions has been inhib-ited by a number of circumstances ranging from the excessive public sector borrowing requirement and the concomitant high level of bank reserve requirements, to the extensive prefer-ential credit regime and associated interest subsidization arrangements, to the statutory limitations and related oli-gopolistic market structures impinging on the environment within which the different types of financial institutions are required to conduct their activities. There exists substantial potential for modification of these factors in ways that will serve to stimulate beneficial competition both within and between the various types of financial institutions.

In any case, as and when recovery of the economy is brought about by the appropriate macro policy measures, and the priority revisions in repressive policies are accomplished, one of the most important liberalizing policy initiatives will be promotion of progressively broadened inter-institutional competition and, thereby, increased functional efficiency in the financial sector of the economy.

Freeing of Financial Market Forces

In order for Mexico's financial intermediary institutions to perform their resource mobilization and allocation activities in a more efficient manner, there must be well-functioning financial markets as well as effective inter-institutional competition. For efficiency-enhancing money and capital markets to evolve, interest rates and other financial prices must be allowed to reflect the forces of supply and demand as determined primarily by the requirements of the ultimate providers and users of transferable financial resources.

Monetary and fiscal policies, of course, will need to play a major balancing role, and there must be adequate prudential regulation as well. But such necessary interventions by governmental authorities should be calculated to complement rather than to frustrate market-driven processes if the fullest possible degree of financial sector efficiency is to be achieved.

Opening to Foreign Competition

The adequacy of domestic financial efficiency will inevitably be tested by the norms prevailing in the international financial services industry. Inefficient domestic financial services place a burden on productive activities and, particularly, on the ability of Mexican enterprises to compete effectively with their foreign counterparts — whether in domestic or external markets. Furthermore, unless the financial services available domestically are competitive in terms of both cost and sophistication, those able to do so will arrange for access to such services externally — thereby imposing a burden on Mexico's balance of international payments.

Mexico therefore cannot afford to disregard the rapidly changing standards of functional efficiency and technological sophistication in the international markets for financial services. And one aspect of the effort to establish international competitiveness must be gradually widened exposure of the domestic financial services industry to foreign competition within Mexico.

Re-Establishment of Effective Central Banking

The final observation to be made with respect to the "progressive liberalization" agenda is that Mexico's ability to reform the financial sector in these directions is fundamentally dependent on success of the financial stabilization program and, particularly, its fiscal and monetary policy elements. More specifically, the essential prerequisite for financial liberalization and realization of the efficiency-enhancing benefits potentially available from following such a course, is sufficient further correction in the fiscal area to permit primary reliance on traditional market-oriented central banking procedures. Efforts to pursue a program of financial sector liberalization will be doomed to failure unless the effectiveness of Banco de Mexico as the principal agent of government for stabilizing management of monetary and credit policies is first re-established.

RECENT AND PROSPECTIVE ACTIONS

A number of actions have been taken in recent months which clearly indicate governmental commitment to financial sector reform and modernization. Among the most significant have been further curtailment of interest subsidies dispensed by the development banks and associated trust funds, a substantial broadening of the scope afforded commercial banks to mobilize funds in domestic financial markets and to allocate their loans both to the government and to the private sector in accordance with profitability criteria, and more generally removal of limitations on commercial bank deposit and lending rates of interest. There has also been a wide-ranging reform of reserve requirements as administered by Banco de Mexico which has served, along with other related policy changes, to facilitate increased competition between commercial banks and the casas de bolsa in the financial markets.

All of these actions have set the stage for further reforms in accordance with the government's commitments to

the World Bank in connection with the recently-concluded
F-SAL agreement. More specifically, during the balance of
1989 "action programs" are scheduled for substantial restructuring of the development banks and trust funds and for
strengthening of prudential supervision and regulation of
banking system institutions. While the new development plan
does not contain a fully articulated program for financial
sector modernization, it does indicate that substantial
emphasis during the coming several years will be placed on
promotion of efficiency and assurance of soundness throughout the domestic financial system. It should be noted in
this context, however, that there has been no indication of
willingness on the part of government to reconsider the wisdom of the commercial bank nationalization action taken in
1982.

It is worrisome that the recent and prospective actions
are somewhat inconsistent with the prescriptions contained
in preceding sections of this paper regarding sequential
ordering requirements for successful financial sector reform
and modernization. Given the continuing uncertainties about
the prognosis for the government's macro stabilization program, and also the delayed response to evident problems in
the development banking and prudential regulation areas,
there is a risk that the liberalizing reforms already introduced in the commercial banking area may have been somewhat
premature. Let us hope that the future course of events
will prove otherwise.

LONGER-TERM PLANNING HORIZON

It is one thing to hypothesize that Mexico is on the
verge of success in devising a novel and workable development strategy, and on this basis to speculate about the
likely implications for financial sector reforms. It is
quite another to envisage in a larger and longer-term framework the directions toward which macroeconomic recovery and
financial sector improvement might naturally lead or ought
consciously to be directed. Speculation about these latter
matters might seem to be fanciful in the contemporary context, but it is useful to outline the distant horizons --
however vaguely -- in order to stimulate thinking about the
financial system characteristics that would best serve Mexico's longer-term aspirations.

I do not want to stray off into the realm of an ideo-
logical/geopolitical never-never land, nor do I intend to
transgress into an area of strictly Mexican prerogatives.

Nevertheless, it might be pardonable to point out that if, for whatever combination of national preference and external pressure, Mexico's future lies in the direction of a progressively closer economic orientation toward North America, this would have important implications for what should be done along each step of the way toward restructuring and modernizing of the existing financial system. More particularly, if the longer-term objective for Mexico's financial development is that of establishing a competitive modus vivendi within the North American context, then preparations should be started sooner rather than later. Not only might this make it easier to achieve more rapid progress initially toward realization of benefits from the financial modernization initiative, but also by adopting this orientation during the current stage of the rebuilding process the burden of a further restructuring of the financial system later on could be avoided.

Finally, whatever the longer-term orientation of the financial sector planning process, there probably is a good deal Mexico could learn from Canada about how best to proceed -- since Canada has been quite successful in modernizing its own financial system and in devising ways to survive and prosper in direct financial competition with the United States. Similarly, there quite likely is much to be learned from contemporary Spain about how to prepare for open competition with financially more developed neighboring countries. But above all there exist in Mexico's own financial history, particularly the relatively recent period running from the early 1950s to the early 1970s, indications of the objectives and guidelines that would serve the country well as the basis for establishing the longer-term horizon for planning future financial development.

NOTES

1. The full title is as follows: Problem Areas and Policy Issues in the Financial Sector of the Mexican Economy, Final Report on the Financial Sector Studies Program, January, 1989 (253 pages + 10 appendices).

2. The F-SAL agreement was reviewed by Nacional Financiera in El Mercado de Valores, Num. 13, Julio 1, 1989, pp. 7 and 10.

3. Secretaria de Planeacion y Presupuesto.

4. Comision Nacional Bancaria y Seguros.

5. Comision Nacional de Valores.

6. Plan Nacional de Desarrollo 1989-1994.

7. Ronald I. McKinnon, <u>Money and Capital in Economic Development</u> (Brookings Institution, 1973); Edward S. Shaw, <u>Financial Deepening in Economic Development</u> (Oxford University Press, 1973).

8. Fideicomiso para la Cobertura de Riesgos Cambiarios.

9. Fondo de Apoyo Preventivo a las Instituciones de Banca Multiple.

TABLE 1. Estimated Subsidies in Preferential Credit Operations of Development
Banks and Official Trust Funds[a] (% of GDP)

	1978–81 (Avg.)	1982	1983	1984	1985	1986	1987
Total Estimated Subsidies	0.9	5.4	6.6	2.0	2.1	3.2	1.8
Of Which Reflected in Direct Transfers by Government to Dev. Banks and Trust Funds	1.0	1.7	1.6	1.0	0.8	1.1	0.4
Recipients by Sector:							
Agriculture (incl. Sugar and Fishing)	0.4	1.1	1.3	1.2	1.3	1.7	1.0
Industry	0.2	2.1	2.8	0.4	0.4	0.6	0.5
Housing and Urban Development	0.2	1.9	2.2	0.4	0.3	0.6	0.1
Trade, Consumption, Tourism, etc.	0.1	0.3	0.3	0.1	0.1	0.3	0.2
	*	*	*	*			
Public Sector (incl. States, Municipalities & D.F.)	n.a.	3.8	3.7	1.5	1.8	n.a.	n.a.
Private Sector (incl. Enterprises, Individuals, & Other)	n.a.	1.6	2.9	0.5	0.3	n.a.	n.a.[b]

[a]Figures shown are preliminary estimates subject to revision.
[b]Letters n.a. indicate not available.

Source: Direccion General de Planeacion Hacendaria, SHCP.

TABLE 2.   Indicators of Soundness of Commercial Banking
           System

	1982	1983	1984	1985	1986	1987
			(% Ratios)			
Total Capital:						
Total Credit	5.4	5.5	4.9	4.7	5.0	6.4
Paid-in Capital	1.6	1.0	0.7	0.4	0.3	0.2
Reserves & Retained						
Profits	1.4	1.1	1.1	1.2	1.0	1.5
Asset Revaluation	1.5	2.6	2.0	2.0	2.3	2.9
Current Profits	0.9	0.8	1.1	1.1	1.4	1.8
Non-Performing Loans:						
Total Credit	3.9	4.4	2.4	2.1	1.2	0.5
Total Capital	71.4	78.9	48.9	44.1	22.8	8.0
Financial Losses:						
Total Capital	6.1	10.0	7.4	7.4	7.7	5.2
Net Profit	37.1	70.4	31.4	29.2	27.2	18.7
Financial/Other						
Operating Losses:						
Net Profit	49.1	81.5	47.9	40.4	36.7	30.8

Source: Comision Nacional Bancaria y Seguros.

TABLE 3. Indicators of Soundness of Development Banks

	1982	1987
	(% Ratios)	
Total Capital: Total Credit	2.6	1.5
Paid-In Capital	1.9	1.1
Reserves & Retained Profits	0.5	0.4
Asset Revaluation	0.1	0.2
Current Profits	0.1	(0.2)
Non-Performing Loans:		
Total Credit	0.9	0.3
Total Capital	35.4	23.2
Financial Losses:		
Total Credit	0.0	0.6
Total Capital	1.1	36.2

Source: Comission Nacional Bancaria y Seguros

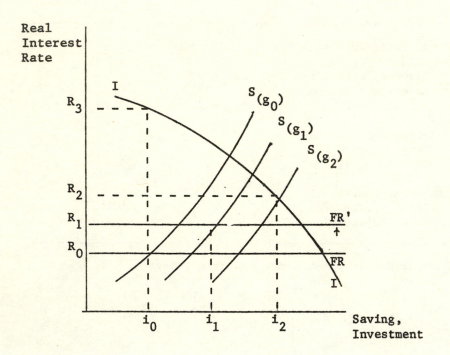

Based on Maxwell J. Fry, <u>Money, Interest, and Banking in Economic Development</u> (Johns Hopkins University Press, 1988), pp. 16.

Figure 1. Diagrammatic Formulation of Financial Liberalization Theory

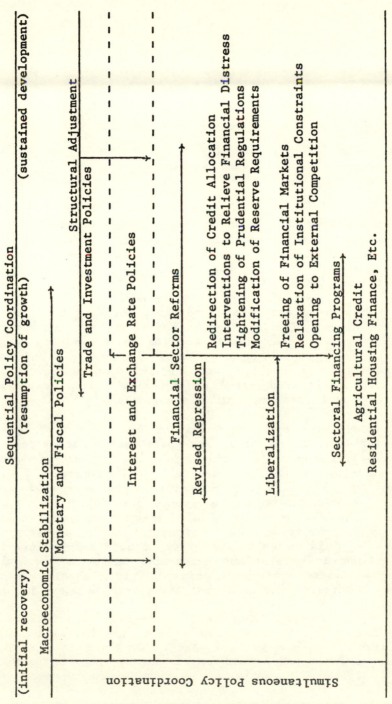

Figure 2. Conceptual Framework for Planning of Financial Sector Reforms

Comments

Jesus Marcos
Director of Economic Studies, Banco de Mexico

My comments on the paper presented by Dwight Brothers
will focus on the relationship between macro adjustment policies and financial sector reform in Mexico. Before express-
ing my point of view on this issue, however, I shall quote
Brothers' position:

> ...I believe that the immediate priority for Mexico is
> not so much freeing financial institutions and markets
> from governmental 'repression' as it is revising exist-
> ing policies impinging on these institutions and mar-
> kets in ways that are consistent with and supportive of
> macro policies directed sequentially toward stabiliza-
> tion, structural adjustment and growth.

In Brothers' opinion, "revision of repression" should
be Mexico's first priority. The government should strength-
en prudential supervision and regulation and address problems relating to the preferential credit regime and distressed debtor-creditor relationships. "Progressive liberalization" should follow as the second priority. This order
Brothers supports in spite of his recognizing some overlapping and imprecision with respect to the sequence of
reforms. It is my belief, however, that freeing financial
institutions in general and commercial banks in particular
should be Mexico's first priority. This financial sector
reform is necessary to carry out the country's macro adjustment program.

When the Mexican stabilization program was initiated at
the end of 1987, no structural reform or liberalization of
the financial sector was envisaged. On the contrary, more
regulations were imposed on the banking system. In particular, a ceiling on credit to the private sector was established.

However, once the fiscal effort consistent with price stability was determined and implemented, the exchange rate fixed, and the economy rapidly opened to foreign competition through foreign trade, any deviations from the expected course of the stabilization program due to internal or external shocks had to be confronted mainly with monetary policy.

Moreover, the credit ceiling proved ineffective in controlling private credit due to the fast development of the informal and uncontrolled credit market. Accordingly, it became clear that the stabilization program required much more flexible interest rates. No other short-term policy instruments were available to reduce the risks of program failure.

More specifically, the main nominal anchor for the Mexican stabilization program is the exchange rate. Needless to say, this anchor can hold firm only if the fiscal deficit is reduced to a level that can be financed with noninflationary resources. In other words, the equilibrium between the supply of and the demand for money, using the broadest definition of this aggregate, must be maintained. Under the circumstances this condition requires allowing the interest rate to adjust to the appropriate level. Otherwise, if for any reason the supply of money exceeds the demand, foreign reserves of the central bank would be depleted and the exchange rate would become unsustainable, thereby threatening the stabilization effort.

At the inception of the stabilization program, a rather large and relatively free market for government securities was already in existence. Growth of this market had been stimulated by the ceilings imposed on interest rates paid on bank deposits, and was therefore achieved largely at the expense of traditional banking operations.

During most of 1988 efforts were made to achieve the necessary degree of interest rate flexibility in the government securities market alone, but this policy proved insufficient. Moreover, it introduced distortions with undesirable consequences for the structure of the financial sector. Maintaining a policy that did not allow flexibility in banking operations would have produced lasting deleterious effects on banks, constraining significantly their contribution both to the structural change being induced by the bold liberalization of foreign trade and to the allocation of savings to their most productive uses. Furthermore, the restrictions on commercial banks were unsustainable because of their unfairness vis-a-vis the treatment of non-bank intermediaries.

As a result of the ceilings imposed on both bank credit granted to the private sector and the interest rate paid on bank deposits, during 1988 bank deposits contracted very rapidly, while lending to the government increased substantially. Furthermore, informal credit markets developed outside the control of the monetary authorities.

In this process, loans to the government became the main asset of the banking system. Consequently, the interest rate paid on these loans became a crucial issue in the rather difficult negotiations between the government and the banks. The agreed-upon rate became, in fact, a mechanism for subsidizing commercial banks, with an unfavorable impact on government finances at a time when considerable effort was being made to achieve a major fiscal correction.

The consequences of the limited flexibility of interest rates made inevitable the liberalization of banking operations so that banks could grant loans to the private sector and set the interest rate paid on their commercial deposits. Not only did this pave the way for more competition among banks and even more importantly between them and informal credit markets, but in conjunction with the development of the government securities market it helped consolidate the role of open-market operations as an instrument of monetary policy. A sufficiently large market for government securities and reduction in the fiscal deficit were important prerequisites for financial liberalization: without them, pressures for continued reliance on interest rate ceilings and high reserve requirements to obtain necessary financial resources would have been irresistible.

Besides supporting the stabilization program, commercial bank liberalization warrants first priority in order to open the economy to foreign trade competition. To compete with their foreign counterparts, domestic producers need a flexible and competitive domestic financial system. Otherwise, financial intermediation margins would be artificially high. This high margin of financial intermediation would clearly be a handicap for domestic producers trying to combat foreign competition.

A flexible and competitive financial system is also required to foster structural changes in the economy. With the opening of the economy to foreign competition, some sectors will prosper and others will stagnate or contract. In the end, these changes will permit a better allocation of resources, with ensuing productivity gains. Clearly, the speed with which the benefits of structural changes will become apparent depends on the degree of resource mobility. The financial system can play a very important role in fostering and supporting structural changes through its influence on the mobilization of resources. But to perform this important function, it must be flexible and competitive so that it can allocate savings to the more dynamic productive activities.

Finally, I would like to make some remarks on related microeconomic issues.

First, the recent commercial bank reform freed these institutions from the preferential credit regime imposed by the financial authorities, so that they need no longer grant interest subsidies. This reform was cited by Brothers as one of the initial priorities.

Second, the banks have also received explicit instructions from the government to be profitable institutions. Needless to say, this injunction provides a new element for evaluation of the performance of bank administrators.

My third point concerns the quality of the commercial banks' loan portfolios. Because of the ceiling on their credit to the private sector, a very large portion of their portfolios was invested in riskless government loans. Moreover, the private firms had a net creditor position with the financial system before the liberalization. Accordingly, at the time of the liberalization actions the soundness of the asset portfolio of the commercial banking system was not in serious doubt.

Fourth, because real interest rates have remained at relatively high levels during the past twelve months, and because commercial banks are now free to determine the rates they pay on deposits and thereby to compete more effectively with other intermediary institutions, prudential regulation and supervision clearly must be strengthened. Since the banks are government owned, this is of the utmost importance. In these circumstances and on the basis of past experience, depositors believe that their deposits are insured and that there exists no capital risk. However, bank administrators may have an incentive to grant riskier loans in order to be able to offer higher returns on deposit liabilities and thus increase their market shares. Clearly the regulatory authorities must take the actions necessary to catch up with the liberalization process, to minimize the risks of bank failures and thereby to consolidate the commercial bank reforms.

Prudential Regulation and Financial Stabilization

Aristobulo de Juan
Managing Director, de Juan y Asociados

INTRODUCTION

This paper discusses prudential regulation of banking broadly defined to include supervision and restructuring. The basic argument is that the short-term effects of financial stabilization and economic deregulation programs may exacerbate problems of insolvency in banking systems and that governments may have to respond by strengthening bank regulatory procedures.

Because the author's knowledge of the Mexican financial system is limited, the picture described in this paper is not necessarily fully applicable to Mexico. But experience has taught me that in many developing countries bank deregulation has been applied too abruptly in an environment of inadequate disclosure and prudential supervision and in the context of financial stabilization programs involving tight monetary policies which put additional stress on the system. If, as I suspect, symptoms of financial distress and bank insolvency are already evident in the Mexican system or are likely to show up in the near future, it seems relevant to consider which remedies are appropriate.

INSOLVENCY AS AN EPIDEMIC

During the 1980s in many developing countries bank insolvency has become an epidemic which may continue to spread well into the 1990s unless treated appropriately and with determination. The concept to underscore, based on experiences of both success and failure, is that bank insolvency is a financial system disease requiring careful diagnosis and prescription. Governments are becoming increasingly aware that they must deal with bank insolvency in order to remove a serious obstacle to economic growth, fiscal soundness and monetary stability. Argentina, Bolivia, Chile, Ghana, Nigeria, the Philippines and Turkey are just a few examples of countries where this heightened awareness exists even though nationalized banks predominate and the conventional wisdom is that insolvency does not matter.

The situation may be deemed an "epidemic" when over 50 percent of the banks in a system are technically insolvent or, to use a different measure, when more than 30 percent of banking system assets are comprised of bad or doubtful claims on debtors. Commercial as well as development banks become insolvent, but the latter are frequently in worse shape because (often futile) attempts to achieve development and social objectives by means of directed credit schemes and related financial subsidies lead to a diluted sense of risk, relaxed controls and concealment of losses. Similarly, although insolvency affects private as well as publicly owned banks, the latter are frequently worse off, especially if they are run as government agencies and political factors override economic considerations.

While banks may show a reasonable level of capital adequacy on the books, a considerable part of their formal equity may be "reserves" derived from asset revaluations that exceed real market values. Banks in this situation often actually have a negative net worth and current losses. A particularly significant indicator is a high proportion of non-performing and lost assets carried both on and off the balance sheet. These concealed losses in some cases amount to as much as 50 percent of total assets, or several times the equity capital. The losses are primarily in the loan and guarantees portfolio, but can often be detected as well in real property, financial investment and foreclosure accounts. Within the loan portfolio, losses are found not only in term lending but also in working capital advances used to finance borrowers' losses. The use of overdrafts or open lines of credit facilitates the concealment practice and makes it harder for both bankers and supervisors to detect the losses. Of course, most non-performing assets produce no income; nor do real estate, foreclosures or reserve requirements. Actual results can therefore hardly be positive -- indeed, the flow of losses tends to grow cumulatively because these assets, plus the stock of previous losses, have to be financed with resources that involve high service costs.

The negative net worth and current losses often do not show up on a bank's books. As the president of the central bank of a major developing country recently put it, "Most of our banks incur big losses, but they all declare profits -- and pay taxes and dividends." This lack of disclosure occurs because of poor accounting rules and practices, poor supervision by government agencies, unreliable external audits and the determination of many bankers to keep their problems hidden. When governments also wish to hide insolvency in the system because they fear losing public confidence or lack the proper mechanisms and political will to deal with the situation, the effects are compounded. Governments, insolvent banks and distressed borrowers become accomplices in the art of non-compliance and cover-up. A typical example is the present state of the saving and loan associations in the United States. In such situations, the worst loans will rarely be recognized as bad, but rather will be labelled as "current loans" in the books, with unpaid interest being capitalized and accounted for as income. Rolling over bad loans "sine die" to keep them "evergreen" and capitalizing interest may make these practices formally legal if regulations are loose. But any resemblance between the net worth and profit figures shown in the accounts and the reality of the situation becomes merely coincidental.

Governments frequently require the banks to allocate a major portion of their deposits to government securities in order to finance the budget deficit, as well as imposing high and unremunerated reserve requirements in an attempt to check inflation and regulate monetary flows. Banks may also be forced to allocate another (and sometimes very significant) part of their deposits to finance development projects or privileged circuits of credit within which resources are mandatorily allocated to borrowers with favorable treatment in terms of interest rates and maturities. What then remains for a bank to lend freely for proper remuneration? Clearly a series of policies like those described here involves a serious burden on bank profitability and leads to high lending rates on the small portion of deposits they can freely lend, as explained below.

Bank operational costs often are disproportionate to the volume of business transacted. A proliferation of branch offices, staff and paperwork, as well as extravagant spending for public relations purposes, is typical of banks in distress. In periods of abrupt deregulation and high inflation, banks tend to open more branches than they need, hire more staff than necessary and pay higher salaries than the market requires. Inflation also leads to operations with shorter terms, both on the liability and on the asset side, involving large amounts of paperwork and processing expenses. When inflation is controlled, the volume of banking business tends to shrink in real terms, but operational costs seldom decrease proportionately as inertia prevails. Some governments limit the freedom of bankers to close branches in order to service remote or unprofitable areas, while concerns over possible signals of distress and gradual liquidation as well as union reactions make the bank managers themselves reluctant to close others. Heavy paperwork and processing also remain in place because confidence in the system is slow to return and short-term operations prevail for a long time. Of course, proper computerization might help, but bank managements often think there are other priorities.

If financial deregulation is introduced abruptly, deposit rates tend to soar as the fight for deposits exceeds the limits of normal competition and comes to resemble a struggle for survival. Inexperience of banks in competitive pricing and ill-advised striving for "prestige" through growth in market share contribute to this process. But when banks are in distress, high remuneration of deposits generally indicates the need for liquidity at any cost. The banks use the new deposits to meet their current interest payments and other operational costs, even though these expenses exceed the spread between deposit and lending rates. Only part of the new deposits is accordingly available for new lending. Such aggressive competition for new deposits in order to avoid illiquidity therefore often leads to increasing losses, as will be explained below. Banks have little money to allocate freely because a sizeable part of their resources have to be allocated to reserve requirements, forced investment and the privileged circuit, as mentioned above. Another part is increasingly stuck in non-performing loans.

The obvious result is skyrocketing lending rates and, worse, a perverse selection of borrowers. Those who accept high lending rates tend to be speculators or high-risk operators who will ultimately prove unable to repay. Some of them know this from the beginning. So do some of the bankers.

In these circumstances loan portfolios deteriorate faster and faster not only because of the perverse selection of borrowers but also because new lending tends to be concentrated on non-performing borrowers related to the banks or on other borrowers holding large credits that can not be repaid. A number of bankers feel they cannot afford to "stop the bicycle" and have a large client fail because then their own insolvency will be unveiled. The implication of this pattern for portfolio quality is obvious.

The sequence outlined above is particularly typical of development banks with subsidiaries for four reasons. First, because of the parental relationship between the bank and the subsidiary, loans made according to less rigorous criteria may constitute a high proportion of the bank's capital. Second, the attitudes of the subsidiary's management may deteriorate because of their easy and systematic access to credit. Third, the bank's representatives on the subsidiary's board may develop so close a relationship with the people they are supposed to supervise that they become an obstacle to information and control rather than a proper conduit for both. Fourth, the parent bank will seldom recognize a loan to a subsidiary as overdue or doubtful. Moreover, in the case of state-owned development banks, social objectives and political pressure may lead to bad loans and losses, whether or not accounted for on the books.

No one pays and no one recovers as a result of poor legal procedures and bad habits. Legal procedures to recover loans are rarely adequate in insolvent systems. Although both borrowers and bankers know that foreclosing on collateral is a very complicated process that may take over five years, they still rely on collateral for loans or open lines of credit, rather than on realistic appraisal of the ultimate destination of the loan and the ability of the borrower to repay. In farming, for example, cattle can be offered as collateral even though, as an African banker used to say, "Those collaterals have legs, so they walk and disappear." Moreover, as mentioned above, when the large and delinquent borrower is in command, the banker does not dare to force reimbursement or foreclose for fear of unveiling his own failure. Sometimes governments complicate matters by establishing indiscriminate and generous schemes obliging banks to reschedule their loans on preferential terms and at below-market interest rates.

Banks are often permeated by attitudes that have little to do with sound banking. Speculation in lending or in para-banking activities becomes the rule, and hiding the truth by means of creative accounting becomes common practice. Worst of all, recovery goes to the bottom of the list of the bank's priorities. Attitudes converge as borrowers are unable or unwilling to repay and bankers continue to neglect recovery. In the case of lending to related parties, this neglect is not coincidental. In state-owned banks, bureaucratic values may add to the vices in corporate bank cultures. State ownership may lead some bureaucrats to ask themselves why they need capital provision, recovery performance or good management controls if the banks exist just to channel government funds into the economy.

CAUSES OF BANK INSOLVENCY

Economists commonly identify macroeconomic policy mistakes as a major source of widespread bank insolvency,(1) but my experience in supervising and dealing with problem banks indicates that mismanagement also plays a major role in bank insolvency. Poor bank supervision and political interference in the areas of lending and recovery are significant as well.

When an economy is subjected to the stresses associated with financial deregulation, the health of its banks is clearly affected. Sharp changes in the relative prices of currencies, property and loanable funds are likely to trigger serious problems in banking systems. Moreover, while beneficial in the long term, adjustment processes and market deregulation will normally create, unleash or unveil new problems in the short term. Reducing fiscal deficits and moving from high inflation to monetary stability will uncover the cracks in the system. The sudden freedom to open new financial companies or set interest rates may also lead to trouble. Other reasons for insolvency like mismanagement, lack of supervision and political pressure are less well known and will accordingly be emphasized below.

Mismanagement is an evil in itself that may cause serious damage to a bank or to a banking system as a whole in good times as well as bad. But the most significant feature of mismanagement is how it introduces a dynamic of deterioration through a behavioral process that proves very difficult to reverse with policies and measures external to the banks. This process is much more likely to occur if banking supervision is ineffective. When a bank is "technically mismanaged" and incurs losses with neither recapitalization nor changes at the helm until its equity is eroded beyond a certain limit, the management is likely to go through a series of stages that can be characterized as "cosmetic management", "desperate management", and "fraud".(2) At the end of the process, a bank that has shown profits on the books and remained liquid may have lost between one-third and two-thirds of its portfolio, or several times its equity capital. The characteristic features of these stages are summarized below.

"Technical mismanagement" may prove very damaging in the following circumstances: a) when a bank grows too quickly and becomes overextended in terms of lending or when it expands into geographical areas or new products with which it is not familiar; b) when it concentrates heavily on large borrowers or in a given economic sector or geographical area; c) when asset and liability terms, interest rates or currency exposures are improperly matched; d) when internal controls are weak; and e) when the bank is unable to anticipate or adapt to change and adopts instead an attitude that "nothing serious ever happens".

"Cosmetic management" means resorting to creative accounting to depositors, shareholders and supervisors in order to cover up capital and profit erosion while waiting for economic recovery or lucky strokes of fortune. Bankers look at income statements "upside down": profits are no longer the remainder of real income less expenditure, but instead are a set objective so that other items are manipulated if the statement won't otherwise come square. Imagination may have no limits in devising cosmetic procedures, but the most typical ones are "evergreening" loans or systematic rollover, capitalization of interest and fictitious or unrealistic collateralization. Provision for losses is inadequate and unpaid interest is accounted for as interest income.

"Desperate management" means the search for speculative and high-risk operations, frequently large exposures that, if successful, might bring about an upturn in the bank's situation. As put by a senior American supervisor, "When banks in Texas began to experience difficulties in their lending for oil rigs and drilling, instead of adjusting and diversifying they doubled their bets and went into real estate; the outcome was disaster." Real estate and speculative investment operations are typical of this stage, as is concentrating large proportions of loans on troubled big borrowers in the hope of a happy ending. These operations are seldom successful and normally multiply the losses rather than reducing them. Since cash flow suffers, the obvious "desperate" reaction is to seek new deposits at any cost, again fueling the spiral of risk and losses while hiding liquidity problems. Playing with interest rate risk is another typical reaction.

The concept of fraud does not require much elaboration. One could summarize this stage by saying that "There are one thousand ways to skin...a bank," but lending to related parties, whether directly or indirectly, stands out among the fraudulent practices that contribute to bank failure.

Poor supervision is also a decisive element in bank failure and insolvency. For the sake of simplicity, the general concept can be broken down into three components: the regulatory framework, verification activities and enforcement. During macroeconomic shocks and particularly in periods of adjustment or economic deregulation, a strong

prudential regulatory framework is indispensable for damage
control. But in order to implement proper regulation, the
market and the government should be in a position to supervise banks through proper disclosure of information and
institutional verification mechanisms. If problems are then
unveiled, effective and prompt enforcement of remedial
action is the necessary supplement so that the problems
won't get out of hand and discredit both the regulatory
framework and the supervisory mechanisms. Needless to say,
these protective devices do not exist where bank insolvency
is widespread.

Many developing countries have flaws in their regulatory framework, and four major gaps commonly exist. First,
while exit from the market seldom occurs, entry requirements
are either very loose or based on the wrong criteria. Second, the requirements for capital adequacy are set at a
level that proves too low to cushion losses and allows for
components of "capital" that hardly deserve that name (for
example, fictitious assets revaluation reserves) and yet are
measured as a proportion of total deposits or assets regardless of the risks involved. Third, accounting systems are
poor, especially in the area of loan classification, which
is often unregulated and based only on formal aspects of
loans rather than on the actual riskiness of the borrower.
If a loan is overdue or the borrower is bankrupt, the loan
should be classified as overdue or in arrears. However, in
practice if the debtor is high risk and in serious trouble
but his loans are rescheduled or rolled over and therefore
not technically in arrears, the loan can -- and will -- be
classified as current, no provisions will be made and interest will be accrued by the bank on its books. Fourth,
limits to large exposures or loans to related parties do not
exist or are very lax (amounting to one to three times the
bank's equity in some cases). Frequently, these limits
apply to loans to each particular person or company but not
to groups or conglomerates. This laxity is particularly
serious because loan concentration is the main reason for
individual bank failures around the world.

Flaws in supervision are also prevalent. All countries
have an institution responsible for verification. Common
names include "Superintendency of Banks", "Bank Control
Commission", "General Inspectorate of Banks" and "Bank
Supervision Department". They normally operate within the
Central Bank or the Ministry of Finance or as a separate government institution. But as a rule, their staffing is insufficient in quality and poorly remunerated, with no regular
training programs in place. Their work is based on poor

accounting systems and sketchy or meaningless prudential reports required from banks. The paperwork is often overwhelming for the banks and not very enlightening for the supervisor. Off-site surveillance involves little use of computer and analytical methods and on-site verification focuses on compliance with administrative regulations rather than on the banks' health problems. Bank inspections take place after long time spans (three to eight years in some countries) and credit analysis in conspicuous by its absence. Risk assessments are therefore hardly ever made, problems are unidentified and the supervisory authority works in the dark.

As a supplement to the government's role in verification, external audits of banks by independent public accountants is common practice in most countries. These audits are usually statutory in nature and focus on bank compliance with generally accepted accounting principles. Although most of them are supposed to establish whether the banks' accounts are a fair and true view of their financial situation, they seldom unveil existing problems of bank insolvency, in part because of the laxity of requirements for loan loss provisions and identification of interest accruals. Poor skills, lack of interaction with the government supervisors and lack of independence may play a role as well.

Even with poor regulation and supervision, some administrative and minor institutional health problems are occasionally detected. But more often than not, insolvency problems are discovered not as a result of any early warning or bank rating system but because problems of illiquidity surface (often too late, after repeated insolvencies) or because fraudulent activities become known to the public. Enforcement of remedial action, which is the key to solving problems at any stage, but especially when a bank proves to be insolvent, is often very weak. In some cases, the legal framework is such that regulators lack the necessary powers to apply good remedies. But even when regulations are sufficient, they are hardly ever enforced: no provisioning for bad debts is required, no recapitalization is implemented, no board members or managers are removed and no suspension of dividend payments is demanded for loss-making banks. Worse, due to fears of macro dislocation or lack of institutional mechanisms and political determination, insolvent banks are kept alive as "zombie banks" without ever being closed or restructured. Occasional fines or penalties as well as minor harassment by the supervisor are the most common "remedial" actions. The scope for mismanagement is therefore much too wide.

A few months ago the Minister of Finance of a significant developing country observed: "In my country every
minister considers himself to own or control one of our
state-owned banks, and keeps making telephone calls." In a
different country, a bank president said: "All right, our
portfolio is in very bad shape, but we do not have to make
any provisions for losses or recapitalize the bank because
all our bad loans were made under instructions by the government." In fact, in a number of countries lending is
strongly influenced by pressure to achieve developmental,
social or political objectives especially in the case of
state-owned banks. Nor is pressure for non-recovery or
tolerance for non-repayment infrequent. Appointment of
management is also influenced by political factors. The
existence of political pressure is a very good excuse for
lax management and loose accounting practices. Needless to
say, such a context makes it difficult to find competent and
independent professionals to serve as board members or top
bank managers.

IMPLICATIONS FOR THE ECONOMY

The role of banks as a part of the payment system and
as one of the basic pillars in resource mobilization and
allocation makes stability of the financial system a necessity. When made known to the public through evidence of
liquidity problems, insolvency of even a single bank may
trigger a crisis in confidence and affect the stability of a
whole system through deposit runs and related domino
effects, thus contributing to demonetization and generating
capital flight. When insolvency is widespread, even if
unknown to the public, the repercussions in the economy also
constitute serious obstacles to economic growth and the
success of sound macro policies. Growing distortions in
resource allocation, upward pressure on interest rates, a
corporate culture with no sense of risk or disclosure and
growing losses throughout the system are the main areas to
be highlighted.

As described previously in this paper, concentration of
lending on large borrowers is not only one of the main reasons for bank insolvency but also one of its main consequences. An insolvent bank will tend to refinance indefinitely and increase lending to borrowers in trouble in an
effort to avoid precipitating their failure by calling the
loans or foreclosing. This situation becomes particularly
serious when the borrowers in trouble are related to the

bank in any manner. The hope for relief if the economy improves and the need to buy time in order not to unveil the bank's own losses are the main reasons for such behavior. When insolvency is widespread, this behavior means allocating a large part of new deposits to enterprises that have no future and in turn allocate their borrowings to expenditures and losses instead of to productive activities that might have a positive impact on the growth of the economy. The Rumasa holding in Spain is a typical case. Nationalized in 1983 and then re-privatized in 1984, Rumasa owned 20 banks with 5 percent of the banking system's assets and over 200 industrial and service companies. Investigation of the group failure disclosed that through over 500 phantom companies these 200 companies had accumulated 65 percent of the 20 banks' total loan portfolio. Although only the loans to 15 of these companies were performing, not one was formally classified as overdue.

If insolvency is widespread and remains untreated, the excessively high market interest rates that result will adversely affect the behavior of borrowers, prices and growth. In Bolivia, for example, although fiscal deficits and inflation were successfully checked in 1986, interest rates remained extremely high because the problem of bank insolvency had not been addressed and depositors perceived widespread distress in the banking system and therefore demanded a high remuneration to offset the risk. Insolvent banks will pay almost any interest rate to attract deposits, remain liquid and compensate for the lack of yield from their non-performing assets. The resultant high rates for new lending may seriously damage the development of the real economy, prompt disintermediation and distort sound monetary policies.

The corporate culture in the banks deteriorates, as described above. Speculation, lack of disclosure, non-recovery and non-repayment of loans have a strong impact on banks and make the sense of risk and incentives for improvement disappear. Reversing this phenomenon is a lengthy process unless dramatic changes are made in bank management and supervision. And worse, this culture permeates beyond the banks to the corporate world and even to the entire society and its government.

When unaddressed, bank insolvency also causes fiscal and monetary distortions. The losses in the system spiral through a dynamic process of deterioration. In many cases governments absorb the losses of private as well as state banks in order to keep the borrowers and/or the banks alive and ongoing. Direct or indirect subsidies to banks and liquidity support through rediscount facilities, special advances by the central banks or special deposits by the treasury or other government institutions are quite common. At least a part of the cost is already being incurred, but the benefit of a solution to end the losses is not immediate. Furthermore, the losses incurred by the government, within the state-owned banks or through subsidies to the banking system in general, remain undisclosed, often as advances on the balance sheet of the central bank. Will these advances be performing? Will they ever be recovered? Probably not. The advances are neither recorded in the budget nor even considered as a quasi-fiscal deficit, in spite of the fact that the fiscal deficit must ultimately record them in full. In the end, losses will grow so large and the situation will become so dramatic that the government -- that is, the taxpayer -- will have to step in, foot the bill and supply the necessary resources because no other options are available to deal with the snowball effect. If addressed promptly, the problem would be much smaller and the cost of its solution much easier to share.

Finally, if untreated, insolvency can make otherwise sound macro policies inappropriate. In the context of a healthy economy and banking system, market deregulation and tight monetary policies are usually recipes for success. However, if applied in a context of bank insolvency, some of these measures may prove counterproductive and fuel the problems policymakers were trying to solve. The policies should therefore be implemented gradually, with bank insolvency problems addressed simultaneously or even beforehand. A few examples follow.

First, deregulation of interest rates is a classic sound policy to encourage financial competition with a view to increasing deposit mobilization. When deregulation is abrupt and banks are insolvent, however, deregulation will lead to a sharp rise in deposit rates to attract new resources. Deposits may grow rapidly, but a considerable proportion of the new resources will be allocated to covering operational costs and addressing liquidity concerns rather than to financing productive investments. Insolvent banks will therefore be unable to compete for good borrowers through low lending rates. As a result of both the scarcity of new resources and the very high cost of deposits and operating expenses, lending rates will also be extremely high and the effects on monetary variables, borrower selection and the quality of portfolio are obvious.

Second, although deregulation of entry into financial markets is typically considered to be a sound policy, when

it occurs abruptly and in a context of distress, the outcome
will often be disastrous. This is especially the case when
the financial institutions established or taken over under
these policies are owned by speculators who want to make
easy money and/or by businessmen who want to ensure financing for their own activities. Experience shows that in
these circumstances, most of the institutions become insolvent and in some countries many of them are then liquidated,
with exit used as the logical counterpart to entry. In the
case of Argentina, the liquidation of some 200 institutions
has brought about a widespread feeling of instability, which
has certainly caused demonetization and capital flight. In
other cases, like Spain, where 52 of the 110 banks became
insolvent between 1977 and 1984, most of the problem banks
had been previously established or taken over by new
bankers.

Third, although desegmentation of banking clearly
favors competition and systems that operate better as a
whole, this policy is not always beneficial if insolvency is
widespread. For example, if competition is increased in
this context by licensing second-tier banks and finance
companies for deposit taking, their new deposits are very
likely to be obtained at a high cost and allocated to
troubled borrowers unable to repay their previous loans.
With easy access to new resources, these banks lose the
incentive to address recovery and discipline borrowers. The
effects will clearly have been counterproductive.

Fourth, increasing reserve requirements is also a typical measure both to check inflation by mopping up liquidity
from the system and to finance fiscal deficits. The cause-
effect relationship is very clear in sound economies, but
when the requirements go beyond reasonable limits and banks
are in distress the implications may be unfortunate for both
the banks and the success of the policy pursued. Because
high and unremunerated reserve requirements seriously reduce
the profitability of banks, their obvious reaction will be
to protect spreads and profits by passing on the cost of the
frozen funds through increases in lending rates for the few
resources they can still allocate freely. The effects of
the measure will thus be a sharp rise in interest rates,
deterioration of loan portfolios, increasing losses and disintermediation.

PRUDENTIAL REGULATION, SUPERVISION AND RESTRUCTURING

The implications of bank insolvency for the economy as
a whole are very serious. Ideally, either the problem of

each particular bank should be solved by its shareholders
through recapitalization and changes in management or the
market should operate and these banks should be closed, let-
ting both shareholders and depositors bear the costs.   If
these corrections fail to occur, however, and the implications of continued insolvency are considered to be profoundly damaging for the economy, government intervention
becomes necessary.   Because the consequences of inappropriate action can be equally serious, a special effort should
be made to establish appropriate principles and practices
based on successful experiences in solving this problem.

Macro and microeconomic policies should be applied
together in order to avoid the cost of permanent subsidization and to secure the benefits of a sound financial system.
The proper choice of measures and sequencing are important
aspects of the correction which, in the author's view,
involves the following basic elements: determining the real
extension and depth of the problem (or how to "get out of
the dark"); enacting proper regulations to set the rules of
the game for bankers to follow and for supervisors to
enforce; dealing with deeply insolvent banks through restructuring, closure or rehabilitation; and taking across-the-
board measures to supplement case-by-case restructuring.
This is the logical sequencing but if obtaining accurate
knowledge of the situation or having the right legislation
in place takes time and insolvency of banks becomes obvious,
restructuring should become a top priority while work proceeds in the other areas.   The acceleration factor should
not forgotten.

"Getting out of the dark" requires primarily a good set
of accounting rules, including those that make it possible
to appraise the quality of assets on the books compared to
their market value, regardless of whether the loans are in
formal arrears.   Getting to know the reality also requires a
good system of verification.   Since information reported by
insolvent banks to the authorities is frequently fictitious,
verification through on-site examination is invaluable.   The
assistance of external auditors, at least while insolvency
prevails and examination resources are scarce, is also essential. Moreover, irrespective of emergency situations, a good
system for disclosure to the regulatory authority should be
devised to serve as an early-warning mechanism focused on
areas such as capital, assets, management, earnings and
liquidity.

With respect to other rules of the game that need to be
established, the key pillars for a sound system are as follows: stringent criteria for entry into markets; capital

adequacy requirements to provide a cushion for potential losses; mandatory provisioning and write-offs of risky loans as well as suspensions of interest accruals; limits to the concentration of lending to individual companies or groups of companies as well as to parties related to the bank; and proper mechanisms and institutions to achieve timely changes in management and ownership as well as effective liquidation or rehabilitation.

Liquidation and rehabilitation are the two principal types of bank restructuring. Although the former is considered the best option according to market principles, not all insolvent banks should be liquidated because of the effect on economic stability when externalities are present. Thoroughgoing rehabilitation -- and emphatically not inaction -- is then the best solution.

Rehabilitation programs should focus on reconstruction of the balance sheet through recapitalization and/or asset clean-up by the central bank or other special institutions so that the bank in question becomes quickly profitable. However, changes in management and ownership are other factors to consider. This is a matter not only of equity, when rehabilitation is accomplished with government money, but also of effectiveness, to avoid repeating previous problems. Mergers and acquisitions are excellent ways to replace former management and ownership when the new units can be strong both financially and managerially, but merging banks simply for the sake of merging leads nowhere.

When possibilities for installing new ownership and management are limited the chances of successful rehabilitation are diminished. Institutional arrangements to own and/ or manage banks temporarily while finding a final solution should then be sought. Rehabilitation mechanisms in combination with deposit insurance can sometimes provide a way to reconstruct banks financially and also to arrange for new management and ownership whether temporarily or permanently.

When bank insolvency problems affect the whole financial system, in addition to treating the worst cases individually along the lines described in this paper, governments should take across-the-board measures to improve the general health of the system. Lowering excessive reserve requirements and partially remunerating reserves should be considered. Reduction of mandatory credit allocation through either investment in government securities or lending at low rates to privileged circuits of the economy also warrants attention.

A number of controversial questions related to bank restructuring still remain. How can the fiscal and monetary

implications of bank rehabilitation be avoided or reduced?
Does rehabilitation mean bailing out bankers? Is moral hazard stronger with or without deposit insurance?   Should
financial markets be restructured before individual institutions?   Should insolvent borrowers be restructured before
banks?   These questions provide ample material for debate
and each could be the subject of a separate paper. But in
the author's view, the benefits of bank restructuring
clearly outweigh the costs if the alternative approach to
bank insolvency is not addressing it at all.

APPLICABILITY TO MEXICO

     In Mexico all banks are nationalized, only 15 percent
of the loan portfolio is placed with private borrowers,
development banks exist primarily to fulfill social objectives and the government has relieved large borrowers from
their foreign currency debt. It might therefore seem that
the picture described in this paper has little relevance.
However, the key elements of sound banking, such as capital
adequacy, good management practices, prudential regulation
and enforcement of remedial action, are important in any
system, whether nationalized or otherwise. Furthermore, as
argued above, in the short run financial stabilization programs of the sort currently being attempted in Mexico may
bring about widespread distress among both borrowers and
banks by revealing the previously veiled cracks of a system.
     In any case, the Mexican authorities may find it worth-
while to consider the implications of objective answers to
the following questions:

     -    Do banks have a proper level of core capital or
          does their equity capital contain a high propor-
          tion of items with doubtful economic substance?

     -    In a system with very high lending rates, where
          the best corporations are net creditors or have
          direct access to disintermediated resources, are
          not the worst borrowers the most likely bank
          clients, even if they are only allocated a small
          part of the loan portfolio?

     -    When freedom to lend is returned to banks in a
          sudden manner, will they be equipped to lend or
          are they likely to have lost the necessary mana-
          gerial skills and sense of risk?

-   Does management behavior in some or all banks correspond to the syndromes described in this paper?

-   Are regulators well informed about their banks' health in time to take effective remedial action, or are they partly "in the dark"?

-   Are disclosure patterns and accounting rules adequate or are asset evaluation and early warning procedures difficult to implement?

-   Are development banks fulfilling a long-term social objective or are the social costs higher than the benefits?

-   Is a thorough overhaul of prudential regulation and effective supervision necessary at the inception of liberalization, a time when banking may become a different kind of game and bankers may lack the necessary training to measure solvency and interest rate risks, wishing instead to grow simply for the sake of growth?

-   Is the present location of the regulatory and supervisory functions appropriate or are they split into separate institutions with inadequate coordination?

-   Is the existing restructuring system (FONAPRE) in a position to solve insolvency problems for good, or does it have serious handicaps, such as the inability to address problems on its own initiative, remove managers or tackle development bank problems?

-   Finally, is financial sector liberalization fully consistent with a banking system where entry into the market is not liberalized?

NOTES

1. Not being an economist, I shall not elaborate on these matters, which are spelled out in a recent paper by a colleague. See Manuel Hinds, "Economic Aspects of Financial Crisis." Policy, Planning and Research Paper No. 104, Country Economics Department (World Bank, 1988).

2.   For a fuller discussion see Aristobulo de Juan, "From Good Bankers to Bad Bankers: Deterioration of Bank Management As a Major Element in Banking Crises," Country Economics Department Working Paper (World Bank, December 1986).

Comments

Francisco Suarez
General Director, Banca Somex

INTRODUCTION

It is a pleasure to comment on Aristobulo de Juan's excellent paper. His remarks and suggestions are derived, as he says, from the school of experience and we can learn much from his education.

De Juan makes a number of major points. Epidemics of insolvency have been one of the diseases affecting many economies in chronic bouts of intensive therapy. Most commonly cited among the developing countries are Argentina and Chile, but Spain is another important case illustrated by the experiences of the good "bank doctor" who authored this paper. There is no doubt about the central role that banks play as "pillars" in mobilizing financial resources and it is equally evident that the financial system and the macroeconomic policy framework interact significantly. Economists have emphasized the influence of policy mistakes on bank insolvency; de Juan emphasizes how bank insolvency due to mismanagement, bad rules and ineffective supervision can severely hamper stabilization policies as well. Adequate prudential supervision therefore plays a major role in the quest for price stability and sustained growth.

Obviously I have no difficulty with de Juan's recommendations concerning "getting out of the dark" -- namely, establishing an adequate diagnosis. In order to forestall a potential crisis, the degree of stress within a financial system must be correctly assessed. The pathway to distress de Juan depicts leading from "cosmetic management" to "desperate management" and then to "fraud" brings clear examples to mind. Insolvent debtors, banks and vested interest groups become accomplices, neither revealing losses nor taking timely remedial action. These phenomena, however, are not exclusive to developing countries. Every effort has to be made to assess the quality of assets and to detect roll-over excesses, inappropriate interest capitalization and improper provisioning and write-offs for bad debts. I also agree with de Juan on the importance of looking at "performing" as well as "non-performing" assets.

The world debt crisis has made it particularly important to achieve technological progress in prudential regulations. The basic measure of capital adequacy should be related to asset risk instead of deposits. Risk concentration should be avoided and standards of profitability raised. Banks tend to rely on tangible guarantees or collateral rather than accurate risk assessments, even though international as well as national experience shows that credit recovery mechanisms are not always effective. The major problem with the various forms of collateral is that they lose value when sold or otherwise disposed of to meet a liquidity crisis and thus leave no alternative to rehabilitation measures when insolvency arises.

SOME GENERAL CONCEPTUAL REMARKS

Agreeing with most of Mr. de Juan's statements, I shall simply add a few comments. "Insolvency" and "financial distress" -- like "elephants" -- may not require precise definitions: the symptoms are quite apparent. Nevertheless because the degree of severity is elusive and may vary with the economic cycle, a more precise conceptual and quantitative framework for the analysis of potential insolvency is required.

The rapid transformation of the inflationary environment and the financial system in numerous countries certainly poses challenges for supervisors. Some of the main ones are as follows:

- The analysis of bank health must be expanded beyond the traditional concepts of asset and liability management. The analysis has to be broadened to include fee income and operations off the balance sheet. In Mexico, the traditional financial margin may be only 7 percent, while less than 50 percent of the resources mobilized by banks are reflected in their balance sheet.

- Traditional cash and liquidity asset ratios become less adequate to safeguard liquidity and solvency in the context of universal banking, where operations off the balance sheet increase faster than traditional ones.

- Regulatory methods have often overlooked the effects of macroeconomic conditions. Consider, for example, a high-inflation non-indexed economy. If regulatory agencies apply international standards, capitalization ratios are likely to be overstated because the values of fixed assets are mechanically upgraded while the real values of financial assets tend to be understated.

SPECIAL CHARACTERISTICS OF THE MEXICAN FINANCIAL SYSTEM

Serious stress in the banking system has been endemic to many developing countries in the 1980s as a result of drastic changes in relative prices, particularly in those that are most relevant to banks -- the exchange rate and the interest rate. These tensions have been aggravated by fluctuations and generally depressed levels of economic activity, a growing transfer of resources abroad and varying inflation rates.

Mexico has certainly not been the exception. Commercial banks, development banks, brokerage houses and insurance companies have been experiencing financial stress -- but so far the Mexican financial system has weathered the storms. In some aspects, several of de Juan's prescriptions have been followed. In others, the clinical pattern he assumes does not apply. The elements that explain why financial stress has been mitigated and widespread insolvency avoided include the following:

- The Mexican system differs from many others in that all commercial and development banks, as well as some major insurance companies, are owned by the government while the major private sector financial institutions are the brokerage houses. The recommendation for making rules of entry into the banking system more stringent does not apply in this setting, and I would venture further to say that the nationalized banking system has proved more successful in dealing with the crisis than would have been the case with a private system.

- A second feature is the effective measures that were taken in the last few years to improve the health of debtor firms. One example is the Ficorca scheme, specifically designed to alleviate private sector liquidity and exchange risk problems. Because exchange rate and commercial policies have also enabled private sector companies to export, a large number of major firms have eliminated their debt overhang and paradoxically become surplus units and active suppliers of funds to the financial markets.

- Some major public sector companies were restructured, prices of the goods and services they produced were raised and some of their debt overhang was absorbed by the federal government.

- Banks allocated a large proportion of their resources to finance the government's budget deficit. However, because this allocation occurred either by holding required reserves remunerated at market rates or through open market operations within a fairly well developed market for treasury bills, it acted as a cushion for banks' profitability when private credit demand was limited.

- Although rate discrimination was not eliminated, widespread progress was made towards allocating credit to preferred sectors at market rates.

- Commercial banks were subject to general austerity measures in the form of ceilings on bank personnel and non-interest expenditures.

- The quality of bank credit and assets generally has been sustained because a large share of commercial bank lending has taken the form of government paper. Moreover, as noted above, major private firms have reduced substantially their debt positions and some government trust funds have enforced high-quality credit supervision on small and medium-sized companies. The combination of these measures has reduced the scope for potential problems.

- The three largest commercial banks represent around 65 percent of the banking system's assets and liabilities. They have maintained adequate profits and capitalizations, as well as very favorable economies of scale. At the other end, small regional banks representing around 8 percent of bank assets are also quite well capitalized. Hence the stress has centered on five or six banks representing a relatively small share of total banking activity. Mergers have been carried out for institutions not considered viable, or to achieve better scales of operations. Also, the banking system has moved from "department" to "multiple" and then "universal" banking, thereby increasing its share in mobilization of financial resources and earning fee income from buying and selling assets of non-bank firms.

-   A "hospital bank" was established for those five or six commercial banks under the most severe stress due to an inadequate level of capital, mismanagement or bad loans. FONAPRE was financed through contributions from all the banks in the system, with no additional fiscal support. To become candidates for its help, institutions had to set up adjustment programs with precise quantitative targets.

These are just some of the regulatory mechanisms established to cope with stress in the Mexican financial system. Since some problems remain, there is, of course, no reason for complacency.

I now turn to an explanation of how the process of stabilization and structural change has interacted with the financial situation and activities of the banking system in Mexico. The banking system has experienced two stages since December of 1987 when the economic adjustment program, the Pacto, was introduced and substantial disinflation began.

During the initial stage which lasted through the first half of 1988, marginal reserve requirements were raised to 100 percent and interest rates on bank liabilities were flexible but determined by financial authorities. Interest revenue flows diminished at a smaller pace than interest expenditure flows and this difference created an important increase in the banks' interest surplus or their "financial margin". Bank profits were substantial, since their non-interest primary deficit did not grow and in some cases even fell in real terms.

Because of severe restrictions on bank credit, informal credit markets surged along with other financial intermediaries. The brokerage houses grew almost tenfold, from 0.5 percent to 4.8 percent of GDP, in less than nine months, and they generated severe competition for banking business. Banks adjusted in a pattern similar to that of brokerage houses, by increasing operations related to mobilizing financial resources for third parties, such as government and commercial paper transactions, instead of concentrating on traditional deposit and credit activities.

Real interest rates were quite high, but not compared to other countries experiencing similar difficulties. On an annual basis banks' real rates reached 22 percent on one-month instruments. This increased yield helped to extend the average maturity of deposits from 26 to about 50 days.

During the banking system's second stage, which began around the end of 1988, the financial bonanza reflected in bank profits began to vanish. The introduction of new types of bank instruments, such as "banker's acceptances" with free market rates and lower reserve requirements, together with a reduction in credit demand caused in part by low economic activity and real interest rates of more than 30 percent annually, pushed financial margins down, in some cases even in nominal terms. As a consequence, profits for the first few months of 1989 were much lower in real terms than those of 1988.

In an effort to modernize further the financial system, the financial authorities decided to engage in a major liberalization program in April of 1989. This program provides for the free determination of interest rates on all types of bank liabilities. It also establishes a simple 30 percent reserve requirement scheme, thereby freeing 70 percent of all bank deposits, and abolishes previous mandatory preferential credit schemes for commercial banks. The program substantially alters the way banking activities have been conducted in Mexico for the last several decades. It responds to both the banks' request for managerial autonomy and the government's overall reform agenda. Nevertheless it brings to our attention the questions that de Juan raises about the possibility of widespread financial distress caused by the timing and intensity of liberalization and deregulation.

CONCLUSION

I shall conclude these remarks with some comments on the effects of financial sector liberalization in the context of a major economic stabilization program. Two aspects need to be addressed: the macroeconomic performance of the financial system and the microeconomic characteristics of bank operations.

-   One of the unsolved puzzles of financial liberalization when accompanied by other stabilization efforts is the persistence of high real interest rates. One example is Chile in the early 1980s, where real rates remained higher than 30 percent per annum for at least two years, despite a major rise in total credit and massive inflows of foreign capital. Even more surprisingly, the liberalization of the domestic financial markets and the existence of high real interest rates hardly affected the overall stock of domestic savings and investment.

-   There is no clear-cut optimal timing for financial liberalization. For banking activities, it has usually meant an increase in the financial cost of funds and higher risks, at least in the short run. Transitional safeguards should be carefully designed to preserve changes designed to foster modernization and development. Certain elements of the stabilization and liberalization sequencing are still pending in Mexico. Three key aspects -- further opening the economy to international trade in goods and possibly services, the economy-wide industrial reconversion and a solution to the external debt problem -- will initiate what we might call the third stage of banking system change.

-   Trade liberalization already has drastically changed the relative prices of tradeable and non-tradeable goods. It has also reduced effective protection in some sectors where rates of 100 to 200 percent once were common.

-   This action could well affect the quality of bank portfolios since credit risk will be enlarged in those sectors that will no longer be able to exploit their monopoly power and enjoy higher than normal profits. Although offset by the credit needs of new firms in new markets due to trade liberalization, this risk enlargement effect is likely to prevail at least for some months to come.

- The external debt has numerous macroeconomic implications that need not be elaborated here. However, the uncertainty that still prevails about both the permanent success of the stabilization effort and the prompt recovery of economic growth creates unhealthy conditions for banking and other financial institutions. The expectation of continued high inflation, real interest and exchange rates will affect the cash flows relating to both bank assets and liabilities. With this influence in mind, bank supervision schemes should be designed to appraise the changes imposed by a highly dynamic economic environment. Regulation will be most effective if contingencies that could develop into a liquidity crisis are considered on an ex ante basis and not, as is sometimes the case, only when the problems arise. Actions that combine these criteria will succeed in reducing adjustment costs and ensuring sound banking institutions.

I would like to conclude my comment with a quotation. "Assuming that financial stability can be sustained, it seems a safe prediction that the problem of financial efficiency will become increasingly central to the activities of monetary and fiscal authorities during the stage of Mexican financial development just beginning." This is the last paragraph of the Brothers and Solis book, Mexican Financial Development, written more than two decades ago.

Role of the Central Bank in Financial Modernization

Sergio Ghigliazza*
General Director, Banco de Mexico

1. INTRODUCTION

Although the theoretical role of a modern and efficient financial system in enhancing economic growth remains controversial (indeed, the differences of opinion within Banco de Mexico alone have been at times quite heated), consensus has been reached on one basic point: inefficiencies in the financial intermediation process inhibit economic growth. The more costly it is to transfer savings to their most productive uses, the less an economy will save and therefore the less it will invest. Technology and market developments determine at each point the measures through which authorities can induce an efficient performance of financial institutions. But precisely because technology and markets are dynamic, it takes a great effort on the part of authorities to respond in a timely and flexible fashion to ensure this efficiency.

One of Banco de Mexico's permanent concerns is therefore to modernize banking and the financial system as a whole. With the advantage of historical perspective, several of its actions appear to have been important steps towards this modernization. These include creating financial groups (grupos financieros) and multiple banking (banca multiple), formalizing capitalization criteria based on the riskiness of assets rather than liabilities, and providing Mexican banks with access to international markets.

---

*The ideas, opinions and conclusions presented in this paper are the sole responsibility of the author and in no way represent the views of Banco de Mexico on the topic at hand.

Although these steps have made Mexican banks more flexible, versatile and technologically advanced, the process
has been discontinuous. Not only have some of the monetary
authorities' proposals been incorrect, but macroeconomic
policies have at times hindered the efficacy of the measures
adopted and both politicians and bankers have resisted some
innovations. Inflation is the first macroeconomic hindrance
to come to mind, but fiscal deficits have also constrained
the development of financial institutions; and it is not
uncommon for politicians to oppose interest rate increases
because of their direct and indirect impact on both public
and private finances.

These arguments point to the critical role of the Central Bank in promoting an efficient financial system, most
notably in three categories of action. First, the Bank par-
ticipates directly or indirectly in defining the regulatory
framework within which financial intermediaries operate. It
sets guidelines to induce competition among market participants, to avoid undue risk-taking by institutions and to
provide guarantees that avert bank runs. Fostering healthy
competition in this manner not only reduces intermediation
costs but also strengthens and stabilizes the market, thus
making monetary policy management more effective. Second,
the Central Bank can play a critical role in expanding the
financial market by establishing trading patterns and promoting new instruments of monetary control. In particular, the
development of a public debt market has facilitated the use
of open market operations as a means of monetary control.
In the third category are all the monetary policy actions
promoting price stability. In a very important manner, stability makes the intermediation process more transparent and
less prone to costly distortions that constrain the efficiency of the financial system and thus preclude a fair distribution of benefits among market participants.

Notwithstanding the ample means at the Bank's disposal,
introducing significant measures for financial modernization
requires a rare conjunction of economic and political circumstances in addition to the initiative of the monetary authorities. Such a set of circumstances exists in Mexico today.
After years of serious economic upheavals, the stabilization
program launched towards the end of 1987 has created a climate propitious for a market-wide liberalization of interest
rates. The real fiscal deficit has abated, a large market
for government securities has developed, the economy has
been opened to trade, and with price and exchange rates
rising at a moderate pace, interest rates can perform once
again their role of signaling financial market conditions.

In this context and in the absence of foreign credit, interest rate controls had to be removed in order to stimulate
and retain savings in the domestic market and consolidate
economic growth. However, this liberalization also made it
imperative to deregulate banks, particularly with respect to
the selective credit regime, so that they could channel
their resources to their most profitable uses.

This paper shares the experiences of Banco de Mexico in
the process of financial system modernization and puts in
historical perspective the measures being implemented during
the current stabilization effort. Perhaps one of the most
important points is the complementary relationship between
macroeconomic conditions and structural change. In this
context structural constraints preclude an efficient operation of the financial system and of macroeconomic policies
in general. At the same time, unless macroeconomic policies
are managed properly, eliminating structural constraints is
difficult. I believe that the most expedient way to develop
these ideas is to follow the course of history. Hence the
paper begins with the 1960s, when banks as well as the economy expanded briskly and healthily, and concludes with the
current process of stabilization and liberalization. The
paper emphasizes the constant impetus for modernization within Banco de Mexico and identifies some of the obstacles that
still exist.

2. HISTORICAL PERSPECTIVE

2.1 The Stabilizing Growth Period

Mexico shared in the general stability that characterized the international economy during the postwar years.
The most outstanding features of the period from the late
1950s to the early 1970s were the country's financial stability and rapid economic growth. The 1954 devaluation of the
peso ushered in a period during which macroeconomic policy
was managed with the persistent objective of ensuring a stable exchange rate. Such a policy was considered consistent
with sustained growth. Thus, the size of the public deficit
was kept within the bounds of non-inflationary financing and
interest rates were maintained at a level that stimulated
domestic savings. Because of the confidence this macroeconomic policy generated, Mexico attracted a largely voluntary
inflow of external savings although official foreign loans
played a minor role. External financial resources were
attracted both by higher yields offered in the Mexican

financial system than those prevalent abroad and by the opportunities open to direct investment in a burgeoning economy. Furthermore, the required inflow of foreign savings was fairly modest due to the relatively small magnitudes of the current account and fiscal deficits.

Such an environment was quite propitious for the development of the financial system as a whole and the banking sector in particular. Financial intermediation, measured by the ratio of M4 to GDP, increased from 18.2 percent in 1960 to 35.9 percent in 1972.(1)

The banks dominated the financial system of Mexico and specialized banking (banca especializada) prevailed. Deposit banks (bancos de deposito), investment banks (financieras) and mortgage banks (hipotecarias) were theoretically distinct entities, subject to different reserve and investment portfolio requirements. In fact, however, those institutions were often closely linked. Most financieras existed only in name, their operations being controlled by one of the commercial banks. The banks coexisted with other financial institutions such as insurance companies and brokerage houses (casas de bolsa). These non-bank institutions were usually linked to banks and operated in close coordination with them. This form of financial organization changed in 1970 with the formal recognition of financial groups (grupos financieros). These groups were formed by the integration of the major deposit-taking bank with at least one investment bank and mortgage bank. Their official authorization was intended to reduce operating costs and enhance the flexibility with which the system could address the needs of savers and borrowers, and the rules applied to their investment portfolios were somewhat eased.

During this period banks expanded their operations substantially and recorded high profits. But numerous regulations make their efficiency difficult to judge on this basis alone. Throughout the period Banco de Mexico set the rate of interest on bank instruments, usually at a high level by international standards. At the same time, rapid economic growth and fiscal distortions that favored debt financing over equity financing maintained a strong level of credit demand. Banks were therefore in the comfortable position of financing mostly low-risk companies, often belonging to the same financial group.

On the other hand, the banks were forced to channel part of their resources at subsidized rates to activities to which the government gave priority. The reserve requirement ratio was relatively high and acted as an instrument both for monetary control and for financing the public sector.

Yet, reserve requirements were greatly remunerated at a rate covering the financial and administrative costs to banks.

As the reserve requirement ratio was gradually increased the government became the main borrower from the banks. Particularly during times of weak credit demand from the private sector, the outcome of negotiations regarding the rate of remuneration on reserve requirements became the strategic factor determining profitability in the banking sector.

The relatively high rates charged by banks on loans to private borrowers reflected a degree of market power arising from an insufficiently developed competitive system and from barriers imposed on non-banks and on foreign institutions. Notwithstanding the artificially high rate of profit in the banking sector, however, several arguments support the assertion that banks in general fulfilled their intermediation role satisfactorily and did not take undue advantage of their prerogatives. For example, new banks were founded, geographic coverage was extended and no significant volume of intermediation took place outside the institutional system.(2) The nominal interest rates, although fixed by Banco de Mexico, seem to have been appropriate. Even though they were 2 or 3 percentage points higher than those prevailing abroad, the rapid growth of the economy reflected a high rate of productivity that justified these high real interest rates in the financial market.

Monetary policy instruments were limited by the rudimentary state of financial market development. Without the elements to conduct open market operations, Banco de Mexico had to resort to direct intervention through interest rate ceilings, changes in the reserve requirement ratio, quantitative credit controls, and the rate of remuneration on its deposits. Yet, through informal gentlemen's agreements (convenios) banks occasionally purchased bonds from Banco de Mexico at a rate negotiated between the parties involved. Moreover, because of the underlying stability of the system, only sporadic policy actions were needed.

Finally, in order to make the support to preferential sectors more effective, the authorities created development banks and trust funds explicitly to grant financing at subsidized rates. Whereas trust funds derived their resources directly from the government or through government guaranteed foreign loans, the development banks also competed with private banks and other financial intermediaries to attract private savings. In so doing, because of the differential between lending and deposit interest rates, they incurred operating losses which were covered by the government.

Development banks were subjected to less stringent regulations. However, since their expansion depended on government support (or subsidies), they were never able to compete
seriously with private banks and their share in domestic savings mobilization remained relatively low.

In retrospect the period from the late 1950s to the
early 1970s provides several lessons. The first and fore-
most is that the macroeconomic environment of price and
exchange rate stability was the major ingredient in promoting financial development. Despite the numerous regulations
affecting banks, the certainty that derived from a climate
of stability instilled confidence in savers who then deposited their resources at banks and in borrowers who were then
willing to incur long-term debt. Stability also made more
transparent the assessment of costs imposed on banks because
of the subsidized credit policy and the high reserve ratio;
thus, these costs could be more accurately reflected in the
rate of remuneration on reserves. Bank regulations may have
created distortions; in particular, the requirement to allocate credit to preferential sectors generated inefficiencies
in resource allocation. Nevertheless, the climate of stability made it less difficult for the economy to bear the burden of such inefficiencies.

Another lesson is that in the virtual absence of
exchange rate risk domestic banks were better placed to compete against foreign banks both in attracting savings and in
granting credit. In spite of the regulatory framework,
financial deepening proceeded at a rapid pace.

2.2 Financial Disintermediation During 1972-1982

International stability began to falter towards the end
of 1960. The Bretton Woods Agreement had to be modified in
1967 by the Sterling Pound devaluation, the U.S. economy suffered a recession in 1970 and inflation began to increase.
More importantly, international interest rates reached historically high levels in 1973 and commodity prices fluctu-
ated widely, marked by particularly sharp increases in grain
and oil prices.

The administration that took office in December of 1970
applied a development strategy aimed at accelerating growth.
However, this strategy was challenged in 1973 by inflation
of 21.3 percent, more than four times the rates observed for
the last 14 years.(3) The monetary authorities responded
sluggishly to this shock. Failure to adjust nominal interest rates had an immediate impact on the real interest rate,

which went from positive 2.4 percent in 1972 to negative 10.7 percent in 1973.(4) Financial intermediation faltered and the ratio of M4 to GDP declined from 33.5 percent in 1973 to 25 percent in 1977. Furthermore, the excess liquidity that the Central Bank was forced to inject into the system in order to finance the fiscal deficit generated foreign reserve losses. In 1976 the peso finally had to be devalued.

After 1977 the sharp improvement in Mexico's terms of trade, the increase in revenues from oil exports and the ample availability of foreign credit helped to dissipate expectations of exchange rate devaluation. The government initiated an aggressive development program and GNP grew at an average rate of 8.6 percent from 1978 to 1981. Inflation, however, remained high and with a relatively stable parity the real exchange rate became overvalued. In conjunction with the rapid expansion of domestic demand this overvaluation led to a contraction of non-oil exports and an increase of imports, thus making the balance of payments quite vulnerable to the availability of foreign credit and oil prices. Internally, the growth based on oil exports was also distortional. Real wages rose faster than productivity so that non-oil international competitiveness was eroded. However, until 1981 the enormous volume of foreign credits allowed a solution to these problems to be postponed.

The financial intermediation coefficient (M4 to GDP ratio) increased from 27.6 percent in 1978 to 32.1 percent in 1981. This recovery occurred because domestic interest rates, given the exchange rate stability, were substantially higher than abroad, even though real interest rates remained negative.(5) This increase in the ratio was also due to the rapid economic growth and the financial intermediation measures introduced during this period as discussed below.

The public's perception of exchange rate risk never completely abated after the 1976 devaluation and with the encouragement of the authorities, banks promoted instruments denominated in foreign currency. The market responded asymmetrically: these instruments helped arrest capital flight, especially during 1981 and made savers feel secure, but borrowers seem to prefer the previously lower interest rates to the smaller exchange rate risk now offered.(6)

Though investment and production continued to grow, this period represented a serious setback to the financial system. Foreign financial institutions captured part of the intermediation business and the domestic system assumed a hidden but unsustainable exchange rate risk against which it was uninsured as a whole. By creating dollar-denominated deposits, the banking system was in effect issuing dollars which the ultimate borrower (the Mexican government) did not have for repayment. The banking system was therefore quite vulnerable to external shocks. When a large one occurred in 1981 with a drop in the international price of oil, the guarantee of dollar-denominated instruments was considered insufficient and savers transferred their deposits abroad, reducing foreign reserves significantly. The grossly overvalued exchange rate was maintained by massive recourse to short-term foreign loans, but when this flow came to an end in February of 1982 the Central Bank was forced to devalue. In August of the same year, a second substantial devaluation took place, and this time domestic banks could not honor their obligations denominated in foreign currency. These deposits therefore were converted to pesos by government decree and redeemed in the national currency at a rate that implied a capital loss to savers. Both the macroeconomic and the financial crisis provided the scenario in which the nationalization of the banking system took place, in September of 1982.

As inflation worsened throughout the period, some distortions not evident during the years of financial stability became quite burdensome and required direct action by the monetary authorities. The lack of competition among banks aggravated these distortions. First, maintaining relatively constant lending rates of interest on compulsory credit allocations to preferential sectors made the subsidy element more onerous as inflation rose. Commercial banks were thus compelled to increase the intermediation margin on their unregulated portfolio and the development banks' operative losses grew. Now only was this subsidization inefficient, but it stimulated in turn an increase in the demand for credits, thus making the subsidy even larger. Second, since commercial banks could not shift the costs of the credit subsidies entirely to regular loans, they tried to obtain from the Central Bank a higher rate of remuneration on their reserve requirements, and this effort led to a complicated system of reserve remuneration. Furthermore, as fiscal deficits rose, the average reserve requirement ratio had to be increased, exacerbating this problem.

Several important advances in modernizing the financial system nevertheless occurred during this period. These measures were undertaken in response to the evident distortions and with the goal of making the banking system more flexible and responsive to the volatility of market conditions.

After the 1976 devaluation, the system was considered excessively liquid because of the widespread circulation of financial instruments carrying a virtual guarantee of repurchase at par and on demand by the issuing institutions. Beginning in 1977 the circulation of these liabilities was gradually eliminated. At the same time, new instruments with short-term maturities were created. As a result, an interest rate structure was established that paid a premium to savers willing to forego liquidity.

Another important action taken during the mid-1970s was the establishment of the legal basis for multiple banking to replace the specialized banking system and the financial groups. Multiple banking was a very important advance because it legalized the integration of the activities performed by different types of banks into a single institution. Moreover, by replacing a very complex system of reserve requirements that applied different ratios according to the type and size of bank, location of bank branches, and so on, with a uniform system, a significant advance was made towards eliminating costly distortions.

By the beginning of 1978 the spectrum of monetary policy instruments was further broadened by the introduction of treasury bills (CETES). The issuance of CETES supplied the market with a liquid instrument of public debt that was also suitable for conducting open market operations (though the thinness of the market at that time prevented it from being used more effectively).

Because the rate of inflation did not abate as rapidly as expected, and since the revision in reserve requirement policy did not completely fulfill the role of regulating liquidity as envisaged, further action was taken in 1979 with the introduction of Monetary Control Bonds (Bonos de Regulacion Monetaria) and deposit-credit auctions administered by Banco de Mexico. While banks were forced to buy the former, purchases of the latter were voluntary. Banco de Mexico then had additional instruments to offset undesirable changes in the liquidity of the banking system. These instruments permitted, at least for a time, the maintenance of a simple reserve requirement.

In 1979 Banco de Mexico established a mechanism for weekly reviews of interest rates on bank deposits denominated in pesos, thus fundamentally transforming a system of infrequent and isolated adjustments to one of periodic revisions, and taking the first step towards introducing interest rate flexibility. Although this new procedure did not prevent real interest rates from becoming negative, given a relatively stable parity, domestic rates could now be adjusted to compensate for foreign interest rate movements.

The authorities proceeded to establish new capital requirements for credit institutions with reference to loan portfolio risk and also to introduce fixed-rate short-term private paper suitable for markets served by the brokerage houses. Existing instruments were likewise promoted by these institutions and new legislation was enacted which made their operations more flexible. The expansive fiscal policy stance was also reflected in an increase in the amount of resources transferred through development banks and trust funds, sometimes to the neglect of due consideration of efficiency and profitability.

The nationalization of banks in the latter part of 1982 changed radically the process of financial system modernization. On the one hand the trend towards universal banking was reversed as it became legally necessary to separate very distinctly banking from non-banking operations. Because of its artificiality, this separation led in time to actions aimed at its circumvention. On the other hand, since the nationalized banks did not receive unambiguous instruction to seek profits (a goal inherent in their formerly private operations), they pursued objectives not wholly consistent with efficiency. The authorities placed themselves in the difficult and contradictory position of being simultaneously owners and regulators of banks, thereby adding inadequate competition and operational inefficiency to the problems of the banking sector.

2.3   The Period of High Inflation: 1982–1987

The problems of excessive foreign borrowing, an over-sized public sector and a vast array of distortions in productive structure and relative prices suddenly became critical when external financing was abruptly interrupted. The government was forced to declare a temporary suspension of its foreign debt service in September of 1982. After the new administration took office in December, the whole macro-economic policy stance had to be shifted. For the first time in the post-war period the country was required to generate a net annual transfer of resources abroad of nearly 6 percent of GDP. Policies were now aimed at extracting more resources from the private sector and increasing public savings. Notwithstanding the advances made in correcting the main structural cause of inflation, namely the fiscal deficit, the foreign debt overhang and the steep deterioration of the terms of trade exacerbated the problem of controlling inflation.

The immediate concern of the authorities was to generate a trade account surplus large enough to rebuild foreign reserves and resume foreign debt service. The main elements of the new program were a restrictive fiscal and monetary policy and a real exchange rate depreciation. Opening the economy was not feasible in the short run, but a policy for gradual liberalization was announced.

The external shocks to which the economy was exposed, combined with the difficulties of coordinating different policy actions, resulted in extreme volatility of nominal and real interest rates and the real exchange rate. That, in turn, made it more difficult to stabilize the economy and to lay the basis for resumed economic growth.

In general, the banking sector's share of the financial intermediation market declined in this period. Although Banco de Mexico strove to foster attractive real returns to depositors, exchange rate risk as well as the uncertainties caused by unfavorable external shocks precluded reversing the declining trend. There were indeed periods of large capital inflows, but as soon as prospects deteriorated these funds flowed out once again. Moreover, as savers sought liquid assets their portfolio shifted in favor of CETES.

On the other side of the market total credit demand did not fall. Despite budgetary adjustments drastic enough to generate a primary fiscal surplus, large debt service commitments kept public sector credit demand at high levels.

Within this context, how did the financial system perform? To begin with, as mentioned in the previous section, banks were nationalized and laws were passed restricting their activities to traditional banking services. Banks had to get rid of their brokerage houses, insurance companies and other ancillary institutions. Furthermore, some nationalized banks were merged in order to have a smaller number of more solid institutions that could compete more effectively with one another and the institutions still operated privately. Unfortunately, many of these mergers were not guided by market forces and the use of administrative criteria resulted in less efficient institutions in some cases.

Interest rate ceilings were maintained while reserve requirements were increased both to limit liquidity and to channel a larger portion of bank resources to the public sector. The rate of remuneration on reserves was also raised, making banking operations much easier because operating profits were assured. Whenever banks had excess liquidity due to weak demand for credit from the private sector, instead of reducing their operations they increased their deposits at the Central Bank with a profitable margin. Thus, the rate of remuneration on reserves became a scheme to subsidize banks.

A major development in the money market was the restoration of the auction system for government securities whereby the government determined the amount to be issued and the market determined the interest rate. With this instrument the monetary authorities regained an indicator of market conditions useful in the determination of interest rate ceilings for banks. Since bank controls had several distortional effects, interest rates on CETES could not be considered general equilibrium rates, but the auction was nevertheless a major improvement in the financial market.

In late 1985, as terms of trade deteriorated sharply and fresh foreign credit could not be contracted, expectations became very volatile. Therefore, in order to avoid large fluctuations in interest rates, the auctions were sometimes constrained by setting an upper limit on the CETES rate. However, unlike bank deposit rates, interest rates on these instruments continued to adjust according to market conditions. Under these circumstances the CETES market share increased as a proportion of M4 from 4 percent in the end of 1981 to over 16 percent by December of 1987. In this context, the introduction of development bonds (BONDES), instruments with a maturity of at least one year and a floating interest rate linked to the yield on CETES, was considered a way to begin development of a domestic bond market.

As inflation had worsened in 1986, the banks' handicap in competing against brokerage houses to attract private savings became progressively more acute. Banco de Mexico maintained interest rate ceilings on traditional bank deposits, but it also actively promoted the development of the money market where instruments were traded at market determined rates. Moreover, as foreign financing to the public sector remained virtually unavailable, Banco de Mexico was forced again to raise the reserve requirement ratio, thus further limiting the banks' lending activities. The banks in turn sought to participate in the intermediation process through non-banking instruments in order partially to overcome the regulations imposed on their traditional activities.

The price index for the stock market increased rapidly during 1986 and the first part of 1987 as a consequence of the incipient reactivation of the economy and the resumption of some financial inflows from abroad. This bubble burst in October of 1987 when the world's stock markets collapsed. Investors then responded to persistent inflation by purchasing foreign currency to cover themselves. Prepayment of private foreign debt also contributed to the fall in foreign reserves. Banco de Mexico tried to contain the outflows by allowing an increase in interest rates, but when this proved to be insufficient it let the exchange rate depreciate freely. As price increases then threatened to reach hyper-inflationary levels, a new stabilization program became necessary.

2.5 A Rapid Disinflation Program: 1988

The crisis in October of 1987 demonstrated that a program of gradual disinflation was no longer viable in Mexico. Given the burden of an excessive public debt, and without new foreign financing, purely orthodox policies would have required a deep recession to break inertial price setting practices. A program was therefore launched to reduce the rate of inflation drastically.

The program plan was to reduce the fiscal deficit and eliminate its financing by the Central Bank. Moreover, by opening the economy to foreign competition internal prices of tradeables were subjected to the discipline of external prices. Very strict monetary controls were applied in an effort to absorb liquidity, requiring substantial increases in interest rates and a ceiling on bank financing to the private sector. However, the basic element of the stabilization program was a stable exchange rate policy supported by the other measures already mentioned. The program was aimed at breaking inflationary expectations through unorthodox agreements (concertaciones) among different sectors for setting the most important prices.

When inflation began to abate and real interest rates became positive, savings deposited in the institutional market (M4) reacted positively. Between the end of January and the end of May, this stock increased 9.8 percent in real terms. On the other side of the market, credit demand remained subdued and consequently Banco de Mexico was able to accumulate foreign reserves.

Towards the end of the second quarter, as credit demand strengthened the interest rate ceilings imposed on commercial banks began to constrain their traditional operations. This posed a difficult dilemma at the Central Bank. It was recognized that a rise in interest rates would immediately affect the fiscal deficit adversely and also undermine the international competitiveness of export industries. On the other hand, the failure of interest rates to rise would involve risking the loss of international reserves and a decrease in the banking system's share in financial intermediation markets. Banco de Mexico decided not to increase interest rates, so international reserves decreased and the banks did lose part of their market share. Implicitly the public sector substituted external for domestic debt thereby reducing current expenditures, and although a definitive correction of the fiscal deficit was not achieved the decision not to raise interest rates was consistent with a sustainable path toward reduced inflation.

The constraints imposed on bank credit and deposit interest rates strengthened the emerging informal intermediation market in which non-bank instruments were employed. The development of a more active informal market lessened the effectiveness of direct monetary policy controls, such as credit limits and interest rate ceilings, which operated only in a shrinking portion of the market. In October and November, Banco de Mexico therefore responded with several actions to restore the ability of banks to compete more effectively with other intermediaries. The most important of these measures was authorization to issue acceptances at rates and maturities determined by market references.(7) Banks were allowed to issue these instruments in unrestricted amounts, the only limitation being that 30 percent of the funds thus raised be invested in government securities.

These measures restored the banks' capacity to compete with the informal market in providing credit to the private sector. However, the attractiveness of the rates offered by the new instrument made the traditional bank controls even more restrictive. The stock of traditional bank deposits fell 46.9 percent in real terms during the last quarter of 1988, thereby limiting the effectiveness of direct monetary controls and reaffirming open market operations as the Central Bank's main tool for managing monetary policy. Even though traditional bank instruments became less competitive, the measures allowing expanded use of acceptances were a significant step in modernizing the system because they served to liberalize bank interest rates and substantially deregulated the composition of bank asset portfolios. Not only did the stabilization program establish the conditions necessary to liberalize the financial system, but this liberalization also contributed to a more comprehensive program of stabilization.

2.6 1989: A Crossroad

The recent stabilization efforts have made extension of the process of financial liberalization imperative. This is a period in which political will coincides with economic

expediency and administrative initiative. From a macroeconomic point of view, sustaining the nominal exchange rate
during the initial phase of the stabilization program
required a combination of flexible interest rates and the
use of previously accumulated foreign reserves. Since 1988
was a presidential election year, the uncertainties produced
by an unfavorable international environment were further
aggravated. But now that the results of the stabilization
effort are becoming evident, it will be necessary to avoid
reliance on foreign reserves, emphasizing instead the flexibility of interest rates in order to support exchange rate
stability, which is the nominal anchor for the stabilization
program.

From a political point of view, the present administration is convinced that modernization requires a reassessment
of public sector involvement in the economy and a revision
of the performance criteria for those enterprises that are
to remain public. This modernization objective has also led
to a strong emphasis on sustainable profits as the guiding
principle for bank operation. Thus, if banks are to operate
under a profit rule they must have the freedom to invest
their resources in the most profitable sectors and to adjust
interest rates as necessary to attract deposits.

From an administrative point of view, since bank nationalization is a fact that cannot be altered, the authorities
are in the difficult position of being simultaneously owners
and regulators of the banks. To ameliorate this situation,
the self-regulating process of competition among financial
intermediaries should replace regulation in determining the
banks' share of financial savings. Banks should be subject
only to those regulations necessary to facilitate market
efficiency and ensure institutional soundness.

The monetary authorities are taking advantage of the
rare coincidence of these factors to advance the process of
bank modernization by consolidating the liberalization
measures adopted in late 1988 focused on bankers acceptances. These measures served to increase the share of
instruments with market-determined rates to almost 80 percent of M4 in December of 1988, but a by-product was to
increase the bias against traditional bank instruments. The
next step was therefore to free the rates on traditional
bank instruments. This liberalization does not pose a destabilizing risk; on the contrary, as banks offer competitive
yields and a wider range of maturities, their position relative to that of other intermediaries will be a result of market preferences, not administrative regulations.

Increasing bank efficiency through competition has required both lifting the constraints on bank asset portfolios and providing adequate pricing policies for other bank services. Regarding the former, authorities have recently eliminated reserve requirements and begun to treat deposits just like acceptances, with a liquidity coefficient of only 30 percent to be allocated freely between government paper and deposits at Banco de Mexico. Credit constraints and bank obligations to grant subsidized credit to preferential sectors have both been abolished and banks are therefore allowed, or rather compelled, to seek the most profitable uses for their own resources. Regarding the latter, charging according to costs prevents an artificial widening of the intermediation margin.

While in some other countries a similar liberalization process was launched at a time when bank portfolios were affected by substantial amounts of non-performing credits, in Mexico the banks' main debtor was the federal government so that their portfolios were virtually risk free. This set of circumstances gave the Mexican banks an advantage, but it has also prevented them in the past from being more active in their lending policies. It was therefore necessary to initiate this new phase with great care. Banks must follow adequate guidelines to assess risk and be somewhat cautious until they regain sufficient experience with credits to the private sector.

As for development banks, the liberalization process requires making the subsidy element more transparent, and their overall operations are being reconsidered on that account. One attractive possibility is to convert these banks into rediscount institutions to support, through commercial banks, certain sectors given high priority status by the government. By this means, the development banks will take over the channeling of funds to preferential sectors that was previously accomplished by the commercial banks under the old selective credit regime.

3.   CONCLUDING REMARKS

The current liberalization trend has advanced rapidly and aroused optimism. However, making this process solid and permanent clearly requires attention to other difficult issues like regulation to ensure the soundness of the financial system by preventing banks from taking excessive risks and elimination of moral hazard problems. These considerations reinforce the view that the main goal of bank administrators should be financial viability instead of market share. The government should consolidate schemes to separate its decisions as bank owner from those as bank regulator.

Finally, authorities should do their utmost to preserve financial stability. The experience surveyed here indicates most persuasively that regulatory actions have an important, albeit limited, impact on the efficiency of the financial system. Price stability is the major factor for instilling both borrowers and lenders with confidence in the financial system.

NOTES

1. M4 is the most comprehensive monetary aggregate in Mexico.

2. Although an informal mortgage market existed for a while, it disappeared shortly after taxes were levied on the income derived from these instruments.

3. The rate of inflation has been measured by the December-December increase in the consumer price index.

4. The real interest rate is an annual compound of the real monthly interest rate calculated as the weighted average of all the interest earning assets in M4.

5. The average real interest rate during the period was -5.8 percent.

6. Public enterprises borrowed abroad where lending rates were much lower than internally, and the government assumed the exchange rate risk. Private firms therefore not only faced credit constraints but were also forced to borrow abroad in order to remain competitive. Competition in this case led the private sector to assume unsustainable levels of foreign exchange risk.

7. These acceptances should not be confused with the instrument known in financial parlance as "bankers' acceptances".

Comments

William White
Deputy Governor, Bank of Canada

A.   INTRODUCTION

This paper is both interesting and timely, particularly because it offers a very useful historical perspective from which to evaluate the reforms of the Mexican financial sector announced in April of this year. But Ghigliazza actually provides both more and less than the title of his paper suggests.

The paper provides more in that in addition to a survey of historical developments in the financial sector it gives the reader a quite comprehensive survey of macroeconomic developments over the past several decades. This is useful in that it reveals the simple but important theme of inter-relationships between macroeconomic conditions and structural reforms. On the one hand, sectoral reforms can clearly have an effect on macro conditions. For example, better functioning financial markets may make a country less prone to inflation in the face of government deficits. On the other hand, macroeconomic circumstances may have an impact on the pace of structural reforms. Some observers contend that favorable performance at the macro level will speed up sectoral reform because it provides the resources required to buy off the vested interest groups. Personally I am more attracted to an alternative view, that sectoral reforms are more likely in an environment of economic performance so bad that it verges on crisis. By stating in his paper that financial reforms could be avoided in the 1960s because other economic circumstances were generally tolerable, Ghigliazza would seem to agree with me.

Ghigliazza's paper also provides less than it promises in that it nowhere makes clear the specific responsibilities or interests of the Banco de Mexico -- as distinct from the interests of the Mexican government more generally. In my judgment, and also implicit in the important reforms now being proposed for the Mexican financial system, the effi- ciency of the financial sector over the last few decades has not been very high. The system was characterized by wide- spread controls on both prices and quantities and serious distortions. As a fellow central banker, I prefer to believe that Banco de Mexico cannot be held responsible for this situation, but the issue is nevertheless worth raising.

What is the appropriate role for a central bank to play in the process of financial modernization? This question cannot be answered without a prior statement of the economic objectives of structural reform in the financial area, and a clear understanding of the international and political con- straints which are likely to condition the pace of financial reform. My comments on Ghigliazza's paper will be presented within the framework of these two themes. In addition to drawing on the Mexican evidence contained in the paper, they will also reflect Canadian attempts over the last forty years to liberalize or modernize our financial markets -- an ongoing process which has not been without its setbacks.

B.   CENTRAL BANK OBJECTIVES IN PROMOTING FINANCIAL SECTOR
     REFORM

Diverse public and private bodies can have legitimately diverse objectives in promoting structural reforms in the financial sector. What specific objectives should a central bank try to promote? I think there are at least three such objectives and although Ghigliazza refers to only one of these explicitly, he seems to endorse the other two at least implicitly in his paper.

1.   Structural Reforms to Promote the Efficiency of
     Monetary Policy

The primary objective for any central bank should be to control domestic inflation. While the central bank must also be aware of the short-term effects of its policies on demand and output levels, as well as the implications for exchange rate movements, such considerations should not be allowed to dominate its primary responsibility. To achieve this objective, it now seems generally (though not univer- sally) accepted that it is best to have financial markets that allow the transmission of monetary policy across as broad a spectrum of economic activity as possible and in as nondiscriminatory a manner as possible. For me, this principle means relying on flexible interest rates across interdependent financial markets and eschewing direct credit controls and credit rationing.

Another advantage of having financial markets in which interest rates can adjust to changing supply of and demand for financial instruments is that there is less potential for fiscal deficits to contribute to inflation. In Canada, for example, the government deficit/GDP ratio is about as high as in Argentina. However, the inflationary implications to date have been much less severe because the Canadian deficit has been wholly financed in financial markets, at rates determined in those markets. The Bank of Canada has thus been able to maintain control over its own balance sheet and in turn over the general rate of monetary expansion.

Canadian experience indicates that a good place to start in modernizing financial markets, along the lines just noted, is with the development of a broader market in short-term government securities. And, of course, this is going on in Mexico now. The Canadian experience also illustrates the important role that a central bank can play in such developments and that such efforts can be successful.

Canada began in the early 1950s with essentially no short-term money market, with interest rate ceilings on certain kinds of bank loans, and with the belief that credit rationing could play a role in the implementation of monetary policy. Things have changed a great deal in the intervening years. Monetary policy actions are now initiated primarily through changes in the amount of cash reserves provided to banks (the clearing medium among themselves), and the interest rate effects are quickly transmitted across a wide range of interconnected markets. Private sector initiatives, based on the search for profit, played a large role in this evolution. However, the process was also encouraged by measures either initiated or supported by the Bank of Canada.

a)   The reforms began in 1953 by offering rediscount facilities at the Bank of Canada to certain investment dealers so that they would be encouraged to make markets in short-term government paper. Such dealers could describe themselves as "jobbers" and gain the prestige (and, potentially, clients) from having a special relationship with the Central Bank. The Bank also offered commissions on institutional purchases of (especially longer-term) government securities provided they were subsequently retailed widely across the country. Finally, the Bank also provided inexpensive wire transfer facilities across the country to facilitate the transfer and exchange of government securities.

b) The Bank of Canada actively encouraged the Canadian chartered banks to provide short-term finance to the jobbers on the basis of discountable collateral. Around the same time (1954), the primary reserve requirements were effectively lowered so that banks subsequently had surplus funds to lend in this way.

c) In June of 1962 the rediscounting of bankers' acceptances was allowed as well.

d) In 1967 the interest rate ceilings on selected bank loans were removed. Increasingly, monetary policy decisions were based on desired levels of interest rates rather than "credit conditions" -- a general term encompassing both prices and quantities in credit markets.

e) More recently, a number of more technical changes have been made to foster the development of competition in the financial markets. In the context of legislative changes designed to "level the playing field for all deposit-taking institutions", the government has committed itself to reduce bank reserve requirements to zero.

f) Finally, the return to a wholly market-based approach has been successful enough that the existence of the jobber as a distinct kind of dealer can now be reconsidered. Along the same lines, the Bank of Canada has increasingly been able to supplement its monetary policy actions with direct interventions in the market for overnight funds. This market is now so closely related to others that the effects of interventions are quickly dispersed over a wide range of instruments.

It is clear from Ghigliazza's paper that reform of Mexico's financial system has proven much more difficult than in Canada. Nevertheless, the steps taken in the last few

years as well as those just recently announced are encouraging and one can only hope they will be successful. As an
aside, one Mexican problem not shared by Canada is a recent
history of very high inflation. This must inhibit the introduction of longer-term government securities, so that getting control of the inflationary process may be more difficult. Again, the issue is how the macroeconomic situation
can make structural reforms more or less likely to succeed.

A central bank might find yet another structural reform
to its liking -- one that would give it more independence
from government authorities on a day-to-day basis. While
the extent of central bank independence varies across the
major industrial countries and is often manifested in
diverse ways, it remains the case that in most countries a
substantial degree of independence is both valued and legis-
latively assured.

2. Structural Reforms to Promote Financial Stability

Financial reforms designed to place greater reliance on
market forces are essential to implement monetary policy
more effectively. Yet the possibility of market inefficiencies and even market failures still remains. Speculative
price movements in important financial markets, the failure
of financial institutions and a loss of confidence in the
solvency of the banking system are phenomena with potentially serious macroeconomic consequences. A central bank therefore has legitimate interests in both the regulation and the
supervision of financial markets to limit these risks. While
the Bank of Canada has no direct regulatory or supervisory
responsibility, it does work closely with the Department of
Finance on the former issue and with the Office of the Supervisor of Financial Institutions (OSFI) on the latter.

Some recent structural developments in Canada have precedents in Mexican experience. For some decades Canada had
four different kinds of financial institutions -- referred
to as the four "pillars" -- with a number of regulatory agencies. This separation was attractively clear and simple,
but it has been breaking down more recently (in part because
of the international forces mentioned in a moment). A whole
series of questions about the legislative and regulatory
framework in Canada have therefore been raised.

Ghigliazza recounts that financial institutions were
separated in Mexico on the basis of their business function
until the early 1970s, then were progressively integrated
("financial groups", "multiple banking") and finally were
separated again after the nationalization of the banking

system in 1982. With this diversity of experience, it would have been interesting to hear how Mexicans have dealt with such problems as: arm's length transactions among different branches of integrated financial institutions, commercial-financial links and insider trading. In fact there is very little in Ghigliazza's paper that deals with these important topics. After the early stages of financial modernization are finished, Banco de Mexico will presumably want to encourage further analysis of such matters.

3.   Structural Reforms to Promote Growth

Ghigliazza refers only tangentially in his paper to structural reforms designed to increase the efficiency of monetary policy and enhance financial stability. But he refers repeatedly and explicitly to the growth objective, which I therefore assume he takes quite seriously. He then goes on to note that the authorities should take steps to "induce (my emphasis) an efficient performance of financial institutions" in order to ensure that savings are transferred at low cost to their "most productive uses". Lying behind this assertion is the idea that a high rate of return actually received by savers (after intermediation costs) will induce a higher savings rate.

I certainly do not object to these points in principle, though I think the proposition that domestic investment is largely dependent on domestic saving has better empirical support than the proposition that savings are interest-elastic. In any case, two further observations seem worth making.

First, lowering inflation is the best way for central banks to promote longer-run growth. Inflation causes a deterioration in the signal content of the price mechanism, even at relatively low levels, and it often interacts with the tax system and administered prices in ways that induce resource misallocation. Ghigliazza provides a classic example when he describes the rise of inflation in the 1970s and the associated increase in the real interest rate subsidies provided by development banks and trust funds among others. And, of course, such rising subsidies also feed fiscal deficits and inflation in turn.

My second point is that the best way to induce more efficient financial institutions may not be (as Ghigliazza says in his first paragraph) through "a great effort on the part of the authorities". Rather, it may be better simply to reduce the government constraints under which financial institutions currently operate. In this regard, the most recent proposals for Mexican financial reform which provide for more flexible interest rates and a substantial deregulation of the composition of their asset portfolios are most welcome. Any improvement in the quality of capital investment in Mexico may help offset the decline in its quantity, which has been an unfortunate by-product of the international debt situation.

Yet although progress is being made, questions about current policy still remain. Why is it that "bank nationalization is a fact that cannot be altered"? Privatization would contribute to: (1) regaining the efficiency which has been lost in this sector since 1982; (2) further removing temptation for traditional government interference; (3) giving a very positive signal to expatriated capital that times have truly changed; and, (4) addressing directly the problem of the government being jointly the owner and regulator of the banking system.

Further, why is it that foreign financial institutions are not allowed to expand their participation in Mexico's financial system? The Canadian experience supports what we all know to be true in theory: competition supports efficiency. Competition is still the best way of ensuring low-cost transfers of savings to the most productive uses. Canada now has over fifty foreign banks and a rising number of foreign dealers, and the fears of nationalists that its domestic firms would be wiped out have proven completely unfounded.

C. THE INTERNATIONAL AND POLITICAL ENVIRONMENT

If there are domestic reasons for welcoming financial reforms in Mexico, recent changes in the international economic environment also point to the necessity for change. The globalization of financial markets is an emerging reality. For example, recent advances in technology have made it increasingly possible for Canadians to carry out many of their financial transactions outside Canada. In response, Canada has had to liberalize and adjust to help its financial institutions stay competitive. For better or for worse, the consequence, has been allowing the creation of integrated financial institutions involved in different kinds of business that used to be strictly separated. With the potential demise of "Glass-Steagall", the United States seems to be going down the same path.

In contrast, Mexico seems to have been moving in the opposite direction, at least since the nationalization of the banking system in 1982. In itself, there may be nothing wrong with this path. For example, my colleague Chuck Freedman recently remarked on the fact that the four most highly developed capital markets in the world exist in countries (United States, United Kingdom, Japan and Canada) where banking business has been rigorously separated from all other kinds of business -- both financial and industrial. Yet the fact remains that there is a growing global market in financial services and that global trends are hard to resist, whether by Mexico or anyone else.

Another global reality has been a highly volatile international macroeconomic environment. In talking about the period 1982-1987, Ghigliazza notes that the "extreme volatility of nominal and real interest rates and the real exchange rate...made it more difficult to stabilize the economy". This was a problem faced by all countries and unfortunately there is no guarantee that these kinds of problems are going to disappear. An unfortunate mix of fiscal and monetary policies still characterizes the North American scene and large international trade imbalances carry the seeds of currency instability and recession. To my mind, the more volatile the external environment, the more desirable is the ability of the financial system to react flexibly to these shocks so that output losses can be minimized.

These international considerations argue for a faster rather than a slower pace of change towards a more competitive and price oriented financial system in Mexico. Two other considerations might be argued in the opposite direction, though only one of them is valid. The valid argument for more measured progress is that due concern must be given to ensuring the stability of the financial system. The pace of reform must reflect the significant short-term costs that may be involved in implementing even the most worthy longer-run reforms. The invalid argument is the one that caters to the status quo and vested interests. Ghigliazza's paper shows clearly how important such influences have been in Mexico. Throughout the period he considers efforts were being made to liberalize and develop markets but it was very much a start-and-stop affair. All that can be hoped is that this phase of Mexico's development has now been superseded by a more modern one.

Distributive Effects of Financial Policies in Mexico

Adalberto Garcia Rocha*
Professor of Economics, El Colegio de Mexico

INTRODUCTION

Mexico's income inequality remains among the highest in the world and progress in addressing distributive issues has been inadequate. Its long-sustained import substitution and protectionist strategy, which biased resource allocation toward capital intensive techniques and implicitly included a wage policy that restrained employment, is largely responsible for the misguided distributive policy. Economic difficulties in the present decade have aggravated the problems of inequality, and inflation and a prolonged recession after 1982 have created new and significant regressive distributive forces. In particular, income transfers through the financial system have become increasingly burdensome for some segments of society.

This paper examines the distributive effects of financial policies in Mexico in the present decade. Despite the importance of the problem, it has begun to receive attention only very recently. Because both the theory and the data are still insufficient to perform formal tests of hypotheses, this paper explores these matters as an initial step toward specification of the agenda for further research.

The paper first gives a brief account of the available information on income distribution in Mexico from 1963 to 1983 in order to establish a context for assessing the relative importance of various redistributive forces. Statistical evidence and the results of previous studies are then

---

*The author wishes to thank Miguel Szekely and Patrick Low for their invaluable help.

examined to determine the orders of magnitude of income
redistributions in the 1980s. The probable mechanisms of
the inflationary tax, interest rate policy and various financial subsidies are examined in the concluding section of the
paper.

INEQUALITY IN MEXICO FROM 1963 TO 1983

The degree of inequality in income shares appears to
have declined steadily from 1963 to the beginning of the
present decade (see Figure 1). The effects of the import
substitution growth policy were quite uneven, however, and
the incomes of a large part of the population did not grow
enough to eliminate widespread poverty. The proportion of
the poor in the total population was an estimated 70 percent
in 1977. This head count ratio takes the average income of
the seventh decile as the poverty line, that is, as the bare
minimum necessary to purchase the basic basket of goods (see
COPLAMER, 1982). Although growth raised the income levels
of the urban middle classes, it also gave rise to substantial income differentials, especially between rural and
urban populations. The declining trend in inequality was
due essentially to a reduction of income disparities between
the very rich and the middle income groups. The lower income
groups realized little improvement in their shares of total
income, as the shares of the poorest 20 percent of the house-
holds indicate (see Table 1).

The economic difficulties during the present decade
have affected predominantly the living standards of the middle classes in the modern urban sector. The data from the
most recent household survey (1983) suggest a reduction of
inequality in the second year of the crisis period, but even
if such a decline in inequality did in fact occur it would
correspond to much lower per capita incomes (see Figure 2).
Although no data are available to assess the distribution of
income after 1983, it is very likely that the deterioration
of real incomes after that year has increased overall income
disparities and caused substantial welfare losses particularly for the urban poor.

REAL WAGES AND FACTOR SHARES IN THE 1980S

Since 1982 the fall in incomes, together with inflation
and very stringent fiscal policies, has caused a notable
shift in factor shares. In Mexico, where a large proportion

of low income groups earn their livings in informal activities, factor shares are not a direct indicator of income disparities. Under the circumstances, however, the fall in real wages and the decline in the share of wages in GDP clearly reflect an unprecedented impoverishment of the middle classes.

Average wages have fallen faster than per capita GDP. The former relatively higher position of wage earners in the income distribution has been reversed. Between 1981 and 1986 real annual wages fell by the unprecedented amount of nearly 40 percent (see Figure 3). Although real wages decreased in all sectors of the economy, the greatest reduction occurred in sectors with higher than average annual wages, so that wage inequality probably declined as well. Indeed, inequality in average yearly sectoral wages can be estimated from national accounts, and the dotted line in Figure 3 shows that this component of total inequality decreased from 1982 to 1986. Although this measure fails to account for inequality among different job positions, the decline suggests strongly that overall wage inequality also fell, since wage bargaining tends to maintain the structure of relative wages by occupations within firms or industries.

The shares of wages measured by national accounts are much lower than those reported by household surveys. The higher wage income shares in the latter imply that wages are the major source of inequality by factor components. A decomposition of inequality by income sources as revealed by household survey data show that over two-thirds of total inequality is due to wage disparities. Thus, the reduction of wage inequality probably had a significant effect on overall inequality and could explain its apparent decrease between 1977 and 1983.

The sectoral composition of the labor force changed in response to falling wage rates, reducing the impact on the wage bill/GDP ratio. Figure 4 illustrates this point by comparing actual wage shares with those that would have been observed if either wages or the 1980 sectoral composition of labor had remained constant. The share of wages in value added would have been higher if real wages had remained constant and lower if the sectoral composition of the labor force had remained fixed. The sectors with higher wages -- and higher productivity -- obviously fared better than others.

EFFECTS OF FINANCIAL POLICIES

This section examines some distributive consequences of financial policies. Although inadequate information and analytical tools make these effects difficult to assess, it is still possible to speculate on orders of magnitude and income groups affected.

The figures referred to in the previous section illustrate in part the effects of fiscal policies. These policies should be considered separately as components of overall financial policies and analysis of their distributive effects should take into account the transmission mechanisms of the financial system.

Budgetary Restrictions

Both the reduction of public expenditure and the mechanisms employed to finance the public deficit since 1982 have had a substantial and regressive impact on income distribution. Total debt service has grown dramatically to 19.5 percent of GDP in 1987 (see Figure 5 and Table 2). The debt service burden as a whole and its domestic component most particularly dominate the time pattern of total government expenditures relative to GDP. The necessary adjustments in federal expenditures have resulted in a reduction in the government payroll and public investment.

The distributive effects of the decrease in public expenditures have probably been quite significant, given the high rate of population growth in Mexico and the inadequate level of public services. Most affected are the urban middle income groups who had previously been the main beneficiaries of public expenditures in education, health, food subsidies, low cost housing programs and government wages.

Debt Financing and Inflation

Mexico's public sector deficits have a regressive distributive effect regardless of whether they are financed by credit from the Central Bank or directly from the public. The inflationary pressures that result from financing the deficits through new money creation transfer resources from the private to the public sector. The size of this inflationary tax depends on the rate of inflation and the public's ability to reduce their cash holdings, and its impact can be substantial when the inflation rate is high and the public's defenses are weak.

The inflationary tax peaked in 1982 at almost 6 percent of GDP, corresponding to an annual inflation rate of nearly 99 percent (see Figure 6 and Table 3). This form of taxation declined during 1983-1985 and then increased again in 1986 and 1987 as the inflation rate exceeded 100 percent. During this latter period the public reacted by reducing their non-interest-bearing holdings of financial assets. This shift, of course, also reflected changes in fiscal policy and in the manner in which the deficit was financed. The lowermost line in Figure 6 and the right-hand column in Table 3 labeled "Composition Effect" measure the change in the operational deficit due to changes in monetized vs. non-monetized debt financing. This effect fluctuates with the rate of inflation but the degree of responsiveness has tended to decline. The reduction of cash holdings induced by inflation has progressively eroded the basis of taxation through inflation.

It is not difficult to understand the highly regressive nature of the inflationary tax. Reducing cash holdings is relatively easy for the wealthy, but not really possible for low income groups. While no current information is available on the impact of the inflationary tax by income groups, an estimate for 1980 indicates that it fell more heavily on the lowest and highest income groups than on the middle groups (see Figure 7). Other evidence also supports the supposition that inflation and deficit financing have had a strongly regressive impact after 1982. The explanation lies partly in the negative or quite minimal savings of low income groups, the limited access of these groups to interest-bearing financial assets in Mexico, and the considerable increase in the disparities between interest rates and inflation since 1982. The financial system gives big savers and short-run account holders a much higher yield than small savers and long-run account holders, and small savers were actually penalized by negative real interest rates in 1986 (see Table 4).

Financing the public deficit through the issuance of treasury bills (CETES) and forced lending on the part of the banks is also likely to have had a regressive effect on income distribution. In this case the holders of claims have received high nominal interest rates more than sufficient to offset the erosion of inflation and to obtain a real return on their financial savings. The mechanism is highly regressive for two reasons. First, since there has been practically no economic growth during the present decade, the positive real interest rates obtainable by the minority of high income recipients has meant in effect that they have received real transfers from taxpayers and other sources of government revenues. Second, tax evasion practices are known to be more frequent among the high income brackets, so that the bulk of the fiscal burden falls on captive taxpayers like the wage earning population.

The order of magnitude of these transfers is probably very high, since service on the domestic debt has risen to 15 percent of GDP (see Table 2). At an annual real interest rate of 11 percent, the income transfer implied in this level of debt service amounts to 1.7 percent of GDP.

CONCLUSIONS

The problem of inequitable income distribution is not new in Mexico. The majority of the population did not benefit significantly from past development policies, and it is this fact, more than the impact of the current crisis, that makes a change in development strategy unavoidable. The need for policy changes, however, has become even more urgent as the crisis has intensified the impoverishment of the wage-earners and their dependents.

During the 1980s income losses have fallen mainly on the groups that formerly benefited from the import substitution policies. The distribution of income is changing extensively and moving towards polarization of the very rich and the very poor. The inflationary tax and related financial policy mechanisms have triggered large regressive transfers. Because of imperfections in the financial and tax systems most of the burden has fallen on low and middle income groups and these effects exacerbate the welfare consequences of the decline in real wages and the increase in open unemployment.

The inflationary experiences of Mexico and other Latin American countries, and the various adjustment programs attempted, have put primary emphasis on macroeconomic policy consistency with very little attention to the distribution of the adjustment costs. The financial system plays a crucial role in determining this allocation among the various social groups, and if it responded less imperfectly to deficit financing the costs could be more justly distributed.

The social costs of inflation, stagnation and adjustment policies have been enormous. They have increased the number of the poor, created social tension and political divisions among organized labor, and caused violence to accelerate in general. The ability of Mexico's political system to contain social unrest within tolerable limits in the face

of such a large decline in the standard of living is
surprising, but the patience of the people may eventually
wear thin.

REFERENCES

Coordinacion General del Plan Nacional de Zonas Deprimidas y
Grupos Marginados (COPLAMAR). Necesidades Esenciales en
Mexico, Situacion Actual y Perspectivas al ano 2000.
Presidencia de la Republica, Mexico, 1982.
Gil Diaz, Francisco. "The Incidence of Taxes in Mexico,
1977," unpublished, October, 1981.
Gil Diaz, F. and A. Fernandez. "Reflexiones Sobre el Sis-
tema Impositivo Mexicano: Consideraciones Economicas,"
unpublished, October, 1987.
Cervantes, Jesus. "La inflacion y la distribucion del
ingreso y la riqueza en Mexico." In Distribucion del
Ingreso en Mexico. Ensayos, Cuaderno 2, tomo II, ed.
by C. Bazdresch, J. Reyes Heroles, and Vera F. Gabriel.
Banco de Mexico, 1982.
Kanbur, S. M. R. "Poverty, Measurement, Alleviation and the
Impact of Macroeconomic Adjustment," Discussion Paper
#125 (Princeton, N.J.: Woodrow Wilson School, November
1985).
Reyes Heroles, Jesus. "Las Politicas Financieras y la Dis-
tribucion del Ingreso en Mexico," Mimeo.
Reynolds, Clark, and Jaime Corredor. "The Effect of the
Financial System on the Distribution of Income and
Wealth in Mexico," Food Research Institute Studies, XV,
I (Stanford).
Trigueros, Ignacio. "El Problema de la Inflacion y las
Estrategias Antiinflacionarias: Algunas Reflexiones en
Torno a la Experiencia Reciente de la Economia Mexi-
cana," ITAM (Octubre, 1988).

TABLE 1. Income Share of the Poorest 20% in Mexico

Deciles	1963	1968	1977	1983.1	1983.2
1	1.0	0.9	1.1	0.9	1.7
2	1.6	1.6	2.1	2.2	3.0
Sum	2.6	2.5	3.2	3.1	4.7

TABLE 2. Public Expenditures: Mexico 1980–1987 (Ratios to GDP)

Item	1980	1981	1982	1983	1984	1985	1986	1987
Total Expenditures	33.5	39.7	44.5	41.0	39.3	39.2	44.8	44.4
Current	23.2	26.4	33.4	33.0	32.1	32.6	38.1	38.7
Debt Service	3.5	5.0	8.2	12.4	11.9	11.5	16.3	19.5
Domestic	2.4	2.9	4.9	7.7	8.0	7.8	11.5	15.2
External	1.1	2.1	3.3	4.6	3.9	3.7	NA	4.3
Net Transfers	4.1	2.9	2.9	2.8	1.8	2.2	2.6	2.0
Government Wages	7.0	7.3	8.0	6.7	6.5	6.6	6.1	6.3
Transfers and Wages	11.1	10.2	11.0	9.4	8.3	8.8	8.7	8.4
Capital Expenditures	9.6	12.9	10.2	7.5	6.7	6.0	5.9	5.5
Public Works	8.0	9.2	7.8	5.3	5.0	4.7	NA	4.2
Other	1.6	3.7	2.4	2.2	1.7	1.4	NA	1.2
Other	0.6	0.5	1.0	0.5	0.5	0.6	0.8	0.2
Total Revenues	26.9	26.7	28.9	32.9	32.2	31.2	3.0	30.2

TABLE 3. Operational Deficit and Inflationary Tax: Mexico
          1978-1980 (Proportions of GDP)

Year	Operational Deficit	Inflation Rate[a]	Inflationary Tax	Composition Effect
1980	8.26	28.0	1.98	0.07
1981	11.59	28.7	1.91	0.07
1982	15.37	98.9	5.52	0.17
1983	5.67	80.8	3.12	0.28
1984	2.03	59.2	2.12	0.17
1985	2.73	63.7	2.20	0.14
1986	5.08	105.7	3.17	0.22
1987	3.38	159.2	3.56	0.20
1988		42.2		

[a]Rate of growth of Consumers Price Index.

Source: Banco de Mexico, Informe Anual, 1987.

TABLE 4. Maximum Real Interest Rates for
          Various Instruments: Mexico, 1986

Instrument	Rate
Savings	-41.7
Interest-Bearing Deposits	-41.1
Bank IOU's	3.3
Other	2.8
Treasury Bills (CETES)	11.9
Commercial Paper	13.7
Oil Bonds	16.0
Average Savings Rate	2.9
Average Loans Rate	13.7

Source: Reyes Heroles, Table 4.

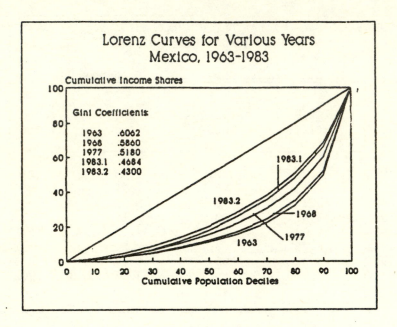

Figure 1.

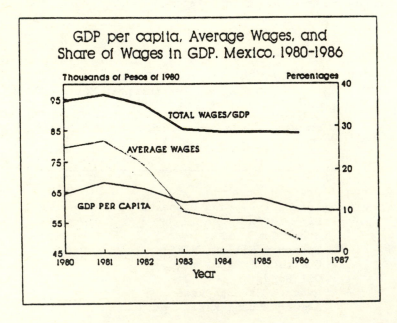

Figure 2.

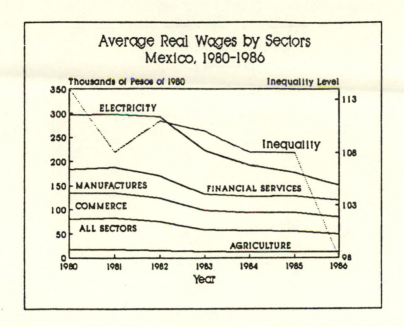

Figure 3

Figure 4

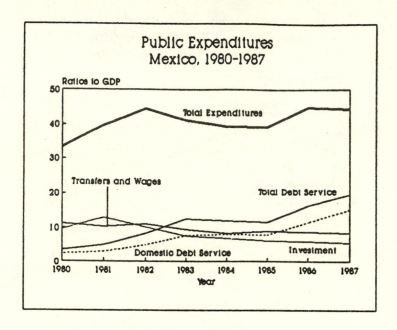

Figure 5.

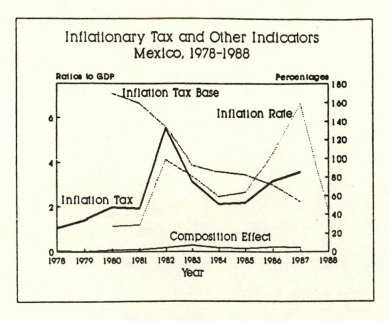

Figure 6.

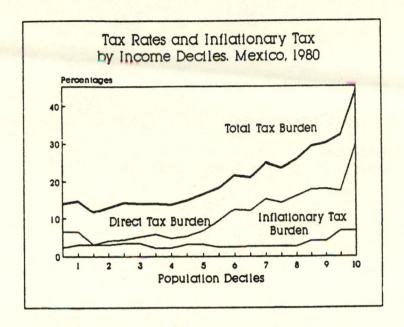

Tax Rates and Inflationary Tax
by Income Deciles. Mexico, 1980

Percentages

Total Tax Burden

Direct Tax Burden

Inflationary Tax
Burden

Population Deciles

Source: Gil Diaz (1981)

Figure 7.

General Comments

Sylvia Maxfield
Assistant Professor of Political Science, Yale University

In the 1990s Mexico is following a path toward financial liberalization paved in the 1970s by countries as varied as Canada and Chile. As economists recognize, this path is fraught with difficulties linked to policy sequencing and timing. But it is also mined with political pitfalls. While debate over the details of financial liberalization plans is often left to lawyers, bankers or economists, in practice politics and politicians shape the implementation of reform. Many studies of the process of financial liberalization neglect the political aspects of engineering change in financial policy. The following comments raise several of the many issues related to the politics of financial liberalization in Mexico.

The first question often posed about financial liberalization concerns whether or not it is a necessary corollary of the broader structural change Mexico is currently pursuing. But given the political obstacles to reform, a more realistic inquiry would ask about the minimal financial reform necessary.

Recent experiences in other countries show that international pressure, rather than economic logic, is the driving force behind financial liberalization. In the Mexican case, the United States has exercised political pressure bilaterally and through the GATT. The World Bank has also made financial liberalization an explicit condition of structural adjustment loans. While these international pressures help to overcome domestic obstacles to reform they may also heighten Mexican nationalism, thereby creating a new political deterrent to reform. In short, since reform has high political costs, it would be helpful if economists could tell us how effective different <u>small</u> steps toward reform could be.

A second question often posed about financial liberalization concerns what this process will look like in Mexico. A scenario of foreign bank entry and increasing competitiveness on the part of domestic financial enterprises is often sketched, but various questions about the politics of this process again immediately spring to mind. First, not one proponent of financial liberalization of whom I am aware has made a strong case for how liberalization can effectively and successfully proceed while domestic banks remain state-owned. State ownership of the banks is now constitutionally mandated and any change would require legislative approval. This is hard to imagine with the PRI opposition increasingly strong in Congress. Politics are central to the question of how to liberalize without re-privatizing the banks. The tremendous variation in competitiveness between the state-owned commercial banks and privately-owned non-bank financial institutions naturally creates disparities of interest and policy preference among diverse and potentially politically powerful actors in the financial community. Can these differences be worked out without re-privatizing commercial banking?

Another political challenge in the reform process will be how to neutralize broad social opposition from old, often inefficient, import-substitution industries; from labor; and even possibly from small-scale agriculturalists and peasants. Structural reform has already created discontent among these sectors and this partly fueled the strong Cardenista challenge to Salinas' presidential campaign. The political symbolism of opening a partly nationalized financial system to foreign banks could easily become fodder for the PRI's opponents. Here lessons from the Canadian experience with financial liberalization are instructive. The 1967 Canadian Bank Act revision was so politicized by the perception of U.S. pressure that a balanced assessment of the costs and benefits was impossible. The nationalists prevailed and the proposed liberalization was only partially implemented. Ten years later, in debate over revision of the Bank Act, nationalism was again a powerful obstructing force.

The Canadian experience suggests that successful, rapid, financial liberalization requires a political strategy. What would that strategy be in the Mexican case? Canadian reform sponsors proposed to nullify nationalistic opposition by limiting the scope for foreign bank operations. These limitations included restricting the leverage of foreign banks to a proportion of Canadian ownership participation in the enterprise, and requiring foreign banks to keep assets in Canada equal to the value of their liabilities.

Emphasizing such limitations is just one of many possible considerations in planning a political strategy for financial reform.

A third and most provocative question about financial liberalization regards its consequences for Mexico. Here many of the concerns that initially spring to mind are economic, but they do have potentially important political implications. First, what specific provisions do financial reformers envision implementing to avoid the potentially destabilizing consequences of liberalization? Mexico's commercial banks, for example, have been dedicating themselves to government lending and are relatively inexperienced in the evaluation of project lending proposals that would be required of them in a more competitive environment. Similarly, what policies can minimize the danger that deregulation and increasing competition would lead to the kinds of illegal activities uncovered in the United States and Japan? The long tradition of anonymous ownership in Mexican financial markets will make control of illegal activities difficult.

A second concern about the consequences of liberalization regards their interaction with public sector debt. In other Latin American countries that have attempted financial reform, interest rates have not fallen as expected. If interest rates remain high in Mexico, the country's staggering domestic debt problem would be aggravated.

Third, how will financial liberalization solve the partly political problem of getting financial resources channeled into long-run productive investment in areas that will contribute to renewed growth? This is a problem that has plagued Mexico at least since the 1930s and some current data highlight the issue. Ninety percent of bank deposits are short term; industrial firms are surviving in a no-growth, high interest rate environment by engaging in short-term financial operations. In Chile, financial liberalization encouraged similar behavior with drastic consequences for the nation's manufacturing base. The question is how to make long-term domestic investment as attractive as short-term international investment when at least part of the calculation revolves around political risk and confidence.

Fourth, discussion of the consequences of financial reform raises questions about efficiency and economies of scale. Some economists suggest that progress toward commercial bank efficiency has been made through recent mergers. Yet these mergers have been dictated not by the market but

rather by the government. How can we be sure they were efficient if market forces were not at work? Furthermore, debate
rages over the extent of the economies of scale in banking.
Do we know where to draw the line in banking between the
inefficiencies of oligopolistic markets and efficiency
gained through economic concentration?

It has been suggested that financial liberalization
will leave a diminished role for monetary policy and
macroeconomic policy more generally. This suggestion raises
two questions: Is this true and is it desirable? In the Canadian debate over financial reform the hypothesized decline
in the autonomy of economic policymaking was considered a
disadvantage. The Bank of Canada protested vigorously that
liberalization would not limit the effectiveness of monetary
policy.

Some Mexican policymakers imply that restricting the
scope of monetary and fiscal policy is a good thing. But
the Keynesian in me wonders whether it is wise to limit the
instruments long-used to stimulate employment in a country
with a rapidly growing and potentially politically powerful
labor force. This is a decades-old debate in Mexican political economy going back at least to the conflict between
Cardenas' Finance Minister Eduardo Suarez and his Central
Bank Director Luis Montes de Oca.

Precisely because of strong inflation and employment
pressures, financial liberalization implies a need for more
rather than less monetary and fiscal policy manipulation
and, in particular, international coordination of these
policies. Discussions of Mexican financial liberalization
should be imbedded in bilateral negotiations between the
United States and Mexico in which the goal is to reach complementary agreements on bi-national flows of capital, labor
and goods. Financial liberalization does imply greater economic interdependence, which must be carefully managed
because of the growing politico-economic pressures in both
the United States and Mexico.

APPENDIX

YALE/MEXICO CONFERENCE PROGRAM PLAN
(April 4-6, 1989)

Schedule/Topics	Speakers	Commentators
THURSDAY, 2:00-5:30 PM: PLENARY SESSION		
Economic and Socio-Political Context	Victor Urquidi, Chair	
Changes in Social Welfare Profile of Mexico during 1980's	Leopoldo Solis	Robert Pastor
Revision of International Economic Policy Environment	Raymond Vernon	Jesus Reyes Heroles
Re-Balancing of Government Direction and Market Guidance	Pedro Noyola/ Jaime Serra	T.N. Srinivasan
Alternative Macroeconomic Scenarios for 1989-94	Sweder van Wijnbergen	Willem Buiter/Luis Tellez
THURSDAY, 7:00-10:00 PM: KEYNOTE BANQUET		
Reaffirmation of Yale/Mexico Connection (before dinner remarks)	Gustav Ranis, Master of Ceremonies Gustavo Petricioli, Toastmaster	
Reappraisal of Mexico/U.S. Economic Relations (after dinner presentations)	Hugo Margain Anthony Solomon	Cathryn Thorup
FRIDAY, 9:00-12:00 AM: PLENARY SESSION		
Macroeconomic Problems and Policy Objectives	Anne Krueger, Chair	
Assessment of Progress Toward Stabilization and Structural Adjustment	Pedro Aspe	S. T. Beza
Comparative Appraisal of Contemporary Adjustment/Growth Problems	Angus Maddison	Gustav Ranis
Reformation of International Trade and Investment Policies	Jaime Zabludovsky/ Herminio Blanco	Koichi Hamada/ Juan Enriquez

Schedule/Topics	Speakers	Commentators
FRIDAY, 12:30-2:00 PM: LUNCHEON SESSION		
Introduction of Speaker	T. Paul Schultz	
Mexico's Contemporary Economic and Socio-Political Problems in Historical Perspective	Enrique Cardenas	
FRIDAY, 2:30-5:30 PM: PLENARY SESSION		
Development Strategies and Policy Instruments	Rodney Wagner, Chair	
Inflation Control and Fiscal/Monetary Policies	Guillermo Ortiz/Luis Tellez	Edwin Truman
Strategies for Domestic and External Debt Management	Rudiger Dornbusch	Angel Gurria
Infrastructure Investment Requirements and Resource Availabilities	Everardo Elizondo	Enrique Espinoza
SATURDAY, 9:00 AM-1:00 PM: ROUND TABLE SESSION		
Financial Sector Reform Agenda	James Tobin, Chair	
Financial Sector Planning and the New Development Strategy	Dwight Brothers	Jesus Marcos
Prudential Regulation and Financial Stabilization	Aristobulo de Juan	Francisco Suarez/Peter Garber
Role of Banco de Mexico in Financial Liberalization/Modernization	Sergio Ghigliazza	William White
Prospective Evolution of Domestic Banks and NBFIs	Sergio Martin	Sylvia Maxfield
Distributive Effects of Financial Policies	Adalberto Garcia Rocha	Sergio Chazaro